15.00

VAT
Guide

VAT
Guide

David G Relf, LLB, ATII
Solicitor
and
Christopher A L Preston
Solicitor

Oyez Publishing Ltd

© 1981
Oyez Publishing Limited
Norwich House, 11/13 Norwich Street,
London EC4A 1AB

ISBN 0 85120 521 6

Printed in Great Britain by
Butler & Tanner Ltd, Frome and London

PREFACE

There has been a need for some time for a practical and easily understood work on value added tax. This *Guide* is offered to fill this need. As such it is designed to be of assistance to both the taxation practitioner who, through the comprehensive indexing of the *Guide*, will be able to find answers to specific problems, and the businessman or non-specialist who wishes to improve his basic knowledge of VAT.

Chapters 1 to 14 of the *Guide* cover the major aspects of the incidence and recovery of VAT specifying in each case the sources of the relevant legislation. These chapters also feature a section on "General Principles" to introduce the reader to the basic law and practice on the topic covered by that chapter before passing on to discuss in greater detail specific problems associated with that topic. The later chapters of the *Guide* concentrate on specialised areas of VAT, for example, Special Categories of Supplier (Chapter 15) and Special Types of Transaction (Chapter 16).

Chapter 11, Customs & Excise Practice, Chapter 13, Appeals and Chapter 14, Conduct of Enquiries, provide a detailed analysis of areas of VAT that are becoming of increasing importance as taxpayers seek to challenge the Customs & Excise interpretation of VAT legislation.

A feature of the *Guide* is its strong emphasis on stating the authorities for particular statements as to the law and the easy cross referencing that it offers to its companion volume, the *VAT Casebook*, by the same authors.

The authors would like to thank Ernst & Whinney who, through Kevin McCormick and James Dixon, have assisted in the production of this *Guide* and the *VAT Casebook*. However, the views expressed remain those of the authors and are not necessarily those of the consultant editors.

The law is stated in the *Guide* as at 30 September 1980.

David Relf
Christopher Preston

London 1980

USING THE GUIDE AND THE CASEBOOK

A reader who wishes to find a general discussion of particular areas of VAT should refer to the *Guide*.

Details of more specific questions relating to VAT may be found through the use of the subject index or the Tables of Statutory and other source material and Cases in the *Guide* and the subject index or the Table of Cases in the *Casebook*.

Cross referencing between the *Guide* and *Casebook* is facilitated by the identical numbering and headings of the chapters and subdivisions of the two works; chapter numbers appear before the decimal point in a reference, subdivision numbers immediately after it. Thus, **5.100** indicates chapter 5, subdivision 1: Input tax, General principles. That subdivision in the *Guide* will discuss general issues relating to input tax while cases illustrating those issues will be grouped under the same number in the *Casebook*. The final two digits of a reference in the Casebook give the individual case number.

Users of the two works will therefore be able to cross refer *from the Guide to the Casebook* (to consult cases which have a bearing on the point under review) or to cross refer *from the Casebook to the Guide* (to consult the "narrative" which has a bearing on the subject matter of a case).

CONTENTS

Contents   xi

Table of Cases

Table of Statutes

Note Because of the very extensive use of statutory and other references throughout the text of the *VAT Guide*, full tables of Statutes, Statutory Instruments, etc, would not be of any real assistance to users of the work, in that each item would have too many page references. Statutes, Notices and Leaflets, therefore, have been tabled so that it can be seen where the most important items form the main source material for the relevant text. Statutory Instruments have not been so tabled but are, of course, extensively referred to in the text.

Bankruptcy Act 1914		s12 (6)–(8)	7.000
s33	15.600A	s13	9.000A
Law of Property Act 1925		s14	16.000A
s109	15.600A	s15	15.300A
Companies Act 1948		s16	6.000
s94	15.600A	s17	6.000
s319	15.600A	s18	6.000
s369	15.600A	s19	15.300A
Finance Act 1972		s20	15.300A
s1	5.000	s21	2.000, 3.000
s2 (1)	4.000	s22	15.400A
(2)	2.000, 9.000A	s23	2.000
(4)	6.000	(2)	15.200A, 15.600A
(5)	2.000	(2A)	15.200A
s3	5.000	s24 (1)	15.000A
(3)	4.000, 6.000	(2)	15.000A
(9)	6.000	(2A)	15.000A
s4	5.000	(3)	15.000A, 15.600A
s5	5.000	s25	4.000
s6	3.000	s26	16.400A
(2)	16.700A	s27	6.000
s7	3.000, 16.300A	s30	17.000
s8	3.000	(1)	17.000
A	3.000, 10.000A	(2)	17.000
B	3.000, 10.000A,	(3)	16.100A
	16.500A, 16.700A	s31	12.000
(3)	7.000	(3)	3.000
s9 (3)	18.100A	s32	14.000
s10	3.000	s33	14.000
s11	3.000, 6.000	s34	17.000
s12	8.000, 10.000A, 16.600A	s35	14.000, 17.000
(1)	9.000A	s36	14.000
(3)	6.000	s37	14.000, 15.600A

Table of Customs and Excise Notices

Table of Customs and Excise Leaflets

Abbreviations

art	article
BIR	Birmingham (Tribunal)
BTR	British Tax Review
CA	Court of Appeal
CAR	Cardiff (Tribunal)
CCAB	Consultative Committee of Accountancy Bodies
CCE Customs & Excise	Commissioners of Customs and Excise
CEMA 1979	Customs and Excise Management Act 1979
Ch D	Chancery Division
DHSS	Department of Social Security
ECJ	European Court of Justice
EDN	Edinburgh (Tribunal)
EEC	European Economic Community
FA	Finance Act
IRC	Commissioners of Inland Revenue
LON	London (Tribunal)
LVO	Local VAT Office
MAN	Manchester (Tribunal)
para	paragraph
Pt	Part
QBD	Queen's Bench Division
r	rule
reg	regulation
RSC	Rules of the Supreme Court
s	section
Sched	Schedule
SI	Statutory Instrument
STC	Simon's Tax Cases
STI	Simon's Tax Intelligence
	Income and Corporation Taxes Act 1970
TMA 1970	Taxes Management Act 1970
VAT	Value Added Tax
VATTR	Value Added Tax Tribunal Reports

Chapter 1

The Charge to VAT

1.000 Sources

The following sources contain the law and practice relating to VAT:

Finance Acts

VAT was introduced by FA 1972, Pt I and Scheds 1–6 and the majority of Finance Acts since 1972 have amended or added to that Act in some way. Major changes were made in F(No 2)A 1975, which introduced the higher rate of VAT (now repealed by F(No 2)A 1979) and FA 1977, which contained the restatement and amendment of VAT in accordance with the requirements of the EEC Sixth Directive. Such restatement involved extensive amendment to and rearrangement of the sections of FA 1972 and made substantial changes of principle in relation to the supply of services. Reference should always be made, therefore, to FA 1972, as amended by FA 1977.

For guidelines as to the interpretation of statutes and the approach adopted by VAT Tribunals in such interpretation, see the *Casebook* **1.300.**

EEC legislation

All EEC Directives and Regulations, rulings and decisions of the European Court of Justice, the Council of Ministers and the European Commission and EEC Treaties are applicable to the United Kingdom by virtue of the United Kingdom's accession to the Treaty of Rome in 1972. Thus, where difficulty is experienced in the interpretation of the UK legislation, reference should be made to any relevant EEC law. Indeed, in the case of a conflict between UK and EEC law, the latter may prevail. For a discussion of this point see **13.800.** However, apart from the EEC Sixth Directive, the impact of EEC legislation has, to date, been limited. Nevertheless, the possibility that a reference of a VAT question may be made to the European Court of Justice should not be overlooked and for this reason any decisions of the European Court of Justice relating to VAT in other European countries should be closely monitored.

Statutory Instruments

One of the difficulties in the practical application of VAT is that FA 1972 and subsequent Finance Acts provide only the skeleton forming the basis of VAT. Many of the detailed rules as to the charge to and application of the tax are contained in subordinated legislation in the form of Orders, Rules and Regulations made by the Treasury and the Customs & Excise. All such Orders, Rules and Regulations must be made by Statutory Instrument (s 43(2)) and fall into two categories.

The first comprises Orders in Council and Orders which:

(*a*) increase the rate of tax;

(*b*) exclude any tax from input tax credit under s 3;

(*c*) vary the provisions as to the zero-rating or exemption of a supply (in the latter case without zero-rating it); or

(*d*) treat a supply of services, made otherwise than for a consideration, as made in the course or furtherance of a person's business.

Statutory Instruments within this category are required to be laid before the House of Commons and cease to have effect if not approved by the House within 28 days of the date on which they are made (s 43(3) and (4)). The failure to pass an affirmative resolution does not, however, invalidate anything already done in pursuance of that Instrument within the 28 day affirmation period.

The second category of Statutory Instrument comprises all other Orders, Rules and Regulations. These other Statutory Instruments are valid unless subject to an annulment resolution passed by the House of Commons (s 43(3)).

A Statutory Instrument, generally, has effect from the date on which it is made unless it specifies a later date on which it is to come into force.

Throughout the Finance Acts, there are provisions enabling Orders etc., to be made. A major problem in practice, therefore, is identifying whether or not such Orders have in fact been introduced. It is also necessary to ensure that Orders which have been made are not invalid as being in excess of the enabling provisions in question. Although this situation will be unlikely, it is open to a taxpayer to question the validity of any Statutory Instrument before the courts.

Customs & Excise discretion and concessions

It is also common in the Act and Regulations for a discretion to be given to the Customs & Excise on a particular point. For example, in Sched 3, para 1, a notice may be given securing the taxable value of a supply "where it appears to the Commissioners" that, *inter alia*, the consideration for the supply has been fixed with a view to the reduction of liability to tax. Also, in the VAT (Special Provisions) Order 1977 (SI 1977 No 1796), art 4(3)(c), a taxpayer may only take advantage of the special margin scheme for certain second-hand goods if he keeps such records and accounts as the Customs & Excise may specify in a Notice published by them "or may recognise as sufficient for those purposes". It is particularly difficult to judge whether any such discretion will be favourably exercised in any given case and equally difficult to challenge any refusal by the Customs & Excise to exercise its discretion favourably (see *J H Corbitt (Numismatists) Ltd* v *CCE*, [1980] STC 231 (*Casebook* **11.101**)). An indication of the view that is likely to be taken by the Customs & Excise can often be gained, however, from the various Leaflets and Notices published by the Customs & Excise from time to time. This subject is discussed in greater detail in Chapter 11.

The actual power of the Customs & Excise to grant concessions in the administration of VAT is limited. Section 12(8) enables the Customs & Excise to waive tax, if it thinks fit, where goods are found in the United Kingdom after having been zero-rated as exported and s 38(8) allows the Customs & Excise to mitigate penalties which would otherwise be imposed for the failure to comply with VAT legislation. Apart from these specific provisions, any forebearance by the Customs & Excise is of questionable legal effect. Thus, it would be open to the Customs & Excise, at any time within the time limits for the making of an assessment or further assessment (s 31, see Chapter 12), to insist upon the correct application of the legislation and the payment of the tax in question (this does raise the issue of whether estoppel would be available against the Customs & Excise: see Chapter 11). In practice, however, the Customs & Excise do apply concessions and are unlikely to raise assessments to deny the effect of such concessions after having done so. Unlike Inland Revenue concessions, there is no general published list of Customs & Excise concessions, however, which consequently remain elusive and cannot be guaranteed to be applied in any given case.

Customs & Excise Notices

As mentioned above, the Customs & Excise has published a number of Public Notices in the form of booklets and leaflets detailing its interpretation of VAT legislation. Notice No 1000 lists these Public Notices which are generally available from the Collectors of Customs & Excise or HM Customs & Excise, King's Beam House, Mark Lane, London EC3R 7HS.

With the exception of, *inter alia*, Notice No 727 (Special schemes for retailers), Notices detailing the margin schemes for second-hand goods and Notice No 700, Pt VI, Records and Accounts, these Notices have no legislative effect and give merely the Customs & Excise's own views as to the application of VAT. Indeed, VAT Tribunals have, on occasions, criticised certain Notices as being unhelpful and contradictory (see *Edward S Nicoll* v *CCE*, EDN/75/9 (*Casebook* **8.302**), which considered a part of Notice No 701). Notwithstanding this, Customs & Excise Notices do give an indication of its views in relation to a particular supply and, for this reason alone, will enable a person to judge whether his interpretation of the law is likely to be challenged by the Customs & Excise. It must be stressed, however, that neither the Customs & Excise nor the taxpayer are bound by these Notices and both may, therefore, choose to take a different view of the law in any given case.

1.100 General principles

VAT is chargeable on the occurrence of:

(*a*) the supply of goods or services in the United Kingdom, after 1 April 1973, where that supply is:

   (i) a taxable supply;
   (ii) is made by a taxable person; and
   (iii) is made in the course or furtherance of any business carried on by such taxable person (s 2(1)); or

(*b*) the importation of goods into the United Kingdom by any person, after 1 April 1973 (s 1(1)); or

(*c*) the "importation" of certain services into the United Kingdom by a taxable person after 1 January 1978 (s 8B). These services are listed in Sched 2A and are:

"1. Transfers and assignments of copyright, patents, licences, trademarks and similar rights.
2. Advertising services.
3. Services of consultants, engineers, consultancy bureaux, lawyers, accountants and other similar services; data processing and provision of information (but excluding from this head any services relating to land).
4. Acceptance of any obligation to refrain from pursuing or exercising, in whole or part, any business activity or any such rights as are referred to in paragraph 1 above.
5. Banking, financial and insurance services (including re-insurance, but not including the provision of safe deposit facilities).
6. The supply of staff.
7. The services rendered by one person to another in procuring for the other any of the services mentioned in paragraphs 1 to 6 above."

The incidence of VAT is linked, therefore, to a number of basic terms. These and certain general points relating to the charge to VAT are briefly outlined in the paragraphs below and are more fully discussed in the following chapters of this Guide.

Supply

The supply of goods and services is widely defined in the Act (s 6(2)) and any obligation undertaken by a person, which is binding on him and for which a consideration is given, is potentially a supply for VAT purposes. Indeed, it is not always necessary for there to be a consideration for the transaction in question.

It is also necessary to determine whether a supply is to be treated as one of goods or services for VAT purposes. The answer to this issue does not always appear to be wholly logical. For example, the hire of goods is regarded as a supply of services (Sched 2, para 1(1)) and the supply of ventilation a supply of goods (Sched 2, para 3). As the nature of the supply will often affect whether VAT is or is not payable, considerable care should, therefore, be taken in this area.

These issues are discussed in Chapter 3.

The United Kingdom

VAT was extended to the Isle of Man under the Value Added Tax and Other Taxes Act 1973, s 50 (this is an Act of Tynwald) and the VAT (United Kingdom and Isle of Man) Order 1973 (SI 1973 No 595). The United Kingdom and Isle of Man form, therefore, a single area for VAT purposes although the Isle of Man does have its own collection and administration facilities. The Isle of Man Act 1979, which came into force on 1 April 1980, prevents VAT being charged under the legislation of both the United Kingdom and Isle of Man in respect of the same transaction. As a result, all references to the United Kingdom in the legislation now include the Isle of Man unless otherwise stated. This convention will be followed in this *Guide*.

The definition of the United Kingdom also includes the territorial sea of the United Kingdom but *not* the UK Continental Shelf. The base lines for calculating the extent of the territorial sea (which extends 3 miles seaward from those lines) are set out in the Territorial Waters Order in Council 1964.

The United Kingdom comprises England, Wales, Scotland and Northern Ireland. It does not include the Channel Islands or the Republic of Ireland.

Taxable and exempt supplies

A taxable supply is defined in s 2(2) as "a supply of goods or services in the United Kingdom or Isle of Man, other than an exempt supply". Those supplies which are exempt supplies are set out in Sched 5 of the Act (s 13).

The making of exempt supplies has three principal effects:

(*a*) no VAT is charged in respect of those supplies;
(*b*) as exempt supplies are not taxable supplies, they are not included in the total value of a person's supplies in determining whether his turnover exceeds, or is likely to exceed, the compulsory registration limits set out in Sched 1; and
(*c*) the taxable person who makes exempt supplies may find that his ability to reclaim tax paid by him on supplies purchased by him for use in his business may be restricted.

Taxable persons and registration for VAT

Section 2(2) defines a taxable person as a person "who makes or intends to make taxable supplies ... while he is or is required to be registered" for the purposes of VAT. Actual registration is not required, therefore, before a person can be regarded as a taxable person and is obliged to charge and account for VAT. This concept runs throughout the legislation simply because the failure to register for VAT could otherwise result in the avoidance of VAT.

Registration is required by Sched 1 of the Act where a person's turnover, ie the total value of all his taxable supplies, exceeds or is likely to exceed certain stated amounts. These amounts are set out at **2.100**, et seq. It must be stressed that these amounts relate to the turnover and not the profits of the taxable person in question.

It is also to be noted that the Act refers to supplies by taxable persons and not by taxable businesses. Thus, registration itself is effected with reference to taxable persons and a taxable person's registration will extend to any number of businesses carried on by him in the same capacity. This applies equally to partnerships, other than limited partnerships, carrying on more than one business; provided that the partners are identical, all such businesses will be covered by the partnership's single registration number. It will be appreciated that this principle can cause considerable practical difficulties (see further Chapter 2).

"Person", in a VAT context, will include an individual, company, partnership, trustee, personal representative, receiver or liquidator. VAT is also extended to supplies by the Crown and local authorities (ss 19 and 20).

Finally, it is interesting to note the definition of a taxable person in the EEC Sixth Directive, art 4. This is:

"1. 'Taxable person' shall mean any person who independently carries out in any place any economic activity specified in paragraph 2, whatever the purpose or result of that activity.
2. The economic activities referred to in paragraph 1 shall comprise all activities of producers, traders and persons supplying services including mining and agricultural activities

and activities of the professions. The exploitation of tangible or intangible property for the purpose of obtaining income therefrom on a continuing basis shall also be considered an economic activity."

As art 4(4) of the Directive points out, the use of the word "independently" in para 1 above excludes employees from falling within the definition of a taxable person.

In the course or furtherance of any business

There is no definition of this phrase in the legislation, although "business" is somewhat unhelpfully defined to include any trade, profession or vocation (s 45(1)). Whether a business is being carried on is a question of fact and "business" in this context has been held to include activities generally regarded as investment rather than trading activities (see *D A Walker* v *CCE*, [1976] VATTR 10 (*Casebook* **4.108**) and also the definition of "economic activities" in the EEC Sixth Directive above).

The phrase "in the course or furtherance of a business" has been applied by VAT Tribunals extremely widely. This phrase expresses the concept employed by the EEC Sixth Directive of a supply by a taxable person "acting as such" (art 2). This concept when taken together with the EEC Sixth Directive's definition of a taxable person (see *Taxable persons and registration for VAT, ante*) may in fact be narrower than its United Kingdom counterpart. If this is the case, the narrower meaning in the Directive may prevail.

Importation

By treating VAT as a duty of customs (s 2(4)), importation effectively means the bringing of goods into the United Kingdom (as defined— see *The United Kingdom, ante*). The importation need not be by a taxable person to be subject to VAT.

The charge to VAT on importation is in addition to any import or customs duty payable in respect of such importation. But, where an exemption from customs duty is afforded to goods on importation, that relief may also apply to any VAT payable at the same time (s 17(1)). Further, where goods of a type specified in Sched 4 (Zero-rating) to the Act are imported into the United Kingdom, no VAT is chargeable on that importation unless Sched 4 provides otherwise in relation to that particular type of goods (s 12(3)). See generally Chapter 6.

Rates of tax and zero-rating

With effect from 18 June 1979, there are two rates of VAT; the standard rate of 15 per cent and the zero-rate, that is nil per cent. Prior rates of tax were:

Date	Standard	Higher	Zero
12.4.1976–17.6.1979	8%	12.5%	0%
1.5.1975–11.4.1976	8%	25%	0%
18.11.1974–30.4.1975	8%	25% (petrol only)	0%
29.7.1974–17.11.1974	8%	–	0%
1.4.1973–28.7.1974	10%	–	0%

The zero-rate of tax is payable on the supply and, unless otherwise provided, the importation of those goods or services listed in Sched 4 of the Act. If a particular supply potentially falls within both the scope of zero-rating (Sched 4) and exemption (Sched 5) the supply will be zero-rated (this follows from s 12(1)).

Zero-rating is not used by the EEC Sixth Directive which refers to supplies only as being taxable or exempt. The United Kingdom is permitted to retain zero-rating, however, under the transitional provisions of the EEC Sixth Directive (art 28(2)) provided that such zero-rating can be shown to have been introduced "for clearly defined social reasons and for the benefit of the final consumer".

Input tax and output tax

"Output tax" is the tax charged by taxable persons on their supplies (s 3(3)). "Input tax" on the other hand is, in general terms, the tax a taxable person himself suffers in respect of the purchases which make up the various elements of his supplies to his customers. To ensure that only the final non-business consumer (in VAT terms the non-taxable person which of course includes persons who make only exempt supplies) bears the cost of VAT, a taxable person is allowed to reclaim input tax incurred by him. This basic principle is subject to two caveats, however:

(a) where a taxable person makes both taxable and exempt supplies, he may not be able to reclaim all input tax paid by him. Such a person is described as being "partially exempt";

(b) tax on certain supplies is specifically not reclaimable. These supplies include motor cars and business entertainment.

Where these caveats apply, a taxable person will incur a VAT cost in his business.

Payment of VAT

VAT is collectable by a supplier from his customer. Whether or not the supplier in fact receives the payment of that VAT, however, the supplier is obliged to account for and pay that tax to the Customs & Excise. The time for such payment to the Customs & Excise is linked to the time of the supply for VAT purposes and the prescribed accounting period in which that time falls. Tax is usually due from the supplier not later than 1 month after the end of the prescribed accounting period in which the supply was made. At the same time as he accounts to the Customs & Excise for such output tax, the supplier will claim, by way of set-off against that output tax, credit for input tax incurred by him. Where input tax exceeds output tax for a particular period, the excess will be repaid by the Customs & Excise.

Administration of VAT

The "care and management" of VAT (which includes its collection) has been placed in the hands of the Commissioners of Customs & Excise (s 1 (2)), referred to in this *Guide* as "the Customs & Excise". A general explanation of the functions of the various officers of Customs & Excise is given in Chapter 14.

Chapter 2

Registration

2.000 Sources

Section 2(2)—Definition of taxable person.
Section 2(5)—Brings Schedule 1 into operation.
Section 21   —Group registration.
Section 23   —Separate registration of divisions of companies permitted.
Schedule 1 —Detailed provisions relating to registration.
VAT (General) Regulations 1977 (SI 1977 No 1759).
   Reg 4—Manner of giving notification of liability for registration.

In addition the following Customs & Excise Leaflets may be helpful:

700/1/80 —Should I be registered for VAT.
700/2/79 —Registration for VAT: Group treatment.
700/3/79 —Registration for VAT: Companies organised in divisions.
700/4/79 —Overseas traders and United Kingdom VAT.
700/11/80—Cancelling your registration

2.100 General principles

A person must register for VAT if he makes taxable supplies and those supplies exceed the limits set out in Sched 1, para 1. Such a person making taxable supplies whilst he is registered, or is liable to be registered, is known as a taxable person and any taxable supplies made by him in the course or furtherance of his business are subject to VAT. It is, therefore, important to note that if a person's taxable supplies exceed the relevant limit (see *Statutory limits, post* for details of these limits) he is liable to VAT on his supplies regardless of whether or not he is in fact registered. Liability to be registered is sufficient to trigger liability to account for VAT. This principle is a fundamental one, therefore, and a person must keep a close watch on the amount of his quarterly turnover and consider his future turnover to see whether he should register. Thus, if a person has failed to register, or registered after the correct date from which he should have registered he must account for VAT, whether or not he has charged and collected VAT from his customers (see *R Duke* v *CCE*, MAN/78/236 (*Casebook* **2.504**)). For detailed consideration of the effective date of registration, see **2.500**, *et seq.*

Furthermore it does not matter that the person has been unable to issue tax invoices because he did not have a VAT number at a time when he should have been registered. Such an argument was raised by the appellant in *B Snowdon* v *CCE*, LEE/75/27 (*Casebook* **2.507**) and rejected by the Tribunal (see also *F S and B E Poulton* v *CCE* LON/78/125 (*Casebook* **2.508**)).

The above may seem inequitable, but in practice problems ought not to arise because the local VAT office will, on receipt of an application for registration, give a preliminary advice of registration which will include the VAT number within a few days of receipt of the application for registration, subject to the clarification of any questions which may have arisen on the registration form. Although no VAT invoices can be issued to customers until the registration is accepted by the Customs & Excise, and a VAT number allocated, a trader should keep records from the date he is liable to be registered and charge VAT to customers, as he will be liable to account for VAT. He will be able to issue proper VAT invoices once his number is known and until such time should notify customers that VAT invoices will be given later, if required.

For a person to be liable to be registered, three factors are necessary, namely:

(*a*) the supplies must be taxable supplies, that is, supplies chargeable at the standard rate or zero-rate. Exempt supplies are non-taxable supplies. For further details of zero-rated and exempt supplies, see Chapters 8 and 9 respectively;

(*b*) the taxable supplies must be made in the course or furtherance of a business (see generally Chapter 4). The Customs & Excise will reject an application for registration if no business is carried on, or about to be carried on (see *M J Walker* v *CCE*, [1973] VATTR 58 (*Casebook* **2.101**));

(*c*) the turnover of taxable supplies must exceed the statutory limits (see *post*).

Statutory limits

The statutory limits for registration are contained in Sched 1, para 1. Basically two tests apply to ascertain whether a person is liable to be registered based on quarterly turnover on the one hand and projected annual turnover on the other hand. Thus:

QUARTERLY TURNOVER

If taxable turnover for a quarter exceeds £4,000 or in the four quarters then ending exceeds £13,500 the person must register within 10 days of the end of the quarter in which turnover exceeds that limit.

If after the first quarter a person's taxable turnover is, for example,

£3,000, he need not register. However, if after the second quarter the
taxable turnover has reached £8,500 he must register, unless the Customs & Excise are satisfied that the person's taxable supplies for that
period and the next three quarters will not exceed £13,500.

It will, therefore, be seen that traders must go through the exercise
of calculating the turnover for the quarter just ended to see if the limit
has been exceeded. Failure to do this and, as a result to register at the
correct time, can lead to the Customs & Excise raising assessments for
VAT that should have been charged, whether or not such VAT is recoverable from customers. The above limits apply from 1 June 1980 and a
quarterly period is one ending on 31 March, 30 June, 30 September
or 31 December (s 46).

ANNUAL TURNOVER

If there are reasonable grounds for believing that the value of a person's
taxable turnover will exceed £13,500 for a period of one year from that
time he must register. Thus, a person who estimates, on starting a business that his taxable turnover will exceed £13,500, must register on commencement of trading. Similarly, if, half-way through his first year, he
calculates that his taxable turnover for the next 12 months, ie taking
him through to 18 months from the commencement, will exceed
£13,500, he must register immediately.

Person to register

It is the person who registers for VAT and not the business so that,
if an individual carries on more than one business, each business is not
registered separately (see **2.200**, *et seq*). Thus, in *C Wiper* v *CCE*, LEE/
74/57A (*Casebook* **2.105**) where a person sold his business but started
a new one before completion of the sale of the first business, the second
business became covered by the registration for the first, notwithstanding that turnover for the second business was below the statutory limit
for registration. The problem in the *Wiper* case would have been avoided
had the first business been sold and the registration cancelled before
the purchase of the second business.

Transfer of registration

There is no provision to enable a registration number to be transferred.
The Tribunal therefore held in *L Reich and Sons Ltd* v *CCE*, LON/H/
73/34 (*Casebook* **2.106**) that it was not possible to make the Customs
& Excise transfer the VAT number on the hive-down of a business from
the company to its **98** per cent subsidiary.

Applications

Applications for registration must be submitted to the local VAT office on Form VAT 1. Where the application is made on behalf of a partnership Form VAT 2 must also be completed giving the names, addresses and signatures of each partner.

Zero-rated supplies

Where a person intends to make zero-rated supplies the Customs & Excise have a discretion to exempt the person from registration (Sched 1, para 11(*a*)), even though his supplies exceed the annual limit. If such exemption from registration is granted the person does not have to complete VAT returns but he is also not able to claim input tax on purchases.

In *Mrs T K Fong* v *CCE*, BIR/77/146 (*Casebook* **2.607**) the Tribunal held that exemption from registration could be granted where there was a preponderance of zero-rated supplies and notwithstanding that some standard rated supplies were made.

2.200 Registered name

As stated at **2.100** it is the person who must register for VAT. Thus, where a person carries on more than one business the person is only registered once (see *K N Weakley* v *CCE*, LON/S/73/142 (*Casebook* **2.203**) and generally *Casebook* **2.200,** *et seq*). The principle has important consequences because, where a person has two businesses, neither of which by itself has a sufficiently large turnover to warrant registration, the person must register for VAT (*R Scanes* v *CCE*, LON/76/209 (*Casebook* **2.204**)), if the combined turnover of both businesses exceeds the limits for registration.

Furthermore, where two distinct partnerships exist with the same partners in each, only one registration can be made to cover both partnerships (see *CCE* v *Glassborrow*, [1974] STC 142 (*Casebook* **2.201**)) although this principle does not apply to limited partnerships (see *H Saunders* v *CCE*, LON/79/226 (*Casebook* **2.202**) and generally **15.400**).

2.300 Voluntary registration

Where a person's taxable supplies are below the level for registration he can, nevertheless, apply to be registered (Sched 1, para 11(*b*)). However, the Customs & Excise have a discretion as to whether or not to accept the application for registration. The discretion is wide as the Act provides that the Commissioners "may, if he [the applicant] so requests and they think fit, treat him as so liable, subject to such conditions as they think fit to impose."

In many instances the Customs & Excise have refused the applications, on the ground that the applicants were not carrying on a business (*Casebook* **2.300,** *et seq*).

Once voluntary registration has been granted, the applicant must carry out all the obligations of a registered person. The Customs & Excise will normally require, as a condition of registration, that the registration shall remain in force for at least 2 years from the date of issue of the VAT certificate. If the Customs & Excise refuse the application they must state their reasons for so doing in writing (Sched 1, para 11(2)).

2.400 Group registration

Section 21 enables companies resident in the United Kingdom or the Isle of Man within a group to make a group registration for VAT. The application for group registration is made by the representative member on Form VAT 1 and Form VAT 50 must also be completed listing the names of companies to be included in the group registration. The effects of having a group registration are:

(*a*) supplies of goods or services made by one group member to another are not liable to VAT;
(*b*) any supply made by or to a member of the group is treated as made by the representative member;
(*c*) the importation of any goods by a group member is treated as made by the representative member, who is accordingly responsible for the payment of any VAT on importation.

Thus, the broad effect of group registration is that one member, "the representative member", assumes responsibility of the obligations under the VAT legislation (other than responsibility for the tax due, which is the joint and several liability of each group member) and all supplies by or to the group are treated as made by the representative member. This may facilitate record keeping as the representative member keeps the records and submits returns on behalf of the group.

Group

For the purposes of s 21 two or more companies will be eligible for group registration if:

(*a*) one of them controls each of the others;
(*b*) one person controls all of them. For this purpose the person controlling the others can either be a company or an individual. Thus,

if Mr X owns more than half of the issued share capital of companies A, B and C Ltd, the companies would be eligible for group registration. It should be noted that not all the companies eligible for group registration have to be included. Thus, in the above example Mr X could elect for companies A and B Ltd, but not C Ltd to be covered by the group registration;

(*c*) two or more persons carrying on business in partnership control all of them. In the above example, therefore, if X and Y carrying on business in partnership own more than half of the issued share capital of companies A, B and C Ltd, the companies would again be eligible for group registration.

A company or individual will be regarded as controlling another company if it would be the other company's holding company for the purpose of the Companies Act 1948; that is to say if it is a member of the other company and controls its board of directors, or holds more than half, in nominal value, of its equity share capital (Companies Act 1948, s 154(1)).

Any change in the control of a company which would affect its position within the group registration must be notified to Customs & Excise by the representative member within 21 days of the change (VAT (General) Regulations 1977 (SI 1977 No 1759), reg 4(4)).

Application

The application (on Forms VAT 1 and 50) should be lodged with Customs & Excise by the representative member not later than 90 days before it is intended the registration should take effect, although the Customs & Excise have discretionary power to accept late applications with retrospective effect *CCE* v *Save and Prosper Group*, [1979] STC 205 (*Casebook* **2.405**). Thus, if a company wishes to apply for group registration to take effect from 1 January 1981, it should apply before 30 September 1980.

The registration takes effect from the beginning of a prescribed accounting period. The Customs & Excise have power to refuse an application if they consider that it is necessary to do so for the protection of the revenue.

If the companies already have VAT numbers prior to the application for group registration the previous numbers will be cancelled and a new one given to the representative member on acceptance of the application. If it is desired to add further companies to the group registration application is made on Form VAT 54 but the group number remains the same. Similarly if it is wished to remove a company from the group registration application is made on Form VAT 56, but the group number is not changed.

Where a company which is not within a group election, but which is eligible for inclusion within the group, makes exempt or partially exempt supplies consideration should be given as to whether to include that company within the group registration. It will be seen at **5.200** that where a person makes taxable and exempt supplies the input tax on which he is able to claim relief is restricted, broadly speaking, to the proportion that his taxable supplies bears to total supplies. Thus, a company with total inputs of £5,000 which makes taxable supplies of £20,000 and exempt supplies of £30,000 would only obtain input relief on £20,000÷£50,000×£5,000=£2,000. It may, therefore, be advantageous to bring such a company into a group with another company (assuming both companies are eligible for group registration) so that the allowable inputs of the group are increased. Example 2.400:1 below demonstrates the advantage of making a group election. In this example, and those following it, the effect of the *de minimis* provisions for partially exempt persons have been ignored (see Chapter 5) in order to illustrate the basic principle of whether or not to make a group registration. Clearly if the *de minimis* rules apply to disregard the exempt supplies there will be no need to consider making a group election.

Example 2.400:1

Company A

Makes taxable supplies of	£50,000
Makes no exempt supplies	—
Has inputs of	£ 4,000
Therefore as no exempt supplies are made the whole of his inputs are allowable	£ 4,000(*a*)

Company B

Makes taxable supplies of	£ 5,000
Makes exempt supplies of	£25,000
Has inputs of	£ 3,000

As exempt supplies are made, the proportion of allowable inputs is restricted to:

$$\frac{5,000}{30,000}\times 3,000 \qquad \text{£ \quad 500(}b\text{)}$$

The total inputs allowable of Company A and Company B are (*a*)+(*b*)	£ 4,500

If a group registration were in force, so that the representative member is treated as making all the group's supplies and incurring all the group's input tax, the position becomes:

Company A and Company B

Group taxable supplies	£55,000
Group exempt supplies	£25,000
Group Inputs	£ 7,000
However, inputs are restricted to	
$\frac{55,000}{80,000} \times 7,000$	£ 4,812.50

By making a group registration therefore the amount of inputs for which relief can be claimed is increased.

It is not always advantageous to apply for group registration, however, as shown in the Example 2.400:2 below.

Example 2.400:2

Company A

Makes taxable supplies	£20,000
Makes no exempt supplies	—
Has inputs of	£ 2,000
As no exempt supplies all inputs allowable	£ 2,000(*a*)

Company B

Makes taxable supplies of	£ 1,000
Makes exempt supplies of	£15,000
Has inputs of	£ 1,200
As exempt supplies are made the proportion of allowable inputs is restricted to	
$\frac{1,000}{16,000} \times 1,200$	£ 75(*b*)
The total allowable inputs of Company A and Company B are therefore, (*a*)+(*b*)	£ 2,075

If a group registration is made the position becomes:

Company A and Company B

Group taxable supplies	£21,000
Group exempt supplies	£15,000
Group inputs	£ 3,200
However, inputs are restricted to	
$\frac{21,000}{36,000} \times 3,200$	£ 1,866

It is therefore not advantageous to be treated as a group as the total allowable inputs falls from £2,075 to £1,866 by so doing.

When group registration is advantageous where partial exemption applies

It is possible to calculate whether or not to have a group registration by applying the following formulae. Note the *de minimus* rules, see p. 16.

Let Company with exempt supplies be B
Let Company(ies) within existing group registration be A

GROUP REGISTRATION SHOULD BE MADE IF:

$$\frac{\text{Total supplies of B}}{\text{Total supplies of A \& B}} \text{ less than } \frac{\text{Inputs of B}}{\text{Inputs of A \& B}}$$

NO GROUP REGISTRATION SHOULD BE MADE IF:

$$\frac{\text{Total supplies of B}}{\text{Total supplies of A \& B}} \text{ more than } \frac{\text{Inputs of B}}{\text{Inputs of A \& B}}$$

Example 2.400:3

If the above formulae are applied to Examples 2.400:1 and 2, *ante* it will be seen that the position is:

As in Example 1
$$\frac{30,000}{80,000} \text{ less than } \frac{3,000}{7,000} = \frac{3}{8} \text{ less than } \frac{3}{7}$$
Group registration is, therefore, an advantage.

As in Example 2
$$\frac{16,000}{36,000} \text{ more than } \frac{1,200}{3,200} = \frac{4}{9} \text{ more than } \frac{3}{8}$$
Group registration, therefore, is not an advantage.

Companies organised in divisions

Section 23(1) enables a company which carries on business in separate divisions to register each division separately for VAT. However, the Customs & Excise have a general discretion as to whether to accept the application or not. The Customs & Excise have indicated in VAT Leaflet 700/3/79 (Registration for VAT: Companies organised in divisions) that the following conditions apply to the registration of separate divisions:

(*a*) all divisions must be registered in the same way. It is not possible for some divisions to remain unregistered even if a particular division's turnover is below the registration limit. Each division must complete Form VAT 1;

(*b*) tax invoices must not be issued for transactions between divisions of the same body corporate;

(*c*) no division must make exempt supplies which exceed 5 per cent or more of the division's total turnover, unless the value of the exempt supplies made by the company (ie all divisions of the company) is less than £100 per month on average;

(*d*) all the divisions must undertake to submit regular quarterly returns, except that if the company as a whole would regularly be entitled to repayments of input tax, all the divisions can make monthly returns. However, whether returns are quarterly or monthly all the divisions must adopt the same procedure;

(*e*) when completing Form VAT 1 the full name of the company should be put in Box 1 and Box 2 should be completed with the name of the division followed by the name of the company;

(*f*) approval will only be given where the Customs & Excise are satisfied that the company would experience real difficulties in operating under a single registration. The Customs & Excise give an example of such real difficulties as being the inability to submit a VAT return for the whole company within one month of the end of a quarterly period.

2.500 Effective date of registration

Where a person is obliged to register because his quarterly turnover exceeds the limit (Sched 1, para 1(*a*), see **2.100**), he must give notice of his liability to be registered within 10 days of the end of the quarter in which the obligation arose. The Customs & Excise must then register the applicant with effect from the twenty-first day of the next quarter. It is possible for the registration to take effect at an earlier date if agreed between the applicant and the Customs & Excise.

Many cases have arisen over the question of what date a registration should be effective from (see *Casebook* **2.500**, *et seq*) as often the Customs & Excise have been able to establish that the quarterly limit had been exceeded earlier than stated by the applicant. In such cases the Customs & Excise have back-dated the registration to take effect from the twenty-first day of the next quarter following the first quarter in which the limit was exceeded. It is clear that this is the correct procedure and therefore care must be taken to notify Customs & Excise as soon as the liability to register arises; failure to do so means the person will have to account for any tax due whether or not it is recoverable from customers and penalties can even be imposed (see **14.400**).

Where a person is obliged to register because his annual turnover is expected to exceed the £13,500 limit (Sched 1, para 1(*b*)), he must notify the Customs & Excise immediately and he will be registered with effect from the beginning of the period in which it is realised that supplies will exceed the £13,500 limit.

Because of the mandatory nature of the limits a careful watch must be kept on supplies so that a trader knows as soon as the limits are exceeded. In practice difficulties may sometimes arise where the annual limit is exceeded for a yearly period which does not correspond with the financial year of the business. Thus, in *E Marks* v *CCE*, LON/77/ 21 (*Casebook* **2.502**), the appellant was held to be liable to register where supplies for the 12 month period ended 30 June exceeded the annual limit, notwithstanding that financial accounts were prepared to 31 December. This just emphasises the importance of keeping quarterly checks on the amount of supplies.

2.600 Deregistration

A registered person will cease to be liable to be registered:

(*a*) after the end of a quarter or prescribed accounting period, if he has been registered for the last 2 years and his taxable supplies in each of those years have been less than £13,500, unless there are reasonable grounds for believing that taxable supplies for the next year will exceed £13,500; or

(*b*) at any time if the Customs & Excise are satisfied that the annual turnover from that date will be less than £12,500.

The above limits apply with effect from 1 June 1980.

Where a person ceases to be liable as provided in para (*a*) above and he wishes to deregister, he should notify the Customs & Excise immediately in writing and the Customs & Excise will cancel his registration with effect from the fifteenth day after receiving the notification, or with effect from such other date as is agreed between the parties (Sched 1, para 9 and VAT (General) Regulations 1977 (SI 1977 No 1759), reg 4(5)).

Where a person ceases to be liable to be registered as provided in paragraph (*b*) above and he wishes to deregister, he should notify the Customs & Excise immediately in writing and his registration will be cancelled from the date that the Customs & Excise are satisfied that the registration is liable to be cancelled (Sched 1, para 10 and VAT (General) Regulations 1977 (SI 1977 No 1759), reg 4(5)).

Provided that where a person ceases to be liable to be registered as described above, and subsequently fails, or has previously failed, to submit returns or account for or pay any tax, the Customs & Excise may, if they think fit cancel the registration from such date as they may determine (Sched 1, para 10A).

In addition to the provisions for cancellation described above, a person must also give written notice to the Customs & Excise if he ceases to make taxable supplies, such notice to be given within 10 days of the date on which he ceases to make the taxable supplies and specifying the date on which the cessation occurred (Sched 1, para 8). The events most likely to give rise to a cessation of the making of taxable supplies are the sale or the closing down of the business.

Whether or not liability to VAT will arise on the cessation of the taxable supplies will depend upon the circumstances surrounding the cessation and for further consideration of this see **4.500,** *et seq.*

As from the date of cancellation no tax invoices can be issued, since these can only be issued by a registered person. Furthermore, no relief can be obtained for input tax, except that exceptionally where the input tax relates to services performed before the cancellation of the registration the Customs & Excise have a discretion to grant relief (VAT (General) Regulations 1977 (SI 1977 No 1759), reg 70(3)); the Customs & Excise have indicated that relief will be granted for input tax on such services where the claim is made within 6 months from the cancellation supported by the relevant invoices (see VAT Leaflet 700/11/80 (Cancelling your registration), para 6), the claim being made on Form VAT 427.

Once the date for cancellation of the registration is agreed, the taxpayer must submit a final return on Form VAT 193 (VAT 197 in Welsh), which return covers the period between the last quarter date and the date of cancellation (VAT (General) Regulations 1977 (SI 1977 No 1759), reg 51(4)). The form must normally be submitted to the Customs & Excise within 1 month of the date of the cancellation.

All records relating to the business must be kept for three years, or such shorter period as the Customs & Excise may allow (s 34(2)), unless the business is being transferred as a going concern in which case all books will be handed to the purchaser, unless, at the request of the transferor, the Customs & Excise otherwise direct (s 25(*b*)).

2.700 Overseas traders

Where a non-resident makes supplies of goods or services in the United Kingdom he will be subject to the normal rules for registration described at **2.100**. It is important to understand therefore, whether a supply takes place in or outside the United Kingdom, which topic is considered in detail at **3.400**. Having regard to the position as discussed at **3.400**

if a non-resident does make supplies in the United Kingdom which
exceed the limit for registration (see **2.100**) he must follow one of the
following courses, depending upon whether or not he has a place of
business in the United Kingdom.

Non-resident trader with a place of business in the United Kingdom

The non-resident must register for VAT in the normal way by completing
Form VAT 1. A person at the UK office must assume responsibility for
submission of VAT returns and generally for complying with the VAT
legislation. If that person is an employee, he shall be given the appropriate authority from his employer. In VAT Leaflet 700/4/79 (Overseas
traders and VAT) the Customs & Excise have indicated that the following
letter of authority will suffice:

> "Draft Letter of Authority for Employee to act in VAT matters
> (name of overseas trader) hereby appoints (name of United Kingdom
> employee) as his/its agent for the purpose of complying with his/
> its legal obligations in connection with Value Added Tax, and auth-
> orises him/it for this purpose to sign return Forms VAT 100 and all
> other documents."

Alternatively, the Customs & Excise may require the non-resident to
execute a Power of Attorney in favour of the United Kingdom responsible
person. Forms of Power of Attorney acceptable to the Customs & Excise
are also given in VAT Leaflet 700/4/79 at Annexe 1.

Non-resident trader with no place of business in the United Kingdom

If the non-resident has no place of business in the United Kingdom but
nevertheless makes supplies in the United Kingdom, for example, from
a stock of goods he maintains in the United Kingdom, he must appoint
a person in the United Kingdom to act for him in VAT affairs. If the
trader has an employee or other responsible person in the United
Kingdom, that person may be appointed, or alternatively the non-resident may wish to appoint a VAT agent to act on his behalf. If an agent
is appointed he must keep separate accounts relating to the particular
non-resident trader, and he must be appointed under a Power of Attorney. However, it is also advisable to have a separate "VAT Agreement"
drawn up appointing the agent which sets out the full terms on which
the agent is to act. The agent would also normally require an indemnity
from the non-resident against any liability that may fall on the agent.
The agent would also usually be paid a fee for the duties he performs.

The mere appointment of such an agent should not of itself give rise to any liability on the non-resident to UK income tax or corporation tax as it would not of itself be sufficient to amount to trading in the United Kingdom. However, the non-resident should take care to have regard to the income tax or corporation tax consequences of his operations.

Chapter 3

Supply

3.000 Sources

3.100 General principles

As mentioned in Chapter 1, at p 4, VAT is chargeable by reference to, *inter alia*, a supply of goods or a supply of services. It is necessary, therefore, to determine the meaning of the concept of a "supply". In this respect, the Act is unhelpful. Section 6(2)(*a*) provides that:

"(2) Subject to any provision made by [Schedule 2] and to Treasury orders under sub-sections (3) to (6) below—
   (a) 'supply' in this Part of this Act includes all forms of supply, but not anything done otherwise than for a consideration;"

Schedule 2 and s 6(3)–(6) largely distinguish between whether a particular supply is to be regarded as a supply of goods or a supply of services (see **3.200,** at p 31) and add no further light on the meaning of a supply itself. However, s 6(2)(*b*) goes on to provide that:

> "(*b*) anything which is not a supply of goods but is done for a consideration (including, if so done, the granting, assignment or surrender of any right) is a supply of services."

The breadth of the phrase "anything ... done" (*Calor Gas Co Ltd* v *CCE*, [1973] VATTR 205 (*Casebook* **3.102**) but see below in relation to the EEC Sixth Directive) arguably leaves open for debate only the question of what is a supply of goods. This is because any other type of transaction will be subject to VAT as a supply of services. This would certainly appear to have been Parliament's intention (see **9.000** for a discussion of this point).

The cases that have come before the VAT Tribunals and courts indicate that the phrase "supply of goods" should not be given a meaning synonymous with that of the sale of goods under the Sale of Goods Act 1979. In *CCE* v *Oliver*, [1980] STC 73 (*Casebook* **3.104**) Griffiths J. stated in a case involving an alleged "supply" of stolen cars by the appellant:

> "I ask myself this question: if any layman had asked the purchaser of one of the stolen motor cars who had supplied him with the car, he would I think have unhesitatingly answered by giving the name of the taxpayer. The fact that it subsequently turned out that it had been supplied under a contract of sale that was in fact void would be neither here nor there, and I am content to adopt the definition of 'supply' for the purposes of this case put forward by counsel for the Commissioners. 'Supply' is the passing of possession in goods pursuant to an agreement whereunder the supplier agrees to part and the recipient agrees to take possession. By 'possession' is meant in this context control over the goods, in the sense of having the immediate facility for their use. This may or may not involve the physical removal of the goods."

Further, in *Carlton Lodge* v *CCE*, [1974] STC 507 (*Casebook* **3.101**) Milmo J. approved a statement in an earlier judgment in a purchase tax case that "the word 'supply' in its ordinary and natural sense means to furnish or to serve".

Both the *Oliver* and *Carlton Lodge* cases were, however, unfortunately decided on the basis of the wording of the Act before it was amended pursuant to the EEC Sixth Directive. In particular, the comments of Griffiths J. above, in relation to the transfer of the possession of goods, are now more relevant to the supply of services than to the supply of goods (Sched 2, para 1(1)(*b*)). The judgments are indicative, however, of the wide scope that the courts have given to the concept of a supply of goods.

Such an approach is to be contrasted with that of the EEC Sixth Directive. Article 5(1) provides that the "'Supply of goods' shall mean the transfer of the right to dispose of tangible property as owner". Article

6(1) provides that the "'Supply of services' shall mean any transaction which does not constitute a supply of goods within the meaning of Article 5". Thus, if the wording of the EEC Sixth Directive prevails (see **13.800,** *post*), for there to be a supply of goods it would appear that the recipient must become the beneficial owner of the entire asset in question. This would most certainly result in the transaction in the *Oliver* case not being a supply of goods. It would also suggest that the concept of a supply of goods is closer to a sale of goods than that adopted by the courts in the United Kingdom to date in relation to the Act prior to 1 January 1978. The question remains, therefore, whether the *Oliver* type of transaction, which falls short of transferring full ownership to the recipient and may, therefore, no longer be treated as a supply of goods, is capable of comprising a supply of services.

For there to be a supply of services under the terms of the EEC Sixth Directive, there must be a "transaction" (Article 6(1)) for which a consideration is given (Article 2—but see **3.800**). A "transaction" is not defined in the Directive. It is defined in the Shorter Oxford Dictionary as:

> "The adjustment of a dispute between parties by mutual concession; compromise; hence *gen* an arrangement, an agreement, a covenant."

The latter part of this definition would appear more relevant in VAT terms. For a supply of services, therefore, there should be some kind of mutual arrangement between the parties involved in the supply. Whether this will be shown to be a narrower concept than that of "anything . . . done" as stated in s 6 must remain an open issue. It can be said, however, that the concept is wide and would appear to be restricted only by the requirement (in most cases) that there should be a consideration for the transaction in question (although, subject as mentioned at p 39 below in relation to Sched 3, paras 1–3, it is not necessary that the consideration is adequate).

Transactions deemed to be supplies

Notwithstanding this breadth of wording, it has been considered necessary in the Act to add provisions to deem certain transactions to be supplies. These provisions are:

SELF-SUPPLIES

The Treasury is empowered by s 6(5) and (6) to specify, by Order, that where a person in the course or furtherance of his business acquires or produces goods (subs (5)) or does anything for the purposes of that business which would be a supply of services if made for a consideration (subs (6)), those goods or services, as the case may be, shall be treated as both supplied to and by him. An indication of the reason for this provision is to be found in EEC Sixth Directive, art 6(3). If a person makes some exempt supplies, he may be unable to set a part of the input tax he suffers on supplies to him against the output tax due by him in respect of his own taxable supplies (see further **5.300**). In such circumstances, that person may supply himself with certain goods or services rather than purchase them from another in order to reduce his costs. As a result this may lead to the distortion of competition between suppliers.

To date, however, Orders have only been made in respect of cars and printed matter (see further **3.700**).

FREE SUPPLIES OF SERVICES

Section 6(4) enables the Treasury to provide, by Order, that, where a person carrying on a business does anything that is not a supply of services merely because it is made otherwise than for a consideration, he shall be treated as making a supply of services. This conforms with the EEC Sixth Directive, art 6(2)(*b*). No orders have yet been made.

DISPOSITION OR PRIVATE USE OF ASSETS

It is provided in Sched 2, para 5(2) and (3) that where goods are either transferred or disposed of at the direction of the person carrying on a business so as no longer to form part of the assets of that business; or are put to any private use or made available to any person for any purpose other than a purpose of the business, a supply is to be treated as taking place. The supplies in such cases are of goods and services respectively.

This provision does not apply, however, to the gift of goods where the cost to the donor is less than £10 (except where a series of gifts is involved), to gifts of industrial samples in a form not ordinarily available for sale to the public, to actual or potential customers or the disposal of a motor car for no consideration and in respect of which no input tax relief has been claimed (VAT (Cars) Order 1980 (SI 1980 No 442), art 7(*c*)).

For the treatment of Business Promotion Schemes see **3.600**.

An example of the operation of para 5(2) is the use of petrol by employees for their own private motoring. The views of the Customs & Excise on this point and its inter-relationship with claims for input tax relief in respect of the petrol are now set out in Notice No 700, Appendix B which is reproduced at **5.100**.

SALE IN SATISFACTION OF A DEBT

It is provided in Sched 2, para 6 that the sale under a power exercisable by any person of the assets of a business of another, in or towards the satisfaction of a debt owed by the taxable person, is deemed to be a supply by the taxable person concerned. This would apply, for example, to sales by receivers.

SUPPLIES ON CEASING TO BE A TAXABLE PERSON

Schedule 2, para 7 deems any goods forming part of the assets of a business carried on by a taxable person as supplied by him in the course or furtherance of his business should he cease to be a taxable person. This does not apply, however, to cases where the business in question is transferred as a going concern to another taxable person (see **4.300**), to persons treated as taxable persons on carrying on the business of persons who have either died, become bankrupt or incapacitated, or if the tax on the deemed supply would be £250 or less.

IMPORTATION OF SERVICES

With effect from 1 January 1978, s 8B provides that certain imports of services by taxable persons are to be treated as supplied by the importer himself in the course or furtherance of his business. The services in question are those listed in Sched 2A (see further **10.200**).

Transactions deemed not to be supplies

The following categories of transactions have been taken out of the wide concept of "supply" discussed above:

THE TRANSFER OF A BUSINESS AS A GOING CONCERN

Provided certain conditions are met, such transfers are not treated as involving a supply of the assets of the business (VAT (Special Provisions) Order 1977 (SI 1977 No 1796), art 12) (see further **4.300**).

REPOSSESSED GOODS OR GOODS TAKEN IN SETTLEMENT

The VAT (Special Provisions) Order 1977 (SI 1977 No 1796), arts 10 and 11 provide that a sale of certain repossessed goods under a finance agreement, or goods acquired by an insurer in settlement of a claim under an insurance policy, or mortgage will, if the sale complies with certain conditions, be neither a supply of goods nor services. The conditions are that:

(*a*) the goods are disposed of in the same condition as they were in at the time of repossession, acquisition or possession; and
(*b*) if supplied by the person from whom they were first obtained, VAT would not have been payable on the supply or not on the full value of the supply; or
(*c*) if the goods have been imported into the United Kingdom, they have borne VAT on import which VAT has not been reclaimed.

The goods that may qualify for exclusion from VAT under the above provisions are:

(*a*) works of art, antiques and collectors' pieces;
(*b*) caravans;
(*c*) motor cycles;
(*d*) boats and outboard motors;
(*e*) electronic organs; and
(*f*) aircraft.

Similar treatment to the above is afforded to the disposal of repossessed used motor cars or used motor cars acquired in settlement of a claim under an insurance policy (VAT (Cars) Order 1980 (SI 1980 No 442), art 7).

See also, in connection with the above, VAT Leaflet 700/5/79.

GROUPS OF COMPANIES

Supplies between companies which are members of a group in respect of which a valid group registration is in force, are disregarded for VAT purposes (s 21—see further **2.400**). It should be borne in mind that a company need not be a taxable person to be included in a group registration for VAT purposes.

Section 21 is to be contrasted with s 23(1) which enables a company carrying on business in more than one division to apply to the Customs & Excise for the separate registration of those divisions. Supplies between such divisions are, however, similarly not subject to VAT.

LOST OR DESTROYED GOODS

Section 31(3) effectively recognises that goods which have been lost or destroyed cannot be supplied, for VAT purposes, by the taxable person in question (see *G Benton* v *CCE*, [1975] VATTR 138 (*Casebook* **3.107**)). That taxable person may, however, claim input tax suffered in respect of such goods in the normal way.

EXCLUSIONS FOR PARTIAL EXEMPTION PURPOSES

Finally, it should be noted that certain otherwise exempt transactions are ignored in the calculation of any restriction to be imposed on a taxable person's ability to claim input tax credit. These transactions are listed in the VAT (General) Regulations 1977 (SI 1977 No 1759), reg 66 and are discussed at **5.300**.

Specific types of transaction

Certain specific types of transaction remain to be considered in connection with the question as to what constitutes a supply for VAT purposes.

CONTRACTS VOID AB INITIO

The position in relation to contracts which are void or cancelled *ab initio* cannot be stated with certainty following the case of *CCE* v *Oliver*, [1980] STC 73 (*Casebook* **3.104**). Such contracts include those induced by fraud where the subject of the fraud elects to rescind the contract and contracts which are novated. In the light of the definition of a supply of goods in the EEC Sixth Directive, art 5(1), it would seem that such a transaction should not be treated as a supply of goods as the recipient of the supply never had the right, as the owner, to dispose of the goods transferred to him. The question remains, however, as to whether the transaction could be regarded as a supply of services.

Where a contract is void *ab initio*, the principle of *restitutio in integrum* applies, that is, the parties to the contract are to be restored to the position in which they found themselves prior to the execution of the contract. Thus, *inter alia*, any price which the recipient of the supply has paid to the supplier must be repaid and the goods supplied must be returned to the supplier. The contractual consequence is, therefore, (if the buyer's right to sue for damages is ignored) to treat the contract as effectively never having been made. It would seem illogical to adopt this approach in contract law but not in relation to VAT. It is hoped, therefore, that a contract which is void *ab initio* would not be a supply of services.

CANCELLABLE CONTRACTS AND SALE OR RETURN

Any cancellable contract, which is cancelled and any sale on approval, where the goods are not accepted, should logically produce the same result in VAT terms as contracts which are void *ab initio*. In such cases, there has been no permanent transfer of the goods or services the subject of the contract although, clearly, there has been a "transaction" between the parties. If any consideration is retained following cancellation or non acceptance, as the case may be, any supply that has taken place is arguably limited to whatever right was purchased by such consideration— in most cases the option to purchase the goods or services or to return them.

This position is in fact adopted by the Act in relation to the fixing of the time of supply where there is a transfer of goods on sale or return. Section 7(2) (*c*) provides that the time of supply is to be "at the time when it becomes certain that the supply has taken place, but not later than 12 months after the removal (of the goods)". This has been interpreted by the Customs & Excise as implying the time when the goods are "adopted" under the contract. Thus, if the goods are returned to the supplier (subject to the 12 months time limit), no supply takes place for VAT purposes.

RESERVATION OF TITLE

The position in the preceding paragraphs is to be distinguished from cases where a supply takes place but the property in the goods does not pass to the buyer immediately on transfer of possession of the goods. This includes, of course, the *Romalpa* style contract where title to the goods does not pass until the full price has been paid (see *Aluminium Industrie Vaassen BV* v *Romalpa Aluminium Ltd*, [1976] 1 WLR 676). In such instance, a supply (of goods where the property in the goods passes under the agreement at a future time not later than the date when the goods are fully paid for: Sched 2, para 1(2)(*b*)) takes place even though the full price has not been received by the supplier (see *Vermitron Ltd* v *CCE*, LON/77/428 (*Casebook* **3.302**) and *M and D Price Bros Ltd* v *CCE*, [1978] VATTR 115 (*Casebook* **3.105**)).

HIRE PURCHASE REPOSSESSIONS

In practice, where the owner repossesses goods sold on hire purchase, it is understood that the Customs & Excise allows the owner to claim a repayment from the Customs & Excise of part of the VAT on the original supply to the hirer and to issue a credit note to the hirer for that amount of VAT. In effect, there is a cancellation of part of the supply (see further **16.400**).

3.200 Distinction between a supply of goods and a supply of services

Although both supplies of goods and services are subject to VAT at the same rate, it is important to determine the category into which a transaction falls. This is because the detailed rules as to the time and place of supply differ according to whether a supply is one of goods or services. This difference is of particular significance in the context of the international supply of goods or services where, although the majority of exported goods are zero-rated, only certain specific services qualify for such treatment.

The basic position is as stated in **3.100**; any transaction which is not a supply of goods but is done for a consideration, is a supply of services. However, Sched 2 contains provisions which deem certain transactions to be supplies of either goods or services and further, the Treasury is empowered by s 6(3) to make similar provision, by Order, in relation to particular categories of supply. Only one such Order has been made to date by the Treasury in connection with exchanges of reconditioned articles (VAT (Special Provisions) Order 1977 (SI 1977 No 1796), art 13).

Supplies of goods

The following transactions are deemed to be supplies of goods by Sched 2:

TRANSFER OF PROPERTY (SCHED 2, PARA 1(1))

The transfer of the whole property in goods is a supply of goods, but the transfer of an undivided share of property is a supply of services.

TRANSFER OF POSSESSION (SCHED 2, PARA 1(2))

A supply of goods is made where there is a transfer of the possession of goods under either a contract:

(*a*) of sale (this would include credit sale agreements); or
(*b*) which expressly contemplates that the property in the goods will pass at some determinable time in the future not later than the time the goods are paid for. This would include hire purchase and conditional sale agreements and *Romalpa* style contracts.

APPLICATION OF A TREATMENT TO GOODS (SCHED 2, PARA 2)

The application of a treatment or process to another's goods so as to produce new goods is a supply of goods (s 6(7) further provides that goods manufactured from other goods are treated as incorporating those other goods).

POWER ETC (SCHED 2, PARA 3)

The supply of any form of power, heat, refrigeration or ventilation is a supply of goods. Numerous attempts have been made by suppliers, who incorporate these items in a supply, to argue that the entire supply is of these items alone, so that the entire supply is entitled to be zero-rated under Sched 4, Group 7. Such attempts have, with one exception (*High Wycombe Squash Club Ltd* v *CCE* [1976] VATTR 156 (*Casebook* **8.702**), failed (see further **8.700**).

LAND (SCHED 2, PARA 4)

The grant, assignment or surrender of a major interest in land is a supply of goods. A major interest in land is defined in s 46 as a fee simple or a tenancy for a term certain exceeding 21 years (see further Sched 5, Groups 1 and 9).

Supplies of services

The following are deemed to be supplies of services by Sched 2.

TRANSFER OF PROPERTY (SCHED 2, PARA 1(1))

The transfer of any undivided share of any property is a supply of services whereas the transfer of the whole of any property is a supply of goods.

TRANSFER OF POSSESSION (SCHED 2, PARA 1(2))

Any transfer of the possession of goods where the contract in question does not satisfy the conditions in paragraph 1(2) is a supply of services (see under *Supplies of goods, ante*). A hire or lease of goods will, therefore, be a supply of services.

NON BUSINESS USE OF GOODS (SCHED 2, PARA 5(3))

A supply of services is deemed to be made where goods are used or made available for any purpose other than for the purposes of the business for which they are held or used. This includes private use but not anything done otherwise than by or under the direction of the person carrying on the business. This is an instance where consideration is not required.

For this paragraph to apply, the goods must remain the property of the supplier. If this is not the case, the supply is one of goods (Sched 2, para 5(2)).

EXCHANGES (VAT (SPECIAL PROVISIONS) ORDER 1977 (SI 1977 NO 1796), ART 13)

A supply of services is made in the case of the supply of a reconditioned article in exchange for an unserviceable article of a similar kind by a person who regularly offers a reconditioning facility in the course or furtherance of his business (see further VAT Leaflet 700/10/79: Processing and repair of goods and supplies of exchange units).

3.300 Time of supply

The basic rules governing the time at which a supply is treated as made are detailed in s 7(2), (3) and (4). Again, however, further provisions are necessary to deal with particular types of supply and the Customs & Excise is given power in s 7(8) to determine, by Regulations, the time of supply in the case of:

(*a*) a supply for a consideration the whole or part of which is payable periodically, or from time to time or at the end of any period;
(*b*) a supply of goods the consideration for which is determined at the time the goods are appropriated for any purpose; and
(*c*) a supply of services under Sched 2, para 5(3) (non-business use of goods), or the subject of a Treasury Order under s 6(4) (no orders have yet been made).

Such Regulations, under s 7(8), may provide for the goods or services to be treated as separately and successively supplied at prescribed times or intervals. The current Regulations are the VAT (General) Regulations 1977 (SI 1977 No 1759) regs 12–22.

Goods

The basic time of supply of goods is the earlier of the time when:

(*a*) the goods are removed (s 7(2)(*a*)); or

(*b*) the goods are made available to the customer (when the goods are not removed) (s 7(2)(*b*)); or

(*c*) a tax invoice in respect of the supply is issued (s 7(4)—for a discussion as to what constitutes a tax invoice see **17.200** at p 331); or

(*d*) a payment is received for the supply (s 7(4)). A returnable deposit is not treated as a payment for the purposes of s 7(4), however.

In the case of (*c*) and (*d*), the supply will be treated as occurring only to the extent that it is covered by the invoice or payment (s 7(4)).

The time of a supply treated as occurring under (*a*) or (*b*) will be delayed (unless the supplier otherwise elects) by the issue of an invoice within 14 days of the occurrence of the event in (*a*) or (*b*). The delay will be to the date of the issue of the invoice (s 7(5)). If no invoice is issued within that period, the time of the supply remains as above. The Customs & Excise also has the power, at the request of the supplier, to extend this 14 day period (s 7(6)).

Particular types of supply of goods

The above basic rules are modified in the case of the following types of supply:

SALE OR RETURN OR SIMILAR SALES

Where goods are removed before it is known whether a supply will take place, the time of supply is "the time when it becomes certain that the supply has taken place" subject to a limit of 12 months following the removal of the goods (s 7(2)(*c*)). In practice, the Customs & Excise regard a supply as having become certain at the time when the goods are "adopted" by the customer. Adoption is interpreted either as the expiry of a fixed time limit, if any, for the return of the goods or their appropriation by the customer for any purpose. The Customs & Excise states (Notice No 700, para 14(*b*)) that a non-returnable deposit or similar payment by the customer would indicate the adoption of the goods.

The rule in s 7(2)(*c*) is subject to the earlier issue of a tax invoice and the issue of a tax invoice within 14 days of the basic time of supply but not the earlier payment rule mentioned in (*d*) above (s 7(4) and (5)).

RETENTION OF PROPERTY

Where the property in the goods is retained by the supplier until the goods are appropriated by the buyer and the whole or a part of the consideration is determined at that time, the time of supply is the earliest of (VAT (General) Regulations 1977 (SI 1977 No 1759), reg 16):

- (*a*) appropriation;
- (*b*) invoice; or
- (*c*) payment.

Again, however, a supply is made in the case of (*b*) and (*c*) only to the extent covered by the invoice or payment. This rule does not apply to sales on approval or sale or return.

POWER ETC.

Supplies within Sched 2, para 3, that is of power, heat, refrigeration and ventilation, take place on the earlier of the receipt of a payment or issue of an invoice (VAT (General) Regulations 1977 (SI 1977 No 1759), reg 15).

LAND

Periodical payments in relation to the grant, assignment or surrender of a major interest in land are treated as separate supplies made on the earlier of payment and invoice dates (VAT (General) Regulations 1977 (SI 1977 No 1759), reg 14).

SELF-SUPPLIES

Goods falling within an Order made under s 6(5) (self-supplies) are supplied when appropriated for use in the taxable person's business (s 7(7)).

DISPOSAL OF BUSINESS ASSETS

Goods falling within Sched 2, para 5(2), that is those which cease to form part of the assets of a business, are supplied when transferred or disposed of (s 7(7A)).

Services

The basic time of supply in the case of services is the time of their performance (s 7(3)) or if earlier the date of issue of an invoice or receipt of payment (s 7(4)). Further, the issue of a tax invoice within 14 days of the time of the performance of the services will delay the time of supply to the date of the issue of that invoice.

Particular types of supply of services

This basic rule is modified, however, in the following cases (references are to the VAT (General) Regulations 1977 (SI 1977 No 1759)):

NON-BUSINESS USE

Supplies falling within Sched 2, para 5(3) are treated as made on the last day of each prescribed accounting period for which they are made available for the non-business use in question (reg 12(1)).

FREE USE OF SERVICES

A similar rule to that in NON-BUSINESS USE, *ante* applies in connection with any services specified in a Treasury Order under s 6(4) (reg 12(2)).

CONTINUOUS SUPPLIES OF SERVICES

A supply, the consideration for which is determined or payable periodically, is treated as successfully supplied at the earlier of each payment or tax invoice date (reg 18(1)). An exception to the tax invoice date rule is given, however, to allow a supplier to issue one invoice for a period (not exceeding 1 year) covering several payments. In such case, the supply will still be treated as occurring on the actual payment dates (reg 18(2)).

ROYALTIES AND SIMILAR PAYMENTS

Where the whole amount of the consideration for a supply of services is not ascertainable when those services are performed and a consideration is given at a later stage for the use of those services, a further supply is treated as taking place each time a payment is received or a tax invoice is issued, whichever occurs first (reg 19). This does not apply to a supply governed by reg 18 (CONTINUOUS SUPPLY OF SERVICES, *ante*).

SUPPLIES IN THE CONSTRUCTION INDUSTRY

Supplies in the course of the construction, alteration, demolition, repair or maintenance of a building or any civil engineering work under a contract which provides for periodical payments, are treated as taking place at the earlier of (reg 21):

(*a*) where the consideration is in money, the receipt of a payment; or
(*b*) the issue of an invoice.

BARRISTERS

Services performed by a barrister are treated as made at the earlier of (reg 20):
(*a*) the issue of a tax invoice (i.e. not a fee note);
(*b*) the receipt of payment;
(*c*) the barrister ceasing to practice as such.

Issues affecting both supplies of goods and services

ACCOMMODATION TAX POINTS

By s 7(6) and (6A), the Customs & Excise may, at a supplier's request, agree that a supply is treated as taking place at an earlier or later time to that determined under the above rules. For example, an extension of 3 months has been agreed between the Customs & Excise and the Law Society under s 7(6). This is commonly known as an "accommodation tax point".

RETENTION PAYMENTS

Where a contract provides for the withholding of any part of the consideration until the full and satisfactory performance of any part of the contract, the supply is treated as made on the earlier of the date a payment is received and the issue of the tax invoice (reg 17).

3.400 Place of supply

A supply is only chargeable when it is made in the United Kingdom. Although the place of supply is fairly easily determined where the supply is one of goods, more complex provisions are required to determine the place of the supply of services. The United Kingdom for these purposes includes the Isle of Man and the territorial waters of the United Kingdom and Isle of Man.

Goods

Under s 8 goods are treated as supplied in the United Kingdom where:

(a) if they are not to be removed to or from the United Kingdom, they are physically present there (s 8(2)). For this purpose, goods which leave and then re-enter the United Kingdom in the course of their supply are not treated as removed from the United Kingdom (s 8(8)); or

(b) they are to be removed from the United Kingdom (s 8(3)).

Goods removed to the United Kingdom are not supplied in the United Kingdom and do not therefore fall within the "supply" head of charge. However, they may fall within the "import" head of charge (see Chapter 6).

Services

The place at which a supply of services takes place is linked with effect from 1 January 1978, to the place in which the supplier "belongs" (s 8A(1)). Thus, a supply of services is treated as made in the United Kingdom if the supplier belongs in the United Kingdom and elsewhere if the supplier belongs abroad. The rules to determine where a supplier belongs are as follows:

(*a*) if the supplier has only one business or other fixed establishment, he belongs in the country in which that establishment is situate. For this purpose, a branch or agency is treated as a business establishment of the person carrying on business through it. Branch or agency is not defined for VAT purposes but has a customary meaning for income tax purposes which may be of assistance in this context. The Customs & Excise in practice take the view that a fixed place of business means, simply, a place from which business is conducted (see also the OECD Commentary, p 59 *et seq* on article 5 of the Model Convention in respect of "fixed place of business");

(*b*) if (*a*) does not apply because the supplier has no such establishment, he is treated as belonging in the country in which he has his usual place of residence. In the case of a company, this is the place where it is legally constituted (s 8A(4)(*b*));

(*c*) if (*a*) does not apply because the supplier has more than one such establishment, he belongs in the country in which the establishment most directly concerned with the supply is situated.

The Treasury is given power by s 8A(5) to vary the above rules generally or only in respect of a particular type of supply.

Services received from abroad

Where services of a type listed in Sched 2A are made outside the United Kingdom, but are received by a taxable person who belongs in the United Kingdom (the test of belonging is the same as that above), that taxable person is treated as if he had himself supplied those services in the United Kingdom in the course or furtherance of his business (s 8B). Section 8B is fully discussed in **10.200.**

3.500 Value of a supply

Section 10 and Sched 3, paras 4–11 lay down the basic rules governing the value of a supply of goods or services. Section 11 covers the valuation of imported goods. Schedule 3, paras 1–3 contain certain anti-avoidance provisions empowering the Customs & Excise to make directions as to the value of a supply "for the protection of the revenue". These three groups of provisions are discussed in the following paragraphs. These provisions do not necessarily apply, however, to a supplier operating one of the special schemes for retailers (see **16.200**).

Before discussing the detailed rules as to the value of a supply, two general points should be mentioned. First, where a consideration is given for a supply and no mention of VAT is made, that consideration is deemed to be VAT inclusive. This follows from s 10(2) and should always be borne in mind by suppliers when quoting a price for a particular supply. It is envisaged that suppliers may shortly be required to specify the VAT element of any charge for supplies. Secondly, where an amount in any currency other than Sterling is involved, that amount must be converted into Sterling in accordance with EEC rules at the appropriate exchange rate at the date of supply in order to establish the value of the supply (Sched 3, para 10(1) and see EEC Regulation 803/68, art 12).

Supply of goods or services

The following basic rules apply:

CONSIDERATION IN THE FORM OF MONEY

If the supply is for a consideration in money (which includes currencies other than Sterling: section 46(1)), the value of the supply is the amount which, together with VAT at the relevant rate thereon, equals that consideration. The consideration is, therefore, the gross amount, the value of the supply, the net amount. To ascertain the value of the supply of a standard rated item, therefore, the consideration should be multiplied by $\frac{100}{115}$, that is, $\frac{20}{23}$.

There is no suggestion in the Act that the consideration, if wholly in money, need be adequate. Neither the Customs and Excise nor a VAT Tribunal is empowered, therefore, to enquire into the price placed on a transaction by the parties, even if they are connected parties, but must take that price as the true consideration for the supply. This is subject to two caveats. First, the inadequacy of the consideration for a particular supply may suggest that there is some other, perhaps undisclosed, supply made by the recipient. A set-off may, therefore, have taken place (see for example *E Mann* v *CCE*, LEE/75/70 (*Casebook* **3.508**), and *Smith and Williamson* v *CCE*, [1976] VATTR 215 (*Casebook* **3.109**)). Secondly, if the supply falls within the anti-avoidance provisions discussed below, the Customs & Excise may give directions as to the value of any future supplies of the same type (Sched 3, paras 1–3).

NO CONSIDERATION OR NOT WHOLLY IN MONEY

If there is no consideration or the consideration given does not consist wholly of money, the value of the supply is its market value (s 10(3)).

"Consideration" for this purpose has its normal meaning under English Law (*Theatre Consolidated Ltd* v *CCE*, [1975] VATTR 13 (*Casebook* **3.501**)) that is, "an act or forebearance of one party or promise thereof, for which the act or promise of the other is bought" (*Exeter Golf and Country Club Ltd* v *CCE*, at tribunal level, CAR/78/124, *Casebook* **15.219**).

"Market value" is effectively defined as the VAT exclusive price that unconnected parties would pay for the supply if money were the only consideration involved (s 10(5)).

CONSIDERATION RELATES TO A SUPPLY AND ANOTHER TRANSACTION

Where the total consideration given relates to both a "supply" and some other transaction, it is to be apportioned and only that part attributable to the supply treated as the consideration given for it (s 10(4)). At first sight this is a curious provision given the scope of the definition of supply. It is intended to cover, however, a transaction which is in part specifically excluded from being a "supply". For example, it would apply where a taxable person transfers both a part of his business as a going concern and also a bundle of further assets which neither formed part of that concern nor a separate business in themselves.

In *CCE* v *Automobile Association*, [1974] STC at p 197c (*Casebook* **3.602**) Lord Widgery CJ. also found that the wording of s 10(4) demonstrated that the draftsman of the Act "obviously had the possibility of apportionment in mind" in the context of apportioning a single consideration between several items comprised in a supply. In such a case, therefore, the consideration should be apportioned between the various items supplied and the rate of VAT in relation to each of those items applied accordingly (see further **3.600**).

DISCOUNT FOR PROMPT PAYMENT

Where a supply is made with a discount for prompt payment and the consideration is not payable by instalments, the value of the supply is to be taken as the discounted price. This principle applies whether or not the customer in the event qualifies for and pays that discounted price (Sched 3, para 4). It also applies to imported goods (Sched 3, para 5).

TRADING STAMPS ETC SUPPLIED FOR A CONSIDERATION

Where tokens, stamps or vouchers entitling the holder to receive goods or services are supplied for a consideration, the value of the supply is treated as only the excess, if any, of that consideration over the value of the goods or services that may be obtained with the token (Sched 3, para 6).

VALUE OF SUPPLY TREATED AS THE COST TO THE SUPPLIER

The value of the following supplies is treated as the cost to the person making the supply (Sched 3, para 7):

(*a*) self-supplies brought into charge by Treasury order under s 6(5);

(*b*) the transfer or disposal of business assets otherwise than for a consideration under Sched 2, para 5(2); and
(*c*) supplies of goods on ceasing to be a taxable person other than as excepted under Sched 2, para 7.

It will be appreciated that this rule can involve a hardship to the supplier where the market value of the assets has fallen since their acquisition. The effect of this rule may be avoided in relation to Sched 2, para 5(2) supplies, by requiring a nominal consideration for the transfer of the assets in question.

The value of the following supplies is taken as the full cost to the taxable person making the supply (Sched 3, para 8). The difference in wording of Sched 3, paras 7 and 8 (that is, "cost" and "full cost") is not considered to be material.

(*a*) services the subject of a Treasury Order under s 6(4); and
(*b*) the private or other non-business use of business assets under Sched 2, para 5(3).

"Cost" is regarded by the Customs & Excise as being the price at which the goods were acquired by the taxable person in question or their cost of manufacture, including overheads (see Notice No 700, para 15(*c*)). In the case of a supply under Sched 2, para 5(3), a proportion of cost is taken dependent upon the period for which the goods are used. In practice, this tends to be an arbitrary figure.

LAND

The Customs & Excise have issued VAT Leaflet 10/74/VMF (Indemnities under property lease agreements), to clarify its interpretation of the consideration for a supply in relation to leases. The relevant part of this leaflet is as follows:

"1. As a general rule, any payment that has to be made by a lessee in order to obtain the grant of a right over land (eg a lease) is the consideration, or part of the consideration, for the supply of the right covered by the lease. This applies whether or not the payment is described as a reimbursement or indemnification of costs incurred by the lessor. Similarly, any payment made by a lessee to a lessor to obtain an additional right is the consideration for the supply of that additional right.
2. Some leasing agreements, however, provide that the lessee shall reimburse the lessor for legal or other advisory costs incurred by the lessor as a result of the lessee's exercising rights already granted under the lease. For example, the lessee may have the right to assign the lease, sub-let or make alterations to the property, and when he does so the lessor may incur legal or surveyor's fees. In such cases, the reimbursement payments by the lessee are not regarded as the consideration, or part of the consideration, for a supply by the lessor to the lessee."

ACCOMMODATION

Where accommodation is provided in an hotel, inn, boarding house or similar establishment for more than 4 weeks, the value of the supply is treated, from the fourth week onwards, as that part of the consideration that is attributable to the provision of facilities other than the right to occupy the accommodation itself (Sched 3, para 9). This reduced value must not be less than 20 per cent of the combined value of the accommodation and the other facilities.

Imported goods

For the value of imported goods see **6.400.**

Imported services

Where a supply is treated as made on the importation of services under s 8B, it is treated as made by the taxable person importing the supply. The basic rules discussed above in relation to supplies of services will therefore apply.

Anti-avoidance provisions

Where it considers it necessary to protect the revenue and it is likely that future similar supplies or imports will be made, the Customs & Excise have the ability to make directions as to the value of such future supplies or imports. This ability to make directions is limited however to cases where it appears to the Customs & Excise that:

(*a*) the consideration for the supply or importation has been determined with a view to securing a reduction of liability to VAT on the supply or importation (Sched 3, paras 1 and 2); or
(*b*) the whole or part of the business of a taxable person consists in supplying goods to a number of individuals who are not taxable persons to be sold by them or by others by retail (Sched 3, para 3).

Notices given under (*a*) or (*b*) must be given in writing and specify the date from which the value stated in the direction is to apply. Such date cannot be earlier than the date of the notice. Any notice given may be varied or withdrawn by a further notice in writing (Sched 3, para 12).

The scope of these provisions is wide and, as the Tribunal noted in *H Tempest* v *CCE*, [1975] VATTR 161 (*Casebook* **3.506**), is not limited, in (*b*) above, to cases where the motive of the supplier is one of tax avoidance. Such motive would appear to be required in (*a*), however, where a subjective test is presumably to be applied.

The exact ambit of Sched 3, para 3 is difficult to state. Clearly, it must extend beyond sales by individuals where some form of agency arrangement or employment can be imputed between the supplier and the individual as such sales would be made by the supplier and already within the charge to VAT without the assistance of Sched 2. The Customs & Excise, in Notice No 700, para 15(*d*), instances the supply to individuals for resale direct to the public by door to door selling and "party plans" as falling within the ambit of Sched 3, para 3. In *H Tempest* v *CCE*, the paragraph was applied to sales of school photographs to parents through headmasters who were given a discount by the supplier on the price charged to parents. "Retail" in that case was held to have its ordinary meaning and to include such sales by headmasters.

3.600 The nature of a supply

It is necessary to determine the precise nature of a supply in each case in order to apply the rules as to consideration and set-off and to ascertain whether the particular supply is entitled to be zero-rated, is exempt or is standard rated. In practice this will only present a problem where a package of goods or services is supplied. The question then arises as to whether the supply is to be treated as either a single supply, comprising the composite whole, or the multiple supply of a number of individual separate supplies. The latter type of supply allows the taxpayer to apportion the consideration among the separate supplies and apply the appropriate tax rate accordingly (see *CCE* v *Automobile Association*, [1974] STC 192, *Casebook* **3.602**)).

The distinction between composite and multiple supplies has become complicated however by the discovery of a third category of supply, that of the "two-part tariff". In effect, a two-part tariff is merely a single supply for which more than one payment is made. However, confusion arises between the multiple supply and the two-part tariff because, in the case of a two-part tariff, a supply often appears to be made at the time of each payment.

The approach to be adopted in determining the nature of a supply was originally thought to have been settled by Lord Widgery CJ. in *Automobile Association* v *CCE*, [1974] STC 192 (*Casebook* **3.602**), where Lord Widgery commented as follows in relation to the Tribunal's question:

"... what does a member get for his subscription? I pause to say that in my judgment that is a perfectly appropriate approach and clearly gives rise to a question of fact. There is no law in that at all ... (The Tribunal) asked themselves what in substance and reality is the service for which the subscription is paid. They concluded that as a matter of substance and reality the subscription is paid for the package of individual benefits and I can see no reason whatever for thinking that they have erred in law or indeed reached other than a perfectly sensible conclusion on the facts of this case."

This approach was followed in *Barton* v *CCE*, [1974] STC 200 (*Casebook* **3.604**) by Bridge J. but was distinguished by Scarman LJ. in

British Airports Authority v *CCE*, [1975] STC 652 (*Casebook* **3.606**), in the following manner:

> "Bridge J ... really addressed himself to the same sort of question (as Lord Widgery CJ), asking: what was the consideration for? Plainly very often an investigation as to the nature of an agreement is no more than an investigation of primary fact. No doubt that was so in the Automobile Association case. But in this case the nature of the agreement has to be determined by a study of its terms, the agreement being a very full and complex agreement in writing. That is a question of law..."

Scarman LJ. did consider, however, that, whether in a particular case the interpretation of the agreement was a matter of fact or law, the court is under an obligation to look at the substance of the agreement and to reach a conclusion as to its nature quite irrespective of form, or the language in which the agreement is embodied.

In *British Railways Board* v *CCE*, [1977] STC 221 (*Casebook* **3.610**), Lord Denning and Browne LJ. also distinguished the *Automobile Association* case on similar grounds to Scarman LJ. in the *British Airports Authority* case and Sir John Pennycuick criticised it as "not an accurate statement of the proper principle". Further Browne LJ. indicated that the "substance and reality" test "may be dangerous if it suggests that one can go behind a written contract". Despite this apparent attack on Lord Widgery's judgment, the test finally approved in the *British Railways Board* case represents a compromise of both Lord Widgery and Scarman LJ.'s positions. The present approach to this question can possibly be summarised therefore in the following passage from the judgment of Sir John Pennycuick:

> "... the first question to be determined was indeed which of these benefits should in substance be regarded as the goods or services supplied by the society or association to its members in return for their subscriptions. Once that question is out of the way, and in the present case it does not arise at all, the applicability of section 12(1) and Schedule 4 Group 10, to the particular service found as a fact to be supplied is one of law".

Characteristics of a composite supply

In *Betty Foster* (*Fashion Sewing*) *Ltd* v *CCE*, [1976] VATTR 229 (*Casebook* **3.601**), the Tribunal noted that on their own the separate components of the supply were worthless and that their individual supply in the absence of the remainder of the components would be "meaningless". Thus, while the Tribunal warned against including extraneous items into an otherwise composite supply with a view to avoiding tax, it considered the supply to be a composite supply entitled to be zero-rated in its entirety.

Two further cases, *CCE* v *Scott*, [1978] STC 191 (*Casebook* **3.611**), and *Mander Laundries* v *CCE*, [1973] VATTR 136 (*Casebook* **3.607**), also show that the central item supplied will dictate the nature of the supply where other items are merely incidental or subsidiary to it and in *Banstead Downs Golf Club* v *CCE*, [1974] VATTR 219 (*Casebook* **3.608**), the practical impossibility of severing the supplies resulted in the decision that the supply was a composite whole.

Characteristics of a multiple supply

The single most important feature of a multiple supply is that the individual items must be capable of being sensibly supplied separately. If this is the case, the fact that a single price is demanded or single invoice issued will not affect the principle that an apportionment of that price will be made. The particular suppliers in question need not be prepared to supply those items separately however. This follows from *River Barge Holidays Ltd* v *CCE*, LON/77/345 (*Casebook* **3.603**), where an apportionment was made between the transport of holidaymakers and their overnight accommodation on board barges, although there was no question of a holidaymaker purchasing only a part of the combined package. Examples of multiple supplies are given by the Customs & Excise in Notice No 700, para 26 and include package tours in the United Kingdom and packs of audio-visual materials (standard rated) together with course books (zero-rated).

Items supplied together, but for which separate charges are made, are usually considered a multiple supply. In fact, the Customs & Excise appears to view the itemising on tax invoices and separate charging of items as necessarily giving rise to separate supplies (see Notice No 700, para 27) even if this would not be the case, in its view, when a single charge is made. It is suggested, however, that the form in which the charge is made is not conclusive as to the true nature of a supply.

The Tribunal retains a discretion as to the manner in which an apportionment is to be made (see *M H Jarmain* v *CCE*, MAN/78/144 (*Casebook* **3.609**)). In practice, the Customs & Excise usually accept any apportionment that is reasonably based. For example, the cost to the supplier of the elements involved, the open market value of each element or the usual mark-up in respect of each element in the trade concerned.

Characteristics of a two-part tariff

It is open to doubt whether the two-part tariff is anything more than an example of a composite supply; both involve two or more transactions which are inter-dependent and cannot exist in isolation. This is seen in *British Railways Board* v *CCE* (*No 2*) [1977] STC 221 (*Casebook* **3.610**), where a student card was supplied for a consideration and enabled the holder to purchase rail tickets at a later stage at a discount.

Neither the possession of a student rail card nor the rendering of the discounted price would, in themselves, have entitled a person to travel by rail. Consequently, the court found that the issue of the card and the sale of a ticket could not be treated as two distinct transactions. Instead, there was a down payment for rail travel in advance when the card was purchased.

In the majority of cases concerning two-part tariffs, the earlier payment is made in order to place the person concerned in a position to be able, at a later stage and in return for a further payment, to benefit from the main supply. As a result, VAT will be chargeable with reference to the nature of that main supply on the aggregate amount of both payments.

Business promotion schemes

A particular instance where goods may be combined in a single supply is in connection with a business promotion scheme. The Customs & Excise details its understanding of the treatment of such schemes in VAT Leaflet 700/7/79. There are three principal types of scheme:

LINKED GOODS SCHEMES

These schemes include the supply of an article with the main object of the supply. The Customs & Excise state that where the article can be regarded as secondary to the main supply, it will be taxable to the same extent as that main supply. Where it is not a secondary supply, it should be taxable in the same manner as it would be taxable if supplied separately. An article is regarded as secondary where it:

(*a*) is not charged to the customer at a separate price;

(*b*) attracts a different tax rate from the main article;

(*c*) costs, in total, no more than 15 per cent of the value (excluding VAT) of the combined supply; and

(*d*) costs the supplier no more than 15 pence (excluding VAT) if included with goods for retail sale, or 45 pence (excluding VAT) otherwise.

DEALER LOADER SCHEMES

In such schemes, the supplier offers a customer additional goods in return for ordering a particular quantity of the supplier's goods. Such additional goods are not gifts but will be taxable in one of two ways:

(*a*) if the supplier regards the price actually paid as the sole consideration for both the main supply and the additional goods, that consideration should be apportioned between those supplies and taxed accordingly;

(*b*) where the consideration relates only to the main supply, the additional goods should be treated as supplies free of charge and VAT accounted for on the market value of that supply under s 10(3).

COUPON SCHEMES

Where a coupon is supplied together with the principal supply, tax will be payable on that supply when made. If the coupon is exchanged at a later stage for an item at no further cost to the customer, the Customs & Excise require that an adjustment is made at the time of the exchange where the rates of tax chargeable on the principal supply and the item exchanged for the coupon are different. In general terms, the difference between the tax paid in respect of the coupons and the tax that would have been paid for the exchanged item had it been supplied instead of and for the same consideration as the coupons were supplied is to be treated as an under or overpayment of tax, in the period in which the exchange is made.

Where, however, a further charge is made on exchange, tax is to be accounted for on the exchanged item at the applicable rate when the exchange is made. Tax is charged on the price charged to the customer plus, where the coupons are price reduction coupons, the face value of the coupons.

3.700 Self-supplies

In VAT terms, a self-supply should not constitute a "supply" if for no other reason than the fact that consideration cannot, in law, pass from a person to himself. There is no consideration, therefore, for a self-supply. This basic principle, although recognised in *FVE Good* v *CCE* [1974] VATTR 256 (*Casebook* **3.702**), has been eroded in several tribunal decisions and is subject to contrary provision in any Orders made by the Treasury under s 6(5).

In *National Transit Insurance Co Ltd* v *CCE*, [1975] STC 35 (*Casebook* **3.701**), a case involving supplies by insurance companies to a committee formed by themselves and Lloyd's Underwriters, the Tribunal commented:

"Despite the superficial attraction of treating the activities undertaken by the Insurers, the Committee and the Appellant as though they were one insurance company, and of looking at the end result, instead of what was actually done step by step, we are driven to the conclusion on the facts before us that a separate service is supplied by the Appellant for a consideration which, whether or not it is aptly termed a handling fee, is quantified in the sum of £4.00 per claim handled. It was contended by Mr Lawton with some force that some part of this service in reality relates to a self-supply, and self-supply of a service is not a taxable supply (section 5(2) of the Finance Act 1972—now s 6(2)). He also contended that, since the Committee has no corporate existence, and was in reality the alter ego of the Insurers, it could not be right that the supply was made to the Committee. Nevertheless, we consider that the better view, since the whole administration of nationalised road transport insurance ... is vested in the Committee and ... the Committee has in turn appointed the Appellant a Service Point to handle claims made ... the service can be properly regarded as supplied by the Appellant to the Committee. We consider this to be the case notwithstanding that the Committee has no legal entity, and even though the Appellant will itself to some degree benefit from the services supplied."

This approach was also adopted by the Tribunal in *Border Flying Company* v *CCE*, [1976] VATTR 132 (*Casebook* **4.204**), which quoted with approval the following passage from *Carlton Lodge Club* v *CCE*, [1974] STC 507 (*Casebook* **3.101**):

"If one analysed the transaction which took place when the member went to the bar and ordered himself a drink, and was then served with a drink, in consideration of his paying the appropriate sum of money the other members were releasing the value of their share of that drink to the member who was paying."

and went on to further comment:

"The same considerations are, in our judgment, applicable to partnership property. Unlike the liabilities of a partnership which are joint and several, the assets are jointly owned even to the extent that if a partner does an act in respect of partnership property which can be justified only by a right to exclusive possession, then he commits the tort of conversion ... Consequently, if a partner makes use of the aircraft for his own purposes it is on the footing that the other partners severally release to him temporarily their interest therein and, for the purposes of VAT the partner so using the aircraft is making to himself a supply of his interest therein."

Some support for the Tribunal's approach in these cases can be found from the fact that VAT is concerned with transactions effected by taxable persons not legal entities. Thus, although in law a partnership has no legal entity distinct from its individual partners, by s 22, registration for VAT purposes may be (and in practice is) in the name of the firm. In this light, a dealing with a particular partner is seen as a transaction between a taxable person and an individual; a normal consumer transaction. Consequently, it is only necessary in s 45(2)(*a*) to provide that the provision by a club or association of facilities or advantages to its members shall be deemed to be the carrying on of a business; such activities already being supplies.

In the above cases, where a supply has been found, the actual recipient of the supply has been different from the actual supplier. It remains to be seen whether a supply by a partnership to another partnership of exactly the same individuals sharing profits, losses and assets in the same proportions will be regarded by the tribunal as a supply. The Authors suggest that it should not be regarded as such.

As mentioned above, s 6(5) gives the Treasury power to specify, by order, that certain types of goods acquired or produced by a person in the course or furtherance of his business which are used by him for the purposes of a business carried on by him and which are not incorporated by him in other goods produced by him, shall be treated as both supplied to him and by him in the course or furtherance of his business.

To date, only two such orders have been made:

(*a*) The VAT (Cars) Order 1980 (SI 1980 No 442), art 5. This Order relates to "motor vehicles" which are not converted into other vehicles or sold by the supplier in the course or furtherance of his business. "Motor vehicle" is defined (art 2(2)) as "any motor vehicle of a kind normally used on public roads which has three or more wheels" except certain specified types of motor vehicle which effectively leaves a residual category of passenger vehicles carrying between two and eleven persons (inclusive).

A car falling within this category may also be unable to qualify for input tax relief on the deemed supply of the motor vehicle (art 4(1), see further **5.400C**).

(*b*) The VAT (Special Provisions) Order 1977 (SI 1977 No 1796), art 14. This Order relates to "printed matter" and only applies to exempt or partially exempt suppliers (art 14(2)(*a*)). The Order does not apply to suppliers who, ignoring art 14, are below the VAT registration limit or where the net loss to the Revenue if the article were not applied would, in the opinion of the Customs & Excise, be negligible (art 14(2)).

Printed matter is defined in art 2(2) and includes printed stationery but does not include anything produced by typing, duplicating or photocopying.

3.800 The need for a consideration: gifts

A transaction is not normally considered a supply unless it is made for a consideration (s 6(2) and **3.100**). This basic principle is over-ridden in the cases discussed in the following paragraphs.

Schedule 2, para 5(2) provides that the transfer or disposal of goods under the direction of a person carrying on a business so that those goods no longer form part of the assets of the business is to be treated as a supply even though no consideration is given for the transfer. This includes the transfer by a supplier of goods to himself (para 5(4)). Paragraph 5 does not apply however to the following transactions which will remain excluded from the charge to VAT:

(*a*) the gift of goods in the course or furtherance of a business where the cost to the donor per donee is not more than £10. In this connection, gifts of gold watches to long serving employees have been held to be in the course or furtherance of the employer's business (*UDS Group* v *CCE*, [1977] VATTR 16 (*Casebook* **4.211**)).

(*b*) the gift of industrial samples in a form not ordinarily available for sale to the public to actual or potential customers of the business.

Paragraph 5(3) further provides that the private use of goods or the making available of goods for any use other than a business use is to be treated as a supply of services.

Finally in relation to services, the Treasury are empowered to specify that anything which is not a supply of services, only because it is not done for a consideration, is to be treated as a supply of services in the course or furtherance of the business of the person concerned. To date, no such Orders have been made.

Chapter 4

Business

4.000 Sources

Section 45 —Definition of business.
Section 2(1)—VAT chargeable on taxable supplies made by a taxable person in the course or furtherance of any business carried on by him.
Section 3(3)—Credit for input tax given to a taxable person where goods or services are used or to be used for the purposes of a business carried on or to be carried on by him (see Chapter 5).
Section 25 —Administrative provision where a business is transferred as a going concern.
Schedule 2, para 7—Deemed supply on ceasing to be a taxable person.
VAT (Special Provisions) Order 1977 (SI 1977 No 1796)
  art 12—Relief for the transfer of a business as a going concern.

In addition the following Customs & Excise Notice and associated Leaflet may be helpful:

700   —paras 8 and 22.
700/9/79—Selling your business as a going concern.

4.100 General principles

Whether a business is carried on or not is of paramount importance in relation to VAT. This is because VAT is only chargeable on taxable supplies made by a taxable person "in the course or furtherance of any business" carried on by him (s 2(1)). If, therefore, a person is not engaged in business he does not need to concern himself with VAT and does not charge VAT on any "supplies" he makes. It should, however, be remembered that even where a business is carried on, but turnover is below the required limits, the person need not be registered for VAT as he is not a taxable person and so not liable to charge VAT, although he may wish to apply for voluntary registration (see **2.100** and **2.300**).

Definition

Business is defined in s **45** as follows:

"(1) In this Part of this Act 'business' includes any trade, profession or vocation.
(2) The following (without prejudice to the generality of anything else in this Part) are deemed to be the carrying on of a business—

  (*a*) the provision by a club, association or organisation (for a subscription or other consideration) of the facilities or advantages available to its members; and
  (*b*) the admission, for a consideration, of persons to any premises.

(3) Where a body has objects which are in the public domain and are of a political, religious, philanthropic, philosophical or patriotic nature, it is not to be treated as carrying on a business only because its members subscribe to it, if a subscription obtains no facility or advantage for the subscriber other than the right to participate in its management or receive reports on its activities.

(4) Where a person, in the course or furtherance of a trade, profession or vocation, accepts any office, services supplied by him as the holder of that office are treated as supplied in the course or furtherance of the trade, profession or vocation.

(5) Anything done in connection with the termination or intended termination of a business is treated as being done in the course or furtherance of that business.

(6) The disposition of a business as a going concern, or of its assets or liabilities (whether or not in connection with its reorganisation or winding up), is a supply made in the course or furtherance of the business."

So far as the general definition of business, as including any "trade, profession or vocation", is concerned (s 45(1)), the definition is not terribly helpful and the question as to whether or not a business exists has been the subject of many Tribunal and some High Court (one Scottish) decisions.

The case which has found favour with the Tribunals and has been cited with approval in the High Court in *The Church of Scientology of California* v *CCE*, [1979] STC 297 (*Casebook* **4.101**) and *CCE* v *Morrison's Academy Boarding Houses Association* [1978] STC 1 (*Casebook* **4.102**) is *IRC* v *Marine Steam Turbines Ltd*, 12 TC 174 where Mr Justice Rowlatt said:

"Now it has been said that the word 'business' is a very wide word and it is a wide elastic word in its extent, of course, but it has two distinct meanings. It may mean any particular matter or affair of serious importance ... I may illustrate what I mean, perhaps, by an example. Of course, it is well known that if a private person goes to see his banker or his solicitor or anyone else he goes very likely upon business although he may not be carrying on any business.... The word 'business', however, is also used in another and very different sense as meaning an active occupation or profession continuously carried on."

It was the latter meaning which Mr Justice Rowlatt preferred. Also in *The Church of Scientology of California* v *CCE*, [1979] STC 297 the court cited with approval the words of Widgery J. in *Rael-Brook Ltd* v *Minister of Housing and Local Government*, [1967] 1 All ER 262, when he said that business meant "a serious undertaking earnestly pursued". Moreover, in *CCE* v *Morrison's Academy Boarding Houses Association*, [1978] STC 1 it was held that business denoted a commercial activity but that it was not an essential feature of a business that it be carried on profitably. It should be further noted that the use of the income tax cases in determining the meaning of business was rejected by the Tribunal in *RA Archer* v *CCE*, [1974] VATTR 1 (*Casebook* **4.105**).

Thus, what emerges from the cases is the concept of business as meaning the continuous carrying on of an occupation, profession or other activity on a commercial basis, without the requirement that the occupation, profession or activity be carried on profitably.

For examples of how these principles have been applied in practice, see *Casebook* **4.100**, *et seq*.

Apart from the general definition of business, certain categories are singled out for special treatment. In particular, s 45(2)(*a*) deems certain activities carried on by clubs and associations to be a business. The position of clubs and associations is dealt with separately in **15.200**, *et seq*.

Section 45(2)(*b*) provides that the admission, for a consideration, to premises shall be treated as the carrying on of a business. The context in which the question arises, as to whether or not such an activity amounts to a business, is usually in connection with clubs or associations and the matter is, therefore, considered in detail in **15,200**, *et seq*. It should be noted, nevertheless, that activities which would not normally be regarded as a business can be brought within the scope of VAT by this provision, for example, in the *Eric Taylor* (*deceased*) *Testimonial Match Committee* v *CCE*, [1975] VATTR 8 (*Casebook* **4.112**), the holding of a testimonial match for which the public were charged admission amounted to the carrying on of a business.

The provisions of s **45(3)** dealing with political and religious bodies etc. are also dealt with in Chapter 15. Further, special rules apply to, *inter alia*, the Crown and local authorities whose position is dealt with at **15.300**.

4.200 In the course or furtherance of a business

By s 2(1) the charge to VAT is limited to supplies made in the course or furtherance of any business carried on by the taxable person. Until FA 1977 introduced the changes in the FA 1972 arising from the United Kingdom's adoption of the EEC Sixth Directive (see **13.800** and **18.300**) the wording used to be "in the course of" only, and the additional words "or furtherance" were not considered by the Tribunals in many of the earlier decisions which have formed the basis of the Tribunals' approach to whether or not supplies were made in the course of a business. However, it is not thought that the additional words would have had any material affect on the cases decided on the interpretation of the old wording, with the possible exception of *The Edward James Foundation* v *CCE*, [1975] VATTR 61 (*Casebook* **4.220**). It is, therefore, proposed in this *Guide* to refer to the new wording "in the course or furtherance of" as introduced by the FA 1977: where reference is made to cases which considered the law pre-1 January 1978; the words "or furtherance of" appear in square brackets. It should be noted, however, that the introduction of the additional words "or furtherance of" by FA 1977, have arguably widened the scope of the tax since the expression "in the course or furtherance of a business" is clearly more embracing than the expression "in the course of a business". Thus, as stated the *Edward James Foundation* case may now be decided differently. However, the relevant article of the EEC Sixth Directive, with which the new expression is intended to comply, is itself narrower in its wording than the term "in the course or furtherance" as adopted in the UK legislation. In particular art 2 of the EEC Sixth Directive provides:

"The following shall be subject to Value Added Tax:

   (1) The supply of goods or services effected for consideration within the territory of the country by a taxable person acting as such."

The wording of art 2(1) would, by means of the words "as such", therefore, appear to restrict VAT to supplies made in the course of a business only. It may, therefore, be argued, if appropriate, that s 2(1) cannot apply where a supply is made in the furtherance of a business and not in the course of it (for an examination of the question of whether the EEC Directives or UK domestic law prevails in such circumstances see **13.800**).

The cases which have come before the Tribunals in relation to businesses fall into five distinct categories.

Does a business exist?

On a general level the Tribunals have had to consider if there is a business at all as clearly, if there is not a business no supply can be made in the course or furtherance of it. In reaching their decisions the Tribunals applied the basic principles mentioned in **4.100** *et seq*, but it is interesting to note how some cases have been distinguished from others.

One of the often cited cases is *Processed Vegetable Growers Association Ltd* v *CCE*, [1973] VATTR 87 (*Casebook* **4.202**), where employees of the Association were transferred to the National Farmers Union ("NFU") so as to be able to take advantage of the NFU pension scheme. The employees were then made available to the Association for a fee equivalent to the employees' salaries onto which the NFU added VAT. On appeal by the Association, it was held by the Tribunal that the activities of the NFU did not constitute commercial activities so that the supply by them of personnel to the Association was not a supply in the course [or furtherance] of a business. This approach was followed in *Allied Schools Agency Ltd* v *CCE*, [1973] VATTR 155 (*Casebook* **4.203**), but in *The Heart of Variety* v *CCE*, [1975] VATTR 103 (*Casebook* **4.205**) and *British Airways Board* v *CCE*, LON/78/191A (*Casebook* **4.206**) the Tribunals distinguished the cases from the earlier ones on the basis that the seconded employees were supplied by the respective companies in the course [or furtherance] of their businesses.

Gifts to employees

Gifts to employees have been the subject of several Tribunal and one High Court decision namely *RHM Bakeries (Northern) Ltd* v *CCE* [1979] STC 72 (*Casebook* **4.208**). There emerges from the cases the concept that something which is done to "promote good industrial relations" between employer and employee is done in the course [or furtherance] of the employer's business, *per* Neill J. in *RHM Bakeries (Northern) Ltd* v *CCE*. In *UDS Group Limited and UDS Tailoring Ltd* v *CCE* [1977] VATTR 16 (*Casebook* **4.211**) the Tribunal further remarked that gifts of gold watches to employees were nonetheless made in the course [or furtherance] of the company's business, notwithstanding that it was not the company's business to supply watches.

For gifts generally see **3.800**

More than one business

In some instances, persons carrying on a business for which they are registered enter into other arrangements outside their recognised business and the question to be determined then is whether the arrangements are effected in the course or furtherance of the recognised business. However, it must be remembered that it is a person who registers for VAT and this registration covers all businesses carried on by him (see **2.200**). The real point of issue, therefore, will be whether the person's additional activities constitute a business (see *LO Clarke* v *CCE*, CAR/77/29 (*Casebook* **4.212**), *DA Redison (trading as DM Motors)* v *CCE*, CAR/77/175 (*Casebook* **4.214**) and *RW and AAW Willamson* v *CCE*, MAN/77/231 (*Casebook* **4.215**)).

Offices

In other cases individuals have taken up offices outside their direct business and the Customs & Excise have maintained that any salary paid in respect of the office is a supply by the individual in the course or furtherance of his business and, therefore, liable to VAT. This is based on s 45(4) (previously s 45(3) but amended with effect from 1 January 1978 as a result of the EEC Sixth Directive). The sub-section is set out in full in **4.100**. Such an argument was put forward by the Customs & Excise in *Lean and Rose* v *CCE*, [1974] VATTR 7 (*Casebook* **4.216**) where a partner in a firm of solicitors took up a part-time employment with a local authority. On the facts he was held to be an employee of the local authority and, therefore, no liability arose. The same argument was put forward in *Hempsons* v *CCE*, [1977] VATTR 73 (noted at *Casebook* **2.216**) in which a partner in a firm of solicitors was clerk to the

Horserace Betting Levy Board Appeal Tribunal. On the facts in the *Hempson* case it was held that the office concerned was a public office at which time there existed an exemption from s 45(3) if the office was a public office. However, following the amendment of FA 1972, as a result of the EEC Sixth Directive, the exemption has been removed from the amendment section (s 45(4)).

It is still necessary, though, for the office to be held by the person "in the course or furtherance of a trade, profession or vocation", which, in itself, begs the question as to when an office is so held. It may be that a partner in a firm is also a director of one or more companies from which he receives director's fees. In such cases the Customs & Excise has indicated (see [1976] ST1 107) it would not normally regard the supply as being made in the course [or furtherance] of the partnership business providing the following conditions are satisfied:

(*a*) the office holding has been arranged with the individual partner and there is no written agreement between the partnership and the organisation in which the office is held; and

(*b*) the office-holding by the partner arises from personal, family or significant financial interest (eg shareholding) in the organisation concerned rather than from his professional qualifications or interests as evidenced by his membership of the partnership concerned; and

(*c*) the duties of the office do not involve significant use of the skills which the individual currently employs in practising his profession (or, if they do, such professional services are separately charged for and invoiced by the partnership).

Disposals of assets

A person may dispose of assets other than stock in trade, eg capital assets and it has been held in *HB Mattia Ltd* v *CCE*, [1976] VATTR 33 (*Casebook* **4.217**) that such a disposal was made in the course [or furtherance] of the business. The case concerned the disposal of vans used in the business and the Tribunal relied on Sched 2, para 3 as it then was (but see now para 7) as authority for the proposition that a sale of capital assets would give rise to a liability to VAT. A similar conclusion was reached in *JE Hughes* v *CCE*, MAN/77/262 (*Casebook* **4.218**), but in the *Edward James Foundation* v *CCE*, [1975] VATTR 61 (*Casebook* **4.220**) the Tribunal distinguished the case on the basis that the asset sold (an antique wall-seat originally settled on the Foundation) was not used for the purpose of the Foundation's business and thus the sale could not be a supply in the course [or furtherance] of its business. It is interesting to note, however, that the Tribunal in *UDS Tailoring Ltd* v *CCE* (see *Gifts to employees, ante*) held that gold watches given to employees were given in the course [or furtherance] of the business notwithstanding that it was not the company's business to supply watches.

Capital assets disposed of during the cessation of a business have also been held to be made in the course [or furtherance] of the business, *M Wolfe (trading as Arrow Coach Services)* v *CCE*, LEE/75/22 (*Casebook* **4.219**), although the legislation has now clarified this point in any event (s 45(5)).

4.300 Transfer of a business

The legislation in respect of the transfer of a business is obtuse and it is, therefore, proposed to give a short summary of the practical position, without citing authority for the statements made, before analysing the statutory provisions in greater detail in the paragraphs below. The Customs & Excise have produced VAT Leaflet 700/9/79 (Selling your business as a going concern) which is a useful summary of the view of the Customs & Excise on the subject.

Stated broadly, the sale of the assets of a business is a taxable supply and the seller should account for VAT, whether he is already registered for VAT or whether he becomes liable to be registered as a result of the sale. However, where the whole of the business is transferred as a going concern, VAT may not be payable as relief from VAT may be given.

There are conflicting decisions of the Tribunals as to whether the transfer of a business as a going concern constitutes a supply in the course [or furtherance] of a business. *J. Proctor* (*Waddington*) *Ltd* v *CCE* [1976] VATTR 184 (*Casebook* **4.301**) and *Briday Ltd* v *CCE*, MAN/77/228 (*Casebook* **4.302**) on the one hand held that such disposals were in the course [or furtherance] of the business, but a contrary finding was made by the Tribunal in *Wensue Coachworks* v *CCE*, LON/78/128 (*Casebook* **4.303**).

Clarifying legislation was introduced in s 45(6) which provides that:

"the disposition of a business as a going concern or of its assets or liabilities (whether or not in connection with its reorganisation or winding up), is a supply made in the course or furtherance of the business".

Section 45(6), however, only provides that the disposition of a business as a going concern is a supply in the course or furtherance of a business. It is therefore necessary also to consider Sched 2, para 7 which provides that:

"where a person ceases to be a taxable person, any goods then forming part of the assets of a business carried on by him shall be deemed to be supplied by him in the course or furtherance of his business immediately before he ceases to be a taxable person, unless ..."

The effect of s 45(5) and (6) (subject to the reliefs available—see *post*) is that the transfer of the whole of the business will give rise to

VAT. Further, if the taxable person ceases to be a taxable person, because, for example, his supplies fall below the statutory limit for registration and he applies for his registration to be cancelled (see **2.600**), the goods then forming part of the assets of his business are deemed to be supplied in the course or furtherance of the business and VAT is accordingly payable. It is quite logical that the latter category of deemed supply should be included since the person would have been entitled to reliefs for input tax, but on ceasing to be registered would not, in the absence of express provision, be liable to account for VAT on supplies made after deregistration.

Reliefs

Relief from the overall effect of Sched 2, para 7(1) is given in sub-paras (*a*)–(*c*) and in para 7(2). Thus, no VAT will be payable on the person ceasing to be a taxable person if:

(*a*) the business is transferred as a going concern to another taxable person; or

(*b*) the business is carried on temporarily on behalf of a person who has died, become bankrupt or incapacitated and who has given notice to the Customs & Excise within 21 days of carrying on the business (VAT (General) Regulations 1977 (SI 1977 No 1759), reg 7 applied by s 23(3)); or

(*c*) the tax on the deemed supply would not be more than £250;

(*d*) the person can satisfy the Customs & Excise

(i) that no credit for input tax in respect of the supply or importation of the goods has been allowed him; or

(ii) that the goods were not acquired by him as part of the assets of a business which was transferred to him as a going concern by another taxable person; and

(iii) that he has not obtained relief for purchase tax under the transitional provisions to VAT.

The requirements set out at (*d*)(i) and (*d*)(ii) above were introduced by FA 1980, s 15 which also raised the limit in (*c*) to £250 with effect from 1 June 1980. The conditions of (*d*)(i) and (*d*)(ii) further restrict the availability of Sched 2, para 7 relief to cases where no credit for input tax has been allowed or the acquisition of the goods took place under a transfer on which no VAT was paid. However, regard must also be had to the additional relief on the transfer of a business under the VAT (Special Provisions) Order 1977 (SI 1977 No 1796).

Further, relief from VAT, where a business is transferred as a going concern, is given by the VAT (Special Provisions) Order 1977 (SI 1977

No 1796) art 12. The relief is given by providing that certain supplies will not be treated as supplies of goods or services, namely:

(*a*) the supply by a taxable person of all the assets of his business where the whole business is transferred as a going concern *to another taxable person* or *a person who immediately becomes a taxable person as a result of the transfer*;

(*b*) the supply, by a taxable person whose business consists of more than one separate concern, of all the assets of any part of his business providing the part sold has been run as a separate concern with separate accounts and is sold as a going concern to a taxable person, or to a person who immediately becomes taxable as a result of the transfer. Attention is drawn in this connection to VAT Leaflet 700/9/79, para 5 where the Customs & Excise states, that to qualify as a separate concern:

"the business being sold must have been run independently of any other business or businesses in his ownership. It would not be a separate concern for the purpose of the relief if it were merely a branch of what would be regarded commercially as a single business. For example, the sale to the particular purchaser of one or more shops from a chain of shops, some of which remain in the same ownership, would be unlikely to constitute the sale of a separate concern or separate concerns, if the activities of the shops had previously been integrated to any appreciable extent. Centralised arrangements for the purchase of stock would normally indicate a normal business, as would the fact that shops have been engaged in the same class of business.

The distinction is between a single business consisting of two or more branches or departments and what are, in the commercial sense, two or more separately run businesses in the same ownership."

Furthermore, the separate business must have separate accounts and an indication of the Customs & Excise view on what is meant by separate accounts is contained in VAT Leaflet 700/9/79, para 6. In essence what is required are separate accounts at least to profit and loss account level and not simply branch or management accounts prepared to enable the owner to see how each branch of his business is performing. The sale of a division of a company organised in separate divisions would normally qualify for this relief;

(*c*) the supply by a non-taxable person, ie one not registered for VAT, of all the assets of his business where the whole business is sold to any other person, whether taxable or not. The seller does not become liable to VAT, therefore, as a result of the sale of all the assets of the business even if he receives more than the statutory limit for registration for them. He will, however, be liable to VAT if he sells only part of the assets (and receives more than £13,500 for them— see **2.100**, *et seq*.), as the sale of part of the business does not qualify for relief and the sale proceeds if more than £13,500 would make him liable to be registered;

(*d*) the supply by a non-taxable person whose business consists of

more than one separate concern of all the assets of the separate concern where the separate concern has separate accounts and is transferred as a going concern. For general comments on separate concern
and separate accounts see (*b*), *ante*.

Again the sale of all the assets of the separate concern is required
as otherwise the person could become taxable as a result of the sale
of part only (see (*c*), *ante*).

Summary of reliefs available

It will thus be seen that the reliefs given under the VAT (Special Provisions) Order 1977 (SI 1977 No 1796) fall into two categories; first
where a *taxable person* sells *the whole of* his business (or a separate
part if the conditions for a separate concern are satisfied) *to a taxable
person* or one who immediately becomes a taxable person as a result
of the transfer, and secondly where a *non-taxable person* sells the *whole
of his business* (or a separate part if the conditions for a separate concern
are satisfied) *to anyone*.

In either case it is the whole of the business (or the whole of a separate
covered by one of the special provisions summarised in the preceding
be taken if all the assets are not being transferred, eg if book debts are
retained to avoid stamp duty, or if goodwill is retained, as VAT will be
payable. This must be borne in mind when negotiating the sale price
of a business since, if no mention of VAT is made, the price is deemed
to be inclusive of VAT (s 10(2) and see **3.500**) and a vendor who retains
some assets will have to pay the VAT out of his net proceeds.

Goodwill

An item often sold as part of the assets of a business is goodwill. The
VAT treatment of a sale of goodwill, where the entire assets sale is not
covered by one of the special provisions summarised in the preceding
paragraph, is unfortunately unclear. It is the Authors' opinion that a sale
of goodwill is caught by the all embracing wording of s 6(2)(*b*), that
is:

"(*b*) anything which is not a supply of goods but is done for a consideration (including,
if so done, the granting, assignment or surrender of any right) is a supply of services".

Thus, although goodwill is an intangible and often difficult to define
in a given situation, its sale will be a supply of services and potentially
subject to VAT if sold as part of a business and the reliefs described
above do not apply. It is understood, however, that at present the Customs & Excise may consider the sale of goodwill as outside the scope
of VAT and, therefore, not subject to VAT on sale.

In particular it is understood that the Customs & Excise consider the intangible aspects of goodwill, for example the fact that customers may continue to patronise the business as being outside the scope of VAT, but would not afford the same treatment to lists of customers, which are sometimes included in a sale under the description of "goodwill"; such customer lists would, in the Customs & Excise view, be liable to VAT.

Administrative provisions on the transfer of a business

Where a business is carried on by a taxable person and is transferred as a going concern, the transferee is treated as having carried on the business prior to the transfer in determining whether he is liable to be registered. Furthermore any records required to be preserved for a specified period under s 34 shall be preserved by the transferee (s 25(1)).

A new provision has been introduced into s 25(2) by FA 1980 which enables the Customs & Excise to make Regulations to secure continuity for VAT purposes where a business is transferred as a going concern. The Regulations envisaged will provide for the transfer of liabilities and the obligation to pay VAT to the transferee and will further enable any credit or repayment due to either the transferor or transferee to be made to either party. However, the transferor and transferee will have to make a joint application for the foregoing to apply. No Regulations have been made to date.

Chapter 5

Input Tax

5.000 Sources

Section 3   —Definition of input and output tax; basic credit provisions.
Section 4   —Quantum of credit where credit is restricted due to partial exemption or supplies made otherwise than in the course or furtherance of a business.
Section 5   —Enabling provisions to give credit to non-UK EEC Member State recipients of UK supplies.
Section 15   —Refund of input tax on supplies to certain bodies.
Section 15A—Refund of tax to persons constructing new homes otherwise than in the course of a business.
Section 16   —Enabling provision to allow relief from tax on importation of goods.
Finance Act 1977 Section 16—Enabling provisions to allow relief from tax on importation of goods for private purposes by taxable persons.
VAT (Cars) Order 1980 (SI 1980 No 442)
   art 4—Disallowance of input tax relief for certain motor cars.
VAT (General) Regulations 1977 (SI 1977 No 1759)
   regs 62 to 69—Rules for input tax relief where partial exemption applies.
   reg 70—Exceptional claims for relief for tax incurred prior to registration or post deregistration.
VAT (Special Provisions) Order 1977 (SI 1977 No 1796)
   art 6—Relief from tax on importation of works of art etc.
   art 7—Disallowance of input tax where a margin scheme operates.
   art 8—Disallowance of input tax on certain goods incorporated in a building.
   art 9—Disallowance of input tax incurred on business entertainment.
In addition the following Customs & Excise Notices and associated Leaflets may be helpful:

700   —paras 14, 15, 18–36, Appendix B.
700/5/79   —Sale of repossessed and surrendered goods by finance companies, insurers and mortgagees.
10/74/VMF —Indemnities under property lease agreements.
700/10/79   —Liability of printed and similar matter.
706   —Partial exemption.
710   —Supplies by or through agents.

5.100 General principles

Section 3(3) provides that:

"... input tax, in relation to a taxable person, means the following tax, that is to say:

(*a*) tax on the supply to him of any goods or services; and

(*b*) tax paid or payable by him on the importation of any goods,

being (in either case) goods or services used or to be used for the purpose of any business carried on or to be carried on by him".

It is a fundamental concept of VAT that a taxable person who incurs input tax should effectively be able to recover that tax from the Customs & Excise. In allowing such a recovery, it is ensured that only the ultimate non-business consumer and those wholly or partially exempt bear the burden of VAT. The manner in which input tax is recovered is primarily by way of credit against output tax due to the Customs & Excise by the taxable person incurring the input tax (s 3(2)). Output tax is defined in s 3(3) as the tax on supplies made by the taxable person in question. Where the amount of input tax exceeds the amount of output tax in a prescribed accounting period, however, that excess may be recovered by way of repayment from the Customs & Excise (s 3(5)). In either case, the recovery of input tax is not automatic; it must be claimed by the taxable person incurring it (s 3(7)). This is done on Form VAT 100 (Return of value added tax) which must be completed by all taxable persons for each prescribed accounting period (see generally, **17.400**). In a House of Commons Written Answer on 18 February 1980, the Chancellor of the Exchequer indicated that 90 per cent of all valid claims for the repayment of VAT are paid within 10 days of receipt by the Customs & Excise (Hansard Vol 979, col 55).

The above definitions of input and output tax lead to the consideration of a number of issues:

Taxable person

The definition of both input and output tax is linked in s 3(3) to taxable persons. While this has the effect that the ultimate non-business consumer and wholly or partially exempt traders may not recover input tax (as is intended) it is interesting to note that no reference is made to registration. As the definition of a taxable person in s 2(2) includes a person who is required to be registered for the purposes of VAT, it would appear that a person who is not actually registered, but should be registered, is capable of claiming input tax relief. Although this is a theoretical possibility, it is likely to be met in practice with resistance from the Customs & Excise and it may be difficult for non-registered persons to obtain a tax invoice evidencing input tax suffered and a VAT

Return Form on which to claim a repayment of that tax. As will be seen below, the production of a tax invoice is a prerequisite for a claim to input tax.

Two exceptions to the above are contained in ss 5 and 15A. Section 5 permits the Customs & Excise to introduce a scheme, by means of Regulations, under which input tax may be repaid to persons who are not carrying on a business in the United Kingdom but are carrying on a business in either an EEC Member State or, if required by an EEC Directive, any other country. Although no such Regulations have been introduced to date, the EEC Eighth Directive requires the introduction of a scheme by 1 January 1981, allowing for the repayment of input tax to persons carrying on business in another Member state. Section 15A allows the recovery of tax on goods incorporated in a dwelling-house by do-it-yourself builders provided that certain conditions are met. This is discussed in greater detail at **5.500**.

Only the recipient of the supply or importer may claim

Section 3(3) states that input tax may only be claimed by a taxable person on supplies "to him". There are a number of marginal cases, however, where it is far from clear as to whom a supply has been made. Some of these cases are discussed below.

INDEMNITY PAYMENTS

If a payment including VAT is made to another by way of indemnity, the payer, even though he is a taxable person, may not recover as input tax the VAT element of that indemnity payment (*Normal Motor Factors* v *CCE*, [1978] VATTR 20 (*Casebook* **3.801**)). This is because the supply in respect of which the payment is made is to the indemnified person not the indemnifier.

Perhaps one of the more common instances of indemnity payments is in relation to the payment of professional fees by a person other than the direct client incurring those fees. The frequency of such cases has led the Council of the Law Society to issue a statement: "Payment of another's costs by agreement" (see the *Law Society Gazette*, 19 September 1973 p 2287), which outlines the recommended practice to be adopted in the case of legal fees. The Customs & Excise has also issued VAT Leaflet 10/74/VMF (Indemnities under property lease agreements) outlining the position in relation to payments by lessees of their lessors' costs.

AGENTS

A supply to an agent acting for a taxable person is, in reality, a supply to the taxable person himself. Only the taxable person and not his agent should be able to recover any input tax on that supply, therefore. It is not always possible to follow this straightforward concept in VAT terms, however. This is particularly the case where the agency in question is undisclosed and the supplier can only make out his tax invoice in the agent's name

Section 24(3) provides, therefore, that:

"Where goods or services are supplied through an agent who acts in his own name the Commissioners (of Customs & Excise) may, if they think fit, treat the supply both as a supply to the agent and as a supply by the agent."

This procedure is normally followed in practice and is discussed in more detail in Chapter 15 and Customs & Excise Notice No 710, para 6(*a*).

As to whether an agency exists in any given case see *R H Norman* v *CCE*, LON/79/174 and the rather curious case of *A L Booth* v *CCE* [1977] VATTR 133 (*Casebook* **5.102**).

Supplies in this context are, of course, only those to the agent as intermediary; the principal cannot recover VAT suffered by the agent in relation to his supply of the agent's own services to his principal as agent (see *Berbrooke Fashions* v *CCE*, [1977] VATTR 168 (*Casebook* **5.108**)).

EMPLOYEES

In certain cases, where the employee has the authority, actual or ostensible, to bind his employer, his position will be one of agent for the employer and the ability of the employer to recover input tax on supplies contracted for by the employee will be as detailed in the preceding paragraph. It is perhaps more usual for no such agency relationship to exist and this would appear in law to place the employer in the position of an indemnifier in respect of costs incurred by his employee again with the consequences detailed above. In the *British Broadcasting Corporation* v *CCE* [1974] VATTR 100 (*Casebook* **5.107**), for example, the VAT Tribunal rejected as "too widely stated" the appellant Corporation's argument that a supply of services to an employee in the course of his duties for the Corporation was a supply to the Corporation itself. In that case, agency was accepted as not applying on the basis that had the employee not paid for the supplies contracted for by him, the supplier would have had no recourse against the Corporation.

This strict position is, however, modified in practice by a concession operated by the Customs & Excise and currently detailed in Notice No 700, para 31 (subsistence expenses), the forerunner to which (Notice No 701 (June 73), para 35) was in fact considered in the *BBC* case. The new para 31 no longer requires a "reimbursement" of actual expenses by the employer but merely that the actual cost should be borne by him, Thus, the employer may pay the supplier direct for a supply ordered by the employee and obtain credit for VAT on that supply. General employee expenses within this concession do not appear to be regarded by the Customs & Excise as subject to apportionment (or output tax under Sched 2, para 5(2)) where a part of the supply can be identified as being for private purposes. The Customs & Excise treatment of petrol expenses is complex and is detailed in Notice No 700, Appendix B (Petrol).

ANY BUSINESS

It should be noted that s 3(2) refers to "any" business carried on by the recipient of the supply and there is, therefore, no justification for disallowing input tax relief because the recipient is carrying on more than one type of activity.

IMPORTATION

A restriction is imposed where goods, which belong wholly or partly to another person, are imported by a taxable person for the private use of either that other person or the taxable person himself. In such circumstances, no input tax relief is allowed to the importer under s 3 unless he can show that a double charge of tax would arise as a result of such disallowance (FA 1977, s 16).

For the purpose of any business carried on or to be carried on

In order for tax to be within the definition of input tax, it must, first, have been incurred by a taxable person in respect of goods or services which are used for the purpose of any business carried on by him and, secondly, the business in question must be carried on or to be carried on when the expenditure is incurred.

In relation to the first of these requirements, it should be noted that the wording differs from that used in connection with the charge to VAT which is expressed to be payable by reference to supplies "in the course or furtherance of" a business. This difference in wording has been construed as suggesting a subjective test in relation to input tax to ascertain the motive for the incurring of the expenditure in question (see *Pye of Cambridge Ltd* v *CCE* [1977] VATTR 33 (*Casebook* **5.112**), *EM Alexander* v *CCE*, [1976] VATTR 107 (*Casebook* **5.113**) and *National Water Council* v *CCE*, [1978] STC at **169** *per* Neill J.). In arriving at this conclusion the Tribunal in the *Alexander* case referred to *Strong and Co of Romsey Ltd* v *Woodfield*, 5 TC 215 where Lord Davey, referring to the words "for the purpose of the trade", said:

"These words are used in other rules, and appear to me to mean for the purpose of enabling a person to carry on and earn profits in the trade. It is not enough that the (expenditure) is made in the course of, or arises out of, or is connected with, the trade, or is made out of the profits of the trade. It must be made for the purpose of earning the profits."

However, the correctness of adopting this subjective test has been brought into question by recent Tribunal decisions on advertising expenditure. Two of these cases, *Hillingdon Shirt Company Ltd* v *CCE*, MAN/78/26 (*Casebook* **5.117**), and *Tallishire Ltd* v *CCE*, MAN/79/42 (*Casebook* **5.120**), concerned the purchase of racehorses and a third, *20th Century Cleaning and Maintenance Co Ltd* v *CCE* LON/79/89 (*Casebook* **5.119**), the purchase of a power boat. These cases would appear to require either some connection between the advertising medium and the business that is being advertised or some reasonable likelihood of benefit to the business through that particular form of advertising before input tax may be recovered.

Two further principles have been applied by Tribunals in connection with the question of whether goods are used for the purpose of a business, namely:

(*a*) there does not have to be any corresponding supply by the taxable person in the course or furtherance of his business for input tax to be claimed (*Sittingbourne Milton and District Chamber of Commerce* v *CCE*, LON/76/178 (*Casebook* **5.111**)) (but see ss 3(7) and 4(1)(*c*) at **5.200**, *post*);

(*b*) it is only necessary that the main purpose for the expenditure is for the purpose of the business (*R Hough* v *CCE* LON/77/106. (*Casebook* **5.121**)). However, where a supply is used only partly for the purposes of the business, the quantum of the credit may be affected (see **5.200**).

Whether a business is being carried on by the taxable person making a claim to input tax relief is a question of fact which will be determined in accordance with the principles discussed at **4.100**. The question of whether a business is "to be carried on" is necessarily more complex and a point on which there is currently little authority. In *Cobbs Croft Service Station* v *CCE*, [1976] VATTR 170 (*Casebook* **5.123**), the Tribunal held that VAT incurred on the purchase of a video cassette by a garage proprietor who said he intended to expand his business, did not qualify as input tax as there was no genuine intention on the part of the garage proprietor to carry on a particular kind of business. Further, it was held that any contingencies upon which the commencement of a business depends must not be too incapable of being overcome.

Special provision is made for the recovery of VAT by certain bodies listed in or pursuant to s 15. These bodies comprise:

(*a*) a local authority;

(*b*) a river authority, a river purification board, the Conservators of the River Thames and the Lee Conservancy Catchment Board;

(*c*) a drainage board within the meaning of the Land Drainage Act 1930;

(*d*) any statutory water undertakers within the meaning of the Water Act 1945, and a regional water board and water development board within the meaning of the Water (Scotland) Act 1967;

(*e*) the London Transport Executive and a passenger transport authority or executive established under Part II of the Transport Act 1968;

(*f*) a port health authority constituted under Part I of the Public Health Act 1936, and a port local authority and joint local authority constituted, under the Public Health (Scotland) Act 1897, Part X;

(*g*) a police authority and the Receiver for the Metropolitan Police District;

(*h*) a Development Corporation within the meaning of the New Towns Act 1965 or the New Towns (Scotland) Act 1968, a New Town Commission within the meaning of the New Towns Act (Northern Ireland) 1965 and the Commission for the New Towns;

(*i*) a general lighthouse authority within the meaning of the Merchant Shipping Act 1894, Part XI;

(*j*) the British Broadcasting Corporation;

(*k*) Independent Television News Limited;

(*l*) any other body specified for the purposes of s 15 by an order made by the Treasury. To date, these are:

> (i) Scottish Special Housing Association (VAT (Refund of Tax) Order 1973 (SI 1973 No 522));
>
> (ii) Certain water authorities (VAT (Refund of Tax) (No 2) Order 1973 (SI 1973 No 2121)); and
>
> (iii) Certain Local Administration Commissions (VAT (Refund of Tax) Order 1976 (SI 1976 No 2028)).

Where any tax is suffered by such bodies, notwithstanding the fact that it is not paid on a supply for the purposes of any business carried on by them, it may be repaid to them under s 15. Tax suffered by such bodies for the purpose of any business remains to be treated under the rules in ss 3 and 4. In any case where it is unclear whether tax is attributable to non-business or business supplies, tax recoverable under s 15 is deemed to be that which is left after deducting from total tax paid, tax considered by the Customs & Excise as being required to be taken into account under ss 3 and 4 (s 15(2)). It is also possible for a s 15 body to recover tax paid on supplies which relate to its exempt supplies where those exempt supplies are considered by the Customs & Excise to be an insignificant proportion of total tax paid on business supplies. "Insignificant" is interpreted by the Customs & Excise as meaning less than £100 per month or less than 5 per cent of total input tax. See further on this point, Customs & Excise Notice No **749** and **15.300**.

5.200 The quantum of tax relief available and the making of the claim

Quantum

Two points arise in connection with the amount of tax that may be recovered by way of input tax credit.

First, only that part of the expenditure that is incurred for business purposes is capable, if all other conditions are satisfied, of qualifying for relief. Where there is a duality of purpose (of necessity with the business purpose predominating) an apportionment must be made in order to ascertain the tax on the supply or importation which is "referable to" business purposes alone (s 3(4)). There is no indication in the Act, Regulations or Customs & Excise Notices as to how such apportionment is to be made and, therefore, any reasonable method that can be substantiated may presumably be used.

Secondly, having established the maximum potential amount of tax that may be recovered, a restriction may be made on that amount either because:

(*a*) the taxable person in question makes some exempt supplies (see **5.300**); or
(*b*) there is a specific disallowance of input tax in respect of that particular type of supply (see **5.400**); or
(*c*) as a result of the application of either s 3(6) or (7) (see *post*).

SECTION 3(6): HELD OVER CREDIT

Regulations may be made by the Customs & Excise to allow input tax to be held over and not immediately repaid either at the taxable person's own request or under general or specific directions given by the Customs & Excise from time to time. Thus, under VAT (General) Regulations 1977 (SI 1977 No 1759), reg 55(2), a person is allowed to estimate a part of his input tax in an accounting period and make any necessary adjustments in a later period.

SECTION 3(7) NO TAXABLE SUPPLIES IN THE PERIOD

Section 3(7) is to be read together with s 4(1)(*c*) as both apply where a taxable person has not made any taxable supplies either in the prescribed accounting period in which the claim for input tax relief is made or in any earlier accounting period of the business. This would apply, for example, to the taxable person commencing business operations who has obtained registration but has not yet made any supplies. In such circumstances, relief is to be granted in respect of such proportion of the input tax paid by the taxable person as the Customs & Excise considers to be fair and reasonable (s 4(1)(*c*)) and subject to such conditions as it thinks fit to impose (s 3(7)).

Evidence required to substantiate a claim

REQUIREMENT OF DOCUMENTATION

Prior to 1 January 1978 it was not necesary for a tax invoice to be produced for a claim for input tax credit to be allowed (*Podium Investments Ltd*, v *CCE* [1977] VATTR 121 (*Casebook* **5.101**)), although some evidence that tax had been suffered was required. This position has largely been amended by s 3(8) which allows for Regulations to be made requiring the production of documentation specified in such Regulations before credit may be given (see VAT (General) Regulations 1977 (SI 1977 No 1759), reg 55). Unless the Customs & Excise "otherwise allow or direct either generally or in particular cases or classes of cases", a taxable person must now produce:

(*a*) an invoice satisfying the conditions of the VAT (General) Regulations 1977 (SI 1977 No 1759) reg 8 (this may be a tax invoice completed by the recipient himself under the consent of the Customs & Excise (reg 8(3)), see (*c*), *post*) if the supply is from another taxable person;
(*b*) an invoice issued by the overseas supplier if the event is an importation of services within s 8B; or
(*c*) a document authenticated or issued by the "proper officer" showing the amount of tax due on the goods (see Notice Nos 702 and 186) if the event is the importation of goods or the removal of the goods from a warehouse.

The Customs & Excise has exercised its discretion as indicated above in respect of certain supplies where, if the VAT inclusive cost is £10 or less, relief may be claimed without a tax invoice. The supplies which qualify for this special treatment are business telephone calls, goods purchased through coin operated machines and taxable parking charges. In such cases, the amount of input tax is calculated by multiplying the tax inclusive cost by three twenty-thirds.

ESTIMATION OF INPUT TAX CREDIT

As mentioned above, reg 55(2) permits the Customs & Excise to allow input tax to be estimated where it is satisfied that a taxable person is not able to claim the exact amount deducted. Estimation is only a temporary measure, however, and the amount claimed must be adjusted in the next accounting period or such later period as the Customs & Excise may allow.

SELF-BILLING

Where a supply is received from a taxable person, the recipient may, with the consent of the Customs & Excise, make out his own tax invoice in respect of that supply. The consent of the Customs & Excise is essential (*J Mangini* v *CCE* MAN/74/24 (*Casebook* **5.203**)) as is the co-operation of the supplier concerned.

The practical difficulties that self-billing can give rise to were clearly illustrated in the cases of *TA Landels and Sons Ltd* v *CCE*, MAN/78/52 (*Casebook* **5.201**), and *Weldstruct Ltd* v *CCE*, [1977] VATTR 101 (*Casebook* **5.202**). In the *TA Landels* case, the Tribunal pointed out that the incorrect operation of a self-billing system by the recipient of a supply who later went into liquidation, failed to absolve the supplier from liability to account to the Customs & Excise for the VAT due in respect of the supply. Further, in the *Weldstruct* case, the Customs & Excise was held to be obliged to allow input tax relief to the appellant where the supplier in question was not traceable and had not accounted to the Customs & Excise for VAT paid to him by the appellant who had also operated a self-billing system. It is clearly in the interest of all concerned, therefore, that a self-billing system should only be operated where all parties understand and are in a position to comply with their respective obligations.

Exceptional claims for input tax relief

Regulation 70(1) and (3) contain provisions dealing with claims for input tax credit which relate to supplies pre-initial registration and *post*-cessation of registration. In both cases, the supplies in question must have been for the purposes of the business covered by that registration.

PRE-REGISTRATION SUPPLIES (REG 70(1) AND (2))

Although it was noted above that the ability to claim input tax credit is not dependent upon actual registration, severe practical difficulties may arise if a non-registered taxable person attempts to claim such credit. Regulation 70(1) offers a means of overcoming these difficulties in the case of supplies of goods still in the possession of the taxable person at the date of his registration. The Regulation permits input tax on such goods to be relieved on the making of a claim by the taxable person within 6 months, or such longer period as the Customs & Excise may allow, of the date of registration. The claim is made on Form VAT 421 and must comply with the conditions set out on that form.

SUPPLIES OF SERVICES INVOICED AFTER DEREGISTRATION (REG 70(3))

Regulation 70(3) applies to persons who have ceased to be both a taxable person and registered for VAT purposes. Where such a person receives a supply of services which relates to and was for the purposes of the business carried on by him while he was registered (whether or not it is still being carried on), he may claim a repayment under reg 70(3) of the tax on that supply. This would cover, for example, lawyers' and accountants' fees billed after registration has been cancelled.

5.300 Partial exemption

It has been seen that the ability to obtain relief for input tax is linked to the claimant being a taxable person (see **5.100** and s 3(3)). A taxable person who makes only taxable supplies (this includes those supplies which are treated as taxable for the purposes of input tax relief) may recover all input tax suffered by him for the purposes of his business. A person who makes only exempt supplies, however, is not within the definition of a taxable person (s 2(2)) and thus cannot qualify for input tax relief. Where a person falls between these two extremes, that is, a person who makes some exempt supplies in addition to taxable supplies (commonly referred to as a partially exempt person), may obtain only a partial credit for input tax. Section 4(1)(*b*) provides, therefore, that:

"(*b*) if (a person's business) is such that some but not all of his supplies are taxable supplies, there is allowable such proportion of the input tax for the period as, *in accordance with regulations*, is attributable to taxable supplies."

Section 4(2), (3) and (4) further provide that such Regulations:

(*a*) may permit all supplies to be treated as taxable where the tax attributable to any exempt supply would be lower than a specified amount, or in other prescribed circumstances (sub-s (2)). The regulation in this respect is the VAT (General) Regulations 1977 (SI 1977 No 1759), reg 68.

(*b*) may introduce provisions to secure a fair and reasonable attribution of input tax to taxable supplies which provisions may (sub-s (3)):

(i) make use of a proportion calculation;
(ii) make adjustments to that proportion over a longer period; and
(iii) dispense with an adjustment under (*b*)(ii) where such adjustment gives rise to a change in input tax relief of less than a percentage, not exceeding 10 per cent, or such amount, not exceeding £10 as specified (in fact £5 is specified in the Regulations). The relevant Regulations are the VAT (General) Regulations 1977 (SI 1977 No 1759), regs 63–69.

(*c*) may allow the Customs & Excise to distinguish and differentiate between particular supplies of goods and services in giving input tax credit (sub-s (4)).

These Regulations are now discussed in the following paragraphs.

Items treated as taxable supplies

Certain *de minimis* provisions apply to treat as taxable supplies, exempt supplies falling below specified limits in any prescribed accounting period (for the meaning of "prescribed accounting period", see **17.400**). These provisions are contained in reg 68 and have the effect that a person whose exempt supplies fall below the relevant limits may recover all input tax on supplies made to him for the purpose of his business.

Regulation 68(2) treats exempt supplies as taxable supplies where in any prescribed accounting period:

(*a*) the value of those exempt supplies is less than either:

(i) £100 per month on average; or

(ii) 5 per cent of the value of all supplies made in that period; or

(*b*) the value of exempt supplies in the period is less than either:

(i) 25 per cent of the value of his total outputs and less than £10,000 per month on average; or

(ii) 50 per cent of the value of his total outputs and less than £5,000 a month on average; or

(*c*) the amount of input tax attributable to exempt supplies is less than 5 per cent of the whole input tax for that period.

It will be appreciated that although known as *de minimis* provisions, the limits in (*a*)–(*c*) are high and can result in substantial exempt supplies in fact being treated as taxable.

The Customs & Excise Notice No 706 provides a flow chart explaining the operation of the provisions in (*a*)–(*c*) and for convenience, this chart is reproduced on p 74.

THE "OUTPUTS RULES"

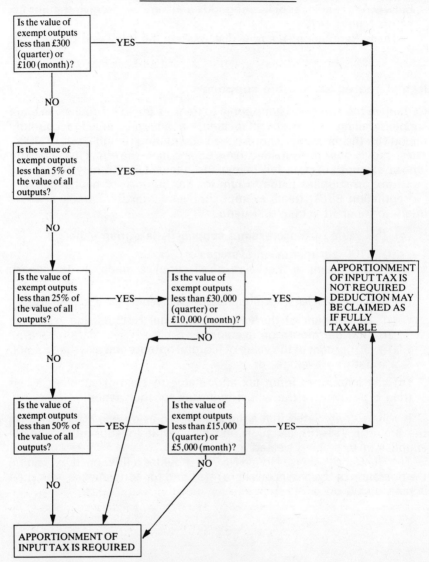

In calculating the limits in (a)–(c), supplies of a type listed under the following paragraph are ignored. The value of any goods of a type specified by Treasury Order under s 3(9) is also to be ignored (see **5.400**).

Exempt supplies to be ignored when operating de minimis provisions etc.

The following exempt supplies are to be ignored both in operating the above *de minimis* provisions and where they are the only exempt supplies made by a taxable person in a prescribed accounting period (reg 68(1) and (4)):

(*a*) the grant, assignment, or surrender of an interest in land habitually occupied in the course of carrying on a business;

(*b*) the issue, transfer or receipt of or any dealing with any security or secondary security within the definition of the Exchange Control Act 1947, s 42, except where the business of the person concerned is, wholly or mainly, the negotiation or undertaking of or making arrangements for such transactions;

(*c*) the assignment of a debt;

(*d*) any transaction within Sched 5, Group 5, item 2 (generally, the provision of an advance, credit or instalment credit finance—see **9.500**) except where the business of the person concerned is, wholly or mainly:

(i) the provision of financial services (other than assignment of debts) within Sched 5, Group 5; or

(ii) the negotiation or making of arrangements for transactions within (*b*) above; or

(iii) the provision of insurance or re-insurance services within Sched 5, Group 2, except by loss or average adjusters, motor assessors, surveyors and other experts and legal services in connection with the assessment of any claim.

(In this Chapter the above supplies will be referred to as "reg 66 supplies".)

Apportionment

If, having operated the rules in reg 68, a taxable person still makes exempt supplies, it is necessary to apportion his input tax between his taxable and exempt supplies. Only the tax apportioned to taxable supplies will then be recoverable by him under s 3. Three principle methods are available under the regulations for apportioning input tax (reg 65(1) and (2)):

METHOD 1

This involves a simple percentage apportionment; that part of the input tax as bears the same ratio to total input tax as the value of taxable supplies bears to the value of total supplies, qualifies for relief.

METHOD 2

Where there is a taxable supply of *goods* in the same condition as they were acquired and the input tax suffered on those goods alone is ascertainable that tax will qualify for relief under this method. All other input tax is apportioned in accordance with Method 1. This method is principally designed for wholesalers and retailers.

SPECIAL METHOD

Any other method may be used, on application to the Customs & Excise, provided that the Customs & Excise are satisfied that it will secure a "fair and reasonable" apportionment of input tax between taxable and exempt supplies. A special method may, for example, allow a partially exempt person supplying services or goods to which he has applied a treatment or process to directly attribute input tax to that supply where it can be clearly shown that such tax was suffered solely in connection with that supply. All other supplies would then again be treated as under Method 1.

A person using a special method may also be permitted by the Customs & Excise to deduct the whole of his input tax if in any period the input tax attributable to his exempt supplies is less than 5 per cent of his total input tax (reg 68(3)). This will, of course, only apply in abnormal accounting periods as the taxable person would otherwise be treated as making wholly taxable supplies under reg 68(2) above.

In operating any attribution method, reg 66 supplies and supplies of a type specified in any Treasury Order made under s 3(9) are ignored (see **5.400**). The exempt supply to be ignored when operating the *de minimis* provisions which is most likely to arise in practice is the disposal of an interest in land, namely a capital sum received from a transaction involving land "habitually occupied" in the course of a person's business. However, land may be sold which while having been used for the business, may not have been habitually occupied in that business. Such land may not be ignored and could give rise to a distortion of a partial exemption calculation. This problem is recognised by the Customs & Excise which has indicated that a Special Method would normally be agreed (even retrospectively) in relation to partially exempt landlords who can demonstrate that little or no input tax is attributable to the exempt side of their business (CCAB TR 371, 11 December 1979, [1980] STI 539).

In operating all the above methods, supplies treated as made under s 8B are to be ignored (s 8B(3)).

Adoption and duration of a method

It is to be noted that a taxable person may himself choose which of methods 1 or 2 to adopt but that a special method may only be used with the prior consent of the Customs & Excise. The Customs & Excise may also direct that a special method is to be used (reg 65(2)).

In the normal event, a method, once adopted, must be retained for at least 2 years and any change must operate from 1 April in any year. The Customs & Excise has the power to allow a change after a shorter interval or on another date (reg 69). For a case where a change was made without notifying the Customs & Excise and the assessment based on the old method was upheld, see *V Lord* v *CCE*, MAN/76/113 (*Casebook* **5.301**).

Periodic adjustments

ADJUSTMENT OF METHOD

An apportionment under one of the above methods, for a particular prescribed accounting period, is initially only provisional and must be reviewed at the end of a "longer period" (reg 67). This revision, or adjustment, is now to be made by the partially exempt person himself (reg 67(1), *cf.* prior reg 26(1)). The Customs & Excise may, however, dispense with an adjustment where a special method is used (reg 67(1)).

The "longer period" is defined in reg 64, generally, as a calendar year. Where, however, the person concerned ceases to be a taxable person during a longer period, the longer period will end on the date he ceases to be taxable.

The adjustment involves applying the same method of apportionment to input tax as was initially adopted in calculating input tax relief but over the longer period. If the amount of input tax calculated for the longer period differs from the aggregate of the input tax for the prescribed accounting periods comprising that longer period, the difference is to be included in the first prescribed accounting period following the longer period (reg 67(1)(c) and (3)(b)).

Although the adjustment calculation is to be applied to all input tax, an adjustment in relation to tax that is not directly attributable to taxable supplies may, on the election of the partially exempt person concerned, be ignored if it is *de minimis* (reg 67(2)). An adjustment is regarded as *de minimis* if the over or under deduction of input tax, as the case may be is no more than the higher of:

(a) 10 per cent of the input tax subject to indirect attribution; or
(b) £5.

APPEAL AGAINST ADJUSTMENTS

There is no longer specific provision for appeal to the Customs & Excise in relation to the amount of any adjustment under reg 67. This follows from the placing of the initiative for the making of the adjustment in the hands of the partially exempt person. There is an appeal, however, against a Customs & Excise refusal to accept an adjustment under the normal appeal provisions, in this case (s 40(1) (*d*), see further Chapter 13).

REVIEW OF TAXABLE SUPPLIES

The operation of the rules in reg 68 discussed above, must similarly be reviewed at the end of each "longer period". If exempt supplies exceed the *de minimis* limits over that longer period, they must be treated as exempt and no longer taxable supplies in making the adjustment (see ADJUSTMENT OF METHOD, *ante*)

This equally applies to the partially exempt person who makes use of a Special Method and is, unusually, treated as making all taxable supplies in a particular period (reg 67(3)).

5.400 Specific disallowance of input tax

Section 3(9) enables the Treasury, by Order, to disallow credit for input tax charged on the supply and importation of such goods or services as may be specified in the Order. To date, Orders have been made in respect of:

(*a*) certain goods installed by builders in new buildings (VAT (Special Provisions) Order 1977 (SI 1977 No 1796), art 8);
(*b*) certain business entertainment (VAT (Special Provisions) Order 1977 (SI 1977 No 1796), art 9);
(*c*) certain motor cars (VAT (Cars) Order 1980 (SI 1980 No 442), art 4);
(*d*) goods under margin schemes (VAT (Special Provisions) Order 1977 (SI 1977 No 1796), art 7).

These are discussed in the following paragraphs.

Items installed by builders

The VAT (Special Provisions) Order 1977 (SI 1977 No 1796), art 8 provides that a taxable person:

- constructing a dwelling, for the purpose of granting a major interest in it, who
- incorporates in any part of the building or its site, goods which are

● not "materials, builders' hardware, sanitary ware or other articles of a kind ordinarily installed by builders as fixtures", cannot recover as input tax VAT on such supplies.

Two major issues arise from this wording. First, the supply must be in the course of the construction of a building which is used as a dwelling and secondly, the correct interpretation of "materials" etc. These issues also arise in connection with Sched 4, Group 8, item 3 and are, therefore, discussed at **8.800**, *post*. It should be noted that there is, however, a minor difference in the wording used in art 8 and Group 8, item 3 (the words "or of" are omitted between "materials" and "builders" in art 8). This is also discussed at **8.800,** *post*.

Business entertainment

Business entertainment is defined in the VAT (Special Provisions) Order 1977 (SI 1977 No 1796), art 2(2) as:

"entertainment (including hospitality of any kind) provided by a taxable person in connection with a business carried on by him, but does not include the provision of anything for persons employed by the taxable person unless its provision for them is incidental to its provision for others."

Entertainment for staff does not generally give rise, therefore, to a disallowance of input tax nor does entertainment provided for an overseas customer (art 9). However, in the case of overseas customers the nature and scale of the entertainment is to be reasonable "having regard to all the circumstances". This proviso possibly adds little to the qualification in both art 9 and indeed s 3(3) that to obtain credit for input tax, the supply must be for the purpose of the business. For this reason also, the ability to obtain credit for unduly extravagant staff entertainment may be open to doubt.

Although entertainment is stated to "include hospitality of any kind", the High Court in *Shaklee International* v *CCE* (*Casebook* **5.406**), held that it was not relevant to consider the motive behind the provision of the supplies in question. Consequently, as the provision of meals and accommodation in that case to an independent sales force was not essential to the provision of training courses for that force, the meals and accommodation amounted to business entertainment. As a result input tax relief in relation to the provision of the meals and accommodation was not allowable.

The close scrutiny given to the incurring of expenditure in this area is also discernible in two similar cases involving the purchase of racehorses. These cases are *British Car Auctions Ltd* v *CCE*, [1978] VATTR 56 (*Casebook* **5.118**), and *Hillingdon Shirt Company Ltd* v *CCE*, MAN/78/26 (*Casebook* **5.117**). In *British Car Auctions*, the motive behind the purchase of the horses, although raced in the appellant's colours, was found to be to induce purchasing agents of customers to the races; the expenditure was, therefore, business entertainment and VAT incurred in respect of that expenditure was not recoverable. In *Hillingdon Shirt Company* (a case already discussed above in relation to advertising), however, an advertising motive was accepted by the Tribunal and input tax relief allowed, albeit with a caveat concerning the need in the future to show tangible advertising results if further credit was to be given for any additional horses. The moral would appear to be that if any purpose other than business entertainment can be identified, input tax may possibly be claimed.

It is to be noted that the Customs & Excise indicate, in Notice No 700, Appendix C that it regards meals, drinks, accommodation, theatre and night club visits, sports or recreational facilities as all falling within the definition of business entertainment.

"Overseas customer" is defined in art 2(2) as any person not ordinarily resident nor carrying on business in the United Kingdom or his agent of similar status, who "avails or may be expected to avail himself in the course of a business carried on by him outside the United Kingdom and the Isle of Man" of the goods or services of the taxable person providing the entertainment. Agents of non-UK or Isle of Man Governments or public authorities are also "overseas customers".

Motor cars

A motor car means:

"any motor vehicle of a kind normally used on public roads which has three or more wheels and either:

(*a*) is constructed or adapted solely or mainly for the carriage of passengers; or

(*b*) has to the rear of the driver's seat roofed accommodation which is fitted with side windows or which is constructed or adapted for the fitting of side windows;

but does not include:

(*a*) vehicles capable of accommodating only one person or suitable for carrying twelve or more persons;

(*b*) vehicles of not less than three tons unladen weight;

(*c*) caravans, ambulances and prison vans;

(*d*) vehicles of a type approved by the Assistant Commissioner of Police of the Metropolis as conforming to the conditions of fitness for the time being laid down by him for the purposes of the London Cab Order 1934;

(*e*) vehicles constructed for a special purpose other than the carriage of persons and having no other accommodation for carrying persons than such as is incidental to that purpose".

The combination of the words "solely or mainly" in (*a*) and (*e*) allows the interpretation that, if a vehicle may only incidentally carry passengers, it is not a "motor car" and consequently, input tax can be recovered. This generally excludes commercial vehicles from the definition of a motor car (*Chartcliff Ltd* v *CCE*, [1976] VATTR 165 (*Casebook* **5.408**)). An estate car used in a business would however, be caught by the definition.

Credit is not disallowed in the following cases (art 4(1)):

(*a*) where the motor car is taken on hire, ie not purchased outright or hire purchased;

(*b*) where the motor car is purchased for conversion into a vehicle other than a motor car;

(*c*) where the motor car is unused and is supplied or imported for the purpose of being sold; or

(*d*) the motor car is unused and is supplied to a taxable person who, as his only business, leases such motor cars to another taxable person whose business in turn wholly consists of the making available of such cars to persons in receipt of mobility allowances.

Margin schemes

Where goods are sold under the benefit of a margin scheme (that is, a scheme whereby tax is charged on only the excess of the sale price of goods over the price at which they were purchased by the supplier (see **16.100**, *post*)), no tax invoice will be issued by the supplier in respect of that sale (VAT (Special Provisions) Order 1977 (SI 1977 No 1796), art 4(3)(*b*)). As a tax invoice is generally required to substantiate a claim to input tax, this alone effectively disallows input tax credit in respect of such goods. However, the VAT (Special Provisions) Order 1977 (SI 1977 No 1796), art 7 specifically disallows credit in such cases. The goods to which margin schemes may apply are:

(*a*) works of art, antiques and collectors' pieces;
(*b*) used motor cycles;
(*c*) used caravans;
(*d*) used boats and outboard motors;
(*e*) used electronic organs; and
(*f*) used aircraft.

5.500 Do-it-yourself builders

Section 15A provides relief for input tax suffered by any person (including taxable persons) in respect of:

● goods

- incorporated in a dwelling or its site (a dwelling includes a garage constructed at the same time as the dwelling and intended to be occupied together with it)
- which goods are "materials, builder's hardware, sanitary ware or other articles of a kind ordinarily installed by builders as fixtures"

where that dwelling has been:

- lawfully
- constructed by that person (construction does not include conversion, reconstruction, alteration or enlargement of any existing dwelling)
- otherwise than in the course or furtherance of any business of the person concerned.

It can be seen that the above section incorporates many of the phrases used in connection with Sched 4, Group 8, item 3 and, therefore, reference should be made to **8.800** for a discussion of those phrases. The following should be noted, however:

(*a*) the section only applies to goods; services may be zero-rated under Sched 4, Group 8, item 2;

(*b*) claims under the section should be made in a single claim within 3 months of the date on which the construction is completed or, exceptionally, at such later time as the Customs & Excise allow (VAT ("Do-It-Yourself" Builders) (Relief) Regulations 1975 (SI 1975 No 649), reg 3). The claim must be accompanied by the following documents:

(i) a certificate of habitation or completion from the local authority;

(ii) an invoice showing the VAT registration number of the supplier in respect of each supply or documentary evidence of importation and payment of tax on the goods;

(iii) documentary evidence of planning permission;

(iv) the certificate of a quantity surveyor or architect that goods in the claim were, or in his judgment were likely to have been incorporated in the dwelling or its site;

(v) written evidence from the local authority that any garage is rated as such.

From the need to produce a certificate of habitation or completion (see (i), *ante*), completion of the building may arguably be the date specified in the local authority certificate. See generally p 137, however, as to the time a building can be said to have been completed;

(*c*) cases before the Tribunals have shown the importance of not only obtaining planning permission but of obtaining it in a suitable form to substantiate any later claim under the section. In particular, in *T Owen* v *CCE* LON/78/345 (*Casebook* **5.503**), the Tribunal laid stress on the fact that the planning permission referred to the "proposed extension to the dwelling house at Beehive Lodge" and went on to hold that the work was consequently excluded from relief under s 15A(3)(*b*);

(*d*) in *S Hardy* v *CCE*, LON/76/46 (*Casebook* **5.501**), the appellant attempted to introduce evidence from Hansard as to the intention of Parliament in enacting the section in order to show that relief should be given to anyone who creates additional housing units. Apart from upholding the principle that Hansard reports are generally not admissible in the interpretation of Statutes, the Tribunal held that work involved in the sub-division of an existing house does not qualify for relief under s **15A**. This is again due to the important bar in sub-s (3)(*b*) that the relief does not extend to work which amounts to the conversion, reconstruction, alteration or enlargement of any existing building.

Chapter 6

Importation

6.000 Sources

Section 2(4) —VAT on importation chargeable and payable as if a customs duty.

Section 3(3) —VAT on importation is input tax.

Section 3(9) —Gives the Treasury power to make orders that no relief as input tax should be available for VAT on importation, and consequently no liability to output tax.

Section 11 —Valuation of goods on import

Section 12(3)—Goods within Sched 4 when imported are not generally liable to VAT.

Section 16(1)—Relief from tax may be given by Treasury Order. Following Orders have been made:

> VAT (Imported Goods) Relief (No 1) Order 1973 (SI 1973 No 327)—goods for use at demonstrations etc.
>
> VAT (Imported Goods) Relief Order 1975 (SI 1975 No 1491)—certain goods of less than £17 value for use by individuals in private capacity.
>
> VAT (Imported Goods) Relief Order 1977 (SI 1977 No 1790)—relates to gold imported by Central Bank.

Section 16(2)—Power given to the Customs & Excise to make Regulations for relief from VAT on goods previously exported from the United Kingdom. Regulations made under this section are:

> VAT (General) Regulations 1977 (SI 1977 No 1759), regs 39—41

Section 16(3)—Power given to the Customs & Excise to make Regulations for relief from VAT on goods temporarily imported into the United Kingdom. Regulations made are:

> VAT (General) Regulations 1977 (SI 1977 No 1759), regs 37 and 38.

Section 17 —Brings VAT within the general statutory provisions of Customs enactments for importation of goods with certain exceptions.

Section 18 —Power given to the Customs & Excise to make Regulations for goods to be imported without payment of VAT. Regulations made are:

> VAT (General) Regulations 1977 (SI 1977 No 1759), regs 33—36.

Section 27 —Provisions relating to supplies made whilst goods are warehoused. The Customs & Excise have power to make Regulations to enable goods to be removed without payment of VAT and the Regulations made are:

> VAT (General) Regulations 1977 (SI 1977 No 1759), regs 33—36 apply.

Section 49 —Relief on reimportation of motor cars exported without payment of purchase tax.

Schedule 4, Group 15—Zero-rates the supply of imported goods before entry for Customs purposes.

FA 1977, s 16—Goods imported for private purposes.

VAT (Special Provisions) Order 1977 (SI 1977 No 1796)
art 6—Relief on importation of certain antiques and works of art.

In addition the following Customs & Excise Notices may be helpful:

702—Imports
465—Outline of import entry procedure.

6.100   General principles

The general purpose of the VAT and Customs enactments is to charge VAT on the importation of all goods into the United Kingdom whether imported by a taxable person or not. Certain categories of goods are, however, excepted from the general charge and these are dealt with in detail in **6.200**, *et seq*. Because of the large number of reliefs available the burden of tax on importation is considerably reduced. The way in which the VAT charge on importation is imposed is by making VAT chargeable and payable as a duty of customs (s 2(4)) and by extending the Customs & Excise legislation to VAT (s 17). By doing this the collection of VAT on importation is brought within the general rules for the collection of import duties and levies and it is for this reason that Customs & Excise procedure for payment of customs duty on importation becomes relevant and why the payment of VAT comes within those rules.

Entry

Before considering the manner in which VAT is paid on importation, therefore, it is necessary to understand some of the principles of importation generally. For example, the importer of any goods into the United Kingdom is required, by law, to deliver a written declaration to the Customs & Excise in respect of the goods. The declaration is referred to as an entry and the term "entry" is encountered frequently in the VAT legislation. The entry will enable Customs & Excise to ensure that the correct amount of duty or VAT is paid. It is important to note that the question as to whether or not any import duty is payable is totally separate from consideration of the VAT position. VAT and import duty may be payable, or alternatively only one of the two may be. Generally, import duties have largely been abolished, but the possibility of an *import* duty or *customs* duty applying must not be overlooked. It is not the purpose of this *Guide*, however, to consider other customs duties.

The form of declaration, or entry, that will usually require completion is Form C10. A list of goods for which a Form C10 should be completed is given in Customs & Excise Notice No 465 (Outline of import entry procedure). The forms are normally provided in a five-part set with different coloured printing on each copy so that the copies can be easily identified and used for the correct purpose. Details of how to complete the Form C10 are given in Notice No 465, as are details of the documents which should accompany the entry. A copy of the form must be kept (the third copy in the package of five being white with green printing) for VAT purposes if the importer is a registered taxable person. The form must be signed by an appropriate person, as listed below, depending upon who the importer is:

Importer	*Signatory*
Individual	The importer, or an employee of his if so authorised in writing by the importer.
Partnership	A partner, or an employee if authorised in writing by a partner.
Company incorporated under the Companies Acts	A director or secretary or other employee authorised in writing by a director or the secretary.
Company incorporated by Statute	A person lawfully entitled to sign for the corporation, or an employee authorised in writing by such a person
Foreign firm or company	A person legally authorised by the law of the country concerned to sign on behalf of the firm or company
Shipping or Forwarding Agent	As agreed between the parties

Postponed accounting system

Although VAT is payable on all imports of goods (subject to the exceptions in **6.200**) it is possible for a registered taxable person to avoid having to pay the VAT on actual importation of goods for use in the course or furtherance of any business by operating what is commonly referred to as "the postponed accounting system". This treatment is not afforded to exempt persons (see *post*), but exempt persons may apply for deferred payment (see **6.400**).

The enabling legislation for the postponed accounting system is contained in s 18 which gives the Customs & Excise power to make regulations to enable goods to be imported by a *taxable person in the course or furtherance of his business* to be delivered or removed without payment of VAT, subject to such conditions as the Customs & Excise may impose, and for the tax to be accounted for on submission of the next quarterly return. Similar power to make Regulations in respect of the removal of goods from warehouse without payment of VAT is given by s 27. Regulations have been made under the VAT (General) Regulations 1977 (SI 1977 No 1759), regs 33–36. The effect of those Regulations is that, to be of benefit, the importer must satisfy the following conditions:

(*a*) be a registered taxable person;
(*b*) have given security within s 32(2), if required; and
(*c*) he must:

(i) include his registration number in the entry (ie Form C10); or

(ii) where the goods are imported through the post and entry is not required include his registration number on the customs declaration; or

(iii) the Customs & Excise have allowed the goods to be removed without entry.

The postponed accounting system, thus means that the VAT on importation need not be paid on actual importation and as that VAT would qualify as input tax (s 3(3)), the VAT never in fact becomes payable. Assuming the goods are supplied by the importer to the consumer during the same accounting period, the output tax will be collected from the consumer and paid to the Customs & Excise in the normal way. The VAT on importation is dealt with by accounting for the tax due on importation in Box 2 of the quarterly return (Form VAT 100) and at the same time claiming a deduction for the tax as an input in Box 6. Failure to comply with the above procedure may lead to the Customs & Excise withdrawing the benefit of this system and consequently the importer may have to pay the VAT on importation in the same way as an exempt person (see *Exempt persons: not eligible for postponed accounting, post*).

As the postponed accounting system applies to registered taxable persons it can apply to persons who make some exempt supplies, providing the person is registered. However, when calculating the VAT deductible as input tax, an apportionment must be made as explained in **5.300**.

It will be seen from the above that the system can only be operated by a registered taxable person on imports for use in the course or furtherance of his business. It follows, therefore, that if the goods are for private use the VAT must be paid on importation. If the goods are partly for private use and partly for use in the course or furtherance of his business, he, again, cannot operate the postponed accounting system and must account for VAT on the whole value of the importation: a repayment may be made later by the Customs & Excise in respect of that part of the VAT attributable to business use (see s 3(4) and **5.200**).

After the entry has been cleared and any tax paid or deferred (see **6.400**) the VAT copy of the entry, authenticated by Customs & Excise will be returned to the importer or his agent. The form must be retained by the importer so as to substantiate the entries in his quarterly return.

Sometimes goods will be imported by a foreign supplier and he or his agent will be liable for completion of the entry. However, where the UK purchaser has consented he may be treated as the importer for VAT purposes and will account for any tax due on importation, although he would normally be able to postpone payment under the postponed accounting system. Where the purchaser agrees to pay for the VAT Form C10 should be amended so that the following declaration is given in Box 57 (see Customs & Excise Notice No 702, para 7):

"The goods are imported for (name of United Kingdom customer) whose VAT registration number is .... and who will account for any VAT due which is not paid to this entry."

Exempt persons: not eligible for postponed accounting

Exempt persons are not eligible for the postponed accounting system, since it only applies to registered taxable persons (VAT (General) Regulations 1977 (SI 1977 No 1759), reg 33). Accordingly, an exempt person must account for any VAT due on importation, unless he is granted deferment facilities (see **6.400**).

Methods of importation

There are various ways in which goods may be imported into the United Kingdom, for example, by air, sea or post, and aspects of these methods are considered below.

SEA

The general rules outlined above apply to entry of goods through ports.

POST

A registered taxable person should ensure that his VAT number is on the customs declaration accompanying the package, and on the package itself, if he wishes to operate the postponed accounting system and avoid having to pay VAT at importation. A Notice of Arrival of goods imported by post, usually Form C170, will be sent to the importer.

AIR

Goods imported through London Heathrow and Gatwick Airports will normally be processed through the London Airport Cargo EDP Scheme ("LACES") (see **6.600**).

6.200 Reliefs

There are several ways in which relief from VAT on the importation of goods into the United Kingdom or Isle of Man is given, namely:

(*a*) by s 12(3) in respect of goods which would otherwise be zero-rated under Sched 4;

(*b*) by Customs & Excise legislation in respect of customs duties and levies, introduced by s 17;

(*c*) by Treasury Order made pursuant to ss 14 and 16(1);

(*d*) by Regulations made pursuant to s 16(2), and (3);

(*e*) by s 49.

The ways by which relief is given on imported goods are dealt with in more detail below.

Zero-rating

Section 12(3) provides that any goods that would qualify for zero-rating under the provisions of Sched 4 (see Chapter 8) may be imported free of VAT, whether the importer is a taxable person or not, except where the application of s 12(3) is specifically excluded from Sched 4. Thus, no VAT will be payable on the importation of any goods of items within Sched 4, except for goods within:

(*a*) Group 8, namely goods supplied for use in the construction of buildings (Sched 4, Group 8, Note 3);

(*b*) Group 12, namely gold (see Sched 4, Group 12, Note 2);

(*c*) Group 14, drugs, medicines, medical and surgical appliances (Sched 4, Group 14, Note 1).

Customs & Excise legislation

As stated at **6.100**, VAT is charged on importation as a duty of customs and s 17 provides that enactments and regulations relating generally to customs or excise on imported goods shall have effect, subject to certain exemptions and the power of Customs & Excise to make regulations, as if VAT were a duty of customs. The effect of s 17 is, therefore, to bring VAT on importation within the general law for customs or excise duties. This would bring the effect of the Customs and Excise (General Reliefs) Act 1979 into operation, but s 17(2A) excludes the majority of the reliefs under the Customs and Excise (General Reliefs) Act 1979 and leaves only ss 7, 8 and 9(*b*) of that Act applying. The result is that the following reliefs are available, being brought into operation by s 17(1), although it must be remembered that registered taxable persons will operate the postponed accounting system so that the reliefs are of more interest to exempt or non-taxable persons:

LEGACIES

Where it is shown to the satisfaction of the Customs & Excise that movable property belonging to a deceased person, which was used by the deceased prior to his death for non-business purposes, is imported by the beneficiary under the deceased's estate the Customs & Excise may remit or otherwise repay the VAT paid on importation (Customs and Excise Duties (General Reliefs) Act 1979, s 7 applied by FA 1972, s 17(1)).

Relief is not available for business goods, cigars, wines or spirits, gifts or items purchased from the legal beneficiaries of the deceased and gifts which the importer receives because of the deceased's "wishes" rather than under a testamentary disposition or intestacy.

Customs & Excise Notice No 368 (Legacies—relief from customs duty, VAT and car tax) sets out the documents which the Customs & Excise will require to substantiate the claim, which stated briefly are:

(*a*) a declaration in the form set out in the Annex to Notice No 368 to be signed by the importer or by a solicitor acting for the importer in connection with the deceased's estate. A list of goods must be included in the Declaration;

(*b*) a certified copy of the Will (or a part thereof) or other legal document;

(*c*) if the legacy is not a specific legacy, a declaration that the goods form part of the estate; this declaration is made by the executor or similar person.

The usual entry Form C10, must be completed and the documents referred to above attached to it. The form should be marked "Legacy-Relief Claimed".

Included in the above, as goods, are cars passing under a testamentary disposition or intestacy.

TRADE SAMPLES

The Customs & Excise have a general discretion to permit the importation of trade samples or goods drawn from imported goods for use as trade samples without payment of VAT where the samples are in connection with goods to be exported. The importation of labels or other articles supplied without charge for the purpose of being re-exported with goods produced or manufactured in the United Kingdom is also permitted without payment of VAT (Customs and Excise Duties (General Reliefs) Act 1979, s 8, applied by FA 1972, s 17(1)).

For further details see Customs & Excise Notice No 118 (Export trade reliefs).

AWARDS FOR DISTINCTION

The Customs & Excise are empowered to authorise the importation without payment of VAT of articles, which are shown to the satisfaction of the Customs & Excise to have been awarded to any person for distinction in art, literature, science or sport or for public services or for other praiseworthy achievement or conduct (Customs and Excise Duties (General Reliefs) Act 1979, s 9(*b*), as applied by FA 1972, 17(1)).

The Customs & Excise have issued Notice No 364 covering this issue (Awards for distinction: relief from customs duty and VAT), which indicates that the relief does not apply to:

"(i) prizes won in ordinary unimportant competitions such as deck games or card games;
(ii) gifts marking anniversaries or other special occasions; or
(iii) customary presentations made by business firms to their employees to mark the completion of long periods of service or commercial association."

The VAT due must be paid on importation and a repayment sought by persons qualifying for the relief although in practice the Customs & Excise will usually allow collection of the goods without payment if satisfactory documentation (see *post*) is produced on entry; registered taxable persons operating the postponed accounting system would not in fact pay the VAT on importation (see **6.100**), so that the relief is only really of interest to exempt or non-taxable persons (or possibly taxable persons who have had the facility of postponed accounting withdrawn). The claim for relief must be supported by documentary evidence, for example, correspondence between the award winner and the presenters of the award, or a declaration by the recipient or the person importing on his behalf on Form C920.

On entry the usual Form C10 should be completed together with, if the importer is an exempt person or a registered taxable person importing otherwise than in the course or furtherance of his business, Form VAT 909. The entry should be marked "Award for Distinction—Relief Claimed" (see Customs & Excise Notice No 364).

If the goods are imported in the recipient's baggage, formal entry is not required but the documentary evidence referred to above is required. Imports through the post should have an accompanying declaration as above, and the package and declaration should be marked as indicated in the previous paragraph. The person to whom the package is addressed will be notified by the Customs & Excise of its arrival (Form C160) and a claim for relief must then be submitted.

TRANSHIPMENTS

Relief from VAT is available in respect of goods imported for transhipment or in transit through the United Kingdom (Customs and Excise Management Act 1979, s 4, applied by FA 1972, s 17(1)). The goods must be duly exported and security is or may be required in respect of VAT (and any customs duty). For further details see Customs & Excise Notice No 198 (Transit and transhipment procedures).

GOODS NOT IN ACCORDANCE WITH CONTRACT

Where goods, which have been imported, are subsequently discovered
to be damaged or not in accordance with the terms of the contract (eg
because they are the wrong goods or wrong quality) and the goods
are destroyed or re-exported before having been used, the VAT paid
may be reclaimed (Customs and Excise Management Act 1979, s 123,
applied by FA 1972, s 17(1)). The relief is not available, however,
in respect of goods bought on sale or return.

Details of how to claim the relief are given in Customs & Excise Notice
No 266 (Goods not in accordance with contract: repayment of import
duty, agricultural levy and VAT) but broadly speaking a registered taxable person need not apply for the relief for the reasons explained earlier.
Partly exempt persons are advised to contact their local VAT office (para
12) whilst exempt persons should follow the procedure for claiming
relief outlined in Notice 266, namely by completing Customs & Excise
Form 1172.

TEMPORARY IMPORTATIONS UNDER INTERNATIONAL LAW

In addition to the relief for temporary importations given under the VAT
(General) Regulations 1977 (SI 1977 No 1759), regs 37 and 38 (see
Customs & Excise Regulations, TEMPORARY IMPORTATIONS), the following
goods are eligible for relief on temporary importation by virtue of the
adoption of statutory enactments by s 17(1):

Private motor vehicles: A private motor vehicle is relieved from VAT on
temporary importation under SI 1970 No 558 as amended by SI 1972
No 838 (applied by s 17(1)), where the importer has been abroad for
at least 12 months out of the 24 months immediately prior to the importation and is visiting the United Kingdom for less than a year. A measure
of relief is also available to a person who has left the United Kingdom
with the intention of living abroad for more than 12 months but who
has not yet completed 12 months residence abroad when he visits the
United Kingdom; in such a case the vehicle may be imported for a 6
month period free of VAT, except that if a person has recently benefited
from this 6 month relief, the period for importing free of VAT may be
reduced to 1 month.

The importer will normally be issued with a Notice No 115D, on which
the date for exportation will be stamped. Full details of the relief are
given in Customs & Excise Notice No 115A (Temporary importation
of private motor vehicles).

Relief will be lost if the vehicle is offered or advertised for sale, hired
or pledged, or otherwise disposed of in the United Kingdom or Isle of
Man. The vehicle must be for the use of the importer or his wife or
dependants.

Commercial vehicles and aircraft: Relief is available on the importation of commercial vehicles and aircraft under The Temporary Importation (Commercial Vehicles and Aircraft) Regulations 1961 (SI 1961 No 1523) (introduced under the Customs and Excise Act 1952, s 40—see now the Customs and Excise Management 1979—and applied to VAT by FA 1972, s 17(1)). To qualify for relief the following conditions must be satisfied:

(*a*) the importer's principal place of business is overseas;
(*b*) the vehicle or aircraft is registered overseas and is owned and operated by a person whose principal place of business is overseas;
(*c*) the vehicle or aircraft is on a journey beginning and ending overseas;
(*d*) the vehicle or aircraft is being used to carry passengers for payment or to transport goods from or to the United Kingdom.

Relief will normally be given for a 3 month period. The importer of a commercial vehicle will receive a Form 115E with the date by which the vehicle must depart stamped on it (see Customs & Excise Notice No 115C (Temporarily imported commercial vehicles)). For details in relation to aircraft see Notice No 115B.

Private aircraft: Similar relief to that available on the temporary importation of private motor vehicles (see *ante*) applies to the temporary importation of private aircraft (see Customs & Excise Notice No 115B).

Containers: These are eligible for relief from VAT on temporary importation (see Customs & Excise Notice No 309, para 16) if the Customs & Excise are satisfied that the containers:

(*a*) are owned by overseas persons with no agreement for ownership to be transferred to a UK person;
(*b*) will not be used in the United Kingdom;
(*c*) will remain in foreign ownership;
(*d*) will be re-exported within 12 months.

Personal effects: Relief may be available on the importation of personal effects under the Customs Duty (Personal Reliefs) Order 1970 (SI 1970 No 558) as amended.

Miscellaneous goods: Certain other goods are eligible for relief on temporary importation. For details see Customs & Excise Notice No 702 (Imports) Section V, para 24. The relevant goods are:

Personal and household effects	Notice No 12
Private vessels	Notice No 8A
Professional effects	Notice No 46
Tourist publicity materials	Notice No 208

Treasury Order

Section 16(1) enables the Treasury to make provision for relief, by Order, having regard to any international agreement or agreements. The persons to benefit from the reliefs are most likely to be non-taxable persons, exempt or partially exempt persons who would not be able to get a full credit for any VAT payable on importation. Registered taxable persons would normally implement the postponed accounting system and would not, therefore, pay the VAT. The Treasury has exercised its power and made four orders for relief as follows:

GOODS FOR DEMONSTRATION

Under the VAT (Imported Goods) Relief (No. 1.) Order 1973 (SI 1973 No 327), relief is granted on the import of goods where it is shown to the satisfaction of the Customs & Excise that the goods are for demonstration or use in the demonstration of any machine or apparatus produced or manufactured outside the United Kingdom or in the construction, furnishing or decoration of a temporary stand of a foreign exhibitor, and the goods will be destroyed or rendered useless as a result of such demonstration. The demonstration must be at a qualifying event, namely:

(*a*) any trade, industrial, agricultural or crafts exhibition, fair or similar show or display, as long as it is not organised for private purposes in a shop or business premises with a view to sale;

(*b*) any exhibition or meeting primarily organised for:

(i) charitable purposes; or

(ii) promoting any branch of learning, art, craft, sport or scientific, educational or cultural activity; or

(iii) promoting friendship between peoples; or

(iv) promoting religious knowledge or worship;

(*c*) any meeting of representatives of any international organisation or international group of organisations;

(*d*) any representative meeting of an official or commemorative character.

The Order does not apply to fuel, tobacco goods or any beverage containing alcohol. Relief is also available on printed advertising or publicity material supplied free of charge from outside the United Kingdom or Isle of Man for free distribution to persons attending the event providing the material relates to goods produced or manufactured abroad. Furthermore, the aggregate value and quantity of the material must be appropriate having regard to the nature and scale of the event.

Where goods are produced during the course of a demonstration the

Customs & Excise may impose conditions to ensure that those goods so produced are destroyed, rendered unfit for use, exported or otherwise disposed of so that they cannot be sold in the United Kingdom without the knowledge and approval of the Customs & Excise.

The Order was made to give effect to the Customs Convention concerning facilities for the importation of goods for display or use of exhibitions drawn up at Brussels on 8 June 1961. The Order affects goods imported permanently for use at exhibitions. Any goods imported temporarily for such use are covered separately under TRADE SAMPLES, *ante*.

Where the importer is a registered taxable person entry form C10 should be completed (see Customs & Excise Notice No 213 (Goods imported for exhibitions or meetings)). An exempt person should endorse the entry "Relief claimed from VAT for the above goods".

GOODS OF LITTLE VALUE FOR PERSONAL USE IMPORTED FROM AN EEC COUNTRY TO THE UNITED KINGDOM OR ISLE OF MAN

The VAT (Imported Goods) Relief Order 1980 (SI 1980 No 1009), relieves from VAT the importation of goods into the United Kingdom. The Order is made pursuant to the EEC Council Directive No 74/651/ EEC, article 2(1), dated 19 December 1974. The purpose of the Order is to reduce tax impediments on small consignments (of a non-commercial nature) of goods between individuals in order to create the characteristics of a domestic market. Relief is available where the Customs and Excise are satisfied that:

(*a*) the value of the goods is £40 or less if from an EEC country and £20 or less if from elsewhere and the goods do not form part of a larger consignment;

(*b*) any excise duty or turnover tax of the EEC country in which the goods were bought has been paid; in respect of goods from a non-EEC country the consignment must be of an occasional nature;

(*c*) the consignment is sent from one private individual to another;

(*d*) the consignment is not imported for any consideration in money's worth;

(*e*) the consignment is for the personal use of the consignee or his family and not for any commercial purpose.

The relief is not available where the goods are brought into the United Kingdom in the personal baggage of the individual claiming relief. This, relief is not due in respect of goods brought back from an EEC country on return from a holiday abroad. Furthermore, the relief does not apply to tobacco products (cigarettes, cigars or tobacco), alcoholic drinks (spirits or wine) or perfumes or toilet water to the extent that such goods are in excess of the limit set out in the Schedule to the Order.

GOLD IMPORTED BY A CENTRAL BANK

Relief from VAT on the importation of gold by a Central Bank is given under the VAT (Imported Goods) Relief Order 1977 (SI 1977 No 1790), made as a result of the EEC Sixth Directive, article 14(1)(*j*), dated 17 May 1977.

WORKS OF ART, ANTIQUES AND COLLECTIONS

The VAT (Special Provisions) Order 1977 (SI 1977 No 1796), art 6 permits the importation of certain works of art and antiques free of VAT. The relief, in respect of works of art, is in addition to that given under the VAT (General) Regulations 1977 (SI 1977 No 1759), reg 40 (relief on reimportation—see *post*). The Order, in relation to works of art, antiques and collections is made under the provision of s 14 and is to bring the VAT position on importation into line with the special schemes operated in respect of works of art, antiques and collections (*see* **16.000**). The relief is available on the importation of:

(*a*) paintings, drawings and pastels, executed by hand and acquired before 1 April 1973;

(*b*) original engravings, prints and lithographs acquired before 1 April 1973;

(*c*) original sculptures and statuary, in any material and acquired before 1 April 1973;

(*d*) antiques, of an age exceeding one hundred years, except pearls and loose gem stones;

(*e*) collections and collectors' pieces of zoological, botanical, mineralogical, anatomical, historical, archaeological, palaeontological or ethnographic interest.

Customs & Excise Regulations

Section 16(2) enables the Customs & Excise to make Regulations for relief from VAT on goods previously exported from the United Kingdom and s 16(3) gives the Customs & Excise power to make Regulations for relief in respect of goods which are only temporarily imported into the United Kingdom. The Customs & Excise have made Regulations contained in the VAT (General) Regulations 1977 (SI 1977 No 1759) as follows:

REIMPORTATION

The VAT (General) Regulations 1977 (SI 1977 No 1759), reg 39 provides that no VAT is payable on the reimportation of certain goods. The relief will be available where:

(*a*) the importer is not a taxable person or, if he is, the goods are not imported for use in his business;

(*b*) the goods were exported originally by or on behalf of the importer;

(*c*) the goods were either originally supplied in or imported into the United Kingdom and purchase tax or VAT was payable on such supply or importation and has not been (and will not be) refunded, or alternatively the goods were made by the importer;

(*d*) VAT or purchase tax was paid on the export of the goods, the goods not being zero-rated;

(*e*) no repair or processing has been carried out to the goods whilst abroad, other than running repairs which have not increased the value of the goods;

(*f*) the goods were, when exported, intended to be re-imported, or have been returned for repair or replacement after rejection by an overseas customer, or the goods were in private use in the United Kingdom or Isle of Man before they were exported.

It will be noted that the above relief only applies to non-taxable persons, or goods reimported by a taxable person other than in the course of his business. The relief is primarily designed, therefore, for exempt persons because an exempt person would have paid VAT in the United Kingdom on the acquisition of the goods (and indeed must have done so to qualify for relief) and it is thus equitable that he should not pay VAT again on their reimportation. A taxable person would not need the relief because he would not, in fact, pay any VAT under the postponed accounting system and would also have zero-rated the supply on export (see **7.100**).

It will also be seen that to be eligible for relief the goods must not have had their value increased by repair or processing overseas (other than running repairs). This is because otherwise any increase in value as a result of the processing or repair would escape VAT. However, a measure of relief may still be available in these circumstances under reg 41 (see REIMPORTATION OF GOODS PROCESSED ABROAD, *post*).

The reimportation must be by the same person who exported the goods (see (*b*), *ante* and *TM Hagenbach* v *CCE*, LON/74/49 (*Casebook* **6.101**)). The application of the relief is further limited by (*f*), *ante*.

Relief must be claimed on entry of the goods by completing Form C10. Full details of the procedure are given in Customs & Excise Notice No 236 (Returned goods relief EEC 1977), para 7.

REIMPORTATION OF GOODS PROCESSED ABROAD

A similar relief is given to that described under REIMPORTATION, *ante* to goods (other than those mentioned below) which have been processed or repaired whilst overseas (VAT (General) Regulations 1977 (SI 1977 No 1759), reg 41). Relief is given by restricting the charge to VAT on reimportation to the increase in value of the goods as a result of the process or repair. The conditions for eligibility for the relief are similar to those outlined above under REIMPORTATION, *ante* but it would appear from reg 41 that the necessity for the goods to be reimported by or on behalf of the same exporter is absent, because reg 41 excludes the condition described at para (*b*) under REIMPORTATION above. However, the Customs & Excise Notice No 702 (Imports) states at page 16 that:

"If goods, other than certain goods mentioned below, were exported from the United Kindgom *by or on behalf of the person reimporting them* ... the goods will be chargeable with VAT only on the increase in their value attributable to the treatment or process plus any import duty payable."

This additional requirement of the Customs & Excise that the importer and exporter be the same person would, therefore, in this particular context, appear to be without authority.

The relief is only available to exempt persons or in respect of goods reimported by a taxable person after process for non-business use. The relief should be claimed in the manner described in Customs & Excise Notice No 235. The reasons for granting the relief are similar to those on REIMPORTATION (see *ante*) but the charge to VAT is retained on the increase in value of the goods as a result of the repairs or processing as otherwise it would be possible to export goods for processing and avoid paying VAT on the increase in the value of the goods attributable thereto.

REIMPORTATION OF CARS AND WORKS OF ART

The VAT (General) Regulations 1977 (SI 1977 No 1759), reg 40 provides relief from VAT on the importation of motor cars and works of art which have previously been exported. To qualify for relief:

(*a*) the motor car must have previously been supplied or imported into the United Kingdom and VAT or purchase tax paid on such an occasion and such VAT must not have been, nor will be, refunded or deducted;
(*b*) the work of art must have been either exported before 1 April 1973 or, if after that date, must have been supplied by the person in such circumstances that VAT would not have been payable on the full value of the supply.

For the purposes of the relief, motor car has the same meaning as in the VAT (Cars) Order 1980 (SI 1980 No 442) (see **5.400**) and work of art means any:

(*a*) paintings, drawings and pastels done by hand;
(*b*) original engravings, prints and lithographs;
(*c*) original sculptures and statuary, in any material.

The work of art, if supplied after 1 April 1973, must have been the subject of a supply to which the special scheme for works of art applies under the VAT (Special Provisions) Order 1977 (SI 1977 No 1796).

Where the value of the motor car or work of art is increased as the result of any repair or process abroad, VAT is restricted on reimportation to the increase in value attributable to the repair or process (reg 40(2)).

So far as motor cars are concerned, regard should also be had to relief on temporary importation under international law (see p 92, *ante*) and s 49 (see p 100, *post*).

TEMPORARY IMPORTATIONS

The VAT (General) Regulations 1977 (SI 1977 No 1759), reg 37 gives the Customs & Excise power to permit goods to be imported without payment of VAT, having regard to the tax on similar goods if supplied in the United Kingdom. To qualify for relief the Customs & Excise must be satisfied that it is intended to export the goods or goods incorporated in or manufactured from the goods. The importer must produce the goods for examination both at the time of importation and subsequently, if required, and must deposit funds with the Customs & Excise or give security to cover any potential VAT. The importer must further keep records as required by the Customs & Excise and must produce those records on request. The goods must be exported within 6 months of importation or such longer period as the Customs & Excise may allow and evidence of the export must be produced on request.

The relief is available to, but not normally needed by, registered taxable persons because they would not pay VAT on importation by virtue of the postponed accounting system, although such persons may wish to claim relief if the facility of postponed accounting has been withdrawn. It will usually be exempt persons who will claim, therefore, and they should do so by separate written letter of application together with Form 990 (see Customs & Excise Notice No 702 (Imports), para 20 and Customs & Excise Notice No 221, para 74).

Regulation 38 gives the Customs & Excise power to grant relief from temporary importations of goods on hire or loan. The Customs & Excise have a general discretion to limit the VAT payable to VAT chargeable on the hiring fee or the value of the loan, although it must be noted that the VAT is payable on importation the importer making a claim for repayment of the VAT after the export of the goods. As a registered taxable person will operate the postponed accounting system, the relief will be utilised primarily by exempt persons.

The Customs & Excise have further power under this Regulation to remit VAT to the extent of that charged in another EEC country, which is not eligible for refund in that country, but note that the Customs & Excise are able to adjust the hiring charge to a comparable charge that would be made in the United Kingdom if the EEC charge is less (see Customs & Excise Notice No 702 (Imports), para 23(*b*) and Customs & Excise Notice No 209 (Equipment on hire or loan temporarily imported).

Vehicles previously exported free of purchase tax

Section 49 provides that where a vehicle which has previously been bought for use outside the United Kingdom, so that purchase tax was not payable under the Purchase Tax Act 1963, s 23 is brought back into the United Kingdom or Isle of Man no VAT is payable. This "relief" is not a real relief however as purchase tax will still be payable on the reimportation.

6.300 Value

The value of imports upon which VAT is payable is calculated by taking the *purchase price* for the goods (assuming there is no consideration) *plus*, if not already included in the sale:

(*a*) all taxes (other than VAT), duties and other charges; and
(*b*) all costs by way of commission, packing, transport and insurance up to importation (s 11).

In any other case their value shall be taken as their open market value, *plus* any of the items at (*a*) or (*b*) if not already included.

Where the goods are offered at a discount for prompt payment, however, the value shall be the discounted price, whether or not the discount is taken up. This does not apply where the price is payable by instalments (Sched 3, para 5 applied by s 11(4)).

A declaration on Form C105 is usually required if the value of the goods exceeds £750 (see Notice 702 (Imports) para 19).

6.400 Deferred payment

Under EEC Directive 69/76 the United Kingdom is required to allow importers to defer payment of customs duties for a 30 day period, subject to adequate security being lodged with the Customs & Excise. FA 1976, s 15, therefore, empowered the Customs & Excise to make Regulations for the deferment of payment of customs duties, and accordingly the Customs Duties (Deferred Payment) Regulations 1976 (SI 1976 No 1223) were brought into force. Since VAT on importation is chargeable as a duty of customs (s 2(4)) and s 17(1) brings the Customs & Excise enactments, in relation to customs and other duties into force (with certain exceptions), the Customs Duties (Deferred Payment) Regulations 1976 apply to VAT.

The Regulations will not be used normally by registered taxable persons who would be operating the postponed accounting system. Deferred payment may be relevant, however, to exempt persons or taxable persons importing goods for use otherwise than in the course or furtherance of their business.

The 30 day period for deferment begins from the date when duty would normally be payable. The security required is a bank guarantee, from a bank approved by Customs & Excise, and payment of the duty must be by way of direct debit. Applications for deferment should be submitted on Form C1200 to the Collector of Customs & Excise in whose collection area entry will be made. Further details of how to claim deferment are contained in Customs & Excise Notice No 101 (Duty deferment).

Certain imports do not qualify for deferment, namely:

(*a*) alcoholic beverages, perfumes, hydrocarbon, oils, matches and mechanical lighters; and
(*b*) goods brought to the United Kingdom or Isle of Man in a person's baggage.

6.500 Agents

A person who supplies goods or services in the United Kingdom may require to be registered for VAT (see Chapter 2). This principle applies wherever the supplier is resident, as it is the supply of goods or services *in* the United Kingdom which is relevant. An overseas trader may, therefore, need to register if he makes taxable supplies in the United Kingdom.

A supply of goods will be regarded as taking place in the United Kingdom if the goods are located in the United Kingdom when supplied.

Thus, an overseas trader importing goods into the United Kingdom has a choice whether to import the goods himself and then to supply customers, in which case he will need to be registered and comply with VAT law, or whether to supply the goods from outside the United Kingdom and appoint an agent to import on his behalf.

For the purposes of VAT where an agent is appointed in the United Kingdom to act as the importing agent of an overseas trader, the agent is treated as a principal. The agent may make the entry as principal and, accordingly, the agent must be able to issue proper VAT invoices and to account for any tax due in his VAT account and return. The agent would operate the postponed accounting system and would charge any VAT due on the ultimate sale.

For further consideration of overseas traders' liability to VAT see **2.700** and see also Customs & Excise Notice No 702 (Imports), para 6 and VAT Leaflet 700/4/79 (Overseas traders and United Kingdom VAT).

6.600 LACES

As indicated at **6.200**. *Methods of importation, ante* importation by air
through London Heathrow and Gatwick airports is usually done through
the London Airport Cargo EDP Scheme ("LACES"). The entry is effected
through a computer and although the facility of preparing the special
coded LACES entry form is available to all importers, the actual input
of the coded information to the computer may only be done by certain
authorised persons. Normally these authorised persons, known as
"LACES paying agents", are approved forwarding agents. If an importer
is unaware of an approved forwarding agent he should be able to obtain
guidance from the Institute of Freight Forwarders, whose address is
Suffield House, 9 Paradise Road, Richmond, Surrey. They will also be
able to give advice as to the rates charged for such services. Alternatively,
the importing airline may be prepared to make the customs entry on
behalf of the importer.

Chapter 7

Exportation

7.000 Sources

Section 8(3)   —Goods to be removed from the United Kingdom are treated as supplied in the United Kingdom.

Section 12(6) —Zero-rates the export of goods.

Section 12(7) —Gives the Customs & Excise power to make Regulations in respect of exports of goods. Regulations made are:

VAT (General) Regulations 1977 (SI 1977 No 1759), regs 42–50.

Section 12(7A)—Gives the Customs & Excise power to make regulations in respect of the export of goods on hire. No Regulations have been made to date.

Section 12(8) —Forfeiture provisions.

In addition the following Customs & Excise Notices may be helpful:

703—Exports.
704—Retail export schemes.
705—Tax free sales of motor vehicles to tourists, etc.

7.100 General principles

This chapter is concerned with the exportation of goods from the United Kingdom. The exportation of services and their treatment for VAT is explained at **10.100**.

Where the Customs & Excise are satisfied that goods have been exported from the United Kingdom or have been shipped for use as stores or for sale by way of retail, on board a ship or aircraft the goods may be zero-rated by the person supplying them (s 12(6)). The Customs & Excise have power to make Regulations providing for the export of goods to be zero-rated (s 12(7)) and have done so. It was held in *Mrs A A Sadri (trading as Hutosh Commercial)* v *CCE*, LON/78/265 (*Casebook* **7.103**) that s 12(6) and (7) must be construed together, so that the Regulations made under s 12(7) must be complied with before goods may be zero-rated. In the *Sadri* case the appellant maintained that the goods had been exported and, therefore, s 12(6) had been complied with. The Tribunal rejected this approach and held in favour of the Customs & Excise as the requisite forms brought into use under powers given to the Customs & Excise in the VAT (General) Regulations 1977 (SI 1977

No 1759), reg 44 had not been completed the goods did not qualify for zero-rating.

As stated regulations have been made under s 12(7) and are contained in the VAT (General) Regulations 1977 (SI 1977 No 1759), regs 42–50 inclusive. The detailed content of each regulation is considered under the appropriate sub-headings in this chapter, and unless otherwise stated references to Regulations are to the VAT (General) Regulations 1977 (SI 1977 No 1759).

In addition to the power to make regulations the Customs & Excise has a general authority in s 12(7) to impose such conditions as they think fit before granting zero-rating on the export of goods. The Customs & Excise has also been given similar authority in the Regulations themselves. The conditions the Customs & Excise require to be satisfied are set out in their respective Notices and reference is made to those conditions as appropriate throughout this chapter. The reasonableness of some of the conditions was challenged with success in *Henry Moss of London Ltd* v *CCE*, [1979] STC 657 (*Casebook* **7.104**). In addition the clarity of Customs & Excise Notice No 703 was criticised in *Middlesex Textiles Ltd* v *CCE*, LON/79/75 (*Casebook* **7.107**). In particular, in the *Middlesex Textiles Ltd* case the Tribunal remarked that Notice No 703:

> "is not a satisfactory document. Various of its paragraphs overlap, and it is extremely difficult to disentangle the words which are alleged to be conditions having the force of law from the remainder of the text."

The Authors would agree with this conclusion. A person is entitled to know what the law is and, if the Customs & Excise is given power to impose conditions they should do so in a clear, concise way, so that the taxpayer is clearly appraised of the position. The Authors understand that the *Henry Moss* case is being taken on appeal to the Court of Appeal and hopefully once the outcome of the case is known Notice No 703 will be revised.

Export of goods generally

In this and the following paragraphs the exportation of goods generally is considered. The position relating to special schemes and special transactions is dealt with at **7.200** and **7.300**. Where the Customs & Excise is satisfied that goods intended for export have been supplied to a non-resident and the goods are actually exported direct by the supplier, the supply, subject to such conditions as the Customs & Excise may impose, is zero-rated providing the person to whom the supply is made is not a taxable person (VAT (General) Regulations 1977 (SI 1977 No 1759), reg 44). It will be seen that the Customs & Excise have a general power to impose further conditions before enabling the supplier to zero-rate the supply. The conditions, imposed by the Customs & Excise vary upon the circumstance in which the export is made, but generally where the export is made directly by the United Kingdom supplier to the non-resident, the supplier must provide proof of export. Normally the commercial documents relating to the sale will be available, for example the contract for the goods, copy invoice, consignment note, freight and packing details and evidence of payment on receipt, and should always be kept for production to the Customs & Excise. In addition, however, the supplier must keep evidence of actual proof of export as detailed in Notice No 703, Part IV (Proof of export). The actual proof of export required by the Customs & Excise depends upon the manner of the exportation. Basically exportation of goods (ignoring the special schemes and special types of export which are dealt with separately below) will either be by sea, air or post and each is considered separately below.

SEA

The exporter needs to retain a copy of the bill of lading or if this is not available, for example because the shipping company does not issue bills of lading for the particular type of export, a certificate of shipment given by a responsible official of the shipping company. For exports through The British Railways Board, who do not issue bills of lading, the Customs & Excise will accept "a shipping advice issued by the Board's Port Superintendent" (Notice No 703, para 23). If the export is arranged by the British and Irish Steam Packet Company Ltd. a shipping advice given by the Company's agent will suffice.

AIR

The supplier should obtain and retain a copy of the air waybill. The waybill should be signed by the airline company and endorsed with the flight prefix and number, and the date and place of departure (Notice No 703, para 24).

POST

A certificate of posting must be produced for each parcel on the appropriate form, as indicated in Notice No 703 para 32. If several parcels containing indentical goods are being sent abroad to the same person under one custom's declaration only one certificate need be obtained. The custom's declaration is made on the appropriate form in the Customs Export Declarations C273 series obtainable from the Customs & Excise.

If several parcels of varying goods are being sent abroad to different persons a list of all the parcels must accompany the certificate of posting. The list of the goods must have the following column headings, "Gross weight", "Quantity", "Description", "Value", "Net Weight" and "Addressee" in that order and should contain similar details to that on the customs declaration. The exporter must make a declaration at the bottom of the list (no space must be left between the last item in the list and the declaration) in the form set out in Notice No 703, para 33(*b*).

The parcel must, in every case where the value of the parcel exceeds £10, have a Form VAT 444 (Value added tax goods exported by post) stuck to it. The form is an adhesive label obtainable from the Customs & Excise. The parcels should be taken to the Post Office with the appropriate Forms duly completed. The certificate of posting will be retained by the Post Office for processing and will be returned in due course and must be kept by the exporter for production to the CCE. Special rules apply if the exporter has an arrangement with the Post Office for parcels to be collected by the Post Office from the exporter's premises, see Notice No 703, para 37.

For cases in which the exportation of goods has been considered, see *Casebook* **7.100**, *et seq*.

Goods supplied to overseas traders for export in their baggage

Where goods are supplied to overseas traders for export in their baggage the goods will not be covered under the rules described above, because the rules explained above apply where the goods, *inter alia*, are exported direct by the supplier. Further, the supply cannot qualify under the retail export schemes described at **7.200**, as those schemes do not apply to overseas traders. Accordingly, the general provisions of reg 44 must be relied on if the goods are to qualify for zero-rating on export. Such goods would qualify for zero-rating as the supply would be within reg 44, subject to the power of the Customs & Excise to impose further conditions. The Customs & Excise have indicated in Notice No 703, para 10 the conditions that must be satisfied before the export of goods by overseas traders in their hand baggage can qualify for zero-rating. The conditions are that:

(*a*) the supplier must keep a special record of the transaction together with evidence that the purchaser was a trader without a place of business in the United Kingdom; and

(*b*) the goods must be exported within one month of the supply; and

(*c*) Proof of export must be obtained. Such proof for this purpose is the certification of a duplicate Form C273 marked "For VAT control purposes only" and the duplicate Form C273 must be returned by the customer to the retailer;

(*d*) the goods must not be used between the time of supply and their exportation.

The reasonableness and validity of condition (*c*) has had doubt cast upon it in the High Court in the case of *Henry Moss of London Ltd* v *CCE*, [1979] STC 657 (*Casebook* **7.104**). In that case the taxpayer company had a substantial export trade and sold goods wholesale over the counter to overseas customers. The company followed the procedure set out above and supplied customers with a stamped, addressed envelope in which to return the certified duplicate Form C273. Nevertheless 99 per cent of customers did not return the forms. The company, therefore, appealed against the Tribunal decision which held that failure to satisfy the conditions was an absolute bar to obtaining zero-rating. In the High Court the appellant company succeeded and Forbes J. commented:

> "Now it really does seem to me to be wholly unreasonable to lay down conditions which result in a trader who has done everything possible to make certain that the necessary proof is available having only a 1 per cent chance of qualifying for exemption from the payment of value added tax ... How can he [the supplier] in fact ensure that he gets back from the trader the necessary certification to prove that the goods have been exported."

It is understood that the case is being taken on appeal to the Court of Appeal, but pending the decision in the Court of Appeal the Henry Moss decision must cast doubt on the enforceability of similar conditions in the retail export schemes described at **7.200B** and **7.200D**.

7.200 Retail export schemes

Special schemes may be operated in respect of goods which are sold retail over-the-counter to visitors to the United Kingdom, or where goods are delivered direct to the visitor's ship or aircraft. The schemes are brought into operation under the VAT (General) Regulations 1977 (SI 1977 No 1759), regs 45–48. Furthermore, under the Regulations the Customs & Excise has a general power to impose such conditions as it thinks fit and notification of the appropriate conditions is given in Notice No 704 (Retail export schemes). The Regulations and conditions vary according to each scheme. Each scheme is, therefore, described separately in detail *post*: there is reproduced on pp 114 and 115 a copy of the flow charts provided by the Customs & Excise in Notice No 703 (Exports) which give a useful visual summary of the position.

A   Over-the-counter: overseas visitors, or community travellers travelling outside the EEC

Where the Customs & Excise is satisfied that goods (excluding cars) have been supplied to a qualifying person and can be carried on the person, in his hand luggage or, if he is travelling by car, in the car and the goods are produced to a proper officer on departure from the United Kingdom, the supply, subject to such conditions as the Customs & Excise may impose, shall be zero-rated (reg 47). At the time of supply the customer must intend leaving the United Kingdom with the goods within 3 months (reg 47(a)(ii)). In general, most goods (apart from cars which are specifically excluded: reg 30(6)) qualify for the scheme but it must be remembered that the goods must accompany the traveller and, therefore, bulky goods will in practice not be within the scheme. Furthermore, if the traveller is travelling by air the airline will normally impose restrictions on the amount or size of luggage that may be taken aboard the aircraft and such restrictions will affect the traveller's ability to benefit from the scheme. If the goods are too bulky special arrangements apply (see *post*) and the goods do not qualify for the scheme (*Helgor Furs Ltd* v *CCE*, LON/78/339 (*Casebook* **7.202**)).

It is important to ensure that the goods are produced to a proper officer as failure to comply with this requirement will render the supply liable to VAT (*Randall Bros (Furs) Ltd* v *CCE*, LON/75/63 (*Casebook* **7.201**)).

A qualifying person is an overseas visitor other than a community traveller, or if the person is a community traveller is one who at the time of supply intended to depart and remain outside the EEC for at least 1 year (reg 47(a)(i)). A "community traveller" is defined in reg 30(2) as being a person whose "domicile, habitual residence or usual place of business" is in an EEC country. It is important to note that the meanings given to "domicile", or "habitual residence" are different from their normal meanings under United Kingdom tax law. In particular, "domicile or habitual residence" means the place where so named in the person's passport or identity card, or lacking these any other identity document recognised as valid in the United Kingdom. It would, therefore, seem possible for a person with a non-British passport which has his overseas address in it where he resides but who is also a resident of the United Kingdom for tax purposes (for example because he is present in the United Kingdom for more than 183 days) to benefit from the over-the-counter scheme. An overseas visitor means a person who in the 2 years immediately before the supply has not been present in the United Kingdom for more than 365 days. A qualifying person cannot be a crew member of a ship or aircraft leaving the United Kingdom. Thus, the persons who are able to benefit from this scheme are non-EEC residents travelling anywhere overseas (including the EEC) and community travellers travelling to countries outside the EEC for at least 12 months. Community travellers travelling to the EEC may, however, be able to benefit from the scheme outlined under heading **B**, *post*.

CONDITIONS IMPOSED BY THE CUSTOMS & EXCISE

The above sets out the position under the Regulations, but as stated the Customs & Excise may impose such further conditions as it thinks fit. In Notice No 704, the Customs & Excise has indicated what those conditions are. In particular, the goods must be exported within 3 months of purchase. The retailer must satisfy himself from the customer's passport or other papers that the customer is a qualified person. The retailer must then complete Section 1, Parts A and B of Form VAT 414, date and sign the Section of the Form and the customer must complete, date and sign Section II of Parts A and B of the Form, including serial numbers or identification marks, where appropriate, so that the goods are clearly identifiable on examination by the proper officer at the point of embarkation. The completed Form 414 should be placed in an unsealed self-addressed envelope marked on the back, "For production to United Kingdom Customs & Excise with the goods". The envelope should then be handed to the customer for him to produce to the proper officer at embarkation.

The customer must produce the goods and envelope containing the Form VAT 414 to the proper officer at the airport or port. The goods and envelope must accompany the customer. The proper officer will examine the goods and certify Part A if satisfied that the goods and customer qualify for the Scheme. Failure to produce the goods for examination will result in the retailer being unable to zero-rate the supply. Further the scheme does not apply if the goods are too bulky to be conveniently produced (see *Randall Bros (Furs) Ltd* v *CCE*, LON/75/63 (*Casebook* **7.201**) and *Helgor Furs Ltd* v *CCE*, LON/78/339 (*Casebook* **7.202**)). Part A is sent back to the retailer by Customs & Excise and the retailer accounts for the sale in his quarterly return. If the retailer is unable to produce Part A of the Form VAT 414 within three months of the supply he will lose the benefit of zero-rating and have to pay the VAT due himself. If Form VAT 414 has been misplaced after certification by the proper officer on exportation, the retailer should immediately write to Customs & Excise at the port or airport that handled the goods. The retailer should include in his letter details of the customer and goods together with the destination and name of vessel or flight number if known (Notice No 704, para 36(*b*)).

B   Over-the-counter: community travellers travelling to the EEC

Where the Customs & Excise is satisfied that goods (excluding motor cars) have been supplied to a qualifying person and the goods can be carried on the person or in his hand-baggage or, if the person is travelling by car, in the car, and the goods are exported to an EEC country, the supply shall be zero-rated (reg 48). The goods must be worth more than £120 in value, including tax if travelling to an EEC country other than Ireland or Denmark (in those cases the limits are £50 and £90 respectively). Bulky goods will not qualify and are the subject of special rules (see *post*).

A qualifying person is one who is a community traveller who at the time of supply intended to leave the United Kingdom within 3 months of the purchase of the goods. For the meaning of Community traveller (see heading **A**, *ante*). The scheme does not apply to members of a crew of a ship or aircraft leaving the United Kingdom.

The Customs & Excise has a general power given to it in reg 48 to impose further conditions before the supply may be zero-rated and those conditions are set out in Notice No 704, paras 10–12. In particular, the retailer must satisfy himself from the customer's passport or other papers that the customer is a community traveller. Once the retailer is so satisfied he must complete, date and sign Section 1 of Form VAT 409 and the customer should complete, date and sign Section 2. The description of the goods on the Form should be sufficiently detailed, including serial numbers or registration numbers, where appropriate, to enable the customs authority at the place of importation to be able to identify the goods. The completed Form VAT 409 should be placed by the retailer in an unsealed, stamped, addressed envelope marked clearly on the back, "For production with the goods to the customs authority at the place of importation in the EEC country of destination".

The envelope should be handed to the customer for production, together with the goods, at the place of importation. The customer must then produce the goods and envelope within 3 months of the purchase to the customs authority at the place of importation. The customs authority will, if satisfied, certify the Form VAT 409 and hand it to the customer. The customer must return the form to the retailer so that the retailer can zero-rate the supply. Relief will only be granted to the supplier if the Form VAT 409 duly certified is produced. Once the certified Form VAT 409 is received by the retailer he should account for the supply in his quarterly return at the zero-rate.

There is an essential difference between these arrangements for community travellers returning to the EEC and the arrangments under heading **A**, *ante* relating to exports by overseas visitors or Community travellers to non-EEC countries, namely that under the previously described arrangements under heading **A**, *ante* it was the Customs officer who returned the certificate of export (Form VAT 414) to the retailer. Here, however, under the community travellers travelling to the EEC scheme, it is the customer who must return the form to the retailer once it has been certified at the port of entry (*contra* heading **A** where the certification was due on embarkation). Whether this placing of the burden on the customer in order for the retailer to zero-rate the supply is a reasonable condition is open to doubt in the light of the decision in *Henry Moss of London Ltd* v *CCE*, [1979] STC 657 (*Casebook* **7.104**). Particulars of the case are considered at **7.100** under *Goods supplied to overseas traders for export in their baggage*. If the Form VAT 409 is lost after certification the customer should be asked to provide further evidence within 6 weeks, in the form of an official receipt for duty or tax, from the EEC country into which the goods were imported (Notice No 704, para 36(*a*)). If such evidence is produced the goods will be zero-rated.

C   Personal export scheme: overseas visitors, community travellers or United Kingdom residents travelling outside the EEC

This scheme applies to the exportation of goods by overseas visitors travelling to any destination or to Community travellers or United Kingdom residents travelling to a destination outside the EEC for a period of at least 1 year. The scheme enables the aforementioned persons to purchase goods at a zero-rate (other than motor-cars) and have the retailer deliver the goods direct to the ship or airport on their behalf. The goods must be produced to a proper officer on exportation and exported in the ship or aircraft upon which the exporter is travelling (VAT (General) Regulations 1977 (SI 1977 No 1759), reg 45). The Customs & Excise has a general power to impose such further conditions as they think fit and have stipulated (see Notice 704, paras 28–32) that the following conditions must be satisfied.

The retailer must be satisfied that the customer is entitled to benefit from the scheme by examining his passport or similar documentation. If the retailer is so satisfied he should complete, sign and date Section 1 of Parts A and B of Form VAT 413, and the customer must then complete, sign and date Section 2 of Form VAT 413. The goods must then be sent by the retailer to the railway, shipping company or airline concerned with the Form VAT 413 in an envelope securely attached to the goods. The package must be clearly marked "VAT 413 No's .... For production to Customs and Excise before shipment". The goods must be sent direct in this way and must not be sent to the customer. The railway, shipping company or freight forwarder acting for the retailer must produce the goods and documents to the proper officer of the Customs & Excise not later than the customer's arrival for embarkation. The retailer's agent must transfer the goods to the ship or aircraft and return the certificate of export (Part A of Form 413), once certified by the proper officer, to the retailer. On receipt of the certificate the retailer should enter the supply in his next quarterly return as zero-rated. If the certificate is lost the retailer should follow the same steps as the retailer under heading **A** *ante* under similar circumstances.

Failure to comply with the above conditions will mean that the retailer will be unable to zero-rate the supply and will have to pay the VAT on the supply himself.

If the goods cannot be delivered to the ship on which the customer is travelling before its departure, they may be exported later as "unaccompanied baggage". The procedure outlined above should be followed except that Form VAT Form 413 should be headed "For export as unaccompanied baggage in [ship's name] and [port] on [date]".

D Personal export scheme: community travellers travelling to the EEC

This scheme applies to the exportation of goods worth more than £120 by either Community travellers exporting the goods to an EEC country, (other than Ireland or Denmark) or United Kingdom residents leaving the United Kingdom for at least a year and taking the goods ultimately to an EEC country (other than Ireland or Denmark). The scheme enables the retailer to zero-rate the supply of goods worth more than £120 (other than motor cars) to the aforementioned persons if the supplies are delivered direct to the purchaser's ship or aircraft. The goods must subsequently be exported on board the ship or aircraft (VAT (General) Regulations 1977 (SI 1977 No 1759), reg 46). Where the traveller is travelling to Ireland or Denmark the goods must be worth at least £50 and £90 respectively.

The Customs & Excise has a general power to impose further conditions and the relevant conditions are set out in Notice No 704, paras 21–25. In particular, the retailer must examine the passport or similar papers of the purchaser and satisfy himself that the customer is entitled to benefit under the scheme. If the retailer is so satisfied he must complete, date and sign Section 1 Parts A and B of Form VAT 408 and the customer must complete, date and sign Section 2 of the same form. The completed Form VAT 408 should be handed to the customer who must produce the Form together with the goods at the place of importation in the respective EEC country. The appropriate officer at the place of importation will, if satisfied, certify the Form VAT 408 and the customer must return the certificated Form to the retailer. Whether it is reasonable to place the burden on the customer, by getting him to return the certificate Form VAT 408, in order for the retailer to be able to zero-rate the supply is open to doubt in the light of the decision of the High Court in *Henry Moss of London Ltd* v *CCE*, [1979] STC 657 (*Casebook* **7.104**). Particulars of this case are considered at **7.100** (under the heading *Goods supplied to Overseas traders for export in their baggage*). The goods must be delivered direct to the ship or aircraft by the retailer or his agent (freight forwarder etc) for delivery to the customer on embarkation.

Once the retailer has received the Form VAT 408 duly certificated he should account for the supply in his quarterly return at the zero-rate. If the Form VAT 408 is lost after it has been certified the retailer should write to the customer requesting him to provide alternative evidence with six weeks. The further evidence should take the form of an official receipt for tax or duty in the country of importation (Notice No 704, para 36(*a*)).

If it is not possible for the goods to be delivered to the ship or aircraft prior to the departure of the customer, the customers must make their own arrangements for certification at importation (Notice No 704, para 32).

The above schemes all apply to goods which can be carried on the person or in his car or hand-baggage and which can conveniently be produced for examination at the place of departure (**A** and **C**) or importation (**B** and **D**). The schemes do not therefore apply to bulky goods (see *Randall Bros (Furs) Ltd* v *CCE* (*Casebook* **7.201**) and *Helgor Furs Ltd* v *CCE* (*Casebook* **7.202**)), for which special arrangements apply as set out below. Furthermore, the schemes do not apply to overseas traders for which special arrangements apply as set out at **7.100** *Goods supplied to overseas traders for export in their baggage.*

E   Retail export scheme inappropriate: bulky goods

If goods are too bulky they will not qualify for the schemes described at **A–D**, *ante*. In addition, if the customer is travelling by air it may well be that the personal export scheme cannot apply as the airlines do not usually accept goods for production at embarkation. Accordingly, if the over-the-counter scheme or personal export scheme is inappropriate special conditions apply (see Notice No 703 (Exports), para 12). In particular having satisfied himself that the purchaser was not resident in the United Kingdom the supplier must keep a separate record of the transaction.

The goods must be exported within 3 months and proof of export obtained by the supplier within one month of the exportation of the goods. The proof of export required is the certification of a duplicate export entry Form C273. The Form C273 is not normally certificated, but the customs officer will do so if requested in these cases. The original form should be marked "Export of goods otherwise than as manifested cargo" and the duplicate should be marked "For VAT control purposes only" (see Notice No 703, paras 12(*a*)(iii) and 30).

The Form C273 and goods must be produced to the proper officer for certification. The duplicate will be handed to the customer who must return it to the retailer. Whether or not this last condition is enforceable

PERSONAL EXPORT SCHEME

(For goods delivered direct to ship or aircraft, but see also paragraph 2(b))

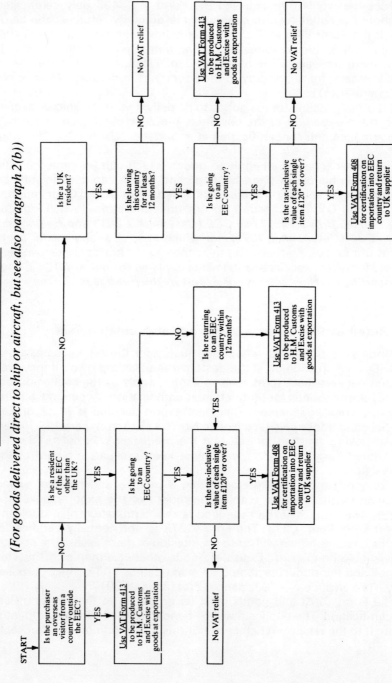

*The limits are £90 and £50 for Denmark and Ireland respectively.

OVER-THE-COUNTER SCHEME

(For goods handed over to purchaser at time of sale)

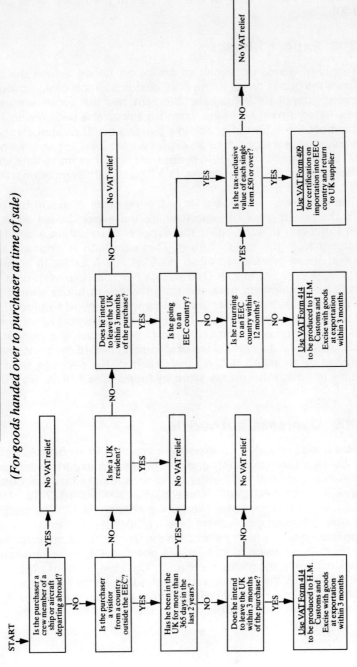

is open to doubt in view of the decision in the *Henry Moss* case (see **7.100**).

7.300 Export houses

A supply of goods on behalf of an export house, where the supplier delivers the goods direct to the port, customs airport or approved inland clearance depot for immediate shipment and the goods are exported, is zero-rated. An export house, includes any taxable person who arranges or finances the export of goods in a transaction. The supplier may, alternatively deliver the goods to an export packer who in turn is responsible for the delivery of the goods to the port etc. and their immediate shipment to the order of the export house (VAT (General) Regulations 1977 (SI 1977 No 1759), reg 42).

The supplier is responsible for obtaining proof of export but may not have the actual proof of export where the export house arranges the final shipment. In such cases the supplier must obtain a certificate of shipment from the export house. This condition is imposed under a general power given in reg 42 to the Customs & Excise to impose such conditions as they think fit (see Notice No 703 (Exports), para 7). The certificate of shipment obtained from the export house should include the purchase order number and the supplier's invoice number, the bill of lading or air waybill number, the name of the ship on which the goods will be exported or alternatively the flight number, the port or airport of departure, the date and place of shipment, and (if the goods are being exported by an export packer) the details of the package, container or vehicle in which the goods were included (see Notice No 703, para 28).

7.400 Overseas authorities

Where goods intended for export are supplied to an overseas authority not being a taxable person and the goods are exported the supply is zero-rated, provided the further conditions imposed by the Customs & Excise are observed (VAT (General) Regulations 1977 (SI 1977 No 1759), reg 44(*a*)(iii)). An overseas authority for this purpose is, for example, a foreign government (see reg 30(10)). The provision enables supplies of goods which are made in the United Kingdom to, for example, the High Commission of an overseas government, to be zero-rated provided, of course, the goods are actually exported. Proof of export is therefore required by the supplier, and this should take the form of a certificate of shipment obtained by the High Commission or other United Kingdom agent. The Certificate should contain the details set out in the previous paragraph (see **7.300**).

7.500 Cars

It is possible in certain circumstances for new cars to be purchased from the manufacturer free of VAT where the car is to be exported from the United Kingdom and the purchaser intends to live outside the United Kingdom for at least twelve months. Two types of scheme apply depending upon whether the purchaser is an overseas visitor or not. Each scheme is considered below.

(A) Overseas visitor

Where an overseas visitor buys a car from a United Kingdom manufacturer and intends leaving and living outside the United Kingdom for at least 1 year the supply may be made free of VAT. It should be noted that the supply is not zero-rated as such, but is made without payment of tax. The purchase can be made at any time within twelve months of the purchaser's intended departure. The car must be new and must be bought direct from the manufacturer and not from a dealer (VAT (General) Regulations 1977 (SI 1977 No 1759), reg 49). The Customs & Excise have indicated (Notice No 705 (VAT and car tax), para 1(*a*)) that a sole selling agent in the United Kingdom of a foreign car manufacturer may be treated as a manufacturer for the purpose of this relief.

The Customs & Excise has a power to impose further conditions before granting the relief. Accordingly, the manufacturer must be approved by the Customs & Excise. Application for relief from VAT must be made by the purchaser on Form VAT 410. The Form should be completed and returned to the manufacturer. Details of the conditions imposed by the Customs & Excise are given on the Form VAT 410. In essence those conditions are:

(*a*) only the applicant may take delivery of the car;
(*b*) only the applicant, or a person with similar entitlement to benefit under the scheme, may use the car;
(*c*) the applicant must export the car within twelve months of its purchase and the date by which the car must be exported will be entered in the registration book;
(*d*) the car must not be lent, hired or disposed of in the United Kingdom, nor offered for such transactions.

The relief is available to overseas visitors, although a similar relief is available to any person as described under (*B*) *Any person, post*. An overseas visitor is defined in the VAT (General) Regulations 1977 (SI 1977 No 1759), reg 30(11), as being a person who either has not been present in the United Kingdom for more than 365 days out of the 2 years immediately prior to the application, or alternatively has not been present in the United Kingdom for more than 1,095 days in the 6 years immediately prior to the application. The qualifying periods are alternatives and only one has to be satisfied. The 6 year period only applies for the purpose of this relief.

If the applicant discovers that he will be unable to export the car within the time limit he should report the matter immediately to the Customs & Excise and pay the VAT otherwise payable. If the vehicle is found to be in the United Kingdom after the date by which it should have been exported it is liable to forfeiture.

(B)   Any person

Where any person, whether a United Kingdom resident or not, buys a new car from a United Kingdom manufacturer and intends leaving and living outside the United Kingdom for at least 1 year, the car may be supplied free of VAT. The purchase can be made at any time within 6 months of the purchaser's intended departure. The car must be new and unused and bought direct from the manufacturer and not a dealer (VAT (General) Regulations 1977 (SI 1977 No 1759), reg 50). However, the Customs & Excise allow a purchase from a sole United Kingdom selling agent of an overseas manufacturer to be treated as a purchase from a manufacturer for this purpose.

The Customs & Excise is given power in reg 50, to impose further conditions before granting the relief, and the conditions are similar to those described under *Overseas visitor, ante*, except that the period in which the car must be exported is reduced from twelve months to six months. The appropriate form of application for the relief must be submitted duly completed to the authorised manufacturer, namely Form VAT 411. Similar rules apply as outlined under *Overseas visitor, ante* if the car is found in the United Kingdom after the date by which it should have been exported.

7.600 Record-keeping

An exporter must keep the usual records described in **17.300**. However, the following special procedures in relation to exports should be noted.

Where goods are exported directly by the supplier the supply may be treated as zero-rated at the time of the supply. However, if no proof of export is provided within 3 months, VAT must be accounted for at the rate in force at the time of supply. If this occurs the exporter's VAT records will require amendment: the tax payable on the supply must be entered in the "tax due" side of the VAT account and must be included in Box 1.

If evidence of export is produced subsequently the supply may be zero-rated in the next quarterly return.

Special rules apply if the exporter is operating one of the special schemes for retailers (Notice No. 703 (Exports), para 19(*a*)).

Where the supply is of goods to an overseas trader for export in his baggage, or is made under a retail export scheme, the supply should not be zero-rated until proof of export is obtained. If the proof of export is not obtained within the appropriate time limit, the supply should be charged at the standard rate and the tax accounted for in the next quarterly return.

7.700 Forfeiture

Where a supply of goods has been zero-rated under the export provisions and the goods are subsequently found to be in the United Kingdom, or any of the conditions imposed by the Customs & Excise are found not to have been observed, the goods are liable to forfeiture under the Customs and Excise Management Act 1979 (s 12(8)). The tax also becomes immediately payable, although the Customs & Excise has a general discretion to waive the tax, if it thinks fit.

Chapter 8

Zero-Rating

8.000 A Sources

Section 12—The basic provisions applying zero rating to certain categories of supply.
Schedule 4—The categories of zero-rated supply.
In addition the following Customs & Excise Notices and associated Leaflets may be helpful:

701	—Scope and coverage
700	—General guide, para 12
708	—Construction industry
709	—VAT: hotels, catering and holiday services
714	—Young children's clothing and footwear
715	—Construction industry: alterations and repairs and maintenance
1/78/VAH	—Gross tonnage of unregistered ships and boats.
4/78/VAH	—Ships' managers and port agents.
5/78/VAH	—Passenger transport: taxis and hire cars.
3/75/VLB	—Off-shore oil and gas installations.
17/74/VLC	—VAT: The borderline between alteration and repair or maintenance as applicable to roads and other civil engineering works.
701/1/79	—Charities.
701/2/79	—Freight forward services in connection with international movements of goods.
701/3/79	—Handling services in ports and customs and excise airports.
701/4/79	—The supply, repair and maintenance of ships and aircraft.
701/6/79	—Donated medical and scientific equipment.
701/7/79	—Aids for chronically sick and diabled persons.
701/10/79	—Liability of printed and similar matter.

8.000B   General principles

Categories of zero-rated supply

Two categories of supply are entitled to be zero-rated. These are:

(*a*) the supply of goods or services or the importation of certain goods falling within one of the groups listed in Sched 4 (s 12(2) and (3)); and

(*b*) the exportation of goods to a place outside the United Kingdom (s 12(6)).

This chapter concerns only the first of these categories. The exportation of goods and the conditions that must be fulfilled before zero-rating may be claimed in respect of such goods are discussed in Chapter 7. The international supply of services is discussed in Chapter 10.

It is most important to realise that a zero-rated supply is a taxable supply for VAT purposes. This follows from the definition of a taxable supply in s 2(2) and is stressed in s 12(1) itself. The wording of s 12(1), which provides that a supply which is zero-rated shall be treated as a taxable supply "whether or not tax would be chargeable on the supply apart from this section", has the effect that where a supply is capable of being both zero-rated and exempt, the zero-rating of that supply shall prevail. The fact that zero-rated supplies are taxable supplies also has the effect of:

(*a*) requiring the value of those supplies to be brought into the calculation of a person's turnover in applying the VAT registration limits (see Chapter 2); and
(*b*) of not restricting a taxable person's ability to claim input tax relief in respect of supplies to him for the purposes of his business (see Chapter 5).

Schedule 4

The Treasury is given power by s 12(4) to vary the content of Sched 4 by both adding to and deleting from that Schedule particular types of supply. Advantage of this power was taken in 1978 when Group 9 was entirely altered by the VAT (Consolidation) Order 1978 (SI 1978 No 1064).

The Tribunal has rejected in the past (see *En-Tout-Cas Ltd* v *CCE*, [1973] VATTR 101 (*Casebook* **8.004**), although a minority of the Tribunal in that case expressed sympathy with a similar argument in the earlier case of *Blackpool Pleasure Beach Company Ltd* v *CCE*, MAN/73/7 (*Casebook* **8.1003**) the idea that there is any underlying theme or concept to Sched 4. Instead, it was held that each supply must be examined individually to determine its nature and the Schedule then applied objectively to ascertain whether the supply in question falls within any of its Groups. In this respect, the nature of a supply is a question of fact and whether it falls within a zero-rated Group, one of law (see *British Railways Board* v *CCE* (*No. 2*), [1977] STC 221 (*Casebook* **3.610** and **8.002**). This approach ignores, however, the fact that the United Kingdom is only permitted by the EEC Sixth Directive to retain zero-rating during a transitional period if it can be shown that the supply has been zero-rated "for clearly defined social reasons and for the benefit of the community" (art 28(2)). In this connection also, it is worth noting the comments made in the House of Commons when Sched 4 was first debated (see **9.000B**) which do suggest that such a motive was present.

Section 46(2) provides that Sched 4 is to be interpreted in accordance with the notes to that Schedule. Care must be exercised in applying

Sched 4, therefore, as these notes often severely limit what would other-wise appear, from reference to the items within the Groups to Sched 4 alone, to be zero-rated supplies. These notes may also be changed by Treasury Order.

In interpreting the items within the various Groups of Sched 4, too great an emphasis should not be placed on the headings to the Groups themselves. Section 46(3) specifically states that such headings are for ease of reference only and do not affect the interpretation of the Groups.

Finally, Customs & Excise Notice No 701 lists, by reference to each group of Sched 4, the supplies the Customs & Excise consider to be within those Groups. Reference should be made to Notice No 701, there-fore, where there is any doubt as to whether a given supply is within a particular Group.

8.100 Group 1: Food

The supply of anything comprised in the general items set out below, except—

(*a*) a supply in the course of catering; and

(*b*) a supply of anything comprised in any of the excepted items set out below, unless it is also comprised in any of the items overriding the exceptions set out below which relates to that excepted item.

General items

Item No.
1. Food of a kind used for human consumption.
2. Animal feeding stuffs.
3. Seeds or other means of propagation of plants comprised in item 1 or 2.
4. Live animals of a kind generally used as, or yielding or producing, food for human consumption.

Excepted items

Item No.
1. Ice cream, ice lollies, frozen yogurt, water ices and similar frozen products, and prepared mixes and powders for making such products.
2. Chocolates, sweets and similar confectionery (including drained, glacé or crys-tallized fruits); and biscuits and other confectionery (not including cakes) wholly or partly covered with chocolate or some product similar in taste and appearance.
3. Beverages chargeable with any duty of excise specifically charged on spirits, beer, wine or made wine and preparations thereof.
4. Other manufactured beverages, including fruit juices and bottled waters, and syrups, concentrates, essences, powders, crystals or other products for the pre-paration of beverages.
5. Any of the following when packaged for human consumption without further preparation, namely, potato crisps, potato sticks, potato puffs, and similar pro-ducts made from the potato, or from potato flour, or from potato starch, and savoury food products obtained by the swelling of cereals or cereal products; and salted or roasted nuts other than nuts in shell.

6. Pet foods, canned, packaged or prepared; packaged foods (not being pet foods) for birds other than poultry or game; and biscuits and meals for cats and dogs.
7. Goods described in items 1, 2 and 3 of the general items which are canned, bottled, packaged or prepared for use in the domestic—
    (*a*) brewing of any beer;
    (*b*) making of any cider or perry;
    (*c*) production of any wine or made-wine.

Items overriding the exceptions

Item No
1. Yoghurt unsuitable for immediate consumption when frozen.
2. Drained cherries.
3. Candied peels.
4. Tea, maté, herbal teas and similar products, and preparations and extracts thereof.
5. Cocoa, coffee and chicory and other roasted coffee substitutes, and preparations and extracts thereof.
6. Preparations and extracts of meat, yeast, egg or milk.

Notes:

(1) "Food" includes drink.
(2) "Animal" includes bird, fish, crustacean and mollusc.
(3) A supply of anything in the course of catering includes any supply of it for consumption on the premises on which it is supplied.
(4) Item 1 of the items overriding the exceptions relates to item 1 of the excepted items; items 2 and 3 of the items overriding the exceptions relate to item 2 of the excepted items and items 4 to 6 of the items overriding the exceptions relate to item 4 of the excepted items.
(5) Any supply described in this Group shall include a supply of services described in paragraph 1 (1) of Schedule 2 to this Act.

The provisions generally

The provisions of Group 1 are particularly tortuous. The four general items listed will be zero-rated unless they are either:

(*a*) supplied in the course of catering (see further, *post*); or
(*b*) mentioned as one of the "excepted items". If this is the case, however, reference must also be made to the list of items overriding the exceptions. This is because a supply within one of the items within this list will, indeed, be zero-rated. Note (4) at the end of the Group specifies to which excepted items the items overriding the exceptions apply.

The majority of the excepted items in Group 1 are of a particularly specialised nature and it is not planned to discuss these items in this *Guide*. Reference should be made, therefore, to Customs & Excise Notice No 701, pages 5–13 for an extensive list of examples of what supplies the Customs & Excise consider to be zero-rated and standard rated by reference to this Group.

In the course of catering

Note (3) provides that "a supply of anything in the course of catering includes any supply of it for consumption on the premises on which it is supplied". This phrase has been the subject of a number of Tribunal decisions and the principles set out in the following paragraphs (*a*)– (*e*) can be identified as being applied by Tribunals when considering this issue. Customs & Excise Notice No 709 (VAT: hotels, catering and holiday services, as amended by VAT News No. 13, may also be of assistance here).

(*a*) although Note (3) is couched in terms of an inclusive definition, the Tribunal in *BR James* v *CCE*, [1977] VATTR 155 (*Casebook* **8.103**), rejected the Customs & Excise argument that any supply in the course of catering was excluded from being zero-rated. The Tribunal considered that Parliament had intended in setting out Note (3) to contrast supplies on and off premises, the latter being entitled to be zero-rated;

(*b*) an early test as to whether food was supplied in the course of catering was that of whether it was supplied for immediate consumption (*Bristol City Supporters Club* v *CCE*, [1975] VATTR 93 (*Casebook* **8.102**). This test was, however, rejected in *BR James*, (*ante*) as it might give rise to anomalies in the context of the requirement that a supply was to be zero-rated unless supplied on premises;

(*c*) in an opinion adopted by the Tribunal in the *BR James* case Lord Dilhorne in *Maunsell* v *Olins and another*, [1975] 1 All ER 16, stated that "premises" is "an ordinary word of the English language which takes colour and content from the context in which it is used". Accordingly, it was not correct "to conclude that (premises) is intended to have the meaning that conveyancers attach to it unless a contrary intention appears". Such interpretation in the *BR James* case allowed the conclusion that a hot dog stall could constitute "premises". However, as the hot dogs were taken away from the stall by customers, they were consumed off the premises and therefore entitled to be zero-rated. This interpretation is also now recognised by the Customs & Excise (VAT News No 13, page 37);

(*d*) the premises in question need not belong to the party making the supply (see *Bristol City Supporters Club* v *CCE*, [1975] VATTR 93 (*Casebook* **8.102**) and *Burnham Radio Recreational and Welfare Club* v *CCE*, CAR/77/157 (*Casebook* **8.104**);

(*e*) although Tribunals have consistently avoided defining premises (other than to say that it should be given its ordinary meaning—see (*c*), *ante*), it seems that where the point at which the supply is made is mobile, that point itself will comprise the premises. If, on the other hand, it is fixed or, in cases such as football matches, brought to a location for a period of time, the extent of the premises will be the extent of the environs of that location. This is, of course, itself an arbitrary rule, for example, a hot dog bought from a stall outside a football ground will be zero-rated even if taken into and eaten in the ground, whereas a hot dog bought from a stall in the ground will be standard rated. A more satisfactory test has yet to be established, however.

General item 1

This item zero-rates the supply of food for human consumption.

By Note (1) food includes drink. Excepted items 3 and 4 subject to overriding items 4, 5 and 6 limit the ambit of "drink", however.

In *Marfleet Refining Company Ltd* v *CCE* [1974] VATTR 289 (*Casebook* **8.101**) the Tribunal considered at length a number of factors put to it by the Customs & Excise and the appellant which, it was suggested, governed whether an item was "food" or was "of a kind used for human consumption". The Tribunal declined to identify any particular factor as decisive, stating only that it was "relevant to consider what the ordinary man or woman or housewife understands it to mean". Palatability appears to have been regarded as an important characteristic of food, however, as does its nutrative value (see *Girdhartal Ratanji Soni* v *CCE*, MAN/78/251 (*Casebook* **8.101A**).

General item 2

This item zero-rates animal feed.

Note (2) extends "animal" to include birds, fish, crustaceans and molluscs.

Two important limitations to this category should be noted. First, pet foods are excepted items (excepted item 6) if they are in canned, packaged or prepared form. Whether foods fall within this category may give rise to difficulties but the Customs & Excise appears, in practice, to accept the trade's differentiation as to whether a particular food is considered to be pet food. Secondly, *CCE* v *Bushby*, [1979] STC 8 (*Casebook* **8.109**), shows that where the supply of animal feed stuffs is part of a composite supply it will be subject to the rate of tax applicable to the composite supply itself.

General item 3

Seeds or other means of propagation of plants comprised in items 1 and 2 are zero-rated under this item (see Customs & Excise Notice No 701, p 13 for examples of goods within this item).

General item 4

This item covers supplies of live animals of a kind generally used for producing food for human consumption.

A case under this heading concerned the *London Board for Shechita* v *CCE*, [1974] VATTR 24 (*Casebook* **8.110**). In that case, the appellant successfully relied on Sched 2, para 2 (which provides that where a person produces goods by applying to another's goods a treatment or process, he is treated as supplying goods), to claim zero-rating in connection with the slaughtering of animals in accordance with Jewish practice. This "process" was applied to animals which at all times remained the property of the abattoir.

Note (5), which is only likely in practice to apply to general item 4, extends the scope of Group 1 to include the transfer of any undivided share in or the possession (eg on loan or hire) of goods within that Group.

8.200 Group 2: Sewerage services and water

Item No.
> 1. Services of—
>> (*a*) reception, disposal or treatment of foul water or sewage in bulk; and
>> (*b*) emptying of cesspools, septic tanks or similar receptacles.
> 2. Water other than—
>> (*a*) distilled water, deionised water and water of similar purity; and
>> (*b*) water comprised in the excepted items set out in Group 1.

Item 1

This item, which covers services in relation to sewage, is largely self-explanatory. It should be noted, however, that the item relates only to services of reception, disposal, treatment and emptying. Services such as cleaning or maintenance to the extent that they go beyond emptying cesspools etc are not zero-rated nor is the sale of sewerage products. The Customs & Excise regards receptacles which receive foul water etc, from buildings occupied by farm animals as being outside this item.

Item 2

The supply of water in any state, that is, including ice, is zero-rated under this item unless it falls within one of the excepted categories set out in Sched 4, Group 1 (see **8.100**). The supply of most bottled waters would not be zero-rated, therefore, because of this exception.

8.300   Group 3: Books, etc

Item No.
1. Books, booklets, brochures, pamphlets and leaflets.
2. Newspapers, journals and periodicals.
3. Children's picture books and painting books.
4. Music (printed, duplicated or manuscript).
5. Maps, charts and topographical plans.
6. Covers, cases and other articles supplied with items 1 to 5 and not separately accounted for.

Note: Items 1 to 6—
   (*a*) do not include plans or drawings for industrial, architectural, engineering, commercial or similar purposes;
   (*b*) include the supply of services, in respect of goods comprised in the items, described in paragraph 1 (1) of Schedule 2 to this Act.

Eiusdem generis

In its various items, Group 3 provides six separate lists or categories of supplies. Within these items the types of supply are to be interpreted according to the *eiusdem generis* rule of construction (see Chapter 1 of the *Casebook*) and applying the ordinary meaning of the words in question. Thus, in item 1, "leaflets" has been held to mean something of a kind similar to books, booklets, brochures and pamphlets, that is something designed to be read by one person at a time (*E S Nicoll* v *CCE*, EDN/75/9 (*Casebook* **8.302**)). Thus, posters or notices designed to be read by the public at large are not leaflets within item 1. Similarly, "other articles" in item 6 must refer to a supply of a type with covers and cases (*D J Emery* v *CCE*, MAN/75/2 (*Casebook* **8.309**)).

Services

Items in Group 3 do not include supplies of services in connection with the goods mentioned in those items. Consequently, a supply is not entitled to be zero-rated merely because the end product of that supply is incidentally a book, report or musical score. Note (*b*) does, however, zero-rate services which comprise the supply of an undivided share or possession of one of the goods comprised in an item of Group 3, for example, the loan of a book for a consideration.

Plans and drawings

Note (*a*) specifically excludes from zero-rating plans or drawings for industrial, architectural, engineering, commercial or similar purposes.

VAT Leaflet 701/10/79

VAT Leaflet 701/10/79 (Liability of printed and similar matter) is of interest in relation to this group in that it lists at length the type of publications that the Customs & Excise view as falling within this group.

Item 1

This item zero-rates books, booklets, brochures, pamphlets and leaflets.

BOOKS

It seems clear that to constitute a book, the article in question must be complete in itself and capable of being read. As a result, notebooks or account books, which are blank, will not be zero-rated under this item. This need for completeness was commented on in *Butler and Tanner Ltd* v *CCE*, [1974] VATTR 72 (*Casebook* **8.301**). The Tribunal in that case was referred to the Customs Tariff in the Import Duties (General) (No 8) Order 1973 SI 1973 No 1845, Sched 1, tariff heading 49.01. Heading 49.01, which is in identical terms to item 1, was extended by r 2(*a*) to that heading to include incomplete or unfinished articles and the Tribunal stated that Parliament could be seen to have intended not to have extended Sched 4, item 1 to incomplete books for VAT purposes by adopting the identical wording of heading 49.01 without the associated rule.

The requirement of completeness would appear to be subject to the qualification that component parts of a book may, if complete in themselves, be zero-rated under item 1. This principle, which was first expressed in *A E Walker* v *CCE*, [1973] VATTR 8 (*Casebook* **8.310**), is restricted in practice owing to the necessity for parts of a book to be complete in themselves. The *A E Walker* case was one of the first to be heard by a VAT Tribunal (in fact it was heard before the commencement of VAT in March 1973, and was not therefore, binding upon either party) and has been distinguished in all later cases involving binders or folders. It should, therefore, be treated with some caution.

PAMPHLETS AND LEAFLETS

In *Pace Group* (*Communications*) *Ltd* v *CCE*, MAN/77/210 (*Casebook* **8.303**), the format of the pamphlet was regarded as immaterial provided that its function was to "deliver a message of interest to a section of the public". However, it seems that a pamphlet or leaflet is not within item 1 if it takes the form of a poster which is capable of being read by more than one person at a time (*E S Nicoll* v *CCE*, LON/75/9 (*Casebook* **8.302**).

Item 2

This item zero-rates newspapers, journals and periodicals. The Customs & Excise states in VAT Leaflet 701/10/79, para 8 that:

"8. The distinguishing feature of the publications falling within this Item is that they constitute one issue in a continuous series under the same title published at regular intervals, each issue being dated and also frequently numbered. These publications usually consist essentially of reading matter, but they may also be profusely illustrated and may consist mainly of pictorial or advertising matter. Publications such as staff journals, house journals and journals of learned, scientific and vocational associations are within the Item. Publications which are issued annually or less frequently are not normally regarded as falling within this Item; such publications fall within the scope of Item 1."

The meaning of the words in this item has been considered in connection with Sched 4, Group 5 (see **8.500**).

Item 3

This item zero-rates picture and painting books for children. Where the book in question is essentially a toy, possibly for example where it has stand up or moveable or cut out figures, the Customs & Excise considers that it will not fall within the item. The Customs & Excise view in this respect may require modification, however, following the case of *W F Graham* (*Northampton*) *Ltd* v *CCE*, LON/79/132.

Item 4

This item, which covers music whether printed, duplicated or manuscript, is self-explanatory. It does not include blank music paper.

Item 5

Maps, charts and topographical plans are zero-rated under this item irrespective of the manner of printing of those items.

Item 6

Covers, cases and other articles supplied with items 1–5 above may be zero-rated under item 6 provided that they are not separately accounted for. "Other articles" should be construed *eiusdem generis* with "covers" and "cases". It is essential that the covers etc are supplied with the book or other article under items 1–5 (see *Fabbri and Partners Ltd* v *CCE*, [1973] VATTR 49 (*Casebook* **8.311**).

8.400   Group 4: Talking books for the blind and handicapped and wireless sets for the blind

Item No.

1.   The supply to the Royal National Institute for the Blind, the National Listening Library or other similar charities of—

   (*a*) magnetic tape specially adapted for the recording and reproduction of speech for the blind or severely handicapped;

   (*b*) apparatus designed or specially adapted for the reproduction from recorded magnetic tape of speech for the blind or severely handicapped and which is not available for use by other than the blind or severely handicapped;

   (*c*) magnetic tape upon which has been recorded speech for the blind or severely handicapped, such recording being suitable for reproduction only in the apparatus mentioned in (*b*) above;

   (*d*) parts and accessories for goods comprised in paragraphs (*a*), (*b*) and (*c*) above.

2.   The supply to a charity of wireless receiving sets solely for gratuitous loan to the blind.

Note: In items 1 and 2 the supply respectively described therein includes the supply of services of the letting on hire of goods comprised in the items.

This Group zero-rates specialist magnetic tape, tape recorders and wirelesses designed for the blind and not of a type generally used by the public, but only when sold or let on hire to the RNIB, the National Listening Library or similar charities. Wirelesses which are not specifically so adapted are also entitled to be zero-rated if supplied to a charity which then lends them to the blind without charge.

8.500   Group 5: Newspaper advertisements

Item No.

1.   The publication in any newspaper, journal or periodical of any advertisement.
2.   The preparation of any advertisement intended for publication solely or mainly in one or more newspapers, journals or periodicals.
3.   The supply of services for the purpose of securing such a publication or a preparation as is mentioned in item 1 or 2.

This Group zero-rates certain supplies in connection with "newspapers, journals or periodicals". As Group 3, item 2 (see **8.300**) also makes reference to newspapers, journals and periodicals, assistance in the interpretation of these items has been gained by the Tribunals in contrasting Group 3, items 1 and 2. Thus, if a publication is of a type within an item of Group 3 other than item 2, any advertisement in such a publication cannot be a zero-rated supply under Group 5.

Further, it has been held that "newspapers, journals or periodicals" should be applied in accordance with the ordinary meaning of those words. To fall within Group 5, therefore, a publication must contain articles of general or topical interest and must appear in some kind of series with some element of regularity. It would appear from *Tempus Advertising Ltd* v *CCE*, LON/75/93 (*Casebook* **8.501**), where yearbooks were held not to constitute periodicals and consequently advertisements in such yearbooks were not entitled to be zero-rated, that publications issued annually or less frequently would not normally fall within the meaning of the word periodical. It is likely that in practice the greater the length between issues, the greater the tendency for the publication to contain fewer articles of topical interest and for the publication to be more complete in itself, that is more akin to a book. In such cases it will be outside Group 5.

Items 2 and 3 are designed to cover the services of, for example, advertising agencies. By limiting the item to newspapers etc, however, practical problems as to apportionment may be encountered where an advertising campaign covers several media, some of which are and others are not within this category.

8.600 Group 6: News services

Item No.
   1.   The supply to newspapers or to the public of information of a kind published in newspapers.

Notes:
(1) This item does not include the supply of photographs.

It is to be noted that this Group is considered by the Customs & Excise to relate only to news items. In its view, feature articles are not zero-rated under Group 6. The Authors suggest, however, that this may be too restrictive an interpretation to place on the Group. Although the heading to the group would support the Customs & Excise view, headings are specifically stated by s 46(3) to be for ease of reference only and, therefore, cannot affect the interpretation of the Group. The limiting

words to Group 6 would appear to be contained in the phrase "information of a kind published in newspapers". Given the increasing scope
of newspaper articles, provided that the article in question includes some
information, it should fall within Group 6. It is interesting to note, in
relation to this issue, that the Customs & Excise put forward their above
interpretation of Group 6 in *Newsclip (UK) Ltd* v *CCE* [1975] VATTR
67 (*Casebook* **8.601**), but the point remained undecided as the appellant's case failed on another ground.

"Public" in Group 6 is a generic term and as pointed out by the Tribunal in the *Newsclip* case it cannot be extended to include the supply
of information to an individual member of the public.

8.700   Group 7: Fuel and power

Item No.
1. Coal, coke and other solid substances held out for sale solely as fuel.
2. Coal gas, water gas, producer gases and similar gases.
3. Petroleum gases and other gaseous hydrocarbons, whether in a gaseous or liquid state.
4. Hydrocarbon oil within the meaning of the Hydrocarbon Oil (Customs and Excise) Act 1971.
5. Electricity, heat and air-conditioning.
6. Lubricating oils other than those included in item 4.

Notes:
(1) Item 1 shall be deemed to include combustible materials put up for sale for kindling fires but shall not include matches upon which a duty of customs or excise has been or is to be charged.
(2) "Lubricating oils" means agents for lubrication which are neither:
   (*a*) solid or semisolid at a temperature of 15°C, nor
   (*b*) gaseous [at a temperature of 15°C and under a pressure of 1013·25 millibars].
(2) Items 2 and 3 do not include any gas (within the meaning of section 3 of the Finance Act 1971) for use as fuel in road vehicles and on which a duty of excise has been charged or is chargeable.
(3) Item 4 does not include hydrocarbon oil on which a duty of customs or excise has been or is to be charged without relief from, or rebate of, such duty by virtue of the provisions of the Hydrocarbon Oil (Customs and Excise) Act 1971.

The provisions generally

This Group zero-rates the major forms of fuel and power except, generally, road fuels. An extensive list of the fuels zero-rated under this item
is given in Customs & Excise Notice No 701, pp 20–23.

Subsidiary supply of power

In a number of instances, suppliers have attempted to obtain the benefit of zero-rating under this Group where the supply of electricity is an essential element in their particular supply. These cases have involved a laundrette (*Mander Laundries* v *CCE*, [1973] VATTR 136 (*Casebook* **3.607**)) and the facilities for the playing of billiards (*Washwood Heath and Ward End Conservative and Unionist Club Ltd* v *CCE*, BIR/73/12 (*Casebook* **8.701**)) and squash (*High Wycombe Squash Club Ltd* v *CCE* [1976] VATTR 156 (*Casebook* **8.702**), and *St Annes-on-Sea Lawn Tennis Club Ltd* v *CCE*, [1977] VATTR 229 (*Casebook* **8.703**)). Of these cases, only the decision in the *High Wycombe* case was in favour of the taxpayer where it was held that the club was entitled to resell, at any price, electricity supplied to it. The bye laws of the club also obliged members to purchase electricity at a specific price. However, the decision in the *High Wycombe* case has subsequently been criticised (see *St Annes-on-Sea Lawn Tennis Club Ltd* v *CCE* (*Casebook* **8.703**) and must, it appears, now be regarded as incorrectly decided. These "club" cases should it is suggested, be treated as examples of two-part tariffs, that is, a member required to pay an amount for "electricity" when taking advantage of the club's facilities is in reality making a further payment for the advantage of membership of the club.

8.800 Group 8: Construction of buildings etc

Item No.
1. The granting, by a person constructing a building, of a major interest in, or in any part of, the building or its site.
2. The supply, in the course of the construction, alteration or demolition of any building or of any civil engineering work, of any services other than the services of an architect, surveyor or any person acting as consultant or in a supervisory capacity.
3. The supply, by a person supplying services within Item 2 and in connection with those services, of
   (a) materials or of builder's hardware, sanitary ware or other articles of a kind ordinarily installed by builders as fixtures; or
   (b) in respect of such goods, services described in paragraph 1 (1) of Schedule 2 to this Act.

Notes:
(1) Where the benefit of the consideration for the grant of a major interest as described in item 1 accrues to the person constructing the building but that person is not the grantor, he shall for the purposes of that item be treated as the person making the grant.

> (2) Item 2 does not include—
>   (*a*) any work of repair or maintenance; or
>   (*b*) the supply of any services in the course of the construction or alteration of any civil engineering work within the grounds or garden of a building used or to be used wholly or mainly as a private residence; or
>   (*c*) the supply by a person of any services which consist of or include any services supplied to him by some other person otherwise than *in the course of a business* in the course or furtherance of a business carried on by that other person; or
>   (*d*) the supply of services described in paragraphs 1 (1) or 5 (3) of Schedule 2 to this Act.
> (3) Section 12 (3) of this Act does not apply to goods forming part of a description of supply in this Group.

In addition to Customs & Excise Notice No 701, Customs & Excise Notice Nos 708 (Construction industry) and 715 (Construction industry: alterations and repair and maintenance) may be of assistance in the interpretation of this Group.

Item 1

This item zero-rates the grant of a major interest in a building or its site by the person who constructs that building. The following terms need to be considered in relation to this item:

GRANT

In practice the Customs & Excise interpret "grant" in item 1 so as to include the assignment of a lease with at least 21 years of the term unexpired (Notice No 708, para 17).

PERSON CONSTRUCTING A BUILDING

The scope of item 1 is increased by Note (1) to the Group which treats as the grantor of a major interest in land, a person constructing a building if the consideration for the grant accrues to him.

In the *Trustees for the Hulme Trust Education Foundation* v *CCE*, [1978] VATTR 179 (*Casebook* **8.801**), it was held that a person can only be regarded as the person constructing a building if he personally does the work or the work is done by his servants or agents; sub-contracting out the work may result, therefore, in the subsequent grant of the interest in the land being exempt under Sched 5, Group 1 and not zero-rated.

The Customs & Excise states in Notice No 708, para 19, however, that they consider that item 1 extends to a person who commissions the construction of a building if he exercises some measure of control over that construction, for example, over its design or planning. It is understood that this view is still taken notwithstanding the *Hulme Trust* case, *ante*.

The Customs & Excise also regards a construction as taking place where the work in question involves a substantial reconstruction of a building. "Substantial" is interpreted by the Customs & Excise as meaning that the cost of reconstruction, excluding the cost of any associated repair or maintenance work, exceeds 50 per cent of the cost that would have been incurred at that time in constructing the entire building in its new form. The Customs & Excise does not say whether the notional cost of demolishing the existing building must be included as part of the cost of constructing the entire building in its new form.

MAJOR INTEREST IN LAND

A major interest in land is defined in s 46(1) as:

"... the fee simple or a tenancy for a term certain exceeding 21 years, and in relation to Scotland means—

(*a*) the estate or interest of the proprietor of the *dominium utile*, or

(*b*) in the case of land not held on feudal tenure, the estate or interest of the owner, or the lessee's interest under a lease for a period exceeding 21 years."

A grant of any interest in land outside these terms by anyone would be an exempt supply or, if the supply falls within one of the exclusions in Sched 5, Group 1, standard rated. As to this latter, see further **9.100**.

Where a developer wishes to grant leases of land of less than 21 years having developed that land he may, therefore, have a partial inability to recover input tax suffered by him in connection with that building work by reason of the fact that those leases will be exempt supplies. It may be more advantageous, therefore, if he were to sub-contract the development work to another person. That person will be able to zero-rate the supply to the developer under Sched 4, Group 8, items 2 and 3, thereby reducing the developer's costs.

The grant of more than one interest may be zero-rated under item 1 in respect of the same building and site. For example, a person constructing a building may first grant a lease of the land for a term of more than 21 years and then dispose of the freehold reversion. Both supplies will be zero-rated under item 1.

BUILDING

A "building" is not defined in the Act and is, therefore, to be given its ordinary meaning. It is clearly not limited to buildings for human occupation and was found in *E Higham* v *CCE*, LEE/75/35 (*Casebook* **8.803**), to include a structure as basic as four walls and a roof. Item 1 is, however, linked to the granting of a major interest in a building or its site and as a major interest is defined by reference to "land" (the phrase "major interest" not being used in any other part of the Act), it is perhaps possible to infer that the intention of Parliament was to require the building to be of a kind that would in law be classified as "land" in order for the grant of an interest in it to be zero-rated under item 1. If this is the case, the building should be, as the Customs & Excise suggests in Notice No 708, para 6 (as amended), either permanently attached to the land or be sufficiently substantial to be held down by its own weight and have a permanent base on which it rests so that, in both cases, the building becomes a part of the land.

The above line of argument is less strong in the case of item 2, which is only concerned with supplies in connection with the construction of a building not the grant of a major interest in land. The link with the legal definition of land is, therefore, indirect but may be perhaps found from the apparent overall scheme of Group 8. Certainly in *R H R Walle v CCE*, [1976] VATTR 101 (*Casebook* **8.805**), the Tribunal was influenced in its finding that a summer-house was a "building" by the fact that although not bolted to its concrete plinth, it was "intended to and likely to rest on this base by its own weight for an indefinite period of time (meaning at least several years) and that its weight is sufficient for this purpose" (it was this case which led to the amendment of Notice No 708, para 6).

SITE

The wording of item 1 would permit a builder to dispose of the site on which he has constructed a building separately from the building itself. Indeed, it seems that having constructed the building he may retain it and a disposal of the site would remain to be treated as a zero-rated supply.

Although item 1 is expressed in the present tense, it appears to be accepted that the actual grant of the interest may post date the completion of the construction. If this is correct, then, provided that a builder can show that he intends to construct a building on the site in question, it should also follow that the sale of a site to a person by him prior to his constructing a building on that site for that person may also be zero-rated. The Customs & Excise does not appear to share this view, however.

Item 2

This item zero-rates the supply of services in the course of construction, alteration or demolition of any building or civil engineering work except services of architects, surveyors, consultants or supervisors. Certain further restrictions are added by Note (2) to the item. These restrictions concern:

(*a*) works of repair or maintenance; and
(*b*) civil engineering works in the grounds or garden of a private residence.

The following paragraphs discuss these restrictions and certain other elements of item 2.

IN THE COURSE OF CONSTRUCTION

Supplies after a building has been completed cannot be zero-rated under item 2. It was held in *University of Hull* v *CCE*, LEE/75/31 (*Casebook* **8.806**), that construction ends when the "main structure (of the building) is complete, the windows glazed and all essential services installed". Further, once a building has been occupied, it is clearly no longer in the course of construction. It was also suggested in *Hornby Road Investments Ltd* v *CCE*, MAN/76/131 (*Casebook* **8.830**), that a building is completed at the time of the issue of a completion certificate. However, as several years had elapsed in Hornby since the date the building had, under any test, been completed, the distinction between occupation, completion of the main structure and the issue of a completion certificate was not vital to the decision and remained unsettled.

CONSTRUCTION, ALTERATION OR DEMOLITION

These words apply to both "any building" and "any civil engineering work". To be zero-rated, the supply need not be the actual service of the construction etc of a building or civil engineering work; any service supplied during the construction etc, for example, sub-contracted bricklaying or bulldozer driving may be zero-rated provided that that service is part of an overall work of construction, alteration or demolition.

It was held in *Shirebrook Parish Church* v *CCE*, MAN/77/42 (*Casebook* **8.814**), that "construction" means to place a structure where there was nothing previously and "demolition" the permanent removal of a structure which previously existed. The meaning of "alteration" is considered under ALTERATION, *post*.

It is to be noted that Group 8, Note 2(*b*) excludes the construction or alteration of a civil engineering work in the grounds of a private residence. Any demolition of a civil engineering work in the grounds of a private residence would, however, be zero-rated.

ALTERATION

The meaning of the word "alteration" has been the subject of a number of Tribunal decisions. From these decisions, a number of principles can be identified. These are:

(*a*) the alterations must relate to the structure of the building (*Rentokil Ltd* v *CCE*, [1973] VATTR 31 (*Casebook* **8.809**). In determining whether work involves an alteration of a structural nature, Tribunals tend not to have regard to precedents developed in landlord and tenant cases. However, *Pearlman* v *The Keepers and Governor of Harrow School*, [1979] 1 All ER 365, was cited with approval by the Tribunal in *CCE* v *Morrison and Dunbar Ltd*, [1979] STC 406 (*Casebook* **8.820**). In the *Harrow School* case, Lane LJ. defined "structural" as something which affected the fabric of a building and contrasted such work with the provision of equipment in relation to a building. The provision of equipment is, indeed, a troublesome area in connection with item 2 as not only will there be doubt as to whether it will constitute an alteration to the structure of a building but also as to whether the work is of repair or maintenance. The *Harrow School* case involved the installation of a central heating system which was built into and became a part of the building in question. It was, therefore, an alteration of that building;

(*b*) the alteration must be substantial in relation to the building as a whole but will fall short of "changing the whole building for a new one" (*Michael Gumbrell and Dodson Bros* v *CCE*, [1973] VATTR 171 (*Casebook* **8.810**);

(*c*) it is a question of fact and degree as to whether there has been an alteration to a building. "Alteration" is to be interpreted in accordance with its ordinary and natural usage (*The Parochial Church Council of St Peter's Church, Bolton* v *CCE*, [1977] VATTR 9).

In relation to (*b*) and (*c*) above, there is a discernible divergence of views between Tribunals as to what is and what is not "substantial". For example in *Shirebrook Parish Church* v *CCE*, MAN/77/42 (*Casebook* **8.814**), the external appearance of the building was considered relevant in determining whether there had been an alteration to that building. In the *Cathedral Church of the Holy and Undivided Trinity of Norwich* v *CCE*, LON K/73/162 (*Casebook* **8.818**), however, the building's external appearance was considered a subsidiary factor to the technical design of the changes proposed by the works in question.

(*d*) the removal test originally laid down in *Webb* v *Bevis Ltd*, [1940] 1 All ER 247, was approved by the Tribunal in *John Turner and Smith Ltd* v *CCE*, MAN/74/23 (*Casebook* **8.816**). Thus, if the alteration is only capable of removal with difficulty and of no use in any other location, the work will be, *prima facie*, an alteration within item 2. However, it is still necessary to then apply the test in (*b*) above, that is, whether the alteration is substantial in nature in relation to the building as a whole;

(e) it seems that considerable difficulties will be encountered in attempting to fall within item 2 where the work involves the replacement of an article. Such replacement will tend to indicate the repair or maintenance and not the alteration of a building. If this is the case, the work will not be zero-rated by virtue of the exclusion from item 2, Note 2(a). Similarly, an alteration by way of improvement may also be classed as a work of repair or maintenance (see *T G Davies* v *CCE*, [1976] VATTR 205 (*Casebook* **8.826**)). Where doubt arises in this area, some assistance may possibly be found by reference to land law cases in relation to repairing obligations under the terms of leases. These cases may indicate the degreee of change necessary before a particular work goes beyond a repair and may be classed as an alteration.

REPAIR OR MAINTENANCE

Note (2)(a) excludes from zero-rating works of repair or maintenance. The Tribunal defined these words in *T G Davies* v *CCE*, [1976] VATTR 205 (*Casebook* **8.826**) as follows:

"Repair means the restoration to a sound condition after injury or decay; in its ordinary context it indicates the putting back into good condition of something that having been in a good condition has fallen into a bad condition.
   The word 'maintenance' in the context of 'work of repair or maintenance' is harder to define. We think it extends to the keeping of something in proper order before the thing falls out of condition. It does not in our opinion, exclude improvements. In performing works of maintenance on a building, a householder may substitute one article for a reasonable improvement thereto ... So in our view one may maintain something by ensuring that it remains in the same good condition or by improving it".

Although the above definitions are frequently quoted, their application by Tribunals in practice often appears arbitrary. Also, in *ACT Construction Ltd* v *CCE*, [1979] STC 358 (*Casebook* **8.825**), Drake J. stated that he doubted "whether the Tribunal in the *Davies* case was in fact attempting to define the word 'maintenance': they were merely stating what in their view were guidelines to help them in that particular case". Drake J. went on to find that the Tribunal in considering the works effected by ACT Construction had erred in law in relying solely on the definition in the *Davies* case. In his view, the *Davies* definition did not provide a reliable test in the case he was considering. Drake J. commented:

"I find no fault with the guidelines used by this tribunal and the tribunal in the *Davies* case that 'maintenance' extends to the keeping of something in proper order before it falls out of condition, and does not exclude improvements or a degree of substitution.
   But where alterations, additions, substitutions or improvements to a building are made. I think the question must also be asked whether the building after the work is done is something substantially different in character from that which it was before. If so,

I do not think the work can properly be described merely as maintenance or repair. In my judgment, repair to a building necessarily involves the putting into good order or restoration of the condition of some existing building, whilst maintenance of a building is the keeping of the building in good repair. The two may and often will overlap. But where the work is to replace the building which exists with something substantially and significantly different in character it can no longer properly be called repair or maintenance.

The test of considering whether the work done is such as to alter the character or nature of the premises does of course turn on a question of degree in each case, and, as I have already said, the test is not in my judgment an exhaustive test in considering whether work is or is not repair or maintenance. As the question is one of degree, its application must turn on the facts of each individual case, but I think that some, though by no means all, of the considerations which will arise, are whether the work will: (1) substantially alter the life of the building; (2) significantly affect its saleability; (3) significantly affect its market value; (4) make good a building which had always up to that time been considered defective in the sense that it did not comply with modern building regulations. I emphasise strongly that these are only some of the considerations which I think may be relevant in deciding whether or not a building has been so changed in character that it has become something different. If it has so changed then I think the work done in changing it cannot be 'repair' or 'maintenance'. But the test of a change of character is itself only one consideration to be applied in deciding whether any work is 'repair' or 'maintenance'. Other considerations may be appropriate to other cases, and each case must be considered on its merits."

Adopting the above approach, Drake J. held that the underpinning of a house with totally new foundations separate from the existing foundations was not a work of repair or maintenance. It was, therefore, entitled to be zero-rated. A major factor in Drake J.'s mind in reaching this conclusion seems to have been that the foundations could not have been put right merely by replacing in good condition "whatever was there originally" as the existing foundations did not comply with modern building regulations. The Customs & Excise has taken the *ACT Construction* case on appeal and it is interesting to see that Drake J.'s decision has been upheld in the Court of Appeal.

Finally, two further factors appeared to be of importance in relation to whether work undertaken amounted to repair or maintenance in the *Parochial Church Council of St Luke's* v *CCE*, MAN/78/59 (*Casebook* **8.828**), which involved the restoration of a church gutted by fire. First, the fact that there was an intermediary stage between the state in which the building was initially to be found and its state following the completion of the works was considered significant. Secondly, the fact that the work had merely restored the original function of the building also indicated that the work was of repair and not an alteration.

The Customs & Excise has published, in Notice No 715, examples of supplies which they consider will be classed as zero-rated alterations and those as standard rated works of repair or maintenance.

VAT Leaflet 17/74/VLC (The borderline between alteration and repair or maintenance as applicable to roads and other civil engineering work) may also be useful in determining what is and what is not a work of repair or maintenance in connection with civil engineering work.

EXCLUDED SERVICES

The following services are excluded from zero-rating under item 2:

(*a*) services of architects, surveyors or persons acting as consultants or in a supervisory capacity;
(*b*) by Note (2)(*c*), a supply of services will not be zero-rated if the person actually performing the work on behalf of the supplier is not performing the work in the course or furtherance of a business;
(*c*) by Note (2)(*d*), the hire of goods is excluded from item 2. Such supplies may, however, fall within item 3. The private use of goods is also excluded from zero-rating under item 2 by this note.

CIVIL ENGINEERING

To constitute civil engineering works, the works in question must also be substantial in nature (*Rawlins, Davy and Wells* v *CCE*, LON/77/ 251 (*Casebook* **8.834**)). The meaning of civil engineering is that given to it by the civil engineering profession.

Civil engineering works of construction or alteration effected in the grounds or garden of a building used wholly or mainly as a private residence are excluded from item 2 by Note (2)(*b*).

Item 3

This item zero-rates certain articles supplied by persons supplying services within item 2. The requirement that the same person should be involved in the supply made under item 3 as under item 2 is new. The distinction between the wording of items 2 and 3 made in *Avonside Homes Ltd* v *CCE*, [1974] VATTR 148 (*Casebook* **8.837**), to justify the conclusion that item 3 supplies need not be made by the same person as item 2 services is, therefore, no longer valid.

Item 3 covers both the outright supply and the hire of the goods mentioned in that item.

The phrase "supplies of materials or of builder's hardware, sanitary ware or other articles of a kind ordinarily installed by builders as fixtures" appears in three areas of the VAT legislation. First, in relation to Group 8, item 3. Secondly, claims for input tax by a taxable person constructing a building are only allowed under VAT (Special Provisions) Order 1977 (SI 1977 No 1796), art 8 in respect of goods within that phrase. Thirdly, a person constructing his own dwelling will be entitled under s 15A to a refund of tax suffered on supplies to him of such goods. A difference does exist, however, between the list of items in item 3 and art 8. In item 3, the words "or of" appear between the words "materials" and "builders hardware". This break was considered to be significant in *John Turner and Smith Ltd* v *CCE*, MAN/74/23 (*Casebook* **8.816**). In that case, it was held that, due to the insertion, the words "of a kind ordinarily installed by builders as fixtures" in item 3 only qualified the words "builder's hardware" etc and not "materials". This distinction was not drawn, however, in the earlier case of *Nordic Saunas Ltd* v *CCE*, [1974] VATTR 40, where the qualifying words were applied to "materials".

ORDINARILY INSTALLED BY BUILDERS

In *W and J Taggart* (*Northern Ireland*) *Ltd* v *CCE*, [1977] VATTR 43 (*Casebook* **5.401**), this phrase was interpreted to extend to articles that one would expect to be installed by builders in the ordinary way without special instruction being given to them. Perhaps rather harshly and somewhat illogically, this has been held to exclude articles that are required to be installed by builders either to obtain an NHBRC Certificate (*Rialto Builders Ltd* v *CCE*, [1974] VATTR 14 (*Casebook* **5.402**)) or to comply with Building Regulations (*CCE* v *Westbury Developments* (*Worthing*) *Ltd.*, [1979] STC 665 (*Casebook* **5.403**)). Items installed to facilitate the sale of a property are also excluded (see *W and J Taggart, ante*).

8.900 Group 9: International services

This Group is discussed at **10.100** (the "export" of services).

8.1000 Group 10: Transport

Item No.
1. The supply, repair or maintenance of any ship which is neither—
     (*a*) a ship of a gross tonnage of less than 15 tons; nor
     (*b*) a ship designed or adapted for use for recreation or pleasure.
2. The supply, repair or maintenance of any aircraft which is neither—
     (*a*) an aircraft of a weight of less than eight thousand kilogrammes; nor
     (*b*) an aircraft designed or adapted for use for recreation or pleasure.
3. The supply to and repair or maintenance for the Royal National Lifeboat Institution of any lifeboat.
4. Transport of passengers—
     (*a*) in any vehicle, ship or aircraft designed or adapted to carry not less than twelve passengers; or
     (*b*) by the Post Office; or
     (*c*) on any scheduled flight.

5. Transport of passengers or freight outside both the United Kingdom and the Isle of Man or to or from a place outside both the United Kingdom and the Isle of Man.

6. Any services provided for
(*a*) the handling of ships or aircraft in a port or customs and excise airport; or
(*b*) the handling, in a port or customs and excise airport or on land adjacent to a port, of goods carried in a ship or aircraft.

7. Pilotage services.

8. Salvage or towage services.

9. Any services supplied within or outside the United Kingdom and the Isle of Man for or in connection with the surveying of any ship or aircraft or the classification of any ship or aircraft for the purposes of any register.

10. The making of arrangements for—
(*a*) the supply of, or of space in, any ship or aircraft; or
(*b*) the supply of any service included in items 1 to 9, 11 and 12.

11. The supply of services, performed outside the United Kingdom and the Isle of Man, which are ancillary to the transport of goods or passengers.

12. The supply to a person in his business capacity (and not in his private capacity) who as such belongs in a country other than the United Kingdom:
(*a*) of services consisting of the handling or storage at or transport to or from the place at which goods are to be exported or have been imported or of the handling or storage of such goods in connection with such transport; or
(*b*) of services comprised in paragraph (*a*) of item 6, item 9 or paragraph (*a*) of item 10.

Notes:
(1) "Port" and "customs and excise airport" have the same meanings as in the Customs and Excise Management Act 1979.
(2) In items 1 and 2 "The supply" of a ship or aircraft, respectively comprised therein, includes the supply of any services under a charter of that ship or aircraft.
(3) "Lifeboat" includes any ship used as a lifeboat.
(4) Except for the purposes of item 12 paragraph (*a*) of item 6, item 9 and paragraph (*a*) of item 10 do not include the supply of any services where the ships or aircraft referred to therein are of the descriptions specified in paragraphs (*a*) and (*b*) of item 1 or in paragraphs (*a*) and (*b*) of item 2 respectively.
(5) In items 1, 2 and 3 the supply respectively described therein includes the supply of the service of the letting on hire of craft comprised in the items.
(6) Item 6 does not include the supply of the service of the letting on hire of goods which supply would otherwise be a supply described therein.
(7) Item 12 applies only if the recipient would be treated as belonging in a country other than the United Kingdom or the Isle of Man if, for the purposes of section 8A of this Act, the rules contained therein were applied to him.

Item 1

This item zero-rates the supply, repair or maintenance of certain ships, that is ships of 15 tons or more which are not designed or adapted for recreation or pleasure. A ship for these purposes includes a hovercraft (s 46(1)) and must, it appears, be capable of self-propulsion (see *T M Hagenbach* v *CCE*, LON/74/449 (*Casebook* **8.1001**)). This latter requirement might exclude, for example, the supply of an oil production platform not capable of self-propulsion from zero-rating under Group 10.

This item includes the letting on hire of a ship and the provision of services under any form of charter of a ship within the item. The charter of a ship which does not satisfy the conditions of the item may, however, be zero-rated under Group 10, items 4 or 5.

The Customs & Excise regard the restriction in item 1(*b*), that is, that the ship should not be designed or adapted for recreation or pleasure, as not applying where a ship of that type is supplied to a taxable person for use in his business of providing recreational or pleasure cruises.

The gross tonnage of a ship is generally ascertained under the Merchant Shipping Acts. See the VAT Leaflet 1/78/VAH (Gross tonnage of unregistered ships and boats), however, for the method of calculating the tonnage of ships which have not been ascertained under those Acts.

VAT Leaflets 701/4/79 (The supply, chartering, repair and maintenance of ships and aircraft) and 3/75/VLB (Off-shore oil and gas installations) may also be of assistance in relation to item 1).

Item 2

This item zero-rates the supply, repair or maintenance of certain aircraft, that is, aircraft of 8,000 kilogrammes or more which are not designed or adapted for recreation or pleasure. The weight of an aircraft for the purposes of this item means its maximum take off weight as specified in its certificate of airworthiness or release documents issued by the Ministry of Defence.

This item is similarly extended to cover services under a charter of an aircraft and the letting of an aircraft on hire, (see also VAT Leaflet 701/4/79 (The supply, chartering, repair and maintenance of ships and aircraft) in relation to this item).

Item 3

This item zero-rates the supply to and repair or maintenance for the Royal National Life-boat Institution of any lifeboat. "Lifeboat" includes any ship used as such and a hire of a lifeboat is also zero-rated under this item. The item only applies to supplies direct to the RNLI. The supplier should obtain a certificate from the RNLI that the boat will be used as a lifeboat.

Item 4

The transport of passengers by the Post Office or on any scheduled flight in any vehicle, ship or aircraft designed or adapted to carry not less than twelve passengers is zero-rated under this item. The important restriction to the application of the item is that the vehicle etc should be capable of carrying at least twelve people (which the Customs & Excise interprets as including the "driver"). Taxis and minicabs are, therefore, subject to the standard rate (see also in this context, VAT Leaflet 5/78/VAH (Passenger transport: taxis and hire cars)). The zero-rating of international transport does not impose such a condition, however (see item 5, *post*).

A transport of passengers has been held to mean the carriage of persons from one place to another where the persons concerned do not effectively remain in the same place. This curious definition was evolved principally to exclude amusement rides etc from item 4 (see *CCE* v *Blackpool Pleasure Beach Company*, [1974] STC 138 (*Casebook* **8.1004**).

The zero- and standard rated supplies by reference to this item and in relation to the carriage of vehicles on ferries or sea journeys within the United Kingdom, are listed by the Customs & Excise Notice No 701 at p 46.

Item 5

This item covers the transport of passengers or freight outside the United Kingdom or to or from a place outside the United Kingdom. This item, which overlaps with item 4, therefore, zero-rates the international transport of passengers or freight regardless of the capacity of the carrying vehicle.

A delivery to a dockside in the United Kingdom does not qualify as a transport of freight to a place outside the United Kingdom (*J D Bevington* v *CCE*, LON/76/85 (*Casebook* **8.1008**). The Customs & Excise also considers that any part of the international carriage of goods which is wholly within the United Kingdom and is the subject of a separate VAT invoice is chargeable at the standard rate.

Item 6

Any services of the handling of ships or aircraft in a port or airport or of goods in a port or airport or on land adjacent to a port is zero-rated under this item. The ship or aircraft must be of a type within Group 10, items 1 or 2 as the case may be (Note (4)). Item 6 does not include a letting on hire of goods mentioned in the item (Note (6)). Port and customs & excise airport have the same meanings as in the Customs & Excise Management Act 1979, that is, a port appointed for customs purposes (which includes all seaports in the United Kingdom) and airports designated for the landing or departure of aircraft for the purposes of the Customs and Excise Acts by an Order in Council made under the Civil Aviation Act 1949, s 8.

Examples of supplies within this item are listed in VAT Leaflet 701/3/79 (Handling services in ports and customs and excise airports).

Item 7

This item zero-rates pilotage services in connection with shipping.

Item 8

This item zero-rates supplies of salvage and towage services including such services in inland waters.

Item 9

The supply of any services in connection with the surveying or the classification of any ship or aircraft, in the latter case, for the purposes of any register, is zero-rated under this item. The ship or aircraft in question must satisfy the conditions of item 1 or 2 as the case may be (Note (4)).

Item 10

This item covers the making of arrangements for example by ship or aircraft brokers or travel agents, for the supply of, or of space in, any ship or aircraft or the supply of any service included in items 1–9, 11 or 12.

The ship or aircraft in question must be within item 1 or 2 as the case may be.

An extreme restriction was applied to this item in *British Airport Authority (No 2)* v *CCE*, LON/74/151 (*Casebook* **8.1009**). In that case, the item was construed as applying only where an agency relationship subsists between the party making the arrangement under item 10 and the party making the supply in respect of which the arrangements are made.

See also, in connection with this item, VAT Leaflets 701/2/79 (Freight forwarding services in connection with international movements of goods) and 4/78/VAH (Ships' managers and port agents).

Item 11

The supply of services which are ancilliary to the transport of goods or passengers and which are performed outside the United Kingdom are zero-rated under this item.

Item 12

This item covers the supply to a person in his business capacity (and not his private capacity) who belongs outside the United Kingdom of certain handling and storage services. "Belonging" has the meaning given to it by s 8A, see **10.200**.

The Customs & Excise list the following examples of supplies within this item:

(*a*) the transport of imported goods from a port or customs and excise airport to their first destination in the United Kingdom (the first destination for this purpose is the place in the United Kingdom to which the goods are consigned at importation; if the goods are not consigned to any particular place at that time, it is the first place in the United Kingdom to which they are transported from the port or customs and excise airport);

(*b*) the transport of exported goods to a port or customs and excise airport from the place in the United Kingdom whence they were consigned for export;

(*c*) the packing, repacking and storage of goods which are being transported under (*a*) or (*b*) above; and

(*d*) the storage of imports or exports at a port or customs and excise airport.

8.1100 Group 11 : Caravans and houseboats

Item No.

1. Caravans exceeding the limits of size for the time being permitted for the use on roads of a trailer drawn by a motor vehicle having an unladen weight of less than 2,030 kilogrammes.
2. Houseboats being boats or other floating decked structures designed or adapted for use solely as places of permanent habitation and not having means of, or capable of being readily adapted for, self-propulsion.
3. The suppy of services in respect of a caravan or a houseboat comprised respectively in items 1 and 2, described in paragraph 1 (1) or 5 (3) of Schedule 2 to this Act.

Note:

This Group does not include—

(*a*) removable contents other than goods of a kind mentioned in item 3 of Group 8; or

(*b*) the supply of holiday accommodation including any accommodation advertised or held out as such.

The limits currently laid down for the size of caravans for the purposes of item 1 require caravans to be either more than 7 metres long or 2.3 metres wide before they may qualify for zero-rating under Group 11.

For a discussion of the goods in Group 8, item 3 (see **8.800**).

8.1200 Group 12: Gold

Item No.
1.   The supply, by a Central Bank to another Central Bank or a member of the London Gold Market, of gold held in the United Kingdom.
2.   The supply, by a member of the London Gold Market to a Central Bank, of gold held in the United Kingdom.

Notes:
(1) "Gold" includes gold coins.
(2) Section 12(3) of this Act does not apply to goods forming part of a description of supply in this Group.   .
(3) Items 1 and 2 include:—
     (*a*) the granting of a right to acquire a quantity of gold; and
     (*b*) any supply described therein, which, by virtue of Schedule 2, paragraph 1 of this Act, is a supply of services".

Items 1 and 2 and the Notes applicable thereto were substituted for the former Group 12 by the VAT (Gold) Order 1980 (SI 1980 No 303) with effect from 1 April 1980.

This change followed the abolition of exchange control in the United Kingdom on 28 October 1979 a consequence of which was to bring to an end the status of an authorised dealer in gold on which the former Group 12 relied. As a result, Group 12 now only zero-rates supplies of gold in the United Kingdom involving as buyer or seller a Central Bank. The other party to the supply may be either another Central Bank or a member of the London Gold Market.

For supplies between London Gold Market Members and on the London Gold Market generally, which supplies may be zero-rated under the VAT (Terminal Markets) Order 1973 (SI 1973 No 173), see **16.500**.

8.1300 Group 13: Bank notes

Item No.
1.   The issue by a bank of a note payable to bearer on demand.

The Customs & Excise interpret "issue" to include "reissue". The Group is otherwise self-explanatory.

8.1400 Group 14: Drugs, medicines, medical and surgical appliances etc

Item No.

1. The supply of any goods dispensed, by a person registered in the register of pharmaceutical chemists kept under the Pharmacy Act 1954 or the Pharmacy and Poisons Act (Northern Ireland) 1925, on the prescription of a person registered in the register of medical practitioners, the register of medical practitioners with limited registration or the dentists' register.

2. The supply to the order of a person registered in the register of medical practitioners or the register of medical practitioners with limited registration, to a chronically sick or disabled person, for domestic use, of medical or surgical appliances designed solely for the relief of a severe abnormality or severe injury.

3. The supply to a chronically sick or disabled person, for domestic use, of the following:
   (*a*) electrically or mechanically adjustable beds designed for invalids;
   (*b*) commode chairs, commode stools, devices incorporating a bidet jet and warm air drier and frames or other devices for sitting over or rising from a sanitary appliance;
   (*c*) chair lifts or stair lifts designed for use in connection with invalid wheel chairs;
   (*d*) hoists and lifters designed for use by invalids.

Notes:

(1) Section 12 (3) of this Act does not apply to goods forming part of a description of supply in this Group.

(2) In item 2 "appliances" shall not include hearing aids, dentures, spectacles and contact lenses but shall be deemed to include—
   (i) clothing, footwear and wigs;
   (ii) invalid wheel chairs, and invalid carriages other than mechanically propelled vehicles intended or adapted for use on roads; and
   (iii) renal haemodialysis units, oxygen concentrators, artificial respirators and other similar apparatus.

(3) In item 3 "chronically sick or disabled persons" shall include only a person who as a chronically sick or disabled person is under the care of a person registered in the register of medical practitioners or the register of medical practitioners with limited registration.

(4) In items 1, 2 and 3 the supply respectively described therein includes the supply of the services of the letting on hire of goods comprised in the items.

(5) For the purposes of this Group a person, who is not registered in the visiting EEC practitioners list at the time he performs services in an urgent case as mentioned in paragraph (3) of Article 7 of the Medical Qualifications (EEC Recognition) Order 1977, is to be treated as being registered in that list where he is entitled to be registered in accordance with that Article.

(6) For the purposes of this Group a person to whom paragraph 2 of Schedule 5 to the Medical Act 1978 applies is to be treated as being a fully registered medical practitioner while he continues to be so treated by virtue of that paragraph.

This Group does not apply to imported goods but does apply to goods let on hire (Notes (1) and (4)). For the meaning of "register of medical practitioners" see under **9.700** and Notes (5) and (6) set out above.

Item 1

The supply of goods dispensed by a registered pharmaceutical chemist on the prescription of a registered medical or dental practitioner will be zero-rated under this item. Goods dispensed by a practitioner himself are exempt supplies, however, under Sched 5, Group 7 item 1(*a*) or (*b*) and goods supplied to practitioners are taxable at the standard rate.

Item 2

This item covers the supply to the chronically sick or disabled of certain goods for their domestic use. The supply must be to the order of a registered medical practitioner but made direct by the supplier to the sick or disabled person in question. The supplier should be provided with an order or certificate given by the doctor naming the patient and certifying that the patient is a chronically sick or disabled person and that the appliance is intended for his domestic use.

The Customs & Excise list the examples of items which may and may not qualify as an appliance within this item in VAT Leaflet 701/7/79.

Item 3

The supply of the articles listed in item 3 for the domestic use of a chronically sick or disabled person is zero-rated without the need for those articles to have been supplied at the order of a medical practitioner. Note (3) defines a chronically sick or disabled person for the purposes of item 3 although, strangely, this definition is not extended to item 2 above.

The Customs & Excise list the supplies as eligible and not eligible for relief under this item in VAT Leaflet 701/7/79.

8.1500 Group 15: Imports, exports, etc

Item No.
1. The supply of imported goods before the delivery of an entry (within the meaning of section 37 of the Customs and Excise Management Act 1979) under an agreement requiring the purchaser to make such entry.
2. The transfer of goods or services from the United Kingdom or the Isle of Man by a person carrying on a business both inside and outside the United Kingdom or the Isle of Man to his place of business outside both the United Kingdom and the Isle of Man.
3. The supply to or by an overseas authority, overseas body or overseas trader, charged with the management of any Defence project which is the subject of an international collaboration arrangement or under direct contract with

any Governement or Government sponsored international body participating in a Defence project under such an arrangement, of goods or services in the course of giving effect to that arrangement.

4. The supply to an overseas authority, overseas body or overseas trader of jigs, patterns, templates, dies, punches and similar machine tools used in the United Kingdom or the Isle of Man solely for the manufacture of goods for export.

Notes:

(1) Item 2 does not apply where the person makes other taxable supplies.

(2) An "international collaboration arrangement" means any arrangement made—
  (i) between the United Kingdom Government and the government of one or more other countries, or any government sponsored international body for collaboration in a joint project of research, development or production; and
  (ii) which includes provision for participating governments to relieve the cost of the project from taxation.

(3) "Overseas authority" means any country other than the United Kingdom and the Isle of Man or any part of or place in such a country or the government of any such country, part or place.

(4) "Overseas body" means a body established outside both the United Kingdom and the Isle of Man.

(5) "Overseas trader" means a person who carries on a business and has his principal place of business outside both the United Kingdom and the Isle of Man.

(6) Item 4 does not apply where the overseas authority, overseas body or overseas trader is a taxable person.

Item 1

This item, which zero-rates the supply of imported goods under an agreement requiring the purchaser to enter such goods into the United Kingdom, is designed to prevent the double taxation of imported goods; once when supplied before entry and once on entry. The provision is, of course, primarily of importance to exempt, partially exempt and non-taxable persons who will not be able to reclaim the whole or a part of such VAT.

Item 2

The self-supply of goods or services by a person from his UK to his non-UK place of business is zero-rated under this item. The item is limited by Note (1) however, to supplies by persons who make no other taxable supplies in the United Kingdom.

It is debatable as to whether this item, in fact, has any meaning as a self-supply is not generally a supply for VAT purposes (see **3.700**) and, therefore, cannot be zero-rated under this item. The Customs & Excise would seem to share this view where the person in question makes other taxable supplies in the United Kingdom (see Notice No 703, para 13(*a*)) but, where no other taxable supplies are made, follow the suggestion in item 2 that a transfer of goods or services to a place of business outside the United Kingdom is a supply (Notice No 703, para 13(*b*)). If the Customs & Excise view is correct, item 2 may assist, for example, a non-UK person with a UK place of business (for instance the London branch of a foreign bank) which provides services to its foreign office to recover part of the input tax it suffers on supplies to it for the purpose of its business.

Item 3

This item zero-rates certain supplies of goods or services in connection with international collaboration defence projects. Notes (2)–(5) contain definitions of "an international collaboration agreement", "overseas authority", "overseas body", and "overseas trader".

Item 4

This item zero-rates the supply to an overseas authority, body or trader of certain machine tools used in the United Kingdom solely for the manufacture of goods for export. Notes (3) to (5) define overseas authority, body and trader. Item 4 does not apply where the overseas authority, body or trader is a taxable person (Note (6)).

8.1600 Group 16: Charities

Item No.
1. The supply by a charity established primarily for the relief of distress of any goods which have been donated for sale.
2. The export of any goods by a charity.
3. The supply, for donation to a designated Regional or Area Health Authority in England and Wales, Health Board in Scotland, Health and Social Services Board in Northern Ireland, hospital or research institution, of medical or scientific equipment solely for use in medical research, diagnosis or treatment, where such equipment is purchased with funds provided:
   (*a*) by a charity; or
   (*b*) from voluntary contributions.

Notes:
(1) Where the goods have been donated from his stock in trade by a taxable person item 1 shall only apply to the extent that the cost of the goods to him did not exceed £10.
(2) Item 1 shall apply only if the supply is a sale by the first donee of the goods.
(3) "The relief of distress" means:
   (i) the relief of poverty; or
   (ii) the making of provision for the cure or mitigation or prevention of, or for the care of persons suffering from or subject to, any disease or infirmity or disability affecting human beings (including the care of women before, during and after childbirth).

(4) Item 3 does not apply where—
  (i) the supply is to a person other than the donor of the equipment; or
  (ii) the activities of the hospital or research intitution are carried on for profit; or
  (iii) the donee of the equipment has contributed wholly or in part to the funds provided for the purchase thereof.

For a discussion of supplies by charities generally see **15.100** and VAT Leaflet 701/1/79 (Charities).

Item 1

The supply by a charity as principal of goods donated to it for sale is zero-rated under this item. The charity must be established primarily for the relief of distress. Notes (1), (2) and (3) limit the ambit of this item and define the phrase 'the relief of distress''.

Item 2

The export of any goods by a charity is zero-rated. To the extent that all exports of goods are zero-rated under section 12(6) and (7) if the Customs & Excise are satisfied that they have been exported and certain conditions are satisfied, it is arguable that because these requirements are not incorporated in item 2, a charity may zero-rate exports without the fulfilment of any such conditions.

Item 3

A supply of medical or scientific equipment is zero-rated if purchased by a charity or from voluntary contributions. The equipment must then be donated to a designated health authority for use in medical research diagnosis or treatment. The equipment cannot be zero-rated if supplied direct to such an authority. Further, relief is not given where the activities of the hospital or research institution in question are carried out for profit or the authority has contributed wholly or in part to the funds out of which the equipment was purchased.

See further VAT Leaflet 701/6/79, Donated medical and scientific equipment, which lists the following as eligible and ineligible under the item.

8.1700 Group 17: Clothing and footwear

Item No.
1. Articles designed as clothing or footwear for young children and not suitable for older persons.
2. Protective boots and helmets for industrial use.
3. Protective helmets for wear by a person driving or riding a motor bicycle.

Notes:
(1) "Clothing" includes hats and other headgear.
(2) Item 1 does not include articles of clothing made wholly or partly of fur skin, except—
(*a*) headgear;
(*b*) gloves;
(*c*) buttons, belts and buckles;
(*d*) any garment merely trimmed with fur skin unless the trimming has an area greater than one-fifth of the area of the outside material or, in the case of a new garment, represents a cost to the manufacturer greater than the cost to him of the other components.
(3) "Fur skin" means any skin with fur, hair or wool attached except:
(*a*) rabbit skin;
(*b*) woolled sheep or lamb skin; and
(*c*) the skin, if neither tanned nor dressed, of bovine cattle (including buffalo), equine animals, goats or kids (other than Yemen, Mongolian and Tibetan goats or kids), swine (including peccary), chamois, gazelles, deer or dogs.
(4) Items 2 and 3 apply only where the articles referred to therein are manufactured to standard for boots or helmets approved by the British Standards Institution and bear a marking indicating compliance with the specification relating thereto.
(5) Items 1, 2 and 3 include the supply of services, in respect of goods comprised in the items, described in paragraph 1 (1) or 5 (3) of Schedule 2 to this Act.

All items in Group 17 include the hire of the goods mentioned in those items and private or other non-business use of those goods within the meaning of Sched 2, para 5(3).

Item 1

This item covers clothing which is:

(*a*) designed as clothing or footwear for young children and
(*b*) is not suitable for older persons.

Requirement (*a*) has been held to involve a subjective test and requirement (*b*) an objective test in examining the article in question (*W G Jones and Son* v *CCE*, BIR/74/12 (*Casebook* **8.1703**)). While the question as to whether an article is an item of clothing may be relatively straightforward, that of what is a young child is more difficult.

This difficulty has led to the introduction of certain pragmatic tests by the Customs & Excise. These tests are set out in Notice No 714

(Young children's clothing and footwear). These tests are too numerous to state in this *Guide* and reference should be made, therefore, to that Notice.

Note (1) extends the meaning of clothing to hats and other headgear and Note (2) excludes certain clothing made from fur skin.

Items 2 and 3

These items zero-rate protective boots and helmets for industrial use and helmets for wear by motor cyclists. These articles must, however, be manufactured to standards approved by the British Standards Institution and bear a marking indicating compliance with the relevant specification of that standard.

Chapter 9

Exemption

9.000A Sources

The following Customs & Excise Notices may be helpful:

9.000B General principles

Section 13 provides that a supply of goods or services is an exempt supply if it is one falling within the description of goods or services contained in Sched 5. The Treasury is given power in s 13(2) to vary items contained in Sched 5. No VAT is payable on an exempt supply. Section 2(2) states that a taxable supply is a supply of goods or services made in the United Kingdom, other than an exempt supply. A person who makes or intends to make only exempt supplies is not a taxable person and cannot register and he is unable to recover any VAT on inputs. Accordingly, VAT payable by such persons must be absorbed, as any other expense, within the price charged for the goods or services they supply. A person who is registered and makes both taxable and exempt supplies is entitled to credit for some of the input tax, the actual amount of credit depending upon which method for partially exempt supplies is used (see **5.300**). It may be that a person who makes some exempt supplies will be able to ignore them in calculating the amount of input tax available for credit (see the *de minimis* provisions described at **5.300**).

The advantages of exemption are administrative in that exempt supplies are not taxable supplies (s 2(2)), so that a person making only exempt supplies is not able to be registered and does not have to complete returns.

It will, therefore, be seen that there is a disadvantage in making exempt supplies because of the inability to obtain relief for input tax. Zero-rating on the other hand is a real advantage over standard-rated supplies in that not only is VAT chargeable at a nil rate, but full relief for input tax is available. What then is the purpose of exempting certain supplies as opposed to zero-rating them?

Zero-rating was introduced to cover items of personal expenditure, being either exports or where "the cost enters substantially into the budgets of the less-well-off members of the community; for example with food, fares, fuel and new houses ... In other words the aim [of zero-rating] is to ensure that the tax is fair and does not have a regressive effect." (Mr Patrick Jenkin in Committee Stage of Finance Bill 1972 Hansard, Vol 837, Col 414). Exemption, on the other hand was brought in to apply to certain services and goods supplied ancillary to and in the course of such services. Thus, the services within Sched 5 were brought in largely on social grounds, for example, land, postal services, health, education, burial and trade union and professional bodies. Other exempt services were included because of difficulties in valuing the supplies made, for example, gaming, insurance and financial services.

Where goods or services fall both within the provisions for exemption and zero-rating, s 12(1) provides that the zero-rating provisions shall prevail with the result that the goods will be zero-rated as opposed to exempt.

9.100 Group 1: Land

Item No.
1. The grant, assignment or surrender of any interest in or right over land or of any licence to occupy land, other than:
   (a) the provision of accommodation in a hotel, inn, boarding house or similar establishment or of holiday accommodation in a house, flat, caravan or houseboat;
   (b) the granting of facilities for camping in tents or caravans;
   (c) the granting of facilities for parking a vehicle;
   (d) the granting of any right to take game or fish;
   (e) the granting of any right to fell and remove standing timber;
   (f) the granting of facilities for housing, or storage of, an aircraft or for mooring, or storage of, a ship, boat or vessel; and
   (g) the provision to an exhibitor of a site or space at any exhibition, or similar event, organised wholly or mainly for the display or advertisement of goods or services.

Notes:
(1) "Holiday accommodation" includes any accommodation advertised or held out as such.
(2) "Houseboat" includes a houseboat within the meaning of Group 11 of Schedule 4.
(3) "Mooring" includes anchoring or berthing.

General

The grant, assignment or surrender of any interest in land includes outright sales of freehold land, the grant, assignment or surrender of any lease, or the letting of property generally unless for an excluded purpose, such as holiday accommodation, which is standard rated. Where a lease or tenancy of land includes the provision of services by the lessor or landlord the rent may require apportionment between the constituent elements of the overall supply. The Customs & Excise take the view, in practice, that there is no need to apportion the rent between the supply of land and services where the services are supplied to tenants generally, for example, the provision of a porter or gardener in a block of flats. However, where services are supplied to individual tenants, for example, chambermaid facilities, telephone, telex or heating, the rent must be apportioned and the proportion which is not exempt should be charged at the appropriate rate, ie standard or zero-rated. In the above examples, therefore, the services of chambermaids, telephone or telex would be standard rated, whilst heating would be zero-rated (Sched 4, Group 7 and see **8.700**).

An interest in land would include both an equitable or legal interest in land. An example of the former would be the sale by a tenant-in-common of his share of land.

It should be remembered that the sale, or grant of a lease for more than 21 years, of a newly constructed building by the person who constructed it, will be zero-rated under Sched 4, Group 8 (see **8.800**).

The grant of a lease or licence to remove minerals is also exempt, as is the assignment of such a lease.

Licence to occupy land

A licence to occupy land is also exempt. Several cases have considered whether a right to use premises amounts to a licence to occupy land. For example, the right for taxi-cab drivers to use a "waiting-room" as a base from which to operate was held in *R Ferris and R S Budd* v *CCE*, BIR/76/194 (*Casebook* **9.103**), not to be a licence to occupy land. Further, in the *British Airports Authority (Nos 1–4)* cases, the following were considered:

Principle	*Held*
The right to set up shops at Heathrow airport for the sale of duty-free and non duty-free goods	A licence to occupy land had been granted *BAA (No 1)* v *CCE*, [1977] STC 36 (*Casebook* **9.105**)

Principle	*Held*
The right to cross airport land to make deliveries to aircraft	Not a licence to occupy land *BAA (No 2)* v *CCE* (*Casebook* **9.106**)
The right to use desk facilities	Not a licence to occupy land *BAA (No 3)* v *CCE* (*Casebook* **9.107**)
Licence agreement for the use of desk facilities	Not a licence to occupy land *BAA (No 4)* v *CCE* (*Casebook* **9.108**)

It has been held that market-stallholders have a right to occupy land (*Tameside Metropolitan Borough Council* v *CCE*, MAN/78/243 (*Casebook* **9.109**) even though they occupy the land for less than 24 hours. In this case the Customs & Excise argued that the occupation of the land must be for more than 1 day and in addition that "occupy" in Group 1, item 1 meant occupation as construed in the Rating Acts. Both these submissions were expressly rejected by the Tribunal.

A number of cases have concerned clubs, where club members have the right, *inter alia*, to use the clubs' premises. The courts have, however, refused to accept that any licence to occupy the land has been granted to the member (see *Trewby (Hurlingham Club)* v *CCE*, [1976] STC 122 (*Casebook* **9.111**), *CCE* v *Little Spain Club*, [1979] STC 170 (*Casebook* **9.112**), *Banstead Downs Golf Club* v *CCE*, [1974] VATTR 219 (*Casebook* **9.111**)).

Spectators at a football match have been held not to have a licence to occupy land (*Rochdale Hornets Football Club Ltd* v *CCE* [1975] VATTR 71 (*Casebook* **9.115**)).

Exceptions

Paragraphs (*a*)–(*g*) of item 1 contain several exceptions to the general exemption in relation to land. Each is considered below.

HOTEL AND SIMILAR ACCOMMODATION (*exception (a)*)

The provision of accommodation in an hotel, inn, boarding house or similar establishment, or of holiday accommodation in a house, flat, caravan or houseboat is not exempt. VAT must be charged on such supplies at the appropriate rate.

It will be seen from Note (1) to the Group that "holiday accommodation" includes any accommodation advertised as such. This is important to remember as it is common to advertise property as holiday accommodation to avoid granting tenants the protection of the Rent Acts. However, if accommodation is advertised as holiday lettings, even if, in fact, the letting is not for holiday purposes at all, VAT is chargeable on the rents due from the tenant and the landlord must consider whether he should be registered (*R W Sheppard* v *CCE*, [1977] VATTR 272 (*Casebook* **9.117**)). However, special rules apply to the amount of VAT payable in respect of accommodation in an hotel, inn, boarding house or similar establishment where the period of letting exceeds 4 weeks. In particular, the value of the supply is reduced after 4 weeks to the part attributable to the provision of facilities (other than accommodation) except that the part attributable to accommodation shall not be less than one-fifth of the total supply (see **3.500**).

The provision of accommodation includes the use of hotels, inns, boarding houses or similar establishments for conferences. Accordingly the use of an hotel for a conference is chargeable at the standard rate.

The Customs & Excise consider that the expression "similar establishments" for the purpose of item 1(*a*) means places where overnight lodgings and catering are provided, for example, motels, guest-houses, bed and breakfast accommodation but not public houses that do not provide overnight accommodation (Customs & Excise Notice No 701, p 65).

In Notice No 701, p 65 the Customs & Excise refer to Notice No 709 (Hotels, catering and holiday services) for their interpretation of "holiday accommodation". In particular, Notice No 709, para 6 states that:

> "Holiday accommodation includes any accommodation in houses, flats, houseboats or caravans advertised or held out as such, but it does not include residential accommodation merely because it is situated at a holiday resort. Accommodation within the scope of the charge includes, for example, any which is let where:
>
>   (i) the terms and conditions of the agreement indicate that the occupation of the premises is granted for holiday purposes: or
>   (ii) the accommodation is advertised specifically as holiday accommodation, or under a general heading of 'Holiday Accommodation', or in journals specialising in such accommodation; or
>   (iii) the accommodation has been notified to the local tourist office, local authority, etc., as being available for holiday lettings; or
>   (iv) the accommodation is occupied for the holiday season only."

Whilst the Authors would agree with the view of the Customs & Excise in so far as items (i) and (iv) are concerned, the Authors do not accept the tests laid down at (ii) (so far as advertising under the general heading of "Holiday Accommodation" or in journals is concerned) and (iii). Indeed, the Tribunal in *R W Sheppard* v *CCE* specifically rejected tests (ii) and (iii). Notice No 709 was published before the *Sheppard* case, however, and it may be that the Customs & Excise will revise their practice in the light of the *Sheppard* case.

CAMPING (*exception (b)*)

The granting of facilities for camping in tents or caravans are standard rated. The granting of the right to use a camp-site together with any additional facilities, for example, washing facilities are all taxable supplies. However, camping is regarded by the Customs & Excise as meaning "staying temporarily" so that if a person is granted a right to occupy land, on which he intends to place a caravan, for a long period the supply will be exempt within Group 1. The Customs & Excise regard a long period for this purpose as being "a year or a season" (Notice No 709, para 8).

PARKING (*exception (c)*)

The granting of facilities for parking a vehicle is excluded from exemption and, therefore, chargeable at the standard rate. However, in practice the Customs & Excise accept that where a garage (or other parking facility) is let in conjunction with domestic accommodation the letting of the garage will be exempt. To qualify for this treatment the garage must be part of the house, or alternatively the house and garage if let separately must be in close proximity to each other and let by the same landlord to the same tenant. The Customs & Excise will adhere strictly to this treatment, so that in *F Bondi* v *CCE*, LON/75/70 (*Casebook* **9.122**) the appellant failed to qualify for exemption as the supply was of parking facilities where he rented a garage close to his house, but from a different landlord from whom he rented the house.

GAME OR FISH (*exception (d)*)

The right to take game or fish is excluded from Group 1 and, therefore, taxable at the standard rate. Thus, the grant of a fishing licence is taxable. The Customs & Excise also regard leases or tenancies which have as their main purpose the enjoyment of sporting or fishing rights as standard-rated supplies even though no specific mention of the rights is included in the lease or tenancy. Thus, if a land-owner grants a lease of land to a fishing club which has access and use and enjoyment of fishing rights over a river running through the land, the supply would be standard rated and not exempt.

TIMBER (*exception (e)*)

The grant of a right to fell and remove standing timber is standard rated. The grant must be specifically to fell and remove timber. If a lease of land, with timber growing on it, is granted, the rent will be exempt. There is no need to apportion the rent of the land between the timber removed and the land (Notice No 701, p 65).

STORAGE OF AIRCRAFT OR SHIPS (*exception* (*f*))

The granting of facilities for housing or storage of aircraft, or for mooring or storing a ship, boat or vessel is excluded from exemption under Group 1. These supplies are, therefore, taxable at the standard rate, unless the facilities are the handling of ships or aircraft, or services supplied to a person in his business capacity who belongs outside the United Kingdom relating to the handling of the ship or aircraft, in which case the supplies will be zero-rated (see Sched 4, Group 10, item 6(*b*) or 12(*b*), **8.1000**).

It will be noted that this exception refers to the "granting of facilities" for, *inter alia*, mooring a boat. In *J W Fisher* v *CCE*, LON/75/47 (*Casebook* **9.123**) the Tribunal held that there was no distinction in the groups of exceptions between the use of the phrase "granting of any right" in paragraphs (*d*) and (*e*), and the "granting of facilities" in paragraphs (*b*), (*c*) and (*f*). Thus, the grant of a right to moor a boat amounted to the grant of facilities to moor it and was chargeable at the standard rate.

EXHIBITIONS FOR ADVERTISING OR DISPLAY (*exception* (*g*))

The provision to an exhibitor of a site or space at an exhibition, or similar event which is organised wholly or mainly for the advertisement of goods or services, is excluded from exemption under Group 1 and, therefore, chargeable at the standard rate. However, where the exhibition is not organised wholly or mainly for the display or advertisement of goods or services but is organised primarily for the supply by retail to persons attending the event, the supply is exempt, unless the exhibition is at an hotel, inn, boarding-house or similar establishment within exception (*a*). Examples of exempt supplies on the grant of a licence to use part of an exhibition hall are the annual Boat or Motor Shows.

9.200 Group 2: Insurance

Item No.
1. The provision of insurance and re-insurance by authorised insurers within the meaning of Section 2 to 9 of the Insurance Companies Act 1974.
2. The provision of insurance and re-insurance by the Export Credits Guarantee Department.
3. The making of arrangements for the provision of any insurance or re-insurance in items 1 and 2.
4. The handling of insurance claims by insurance brokers, insurance agents and authorised insurers as described in item 1.

Note: Item 4 does not include supplies by loss adjusters, average adjusters, motor assessors, surveyors, and other experts, and legal services, in connection with the assessment of any claim.

Item 1: Provision of insurance and re-insurance by authorised insurers

Item 1 exempts the provision of insurance and re-insurance by authorised insurers. The item was amended with effect from 1 January 1978 as previously the providers of the insurance did not have to be authorised. Authorisation under the Insurance Companies Act 1974 extends to companies authorised under s 3 of the Act (broadly speaking companies which carried on business before 3 November 1966 or have been authorised specifically by the Secretary of State to carry on insurance business), members of Lloyd's or other associations of underwriters approved by the Secretary of State, friendly societies or trade unions providing provident benefits or strike benefits.

The consideration for the supply of insurance is the premium payable by the insured, and it is therefore the premium that is exempt under this item.

Item 2: Provision of insurance and re-insurance by ECGD

The provision of insurance and re-insurance by the Export Credits Guarantee Department ("ECGD") is exempt. The ECGD is a government department but it aims to run its activities on a commercial basis and to make a profit. ECGD offers, *inter alia*, insurance to exporters and insures against the risk of the exporter not being paid, either because of default by the purchaser or through currency restrictions imposed in the purchaser's country. ECGD further offers insurance in relation to risks undertaken in opening new businesses abroad, for example, against risk of expropriation or war.

If the ECGD insurance cover relates to the export of goods outside the EEC its provision is zero-rated under Sched 4, Group 9, item 8(*a*) (see **10.100**).

Item 3: Arrangement of insurance within items 1 or 2

Item 3 exempts the making of arrangements for the provision of insurance within item 1 or item 2. The arrangements which fall within this item include insurance broking and insurance agency services. It must be remembered that the exemption in item 1 only now applies to authorised insurers, so that the arrangements must also be in relation to insurance provided by authorised insurers.

Arrangements, *prima facie* within this item, may be zero-rated, however, under Sched 4, Group 9 (see **10.100**).

Item 4: Claims

Under this item the handling of claims by insurance brokers, insurance agents and authorised insurers are exempt. The introduction of this item with effect from 1 January 1978 over-rules the decision in *National Transit Insurance Company Ltd* v *CCE*, [1975] STC 35 (*Casebook* **9.201**).

The services may qualify for zero-rating as opposed to exemption if they fall within Sched 4, Group 9, items 6(*d*) or 8(*b*) (see s 12(1) and **10.100**).

The item does not include supplies by loss adjusters, average adjusters, motor assessors, surveyors and other experts and legal services in connection with any claim. Further, such supplies cannot be zero-rated under Sched 4, Group 9, items 6(*d*) or 8(*b*), but may qualify for zero-rating under Group 9, items 5 or 6(*a*).

9.300 Group 3: Postal services

Item No.
   1. The conveyance of postal packets by the Post Office.
   2. The supply by the Post Office of any services in connection with the conveyance of postal packets.

Notes:
(1) "Postal packet" has the same meaning as in the Post Office Act 1953, except that it does not include a telegram.
(2) Item 2 does not include the supply of the service of the letting on hire of goods which supply would otherwise be a supply described therein.

Item 1: Postal packets

Item 1 exempts the conveyance of postal packets by the Post Office. Postal packet means, "a letter, postcard, reply postcard, newspaper, printed packet, sample packet, or parcel and every article transmissable by post", but does not include a telegram which is specifically excluded by Note (1). The postal packet must be conveyed by the Post Office if it is to be exempt.

The consideration for the conveyance of postal packets is the stamps required on the packet: accordingly the supply of new stamps is exempt. Thus, unused current valid stamps are exempt from VAT if bought at face value as would be the case where stamps are bought from the post office to affix to a letter. Where unused current valid stamps are bought for more than their face value, for example, when sold by a stamp-dealer, VAT is chargeable on the excess over the face value (see VAT Leaflet

701/8/79 (Postage stamps and philatelic supplies)). All other stamps, for example, used stamps or unused stamps which are no longer valid, are chargeable to VAT at the standard rate, unless they are over one hundred years old and qualify for the special scheme relating to antiques (see **16.100**). Where a person supplies goods and the price includes a charge for postage and packing, VAT is chargeable on the full price, inclusive of postage and packing (*Mr and Mrs W H G Swinger* v *CCE*, LON/77/127 (*Casebook* **9.301**)).

Where first day covers are supplied, the Customs & Excise takes the view that the whole of the supply, ie the cover, stamps and post-mark, is liable to VAT at the standard rate.

It will be noted that telephones, telex and similar services are not exempt from VAT. The reason for not including telecommunication services within the exemption was stated by the Chief Secretary to the Treasury (Mr Patrick Jenkin) at the Committee Stage of the Finance Bill 1972 to be because of the huge capital investment programme in the telecommunications side of the Post Office which would bear VAT. If telecommunications were exempt, therefore, there would be a large hidden tax charge as the industry would be unable to recover the VAT on construction costs. On the postal side, however, there was small capital investment (some £3 million) so that the postal side could absorb the VAT on its inputs without substantially increasing the cost to the consumer (see Hansard, Vol 837, Col 438).

Item 2: Services in connection with postal packets

Item 2 exempts the supply of services by the Post Office in connection with the conveyance of postal packets. In Notice No 701, p 68 the Customs & Excise give the following list of services they regard as being within item 2 and services outside item 2, by way of example:

Exempt	*Standard Rate*
Business reply services	The impression by the Inland Revenue and HMSO of postage stamps on customers' own material
Cash on delivery services	
Customs clearance of imported postal packets	Printed postage impression services
Express services	
Reply coupon services	Printing performed by private printers for users of the service
Late posted packets services	
Postage forward parcel services	Sales of stationery
Post Office services in respect of railway letters and parcels, and airway letters	

Exempt	*Standard Rate*
Postage services to users of franking machines	Philatelic services (see also the VAT Leaflet entitled "Postage stamps")
Private boxes and bags services	
Railex services	Postmarking (where a separate fee is charged)
Recorded delivery services	
Registration services for letters and parcels	The hire of any goods
Selectapost services	
Special delivery services	

9.400 Group 4: Betting, gaming and lotteries

Item No.
1. The provision of any facilities for the placing of bets or the playing of any games of chance.
2. The granting of a right to take part in a lottery.

Notes:
(1) Item 1 does not include—
    (*a*) admission to any premises; or
    (*b*) the granting of a right to take part in a game in respect of which a charge may be made by virtue of regulations under Section 14 of the Gaming Act 1968; or
    (*c*) the provision by a club of such facilities to its members as are available to them on payment of their subscription but without further charge: or
    (*d*) the provision of a gaming machine.
(2) "Game of Chance" has the same meaning as in the Gaming Act 1968.
(3) "Lottery" includes any competition for prizes which is authorised by a licence under the Pool Competitions Act 1971.
(4) "Gaming machine" means a machine in respect of which the following conditions are satisfied, namely—
    (*a*) it is constructed or adapted for playing a game of chance by means of it; and
    (*b*) a player pays to play the machine (except where he has an opportunity to play payment-free as the result of having previously played successfully), either by inserting a coin or token into the machine or in some other way; and
    (*c*) the element of chance in the game is provided by means of the machine.

Item 1: Placing of bets or games of chance

GENERAL

The provision of any facilities for the placing of bets or the playing of games of chance is an exempt supply. A game of chance is defined for this purpose in the Gaming Act 1968, s 52(1) as:

> "'game of chance' does not include any athletic game or sport, but, with that exception, and subject to sub-section (b) of this section, includes a game of chance and skill combined and a pretended game of chance or of chance and skill combined"

and sub s (b) states,

> "In determining for the purposes of this Act whether a game, which is played otherwise than against one or more other players is a game of chance and skill combined, the possibility of superlative skill eliminating the element of chance shall be disregarded."

An example of a game of chance is bingo. "Spot-the-ball" competitions used to be exempt but the Customs & Excise has indicated that "spot-the-ball" competitions will no longer be treated as games of chance with effect from 1 July 1979.

Furthermore, in *W and D Grantham* v *CCE*, MAN/79/102 (*Casebook* **9.403**) it was held that a shooting gallery at a fun-fair constituted a game of chance and the price for an attempt was exempt. The case should not be taken as a general authority for exempting similar games as the facts in the case were rather special. In particular, the whole of the bulls-eye had to be removed before a winning score could be achieved, which meant shooting four bulls-eyes in a tight group. In tests expert marksmen had considerable difficulty obtaining a winning score.

EXCEPTIONS TO ITEM 1

Admission fees: The payment of an admission fee to premises to take part in betting or gaming activities is chargeable at the standard rate. Thus, where a separate entrance fee is charged it is not exempt (*Fakenham Conservative Association Bingo Club* v *CCE*, LON/S/73/164 (*Casebook* **9.401**)). Where a higher entrance fee was charged to bingo players when additional entertainment was provided the High Court remitted the case to the Tribunal for a specific finding of fact to be made as to whether or not the additional charge was an admission fee (*Tynewydd Labour Working Men's Club and Institute Ltd* v *CCE*, [1979] STC 570 (*Casebook* **9.402**)).

Participation fees: Where a club is registered or premises are licensed under the Gaming Act 1968, Pt II they may charge a participation fee to potential gamblers. Such fees are excluded from item 1 and are chargeable at the standard rate. For a case in which the Tribunal accordingly refused to exempt participation fees, see *Fakenham Conservative Association Bingo Club* v *CCE* (*Casebook* **9.401**).

Membership subscription to gaming clubs: If a person is charged a membership subscription to a club which only provides facilities for the placing of bets or playing of games of chance and is able to participate in the club's activities without further payment, the subscription will be chargeable to VAT at the standard rate.

Gaming machine: The provision of the facilities of gaming machines used to be exempt, but was made a taxable supply of services by F (No 2) A 1975, s 21 with effect from 1 November 1975. The value of the supply is the total takings from the machine after payment of winnings. No other deductions are allowed before calculation of the VAT payable. Gaming machine is defined in Group 4, Note (4) as being a machine which is constructed for playing a game of chance and the player pays to play either by coin or token. The type of machine within the provision includes fruit machines, pin-ball machines and similar games found in amusement arcades.

The person making the supply is the proprietor of the premises on which the gaming machine is located, for example, a publican or club. The receipts from the machines will form part of the business's taxable supplies. Further details in relation to gaming machines are given in VAT Leaflet 9/78/VAH (VAT on Gaming Machine Takings) ; see also **16.1000**, *post*.

Item 2: Lotteries

The grant of a right to take part in a lottery is an exempt supply. A lottery includes competitions for prizes organised under the Pools Competitions Act 1971. Lottery tickets sold by local authorities to the public are included in this item.

9.500 Group 5: Finance

Item No.
1. The issue, transfer or receipt of, or any dealing with, money, any security for money or any note or order for the payment of money.
2. (*a*) The making of any advance or the granting of any credit.
   (*b*) The provision of the facility of instalment credit finance in a hire-purchase, conditional sale or credit sale agreement for which facility a separate charge is made and disclosed to the recipient of the supply of goods.
   (*c*) The provision of administrative arrangements and documentation and the transfer of title to the goods in connection with the supply described in Item 2(*b*) if the total consideration therefore is specified in the agreement and does not exceed £10.
3. The making of arrangements for any transaction comprised in Item 1 or 2.
4. The issue, transfer or receipt of, or any dealing with, any security or secondary security within the definition in Section 42 of the Exchange Control Act 1947.
5. The operation of any current, deposit or savings account.

> *Notes:*
> (1) Item 1 does not include anything included in Item 4.
> (2) This Group does not include the supply of a coin (other than a gold coin which is legal tender in its place of issue) or a banknote as a collectors' piece or as an investment article.
> (3) Item 2(*a*) includes the supply of credit by a person, in connection with a supply of goods or services by him, for which a separate charge is made and disclosed to the recipient of the supply of goods or services.

Item 1: Money transactions

Item 1 exempts the issue, transfer or receipt of, or any dealing with, money, any security for money or any note or order for the payment of money. The item includes the issue of money, dealings in foreign currency (s 46(1)), the issue and discounting of bills of exchange and dealings in commercial bills. Other examples of transactions exempt under item 1 are given in Notice No 701, p 72, as:

> "assignment of debts and the issue of certain bonds, guarantees, and indemnities provided by financial institutions and other commercial undertakings as securities for money. The exemption applies only to a guarantee etc given by a person which is secondary to a contract between two other persons and is a contract of security issued by the guarantor or surety obliging him to pay money to make good, or contribute to, any loss arising from the failure or default of the primary contract."

The services of underwriters are not regarded by the Customs & Excise as financial services within Group 5, so that where a share issue is underwritten, the underwriter's services are not exempt.

Money does not include coins (other than gold coins which are legal tender where issued) or banknotes sold as collector's items or for investment purposes (Note (2)).

The meaning of the phrase "any dealing with money" was considered by the Tribunal in *Williams and Glyn's Bank Ltd* v *CCE*, [1974] VATTR 262 (*Casebook* **9.501**) where the Tribunal held that the expression required the relevant service to have the characteristics of a financial transaction. In the *Williams & Glyn's* case the subject matter of the appeal was the provision of security services supplied to the bank for the transport of money. Applying the above test the Tribunal held that the services were not "any dealing with money".

It will be noted that item 1 does not include any item which falls within item 4 (Note (1)). For more detailed consideration of this point see item 4, *post*.

Item 2: Advances, credit and ancillary matters

The granting of credit is an exempt transaction whether by means of direct loan or advance, or by means of deferred payment. Instalment credit is also exempt, where, for example, the sale is by way of hire-purchase, credit sale or conditional sale providing the charge for the credit is made separately. If the charge for credit is not made separately, the supply is not exempt, therefore, and the whole supply is taxable. Further, where title to goods is transferred under a hire-purchase, credit sale or conditional sale agreement, the fee paid for such transfer of title is exempt if paid under terms in the agreement and the amount is less than £10 (item 2(*c*)).

It is not always obvious that an exempt supply within this item is being made as was discovered by the appellants in *Hedges and Mercer* v *CCE*, [1976] VATTR 146 (*Casebook* **9.505**). The appellants were solicitors and placed clients' money on general deposit at the bank. The interest on undesignated client's accounts accrues for the benefit of solicitors (there are special rules that apply where a substantial sum of money is being held for a particular client for a length of time—usually in excess of one month—so that the interest accrues for the benefit of the client) and the Customs & Excise maintained that the interest represented exempt supplies. The Tribunal held that it was part of the solicitors' business to receive client money and accordingly exempt supplies were made. The effect of the decision was to restrict the partnership's input tax relief. Such supplies are now usually ignored in making any partial exemption calculation (see VAT (General) Regulations 1977 (SI 1977 No 1759), reg 68(1), (4) and the statement in the *Law Society's Gazette*, 8 February 1978 at p 130).

Item 3: Arranging transactions in item 1 or item 2

This item exempts the arranging of transactions within Group 5, item 1 or item 2. Thus, mortgage brokers' fees are exempt under this item, as are commissions paid by building societies to agents for the introduction of customers' funds. Item 3 specifically does not cover the making of arrangements for transactions within item 4 so that UK managers of UK bond issues must charge VAT on their fees. The provision of cheque clearing facilities was held in *The British Hardware Federation* v *CCE*, [1975] VATTR 172 (*Casebook* **9.502**) to be exempt as financial transactions where the Federation received interest on cheques deposited with it, against payment by it of several bills of the depositor.

To fall within item 3 the arrangements must be closely associated to a financial transaction within item 1. Thus, in the *Williams & Glyn's* case (see item 1, *ante*) security services were not within item 3 as they did not themselves have the characteristics of a financial transaction.

Item 4: Securities and secondary securities

This item exempts the issue, transfer or receipt of, or any dealing with securities or secondary securities within the Exchange Control Act 1947, s 42. Because item 3, relating to the arrangements of transactions within item 1 or item 2, does not apply to transactions within item 4, it is important to understand the difference between securities and secondary securities within item 4 and securities for money within item 1.

Item 4 only applies to securities or secondary securities within the Exchange Control Act 1947, s 42 which defines "security" as:

"shares, stocks, bonds, notes (other than promissory notes), debentures, debenture stock, units under a unit trust scheme and shares in an oil royalty."

and "secondary security" as:

"any letter of allotment which may be renounced, any letter of rights, any warrant conferring an option to acquire a security any deposit certificates in respect of securities (but not including a receipt by an authorised depository for any certificates of title pursuant to this part of this Act), and any such other documents conferring, or containing evidence of, rights as may be prescribed."

The meaning of "security" in item 1 and item 4 was considered by the Tribunal in *Dyrham Park Country Club* v *CCE*, LON/78/284 (*Casebook* **9.503**) where, on joining the club, members were required to subscribe for an amount of bonds in a limited company. The club maintained that the bonds were exempt either under item 1 or item 4. The Tribunal commented that the word "security" in item 1 did not mean a document which gave a charge on specific property but was used in item 1 in the same context as in the Moneylenders Act 1927, s 1(3)(c).

The Tribunal stated:

"in our view 'security for money' in Schedule 5 Item 1 means a document under seal or under hand at a consideration containing a covenant, promise or undertaking to pay a sum of money. In our view a document to be a 'security for money' does not have to be either 'marketable' or 'transferable' or 'negotiable'."

The Tribunal concluded in *Dyrham Park Country Club* v *CCE* that bonds were, therefore, not within item 1 but within item 4.

As stated, item 3 (arranging transactions within item 1 or item 2) does not apply to item 4, so that in *CCE* v *Guy Butler* (*International*) Ltd, [1976] STC 254 (*Casebook* **9.507**) the arranging of a loan secured by a certificate of deposit by the appellants, a firm of money brokers, was not exempt as the service provided related to the arrangement of a transaction within item 4.

A fuller example of a situation where item 3 would not exempt the arranging of financial transactions is the managing or underwriting of a Eurobond issue. The manager or underwriter in the United Kingdom would be providing services in connection with the issue of the bonds.

Since the bonds would be within item 4 the manager or underwriter would charge VAT on his respective fees. It may be that the issue is by a non-resident in which case the manager or underwriter's services may be zero-rated under Sched 4, Group 9, items 5 or 6 (see **16.600**).

Item 5: Bank accounts

Item 5 exempts the operation of a current, deposit or savings account and includes services normally supplied by banks in relation thereto.

It should be noted that the British Bankers Association has reached agreement with the Customs & Excise aş to the rate of tax applicable to various services supplied by member banks and have also negotiated a special method of calculating the amount of input tax relief available where partially exempt supplies are made.

Finally, it is useful to note that in Notice No 701 the Customs & Excise list the following services as not being financial services within this Group, and, therefore, as not being exempt:

Account preparation services and data processing.

Debt collection, credit control and sales ledger accounting services.

Equipment leasing.

Executor and trustee services and the administration of estates.

Investment, finance and taxation advice.

Management consultancy.

Management of trust funds.

Merger and takeover advice.

Nominee services.

Paying agents' services.

Portfolio management.

Registrar services.

Safe custody services.

Service companies' activities—administration, payment of salaries and wages etc.

Underwriting services.

9.600 Group 6: Education

Item No.

1. The provision of education by a school or university.
2. The provision, otherwise than for profit, of—

   (*a*) education if it is of a kind provided by a school or university; or
   (*b*) training or re-training for any trade, profession or employment.
3. Private tuition, in subjects (except those of a recreational or sporting nature) which are normally taught in the course of education provided by a school or university, to an individual pupil by a teacher acting independently of any employer or organisation.
4. The supply of any goods or services incidental to the provision of any education, training or re-training comprised in Items 1 and 2.
5. The provision of any instruction supplemental to the provision of any education comprised in Items 1 and 2.
6. The provision by a youth club of the facilities available to its members.

Notes:
(1) "Education" includes training in any form of art.
(2) "School" in Items 1, 2 and 3 means an institution which, within the meaning of the Education Acts 1944 to 1976, the Education (Scotland) Acts 1939 to 1976 or the Education and Libraries (Northern Ireland) Orders 1972 and 1976, provides primary or secondary education or both, and which—
    (a) within the meaning of the aforesaid legislation, either is provisionally, finally or deemed to be registered as a school in a register of independent schools or is a school in respect of which grants are made by the appropriate Secretary of State to the proprietor or managers of that school; or
    (b) is a voluntary school within the meaning of the Education Act 1944 or the Education and Libraries (Northern Ireland) Orders 1972 and 1976.
(3) "University" means a United Kingdom university and includes any college, institution, school or hall of such a university.
(4) Paragraph (a) of Item 2 does not include recreational or sporting activities except when provided as part of a general educational curriculum.
(5) Item 4 applies only where the supplies described therein are made to the persons receiving the education, training or re-training comprised in Items 1 and 2, by the same person who provides them with that education, training or re-training.
(6) Item 5 applies only where the instruction described therein is provided to persons receiving education comprised in Items 1 and 2 by the same person who provides them with that education.

General

In items 1 and 2 the provision of education relates to the provision by independent schools, as opposed to local authority schools and universities. Local authority schools are not covered in Group 6 as the provision of education in local authority schools is not regarded as a business for VAT purposes. Since local authorities are not carrying on a business for VAT purposes when they provide education they do not charge VAT on the provision of education. However, the local authority schools will have to pay VAT on supplies made to them, and in order to avoid the local authorities being unable to recover the VAT paid on supplies to, *inter alia*, schools, special provision is made in s 15 to enable local authorities and other similar bodies to recover input tax in respect of non-business activities. Further consideration of local authorities generally is given in **15.300.** Section 15 is discussed in **5.100.** There is no obligation on the part of the local authority to ensure that refunds of VAT made to local authorities, in respect of VAT on supplies to schools, are used for the benefit of schools or education generally. Similarly, colleges of education and further education establishments run by local authorities are not within Group 6 as they do not constitute business activities by the local authority.

School

For the purposes of Group 6 the school must be registered under the Education Acts or be a voluntary school within the meaning of the Education Acts. This is provided for in Group 6, Note (2) which overrules in part *E Greene* v *CCE*, [1974] VATTR 279 (*Casebook* **6.601**), and *D B Vernon* v *CCE*, LON/75/169 (*Casebook* **6.602**).

The Customs & Excise has expressed the view in Notice No 701 that the facilities offered by the following institutions are not exempt:

> "commercial language, management, marketing, computer, business, secretarial, motor, dancing, sports, riding and similar schools or to correspondence colleges, unless exceptionally they come within the scope of Item 2 of the Group."

University

University means a United Kingdom university and includes any college, institution, school or hall of such a university. The definition does not extend to colleges of education generally as the reference in the definition is qualified to apply to colleges which form a part of a university, for example one of the colleges forming a part of Oxford or Cambridge University. Colleges of further education will normally be administered by local authorities and are not within Group 6 as the local authority is not regarded as carrying on a business when it supplies educational facilities (see under *General, ante*).

Education

The school must provide full-time primary or secondary education to pupils who have not attained the age of 19 years. In *E Greene* v *CCE*, [1974] VATTR 279 (*Casebook* **9.601**) it was held that full-time education meant more than mere academic study and included the provision of spiritual, moral and physical development too. It should be noted that the *Greene* case has been partly overruled as it is now a requirement that the school is registered or voluntary registered; this requirement being introduced by the VAT (Education) Order 1976 (SI 1976 No 2024) which amended Group 6, Note (2), with effect from 1 April 1977.

Education includes training in any form of art.

Item 1: The provision of education by a school or university

As stated under *General, ante* the schools referred to in item 1 are independent schools. Universities are also exempt. The meaning of education is considered above under *Education, ante*.

Item 2: The provision of education otherwise than for profit

Item 2 exempts the provision of education otherwise than for profit where the education is provided by a school or university or where the education is training or re-training for any trade, profession or employment. In both cases the education must not be provided for a profit. The Customs & Excise takes the view that, for the purpose of determining whether the education is provided for profit, it is the overall status of the institution supplying the education that matters and not the financial arrangements. Thus, the exemption is aimed at the provision of education by charities and other bodies who are not able to distribute profits. Further, the Customs & Excise has recently revised their practice and, in addition, now maintains that the bodies concerned must demonstrate their non-profit making status by reference to outside funding, which funding must be unconditional (see VAT Notes 1980/81, para 10). However, it is the Authors' view that the Customs & Excise interpretation of the expression "otherwise than for profit" is unnecessarily restrictive.

Item 3: Private tuition

Where a teacher, acting independently of his employer, provides tuition to an individual pupil on a subject which is normally taught in schools or universities the supply is an exempt supply. Recreational or sporting activities are, however, specifically excluded from this item. The exemption does not apply if there is more than one pupil being taught at a particular time, for example, if a group of pupils are taken for private tuition together.

There is no definition of teacher for the purpose of this item but it is the Authors' view that the exemption only applies to a person who is employed as a teacher and who gives private tuition in his free time. Where an individual outside the teaching profession gives private coaching the fees would, by analogy with *Dr A R Evans* v *CCE*, [1976] VATTR 175 (*Casebook* **9.702**) be liable to VAT. In the *Evans* case the appellant was an acupuncturist as well as a qualified nurse. In supplying treatment as an acupuncturist he was not acting as a qualified nurse and his supplies were, therefore, not exempt under Group 7.

Item 4: Incidental supplies

The supply of any goods or services incidental to the provision of education, training or re-training in items 1 or 2 is exempt. However, the supplies are only exempt if made to the recipient of the education by the person supplying the education as well (see Note (5)). In its original form it was possible for the supplies to be by some person other than the provider of the education. Thus, in *J McMurray (a Governor of Allen*

Hall) v *CCE*, [1973] VATTR 161 (*Casebook* **9.606**) the Tribunal allowed an appeal by the Hall and held that the supplies by a hall of residence at a university were incidental to the provision of education. The *McMurray* case has been reversed on its facts by Group 6, Note (5). It was also possible for the supply originally to be to persons other than the recipient of the education (see *R A Archer* (*No 2*) v *CCE*, [1975] VATTR 1 (*Casebook* **9.603**)—the provision of car parking facilities to a lecture, which has also now been reversed on its facts by Note (5)).

Although the cases of *McMurray* and *Archer* have been reversed on their facts, the facilities provided, namely a hall of residence and car parking respectively, could still amount to incidental services for the purposes of item 4 if provided by the person supplying the education to the pupils or students.

In Notice No 701 the Customs & Excise states that catering supplied by outside caterers to students is taxable unless supplied as agent for the educational establishment. This view would correctly follow from *Woodard Schools* (*Midland Division*) *Ltd* v *CCE*, [1975] VATTR 123 (*Casebook* **9.604**), where it was held that the supply of clothes from a school shop was not incidental to the provision of education. The provision of meals to staff is not strictly speaking, exempt in the light of Note (5) but the Customs & Excise has recently introduced a concession whereby the catering supplied to staff or visitors may be exempted where staff and visitors use the same dining facilities as students and it is not possible to differentiate between the two classes of user at the time of supply (see VAT Notes 1980/81, para 11).

Item 5: Supplemental instruction

The provision of any instruction which is supplemental to the provision of education in items 1 or 2 is exempt. However, the supplemental education must be supplied by the person providing the education and be supplied to the persons receiving the education. The type of supplementary instruction included in this item is music lessons or sporting activities which complement and form a part of the total education.

Item 6: Youth clubs

The provision by a youth club of facilities to its members is an exempt supply. There is no definition of "youth club" but the Customs & Excise regard a club as being a youth club if it is "a non-profit making organisation, whose rules restrict membership to young people below the age of twenty and which provides a programme of cultural and recreational activity suitable for the requirements of such young persons" (Notice No 701, p 77).

9.700 Group 7: Health

Item No.
1. The supply of services and, in connection with it, the supply of goods, by a person registered or enrolled in any of the following:
   (a) the register of medical practitioners or the register of medical practitioners with limited registration;
   (b) the dentists' register;
   (c) either of the registers of ophthalmic opticians or the register of dispensing opticians kept under the Opticians Act 1958 or either of the lists kept under Section 4 of that Act of bodies corporate carrying on business as ophthalmic opticians or as dispensing opticians;
   (d) any register kept under the Professions Supplementary to Medicine Act 1960;
   (e) the register of nurses or the roll of nurses maintained in pursuance of Section 2(1) of the Nurses Act 1957 or kept under Section 2 or Section 3 of the Nurses (Scotland) Act 1951 or Section 17(1) of the Nurses and Midwives Act (Northern Ireland) 1970;
   (f) the roll of certified midwives kept under Section 2 of the Midwives Act 1951, Section 3 of the Midwives (Scotland) Act 1951 or Section 17(1) of the Nurses and Midwives Act (Northern Ireland) 1970;
   (g) any roll of ancillary dental workers established under Section 41 of the Dentists Act 1957;
   (h) the register of dispensers of hearing aids or the register of persons employing such dispensers maintained under Section 2 of the Hearing Aid Council Act 1968.
2. The supply of any goods or services by a dental technician.
3. The supply of any services by a person registered in the register of pharmaceutical chemists kept under the Pharmacy Act 1954 or the Pharmacy and Poisons Act (Northern Ireland) 1925.
4. The provision of care or medical or surgical treatment and, in connection with it, the supply of any goods, in any hospital or other institution approved, licensed, registered or exempted from registration by any Minister or other authority.
5. The provision of a deputy for a person registered in the register of medical practitioners or the register of medical practitioners with limited registration.

Notes:
(1) Item 1 does not include the supply of the service of the letting on hire of goods other than such a supply which is in connection with a supply of other services comprised in the item.
(2) For the purposes of this Group a person, who is not registered in the visiting EEC practitioners list in the register of medical practitioners at the time he performs services in an urgent case as mentioned in paragraph (3) of Article 7 of the Medical Qualifications (EEC Recognition) Order 1977, is to be treated as being registered in that list where he is entitled to be registered in accordance with that Article.
(3) Item 3 does not include the supply of the service of the letting on hire of goods.
(4) For the purposes of this Group a person to whom paragraph 2 of Schedule 5 to the Medical Act 1978 applies is to be treated as being a fully registered medical practitioner while he continues to be so treated by virtue of that paragraph.
(5) Item 1 (a) to (g) includes supplies made by a person who is not registered or enrolled in any of the registers or rolls therein specified where the services are wholly performed or directly supervised by a person who is so registered or enrolled.

General

Broadly speaking Group 7 is aimed at exempting from VAT medical and other similar services and medical goods in connection with the supply of such services. The intention of Parliament in relation to health matters generally was to give relief from tax to the sick and disabled. This is done by zero-rating the supply of medicines and medical goods (see **8.1400**) and by exempting the services of the medical profession and supplies of medical goods in connection with that service. The patient receiving drugs etc on prescription pays no VAT as the drugs are zero-rated. Where a patient attends a hospital, either as an in-patient or an out-patient and is fitted with a medical appliance, the supply of both services and the appliance is exempt so that the patient, again, pays no VAT. So far as hospitals and clinics are concerned the vast majority of patients obtain medical advice and appliances under the National Health Service. Some supplies (for example, blankets for use in local authority welfare institutions) are supplied direct by local authorities and no VAT is chargeable on those supplies made by them as these activities do not constitute a business for VAT purposes. The position is analogous with education provided by local authority schools and colleges of education (see Group 6, *ante*). The local authority is able to reclaim VAT on supplies to it under s 15 since the activity of providing such articles is a non-business activity. Hospitals and clinics themselves pay VAT on the supply to them of drugs by manufacturers and because supplies made by the hospitals themselves are exempt, the hospitals must absorb the VAT payable on the supplies to them. Under the National Health Service a statutory charge is sometimes levied on certain items but the charge is not subject to VAT as it is not technically a consideration for a taxable supply. For further consideration of the intention of Parliament in exempting health services see the Committee Stage of the Finance Bill 1972, Hansard Vol 837, col 336, *et seq.*

Item 1: Supply of services and goods by registered persons

Item 1 exempts the supply of services, and in connection with it, the supply of goods, by persons registered or enrolled in the registers listed at item 1 (*a*)–(*h*). The exemption relates principally to the supply of services by such persons and the supply of drugs, dressings and medical appliances in connection with the supply of those services.

The exemption applies whether the services are provided by a registered person himself or by a person who is supervised by a registered person (Note 5). Thus, where a company provides medical services through its staff, who are registered persons themselves, the supply is an exempt supply. Thus, the decision in the case of *Harlow Industrial*

Health Service Ltd v *CCE*, [1974] VATTR 30 (*Casebook* **9.701**) has been reversed on its facts by Note (5) (introduced by the VAT (Medical Goods and Services) Order 1979 (SI 1979 No 246) with effect from 2 April 1979). In the *Harlow Industrial Health Service Ltd* case the appellant company was held not to be making exempt supplies in respect of the services of doctors employed by it, who provided the medical services; as stated the case has been reversed on its facts by Note (5).

The supply of medical and other listed services is exempt provided the person is acting in his qualified registered profession when he provides the services. Thus, in *Dr A R Evans* v *CCE*, [1976] VATTR 175 (*Casebook* **9.702**) the appellant, who was a registered nurse, was held not to be making exempt supplies when he acted as an acupuncturist. Accordingly, the acupuncturist services were standard-rated.

The supply of any goods by a registered person must be in connection with the supply of services. The supply by a dentist, therefore, of dental equipment generally to other dentists failed to qualify for exemption (*A W Roberts* v *CCE*, LON/76/175 (*Casebook* **9.703**)).

Note (1) excludes the letting of goods on hire from item 1, unless the hiring is in connection with the supply of other services which are exempt under item 1. The reason for this exclusion in Note (1) is that the letting of goods on hire is a supply of services for VAT purposes (Sched 2, para 1) so that without the note any lease of goods (including those not connected with medical matters) granted by a registered person would be exempt. A similar restriction is made in respect of item 3.

Item 2: Dental technicians

The supply of any goods or services by a dental technician is an exempt supply.

Item 3: Pharmaceutical chemists

The supply of the services of registered pharmaceutical chemists is an exempt supply. The exemption applies to activities which do not form part of the chemist's trading activities, for example, to analytical services. Drugs supplied by registered chemists on a medical prescription are zero-rated under Sched 4, Group 14 (see **8.1400**).

Item 4: Provision of care in hospitals and approved institutions

The provision of care or medical or surgical treatment in a hospital or other institution approved, licensed, registered or exempt from registration by a Minister or other authority is an exempt supply. The supply of any goods in connection with the supply of such treatment is also exempt. It was held, *obiter dicta*, in *Mrs M Payton* v *CCE*, [1974] VATTR 140 (*Casebook* **9.707**) that a surgical belt fitted by a consultant at a hospital was the supply of goods in connection with the provision of medical care.

The care must be provided by a registered person. This is a strict requirement and failure to register will be a bar to exemption (see *Dr J Ambrosio* (*trading as Branksome Acupuncture Clinic*) v *CCE*, BIR/73/1 (*Casebook* **9.708**) and *Huntley Hair Transplant Ltd* v *CCE*, LON/77/414 (*Casebook* **9.709**)). In the latter case the appellant was only granted exemption from the date of its registration under the Nursing Homes Act 1975.

The meaning of the expression "provision of care" was considered by the Tribunal in *Crothall and Co Ltd* v *CCE*, [1973] VATTR 20 (*Casebook* **9.706**) where the Tribunal commented that the provision of care related to services.

> "which directly contribute to the welfare of a patient but not ... services (such as cleaning) which only indirectly so contribute."

The provision of care must, therefore, be directly related to the welfare of the patient, for example, ward-duties carried out by nursing staff.

Item 5: Deputies

Where a deputy provides the services of a registered medical practitioner the services are exempt. This item was added by the VAT (Medical Goods and Services) Order 1979 (SI 1979 No 246) with effect from 2 April 1979.

9.800 Group 8: Burial and cremation

Item No.
1. The disposal of the remains of the dead.
2. The making of arrangements for or in connection with the disposal of the remains of the dead.

Group 8 exempts the services of undertakers in connection with the burial or cremation of the dead. The exemption extends to the supply of the coffin by the undertakers and the provision of a hearse to take the coffin to the place of disposal. It is not the practice of the Customs & Excise to extend the exemption to the provision of flowers; normally flowers would be supplied by florists at the request of friends and relations of the deceased and would be taxable at the standard rate. If it is necessary to remove and replace a tombstone as part of the burial the new tombstone would be exempt, for example, if a second body was to be placed in a family grave. Normally tombstones and memorials are charged at the standard rate.

Supplies made to undertakers do not fall within the exemption, unless the undertaker has completely sub-contracted the funeral arrangements to another undertaker.

The view of the Customs & Excise is that "the dead" in Group 8 only applies to human beings and not animals.

9.900 Group 9: Trade unions and professional bodies

Item No.

1. The supply to its members of such services and, in connection with those services, of such goods as are both referable only to its aims and available without payment other than a membership subscription by any of the following non-profit making organisations:

   (*a*) a trade union or other organisation of persons having as its main object the negotiation on behalf of its members of the terms and conditions of their employment;

   (*b*) a professional association, membership of which is wholly or mainly restricted to individuals who have or are seeking a qualification appropriate to the practice of the profession concerned;

   (*c*) an association, the primary purpose of which is the advancement of a particular branch of knowledge, or the fostering of professional expertise, connected with the past or present professions or employments of its members;

   (*d*) an association, the primary purpose of which is to make representations to the Government on legislation and other public matters which affect the business or professional interests of its members.

Notes:
(1) Item 1 does not include any right of admission to any premises event or performance, to which non-members are admitted for a consideration.
(2) "Trade Union" has the meaning ascribed in Section 28(1) of the Trade Union and Labour Relations Act 1974.
(3) Item 1 shall include organisations and associations the membership of which consists wholly or mainly of constituent or affiliated associations which as individual associations would be comprised in the item and "member" shall be construed; as including such an association and "membership subscription" shall include an affiliation fee or similar levy.
(4) Paragraph (*c*) does not apply unless the association restricts its membership wholly or mainly to individuals whose present or previous professions or employments are directly connected with the purposes of the association.
(5) Paragraph (*d*) does not apply unless the association restricts its membership wholly or mainly to individuals or corporate bodies whose business or professional interests are directly connected with the purposes of the association.

General

This Group was introduced as a result of the EEC Sixth Directive. Its aim is to exempt services (and goods supplied in connection with the service) supplied by trade union and professional bodies.

Services and goods supplied to members in connection with services, are exempt when supplied by the bodies described under the sub-headings, *post*. The supply of services and goods must both be available without payment other than a subscription for membership and the body supplying the services must be non-profit making. The phrase "non-profit making" is not defined but was regarded by the Customs & Excise as having the same meaning as "otherwise than for profit" in Group 6, item 2 (Education), namely that the body, is not able, under its constitution, to distribute funds to members. However, the Customs & Excise has recently reviewed its practice in relation to Group 6 (see **9.600**) and it is not clear yet how the Customs & Excise will treat bodies seeking exemption under Group 9, in the light of that revision. It is the author's view, however, that "non-profit making" in Group 9, item 1 should be given its normal meaning. The body should, therefore, be able to make a profit and use that profit by ploughing it back for the use of members in a similar way to mutual trading and still be regarded as "non-profit making". The supply of goods and services must be referable to the body's aims. The exemption does not cover the admission to premises for which non-members are charged an admission fee. If there is an element of admission charge in the subscription, the subscription must be apportioned between the exempt supplies (not attributable to admission fees) and the taxable supplies (admission fees).

The bodies of persons whose services and goods supplied in connection with those services, are exempt are set out under the sub-headings, *post*.

Trade unions and similar bodies

The actual wording of item 1(*a*) is:

> "a trade union or other organisation of persons having as its main object the negotiation on behalf of its members of the terms and conditions of their employment."

The expression "trade union" is defined in the Trade Union and Labour Relations Act 1974, s 28(1), as meaning an organisation (whether permanent or temporary) which either:

> "(*a*) consists wholly or mainly of workers of one or more descriptions and is an organisation whose principal purposes include the regulation of relations between workers of that description or those descriptions and employers or employers' association; or

(*b*) consists wholly or mainly of—
    (i) constituent or affiliated organisations which fulfil the conditions specified in paragraph (*a*) above (or themselves consist wholly or mainly of constituent or affiliated organisations which fulfil those conditions); or
    (ii) representatives of such constituent or affiliated organisations;

and in either case is an organisation whose principal purposes include the regulation of relations between workers and employers or between workers' and employers' associations, or include the regulation of relations between its constituent or affiliated organisations."

An "employers' association" means an organisation (whether temporary or permanent) which either:

"(*a*) consists wholly or mainly of employers or individual proprietors of one or more descriptions and is an organisation whose principal purposes include the regulation of relations between employers of that description or those descriptions and workers or trade unions; or
(*b*) consists wholly or mainly of—

    (i) constituent or affiliated organisations which fulfil the conditions specified in paragraph (*a*) above (or themselves consist wholly or mainly of constituent or affiliated organisations which fulfil those conditions); or
    (ii) representatives or such constituent or affiliated organisations;

and in either case is an organisation whose principal purposes include the regulation of relations between employers and workers or between employers and trade unions, or include the regulation of relations between its constituent or affiliated organisations."

Group 9, Note (3) enables organisations whose membership consists wholly or mainly of constituent or affiliated associations to benefit from the exemption, where the constituent or affiliated associations would themselves be eligible to benefit under item 1.

An example of a similar body to a trade union for the purpose of this part of item 1, is the "Police Federation" which represents policemen in negotiations with their employers. The Police Federation is not a union as policemen are, by law, prohibited from joining a trade union.

Professional associations

The services, and supplies of goods in connection therewith, of a professional association whose membership is wholly or mainly restricted to individuals who have or who are seeking a qualification appropriate to the practice of that profession are exempt. Examples of professional associations within this definition are the "Law Society" and "The Institute of Chartered Accountants".

In *The Royal Photographic Society of Great Britain* v *CCE*, LON/78/156 (*Casebook* **9.901**) the Society failed to qualify within this Group as its members were not persons who were wholly or mainly seeking a qualification appropriate to their practices or professions.

Learned societies

The services and in connection therewith the supply of goods of an association whose primary purpose is the advancement of a particular branch of knowledge, or the fostering of professional expertise, are exempt. The association must be connected with the past or present professions of its members. The membership of the association must be restricted, wholly or mainly, to individuals whose present or previous professions are directly connected with the purposes of the association (Note (4)). The meaning of "primary purpose" was considered by the Tribunal in *The Bookmakers' Protection Association (Southern Area) Ltd* v *CCE*, LON/79/129 (*Casebook* **9.902**) where the Tribunal indicated that the expression must be interpreted partly according to the objects of the Association and partly according to the expectation of the members.

The bodies included within this part of item 1 are learned societies, The Royal Photographic Society of Great Britain failed to qualify under this head as it did not meet the requirements of Note (4).

Representative bodies on legislation

The supply of services and, in connection therewith, the supply of goods of an association whose main object is to make representations to the Government on legislation and other public matters which affect the business or interests of their members, are exempt. Membership must be restricted wholly or mainly to individuals or corporations whose businesses or professional interests are directly connected with the purposes of the association (Note (5)). It will be noted that corporations may be members as well as individuals.

Chapter 10

International Supplies of Services

10.000A Sources

Section 8A —The place of supply of services.
Section 8B —Charge to tax on certain supplies received from outside the United Kingdom.
Section 12 —International services entitled to be zero-rated.
Schedule 2A—Supplies within s 8B.
Schedule 4, Group 9—International services entitled to be zero-rated.
VAT (General Regulations 1977 (SI 1977 No 1759) reg 13—Time of supply of s 8B services.

In addition the following Customs & Excise Notices may be useful:

700—paras 13(c), 14(j)(v) and 52
701—pp 27–42

10.000B General principles

This chapter is divided into two main sections. The first, **10.100,** covers the "export" of those services entitled to be zero-rated. These services are listed in Sched 4, Group 9 and, as a general guide, are either performed outside the United Kingdom or are supplied to a person who belongs outside the United Kingdom.

The second section, **10.200,** covers the converse situation where certain services are received in the United Kingdom by a taxable person from abroad. These services are set out in Sched 2A and are fewer in number. The consequence of coming within this second category of supplies is that the recipient, if a taxable person, is treated as himself having supplied those services in the United Kingdom. He must, therefore, account to the Customs & Excise for VAT on those services.

The importation and exportation of goods are discussed in Chapters 6 and 7 respectively.

10.100 The "export" of services

Item No.

1. The supply of services relating to land situated outside the United Kingdom and the Isle of Man.

2. The letting on hire of goods for use outside the United Kingdom and the Isle of Man throughout the period of the hiring which:

    (*a*) are exported by the lessor from the United Kingdom or the Isle of Man; or

    (*b*) at the time of supply are not in the United Kingdom or the Isle of Man.

3. The supply of:

    (*a*) cultural, artistic, sporting, scientific, educational or entertainment services; or

    (*b*) services ancillary to, including that of organising, the performance outside the United Kingdom and the Isle of Man of any service in paragraph (*a*)

    where in either case these services are performed outside the United Kingdom and the Isle of Man.

4. The supply of services of valuing goods or of carrying out work on goods where, in either case, the goods are situated and the services are performed outside the United Kingdom and the Isle of Man.

5. The supply to a person in his business capacity (and not in his private capacity) who as such belongs in a country, other than the United Kingdom, which is a member state of the European Economic Community of any service comprised in paragraphs 1 to 7 of Schedule 2A to this Act.

6. The supply to a person who belongs in a country other than the Isle of Man which is not a member state of the European Economic Community of:

    (*a*) any service comprised in paragraphs 1 to 7 of Schedule 2A to this Act other than:

       (i) insurance and re-insurance services described in Group 2 of Schedule 5 to this Act;

       (ii) the issue, transfer or receipt of, or any dealing with any certificate of deposit;

    (*b*) insurance by a person described in item 1 of Group 2 of Schedule 5 to this Act other than that upon or against any risks or other things described in sub-paragraph (*a*), (*b*), (*c*), (*d*) or (*f*) of subsection (4) of section 83 of the Insurance Companies Act 1974;

    (*c*) re-insurance by a person described in item 1 of Group 2 of Schedule 5 to this Act;

    (*d*) services comprised in item 3 or 4 of Group 2 of Schedule 5 to this Act which are in respect of a supply of insurance or re-insurance comprised in this item.

7. The supply of:

    (*a*) insurance (and not of re-insurance) by a person described in item 1 of Group 2 of Schedule 5 to this Act upon or against any risks or other things described in sub-paragraph (*a*), (*b*), (*c*), (*d*) or (*f*) of subsection (4) of section 83 of the Insurance Companies Act 1974 where the supply is in connection with the carriage of passengers, or of goods, to or from a place, other than the Isle of Man outside the member states of the European Economic Community;

(*b*) services comprised in Item 3 or 4 of Group 2 of Schedule 5 to this Act which are in respect of a supply of insurance comprised in this item.

8. The supply:

(*a*) by the Export Credits Guarantee Department or a person described in item 1 of Group 2 of Schedule 5 to this Act of insurance against risks incurred in the making of advances or the granting of credits in connection with goods for export outside the member states of the European Economic Community, other than goods for removal to the Isle of Man; or

(*b*) of services comprised in item 3 or 4 of Group 2 of Schedule 5 to this Act which are in respect of a supply of insurance comprised in this item.

9. The supply of services comprised in item 1, 2 or 3 of Group 5 of Schedule 5 to this Act where the services are in connection with:

(*a*) the export of specific goods; or

(*b*) the transhipment (whether within or outside the United Kingdom and the Isle of Man of goods

the ultimate destination of the goods, in either case, being a place outside the European Economic Community other than the Isle of Man.

10. The supply of services to a person who belongs in a country, other than the United Kingdom and the Isle of Man, of work carried out on goods which, for that purpose, are acquired within, or imported into, the United Kingdom or the Isle of Man for subsequent export and in fact are exported.

11. The supply of services in procuring for another person:

(*a*) an export of goods from the United Kingdom or the Isle of Man; or

(*b*) any of the supplies of services comprised in item 1, 2, 3, 4, 5, 6 or 10 of this Group; or

(*c*) any supply of goods or services made outside the United Kingdom and the Isle of Man.

Notes

(1) Item 1 includes:

(*a*) services in the course of the construction, alteration, repair, maintenance or demolition of any building or of any civil engineering work; or

(*b*) services such as are supplied by estate agents and auctioneers, architects, surveyors, engineers and others involved in matters relating to land;

but does not include any services comprised in paragraphs 1 to 7 of Schedule 2A to this Act.

(2) Item 2 does not include the letting on hire of any means of transport for use in a member state of the European Economic Community.

(3) Item 5, 6 or 10 applies only if the recipient would be treated as belonging in a country described therein if, for the purposes of section 8A of this Act, the rules contained therein were applied to him.

(4) Items 1 to 5 do not include services comprised in any Group of Schedule 5 to this Act.

(5) Items 5 and 6 do not include:

    (*a*) services of education, health or training (which are not comprised in any Group of Schedule 5 to this Act) performed in the United Kingdom other than training supplied to a foreign Government acting in furtherance of its sovereign activities; or

    (*b*) the provision or organisation of conferences, exhibitions or meetings held in the United Kingdom unless those services are comprised in paragraph 2 of Schedule 2A to this Act; or

    (*c*) any services related to these described in (*b*) above.

(6) Item 6 does not include services comprised in any Group, other than those comprised in Group 2 or Group 5, of Schedule 5 to this Act.

(7) Item 7 does not include a supply in respect of:

    (*a*) Boats—

        (i) of a gross tonnage of less than 15 tons; or

        (ii) designed for use for recreation or pleasure;

    except boats which are of a kind used solely as liferafts and comply with the requirements of the rules for the time being in force under section 427 of the Merchant Shipping Act 1894 in relation to liferafts.

    (*b*) Boats adapted for use for recreation or pleasure.

    (*c*) Aircraft—

        (i) of a weight of less than 8,000 kilogrammes; or

        (ii) designed or adapted for use for recreation or pleasure.

    (*d*) Hovercraft designed or adapted for use for recreation or pleasure.

(8) Item 11 does not include the supply of services of procurement by a travel agent for the account of a traveller where the place of enjoyment of the supplies procured is in a member state of the European Economic Community.

(9) In item 6 "certificate of deposit" means a document relating to money, in any currency, which has been deposited with the issuer or some other person, being a document which recognises an obligation to pay a stated amount to bearer or to order, with or without interest, and being a document by the delivery of which, with or without endorsement, the right to receive that stated amount, with or without interest, is transferable.

The law relating to the international supply of services was substantially amended by FA 1977 and the VAT (Consolidation) Order 1978 (SI 1978 No 1064), with effect from 4 September 1978. The result of such amendments is to render of little practical importance the case law built up in this area prior to that date.

The services which are entitled to be zero-rated when exported from the United Kingdom are those listed in Sched 4, Group 9 (International services). It is most important to note that there is no general entitlement to zero-rating where the recipient of a supply belongs outside the United Kingdom. The items which comprise Group 9 are set out above in full and discussed individually in the following paragraphs of this section. It should be borne in mind that a large number of the items in Group 9 are subject to extensive modification in the Notes to that Group. These

Notes are also discussed below in connection with the items to which they relate.

The Customs & Excise Notice No 701, pp 30–42 may also be of use in that the Customs & Excise sets out in those pages examples of supplies which it considers should, or should not, fall within the various items of Group 9. Further, the Customs & Excise in Notice No 701, p 31, identifies five underlying principles to the zero-rating of supplies under Group 9. These are that such supplies should either:

(*a*) relate to land outside the United Kingdom;
(*b*) be performed outside the United Kingdom;
(*c*) be supplied to a person who belongs outside the United Kingdom (certain services only);
(*d*) relate to an insurance risk outside the EEC and Isle of Man; or
(*e*) consist of particular financial or agency services relating to imports, exports or transhipments.

Item 1: Land outside the United Kingdom

This item zero-rates the supply of services relating to land outside the United Kingdom in accordance with the EEC Sixth Directive, which requires that the situation of the land in question should determine the place of the supply for VAT purposes.

The crucial factor in relation to this item is the location of the land. If the land is situated outside the United Kingdom and Isle of Man, it is irrelevant that the supplier of the recipient belongs or the services are performed in the United Kingdom

Note (1) lists some of the services which are to be regarded as within item 1. This list is expressed to be inclusive and should not, it is suggested, be regarded as an exhaustive list of services zero-rated under item 1.

Services in Sched 2A are not included in item 1. However, services mentioned in Sched 2A, para 3 may be zero-rated if they relate to land outside the United Kingdom due to the double negative that results from combining item 1 and para 3.

Exempt services listed in Sched 5 are not included in this item (Note (4)).

Item 2: Letting of goods on hire outside the United Kingdom

This item covers the hire of goods which are used outside the United Kingdom throughout the term of the lease provided that the goods are either:

(*a*) exported by the hirer; or
(*b*) are outside the United Kingdom at the time of the supply.

The first of these alternatives should not present a problem to a supplier in practice. In relation to the alternative requirement, it is important to realise that under the VAT (General) Regulations 1977 (SI 1977 No 1759), reg 18(1), a supply will be treated as made each time a payment is received or, if earlier, a tax invoice is issued by the supplier. Thus, should the goods be in the United Kingdom when a particular rental payment is made, although that rental payment will not qualify for zero-rating under this item, future payments should not be prejudiced. Those future payments may be zero-rated if the goods are outside the United Kingdom at the time they are made and the requirement that the goods are let for use outside the United Kingdom throughout the hire term is satisfied. This alternative requirement is in line with the EEC Tenth Directive which proposes that the hire of tangible movable property other than forms of transport should be treated as taking place in the country in which the property is made available to the hirer.

Item 2 does not include the letting on hire of any means of transport for use in an EEC Member State (Note (2)) or any supply listed in Sched 5 (Note (4)).

Item 3: Cultural etc services

The performance of cultural, artistic, sporting, scientific, educational or entertainment services or services ancillary to such services, outside the United Kingdom is zero-rated under this item. There is some overlap between this item and Sched 5, Group 6. The exempt schedule will prevail where this occurs (Note (4)) and the services in question cannot be zero-rated.

The Customs & Excise gives as an example of a service coming within this item "services connected with off-shore oil and gas exploration, including on-rig catering or similar support services". This is because such services are regarded as either scientific services or services ancilliary to scientific services.

Item 4: Valuations etc

The valuation or performance of work on goods may be zero-rated under item 4. It is a requirement, however, that both the goods and the place of performance of the services are outside the United Kingdom. Furthermore, services listed in Sched 5 are not within this item (Note (4)).

Items 5 and 6(*a*): Sched 2A supplies

These items are discussed together as both relate to the "export" of Sched 2A supplies. This is the converse of s 8B discussed in **10.200**. Schedule 2A supplies comprise the following:

"1. Transfers and assignments of copyright, patents, licences, trademarks and similar rights.

2. Advertising services.

3. Services of consultants, engineers, consultancy bureaux, lawyers, accountants and other similar services; data processing and provision of information (but excluding from this head any services relating to land).

4. Acceptance of any obligation to refrain from pursuing or exercising, in whole or part, any business activity or any such rights as are referred to in paragraph 1 above.

5. Banking, financial and insurance services (including re-insurance, but not including the provision of safe deposit facilities).

6. The supply of staff.

7. The services rendered by one person to another in procuring for the other any of the services mentioned in paragraphs 1 to 6 above."

The scope of paras 1–7 is also discussed in **10.200.**

A fundamental difference between items 5 and 6(*a*) is, however, that while item 5 does not include any services which are within the exempt schedule (Sched 5), item 6(*a*) may include those exempt supplies in either Group 2 (insurance) or Group 5 (finance) of Sched 5. Those insurance and financial services not within Groups 2 or 5 may be zero-rated, however, under Group 9, either item 5 or 6.

By Note (5), items 5 and 6 do not include:

(*a*) services of education, health or training (which are not comprised in any Group of Sched 5 to this Act) performed in the United Kingdom or the Isle of Man other than training supplied to a foreign Government acting in furtherance of its sovereign activities; or

(*b*) the provision or organisation of conferences, exhibitions or meetings held in the United Kingdom unless those services are comprised in Sched 2A, para 2; or

(*c*) any services related to those described in (*b*) above.

The country in which a recipient of a supply belongs is to be determined in accordance with s 8A (Note (3)). Section 8A lays down the following tests:

(*a*) if the supply is made to an *individual* in his *private capacity* (meaning that it is received otherwise than for the purposes of any business carried on by him), he is treated as belonging in whatever country he has his usual place of residence (s 8A(2));

(*b*) in all other cases a person is treated as belonging in the country in which (s 8A(3)):

(i) he has his only business or some other fixed establishment (a person carrying on a business through a branch or agency in a country is treated as having a business establishment there);

(ii) if he has no such establishment, he has his usual place of residence (in the case of a body corporate, this means the place where it is legally constituted);

(iii) if he has more than one such establishment, the establishment at which the services are, or are to be, most directly used, is located.

Items 6(*b*), (*c*) and (*d*), 7 and 8: Insurance

These items cover those classes of insurance services which are entitled to be zero-rated. Generally, the insurance must be provided by an authorised insurer within the meaning of the Insurance Companies Act 1974, ss 1–9 or the Exports Credit Guarantee Department (item 8). Under item 6 the insured must be a person who belongs outside the EEC (see s 8A and under items 5 and 6(*a*), *ante*) and under item 7, the insurance must relate to the carriage of passengers or goods to or from a place (other than the Isle of Man) outside the EEC. Item 8 zero-rates insurance in relation to the export of goods outside the EEC (again excluding the Isle of Man). Notes (5) and (6) apply to item 6 (see under item 5 and 6(*a*), *ante*) and item 7 does not include a supply in respect of (Note (7)):

"(*a*) Boats—
  (i) of a gross tonnage of less than 15 tons; or
  (ii) designed for use for recreation or pleasure; except boats which are of a kind used solely as liferafts and comply with the requirements of the rules for the time being in force under section 427 of the Merchant Shippning Act 1894 in relation to liferafts.
(*b*) Boats adapted for use for recreation or pleasure.
(*c*) Aircraft—
  (i) of a weight of less than 8,000 kilogrammes; or
  (ii) designed or adapted for use for recreation or pleasure.
(*d*) Hovercraft designed or adapted for use for recreation or pleasure."

The relevant exclusions in the Insurance Companies Act 1974, s 83 for the purposes of item 6(*b*) are contracts of insurance:

"(*a*) upon vessels or aircraft, or upon the machinery, tackle, furniture or equipment of vessels or aircraft;
(*b*) upon goods, merchandise or property of any description whatever on board of vessels or aircraft;
(*c*) upon the freight of, or any other interest in or relating to, vessels or aircraft;
(*d*) against damage arising out of, or in connection with, the use of vessels or aircraft, including third-party risks;
(*e*) ...
(*f*) against transit risks (whether the transit is by sea, inland water, land or air, or partly one and partly another), including risks incidental to the transit insured from the commencement of the transit to the ultimate destination covered by the insurance."

Item 9: Financial services relating to the export of goods

Where the ultimate destination of goods exported or in transhipment is outside the EEC, financial services within Sched 5, Group 5 (for example, the making of any loan or credit facility) in connection with such export or transhipment may be zero-rated under this item.

In relation to this item it is to be noted that the supply of the financial services in question need only be "in connection with" the export or transhipment of goods to a destination outside the EEC (excluding the Isle of Man). This is an extremely wide phrase. The Customs & Excise instance a loan to buy machinery which is to be used solely to manufacture goods to be exported to a place outside the EEC as coming within the item. Equally, a loan to purchase a vessel used solely for the shipment of goods would also appear to qualify for zero-rating where the ultimate destination of the goods can be shown to satisfy the item.

It should also be noted that the transhipment may be within the United Kingdom.

Item 10: Work on goods subsequently exported

This item effectively covers the converse type of supply to that in item 4, namely the carrying out of work on goods which are either temporarily imported into the United Kingdom for the purpose or are acquired in the United Kingdom for export where the recipient of the supply belongs outside the United Kingdom. The place where a person belongs is to be determined in accordance with the rules in s 8A (see under items 5 and 6(*a*), *ante*).

The Customs & Excise require the goods to be exported within a "reasonable time" after the work on them has been carried out.

The only case that has been reported under this item is that of *Banstead Manor Stud Ltd* v *CCE*, LON/78/412 (*Casebook* **10.101**).

Item 11: Intermediary services

This item zero-rates the supplies of any person who procures the performance of certain transactions which are themselves zero-rated, or outside the scope of United Kingdom VAT, namely the export of goods, services within items 1–6 and 10 and supplies of goods or services outside the United Kingdom.

This item may, for example, zero-rate the services of a supplier's import agent where title to the goods imported into the United Kingdom passes from the supplier while the goods are still outside the United Kingdom.

This item does not zero-rate, however, the services of a travel agent where those services relate to travel etc, in an EEC Member State (Note (8)).

10.200 Services received from abroad (s 8B)

Section 8B(1) and (2) provide that:

(1) ... where —

  (*a*) services of any of the descriptions specified in Schedule 2A to this Act are supplied by a person who belongs in a country other than the United Kingdom or the Isle of Man;
  (*b*) they are received by a taxable person for the purposes of any business carried on by him, and he belongs in the United Kingdom.

(2) All the same consequences follow under this Part of this Act (and particularly so much as charges tax on a supply and entitles a taxable person to credit for input tax) as if the taxable person had himself supplied the services in the United Kingdom in the course or furtherance of his business, and that supply were a taxable supply.

It should be noted that s 8B only applies to a person who is already a taxable person. The value of s 8B deemed supplies should not be taken into account, therefore, in determining whether a person is required to be registered under Sched 1, that is, whether he is or is not a taxable person.

Section 8B does not apply to any Sched 2A services which also fall within Sched 5 and would, therefore, be regarded as exempt if supplied in the United Kingdom in the normal way (s 8B(3)). Further, s 8B deemed supplies are not to be taken into account in any partial exemption calculations required to be made under s 4.

Finally, supplies within a single legal entity, for example, a supply of staff by a French branch office to a London office of a US corporation, do not fall within s 8B as there is no true supply in such circumstances.

Consequences of s 8B

For the fully taxable person, s 8B does not present any problems apart from the accounting requirements that follow from a supply for VAT purposes. Such a person merely enters in his periodical VAT return (Form VAT 100, see Chapter 17) an amount of tax in relation to s 8B supplies in the period and claims an equivalent amount by way of input tax in that same period. No cost, either real or in cash flow terms is incurred, therefore.

A real cost will be incurred by a partially exempt person, however. Such a person will be obliged to account to the Customs & Excise for tax on a s 8B supply but will not be able to recover all that tax by way of input tax credit. This places the partially exempt person in the same position whether he seeks Sched 2A services from within the United Kingdom or from abroad. Without s 8B, however, it would be more advantageous for him in pure cost terms to take those services from outside the United Kingdom.

A cost will also be incurred by any exempt person to whom a taxable person supplies s 8B services received by him. For example, a UK lawyer taking advice from a French lawyer on behalf of a client will be obliged to account for VAT on the French lawyer's fees under s 8B. When charging his client, the UK lawyer will add VAT on those fees as a disbursement which VAT the exempt client will not be able to recover. If the French lawyer had supplied the services to the client direct, however, no VAT would be accountable for on his fees, in the United Kingdom.

A common example of the application of section 8B in practice is the secondment of personnel by non-UK companies to their UK subsidiaries. In such cases, a s 8B charge will be levied on the UK company which, if it is partially exempt, will be unable to recover part of the VAT comprised in that charge.

Time of supply

Supplies under s 8B are treated as made when they are paid for if the consideration given for the supply is in money. If it is not in money, such supplies are treated as made on the last day of the prescribed accounting period in which they are performed (VAT (General) Regulations 1977 (SI 1977 No 1759), reg 13). The Regulations which modify the time of supply, for example, in cases where there is a continuous supply of services and the provisions in s 7(4) which fix the time of supply at the time of the issue of an invoice would appear not to apply to s 8B services. It would seem, therefore, that a charge under s 8B may be delayed indefinitely if the consideration for the supply is in money and is simply left outstanding. It is recognised that this may not be possible in practice except, perhaps, where the supply is received in the United Kingdom from another company within the same group of companies as the recipient of the supply.

Value of the supply

If the consideration for a s 8B supply is in money, that consideration is taken as the tax value of the supply (s 8B(4)). In any other case, the market value of the supply is the value of the supply for VAT purposes (s 10(3)).

Section 2A services

The services listed in Sched 2A and to which s 8B applies are:

"1. Transfers and assignments of copyright, patents, licences, trademarks and similar rights.
2. Advertising services.
3. Services of consultants, engineers, consultancy bureaux, lawyers, accountants and

other similar services; data processing and provision of information (but excluding from this head any services relating to land).

4. Acceptance of any obligation to refrain from pursuing or exercising, in whole or in part, any business activity or any such rights as are referred to in paragraph 1 above.

5. Banking, financial and insurance services (including re-insurance, but not including the provision of safe deposit facilities).

6. The supply of staff.

7. The services rendered by one person to another in procuring for the other any of the services mentioned in paragraph 1 to 6 above."

This list of services is taken from art 9(2)(*e*) of the EEC Sixth Directive but with two principal differences. These differences and the individual paragraphs of Sched 2A are discussed below:

Transfers and assignments of copyright, patents, licences, trademarks and similar rights (para 1)

In Notice No 701 at p 35, the Customs & Excise gives two examples of what it considers falls within this paragraph. They are:

(*a*) the granting of the rights specified in para 1;

(*b*) the production of cinematographic film for a distribution company.

It is doubtful, however, whether the grant of a right, was intended to be included in the phrase "transfers and assignments". If it had been, it would have been a simple matter to include "grant" in both the EEC Sixth Directive and Sched 2A (it is included in Sched 5, Group 1, for example: "the grant, assignment or surrender of any interest in or right over land . . ."). Thus, unless the grant of para 1 rights falls, in any particular case, within one of the other paragraphs of Sched 2A (perhaps para 4), it would appear that the Customs & Excise first example of a para 1 supply may be misleading.

The Customs & Excise's second example (see para (*b*) *ante*) is also difficult to fit into para 1. The production of a film may be said to create two property rights. First, the physical property of the film itself and, secondly, the copyright in the film. It is, perhaps, the transfer of this more valuable second right to the distribution company that is meant to be covered by para 1. In practice, however, a distribution company is more likely merely to be licensed to use the copyright in the film. As mentioned above, the grant of such a licence may not be within Sched 2A.

Advertising services (para 2)

This is largely self explanatory, although certain points should be noted. First, the paragraph (as does the entire Schedule) only applies to services. Goods which are supplied as incidental items to the main supply off advertising services may fall within the paragraph but goods which are supplied in their own right, albeit as part of a promotion, will not be covered by para 2. Secondly, as the Customs & Excise points out in Notice No 701, the paragraph only covers supplies *by* a person in the course of a business of providing advertising services. Supplies *to* such a person are not para 2 supplies although they may fall within Sched 2A, para 3.

Services of consultants, engineers, consultancy bureaux, lawyers, accountants and other similar services; data processing and provision of information (but excluding any services relating to land) (para 3)

Supplies of services made by the majority of medical consultants do not fall within this paragraph as those supplies are exempt under Sched 5, Group 7. "Engineers" is interpreted by the Customs & Excise as meaning only professionally qualified engineers; this is perhaps open to question. However, by analogy with the decision in *Rawlins Davy and Wells* v *CCE*, LON/77/251 (*Casebook* **8.834**), whether any particular services are those of engineers, lawyers and accountants etc, should possibly be determined by giving those terms the meaning they bear in the respective professions themselves. Thus, a lawyer serving as a director of a company would not, merely by being qualified as a lawyer, be providing services within the "lawyer" head of para 3. He may, however, arguably fall within the "other similar services' heading.

Land is excluded from para 3 as the EEC Sixth Directive requires services relating to land to be taxed in the country in which the land is situated (art 9(2)(*a*)). Paragraph 3 does not entirely achieve this objective, however; by Sched 4, Group 9, item 1, services relating to land outside the United Kingdom are zero-rated, but there is no charge to VAT where services are provided by a person belonging outside the United Kingdom in connection with land in the United Kingdom. It is arguable, therefore, that if the EEC Sixth Directive has direct effect in this area, the proviso to para 3 should read "(but excluding from this head any service relating to land outside the United Kingdom)".

An example of a supply which may fall within para 3 is the grant of a know-how licensing agreement. Such agreements often include not only the provision of information, but also the provision of the services of consultants and engineers. Whether a para 3 supply will be involved will, of course, depend upon the precise terms of the particular agreement.

Acceptance of any obligation to refrain from pursuing or exercising, in whole or in part, any business activity or any such rights as are referred to in para 1 (para 4)

The wording of this paragraph differs from the equivalent in the EEC Sixth Directive which reads:

> "Obligations to refrain from pursuing or exercising, in whole or in part, *a business activity or a right referred to in this point* (*e*)."

The phrase in italics gives rise to two issues. First, the EEC Sixth Directive point (*e*) contains Sched 2A, paras 1–7; it is not limited to para 1 as is the UK version. Secondly, while the UK text makes it clear that "business activity" and "such rights" are distinct concepts, this is less certain in the Directive. Indeed, the EEC Sixth Directive deliberately uses business activity in contrast to "economic activity" which it defines in art 4(2) to determine the scope of the charge to tax. This indicates that a different concept is being employed and arguably requires only those activities within paras 1–7 to be within the meaning of business activity.

Banking, financial and insurance services (including re-insurance, but not including the provision of safe deposit facilities) (para 5)

It should be noted here that any services within Sched 5, Groups 2 or 5 cannot fall within this paragraph, for s 8B purposes. Thus, those services instanced by the Customs & Excise in Notice No 701, at pp 73 and 74 as not within Group 5 may fall within para 5. The making of arrangements for any transaction within Group 5, item 4 or 5 will also come within para 5.

The supply of staff (para 6)

For a supply to come within this paragraph, the recipient of the supply must have some degree of control over the staff supplied. If the recipient cannot direct the manner in which the supplier's staff operate, it is indicative that the real nature of the supply is the end product resulting from the services of the staff and not the staff itself.

The services rendered by one person to another in procuring for the other any of the services mentioned in paras 1–6 (para 7)

Again this is to be contrasted with the EEC Sixth Directive which states:

"the services of agents who act in the name of and for the account of another, when they procure for their principal the services referred to in this point (*e*)."

Although the UK wording arguably implies an agency relationship, it would seem that to come within this paragraph, the agency should be disclosed.

Chapter 11

Customs & Excise Practice

11.100 Discretion

General

There are two kinds of discretion that arise in the context of VAT. First, the Customs & Excise has a general discretion in the administration of VAT, which has been recognised by the Tribunals. Thus, in *E Marks* v *CCE*, LON/77/21 (*Casebook* **11.102**) the Tribunal, whilst acknowledging that it could not force the Customs & Excise to waive the full amount of tax due, expressed the hope that the Customs & Excise would, nevertheless, feel able to exercise a general discretion in favour of the appellant and not insist on payment of the tax strictly due.

Secondly, there is the more precise discretion given to the Customs & Excise in a particular context where the Customs & Excise is given a discretion in relation to specific aspects of VAT and it is this type of discretion with which this part of this chapter is concerned. An example of such a case where the Customs & Excise is given a discretion is, in the context of voluntary registration, where the Customs & Excise is able to accept voluntary registration under Sched 1, para 11(*b*) if "they think fit" and subject to such conditions "as they think fit to impose" (see **2.300**). Also, the Customs & Excise is able to exempt a person from registration under Sched 1, para 11(*a*) if the person makes zero-rated supplies and the Customs & Excise "think fit" (see **2.100**). Another example is the provisions for registering divisions of companies separately (s 23(1)—see **2.400**).

In addition to the above the Customs & Excise is given power to make regulations (s 16(2) and (3)) in relation to relief from VAT on importation and many of those Regulations enable the Customs & Excise to impose such conditions as it may require, see, for example, VAT (General) Regulations 1977 (SI 1977 No 1759), reg 39, relating to the reimportation of goods (see **6.200**). Similar provisions apply in relation to the export of goods where, by virtue of s 12(7), the Customs & Excise is able to make Regulations making provision for the zero-rating of goods on export and impose such other conditions as they think fit.

It will be seen, therefore, that even the above examples of specific instances are, where a discretion is given to the Customs & Excise, capable of being divided into two separate categories. First, those cases where the Customs & Excise has a general power to use a discretion without need to specify for the public any terms of reference within which such discretion will be exercised in favour of the taxpayer, for example, in relation to voluntary registration and cancellation of registration (Sched 1, para 10A). Secondly, there are those cases where the Customs & Excise has to make available to the public the conditions they have imposed, for example in relation to the import and export of goods where the Customs & Excise is given power to make such conditions as it thinks fit. It is important to bear these two categories in mind and to appreciate their distinction in considering the powers of VAT Tribunals to review the exercise of a discretion given to the Customs & Excise as it is the first type with which this part of this Chapter is concerned (see *Discretion: power of review, post*).

In exercising its discretion the Customs & Excise will be bound by the general principles of English law relating to statutory powers. Thus, discretionary powers (*Halsbury's Laws of England*, 4th Ed, Vol 1, p 70):

> "must always be exercised in good faith, for the purpose for which they were granted and within the limits of the Act or other instrument conferring the power. Discretion must also be exercised fairly, not capriciously and in accordance with proper legal principles; and these standards imply that all relevant considerations must be taken into account and that extraneous considerations be disregarded by the person or body exercising the power".

This principle, as stated above, therefore, raises the question as to what remedies are available to a taxpayer who wishes to challenge the exercise of a discretion by the Customs & Excise. This question raises difficult concepts of law and has been the subject of recent case law. It is considered below.

Discretion: Power of review

The question as to the extent to which the Tribunals and courts have power to review the exercise of discretion by the Customs & Excise has been the subject of much comment in *CCE* v *J H Corbitt* (*Numismatists*) *Ltd*, [1980] STC 231 (*Casebook* **11.101**). The facts in the *Corbitt* case were as follows. The company carried on in business as numismatists, dealing in old coins and medals. It operated the margin scheme in respect of antique coins, being coins over one hundred years old. The scheme operates by allowing suppliers to charge VAT on the difference between the cost price and sale price of the goods in question instead of being payable on their full sale price. The scheme has its statutory origin in s 14(1), which states:

> "The Treasury may by order make provision for securing a reduction of the tax chargeable on the supply of goods of such descriptions as may be specified in the order in cases where no tax was chargeable on a previous supply of the goods and such other conditions are satisfied as may be specified in the order or as may be imposed by the Commissioners in pursuance of the order".

Under s 14(1) the Treasury made the VAT (Works of Art, Antiques and Scientific Collections) Order 1972 (SI 1972 No 1971) ("the 1972 Order") which introduced the margin scheme for antiques of an age exceeding one hundred years. The 1972 Order has since been repealed but the points at issue in the *Corbitt* case remain relevant as identical words to those in dispute in *Corbitt* are contained in the VAT (Special Provisions) Order 1977 (SI 1977 No 1796), art 4(3)(*c*), which replaces art 3(5) of the 1972 Order. It was art 4 of the 1972 Order which applied the margin scheme to antiques exceeding one hundred years in age, but certain conditions had to be satisfied before the scheme applied. In particular art 3(5) of the 1972 Order provided:

> "Article 4 does not apply to any supply by a person unless he keeps such records and accounts as the Commissioners may specify in a notice published by them for the purposes of this Order or may recognise as sufficient for those purposes".

Article 3(5) set out the conditions imposed in the 1972 Order by the Treasury, but as authorised in s 14(1) the Treasury gave the Customs & Excise power to impose further conditions. The conditions imposed by Customs & Excise are set out in Notice No 712 (and are the same conditions as apply for the purposes of the VAT (Special Provisions) Order 1977 (SI 1977 No 1759), art 4(3)(*c*)). The company was assessed to VAT on the sales prices of goods as it had not complied with the conditions of Notice No 712. However, it appealed to the Tribunal on the basis that the Customs & Excise had a discretion to operate the margin scheme in its favour, notwithstanding that it had not complied with Notice No 712. It was common ground, therefore, that the company had not complied with the conditions set out in Notice No 712. Its appeal to the VAT Tribunal was, accordingly, based on the last few words of art 3(5) of the 1972 Order, namely the words, "or may recognise as sufficient for those purposes". In particular it was argued on behalf of the company that those words gave the Customs & Excise an additional discretion to review the records of a taxable person and to accept the records as sufficient for the purpose of the 1972 Order, notwithstanding that the strict conditions of Notice No 712 had not been complied with. Furthermore, it was argued before the Tribunal that the Tribunal had power to review the exercise or non-exercise of such discretion and to substitute its own decision for that of the Customs & Excise. Both these arguments found favour with the Tribunal, but, on appeal to the High Court, Neill J. held that the Tribunal had no jurisdiction to review the exercise of a discretion given to the Customs & Excise. The High Court decision was itself over-ruled in the Court of Appeal (Lord Denning MR and Sir Stanley Rees, with Eveleigh LJ. dissenting) but reinstated by the House of Lords (Lords Lane, Simon of Glaisdale, Diplock and Scarman, with Lord Salmon dissenting).

Thus, the position as finally determined in the *Corbitt* case is that the Tribunal has no power to review the exercise of a discretion given to the Customs & Excise. In giving the leading judgment in the House of Lords, Lord Lane reached his decision on the same ground as Neill J. in the High Court. Lord Lane said:

"The answer to that question can be briefly stated. It cannot be and is not disputed that the VAT Tribunal has no jurisdiction to review the requirements as to books and records which the Commissioners had laid down (as the 1972 Act authorises them to do) in the various appendices to the Blue Book [Notice No 712]. Their task on an appeal is confined on this aspect to an enquiry as to whether the trader's books and records in fact comply with the requirements of the Blue Book. That being so, it seems to me to be inconceivable that any different powers should be given to the Tribunal in respect of the second half of Article 3(5), namely, the discretion in the Commissioners to recognise or not recognise records actually kept as being sufficient. The two halves of the Article are part of the same system of approval or non-approval of records, the first set out in terms in the order, the second in the shape of a more flexible discretion. In neither case is there room for review by the Tribunal except on matters of fact as I have indicated. The matter was expressed by Neill J. [1979] (3WLR at p. 298) in words which I am unable to better as follows:–

'It is common ground between the Commissioners and the dealer that insofar as conditions are imposed in Notice No 712 itself, they are not conditions which the appellate body, the Tribunal, can interfere with in the sense that it can substitute its view as to what were the appropriate conditions for the view of the Commissioners. The Tribunal can certainly consider whether or not those conditions have as a matter of fact been complied with. That is something which would be a suitable subject of an appeal. But what it cannot do is to say, "We do not think that Appendix A or Appendix B, or whatever it may be, ought to be in that form; it should be in some other form". Once it is conceded, as I think rightly, that the Commissioners are empowered, subject to the control of the Treasury, to lay down the conditions in a general notice such as Notice No 712 in such a form as they consider proper and that that power is not subject to appeal, it seems to me impossible to contend that the discretion given by the final words of article 3(5) "or may recognise as sufficient for those purposes" is a different kind of discretion which is subject to appeal'.

There is another aspect of the matter. Assume for a moment that the tribunal has the power to review the Commissioners' discretion. It could only properly do so if it were shown the Commissioners had acted in a way which no reasonable panel of commissioners could have acted; if they had taken into account some irrelevant matter or had disregarded something to which they should have given weight. If it had been intended to give a supervisory jurisdiction of that nature to the tribunal one would have expected clear words to that effect in the Act. But there are no such words to be found. Section 40(1) sets out nine specific headings under which an appeal may be brought and seems by inference to negative the existence of any general supervisory jurisdiction".

Lords Simon of Glaisdale, Diplock and Scarman gave short concurring judgments although Lord Simon of Glaisdale made some interesting observations on the role of applications for judicial review, as to which see *post*. Thus, having regard to the types of discretion described at the beginning of this Chapter it will be seen that:

(*a*) where the Customs & Excise is given power to impose conditions and do so (for example in a Notice, such as in Notice No 712 in the *Corbitt* case, or in respect of exports as in Notice No 703) the Tribunal has no power to review the conditions. Either the conditions have been satisfied or not and it will be a question of fact as to whether the conditions have been satisfied (see the remarks of Lord Lane *ante*). The Tribunal's jurisdiction would, therefore, extend only to reviewing the facts to see whether or not as a matter of fact the conditions had been complied with;

(*b*) where the Customs & Excise has a more general discretion, for example, as set out in art 3(5) of the 1972 Order, the Tribunal has no power to review the exercise of such discretion.

Given, therefore, that in the light of the House of Lords' decision in the *Corbitt* case the Tribunal has no power to review the exercise of a discretion given to the Customs & Excise, what remedy does the taxpayer have if he believes a discretion has been exercised unfairly? The position is unfortunately unclear, but it would seem from the comments of Lord Simon of Glaisdale that the taxpayer's remedy lies in applying to the High Court for a judicial order, for Lord Simon of Glaisdale said, in a concurring judgment with Lord Lane:

"Moreover, he [the taxpayer] can, in my judgment, invoke the jurisdiction of the High Court against the exercise of the Commissioners' discretion refusing to 'recognise' his records as 'sufficient' on the grounds, for example, that no reasonable body of Commissioners could so exercise their discretion (or that the discretion was otherwise improperly exercised): this is the normal judicial review, within the short limits which are inherent in such a jursidiction, of the exercise of a legal discretion by any body whether judicial, quasi-judicial or administrative".

Lord Simon was the only one of the judges who, finding in favour of the Customs & Excise, indicated in any detail that this was the position. Lord Lane, in analysing the nature of the appeal by the company stated:

"Was this failure or refusal by the Commissioners to exercise their discretion in favour of Corbitts something which the VAT Tribunal were entitled to review, or was it an exercise of discretion which was subject to review, if at all, only by way of judicial review in the High Court?"

Having raised the possibility of judicial review by the High Court, however, Lord Lane did not return later in his judgment to deal with the point. Lord Salmon did consider the position, however, in his dissenting judgment. He said:

"I do not agree that such a case calls for what is sometimes referred to as a supervisory jurisdiction in the High Court. The jurisdiction of an appellate court or tribunal is to decide whether the judgment or decision appealed from is right or wrong. The principles to be applied when a question arises as to the exercise of a jurisdiction are well established but do not alter the nature of an appeal court's or an appeal tribunal's jurisdiction. In my opinion it would be quite unnecessary and wrong for the taxpayer to take the extravagant course of invoking the High Court's jurisdiction to review what the Commissioners had done since he has the statutory right of appealing to the tribunal against the assessment and therefore against the Commissioners' decision under the second part of Article 3(5)".

Since Lord Diplock simply concurred with the draft judgment of Lord Lane and Lord Scarman concurred with Lord Lane and Lord Simon, the situation is not entirely free from doubt. However, following the decision of the House of Lords the Government has undertaken to review the position (Hansard Vol 982, Col 718—Mr Peter Rees): it can only be hoped that the review takes place quickly to enable the difficulty to be resolved.

11.200 Concession and waiver

The Customs & Excise has a general discretion in the administration of VAT (see *E Marks* v *CCE*, LON/77/21 (*Casebook* **11.102**)). Accordingly, any decision taken by the Customs & Excise not to enforce payment of VAT due is on a concessionary basis only under their power of care and management of the tax (s 1(2)). Similarly there is no general provision in the VAT legislation enabling the Customs & Excise to waive collection of tax due, although it should be noted that s 12(8) gives the Customs & Excise power to waive collection of tax in certain limited circumstances relating to zero-rating of exports. It is, therefore, entirely for the Customs & Excise to decide in any given circumstances whether by concession it will waive tax which is strictly speaking payable. The Tribunals have no power to force the Customs & Excise to waive the collection of tax, although they have expressed the hope that the Customs & Excise would feel able to waive the tax in certain cases (see, for example, *Mr and Mrs W H G Swinger* v *CCE*, LON/77/127, *Cupboard Love Ltd* v *CCE*, LON/76/40 and *J H Tottey* (*trading as Fulwood Pirate Hotel*) v *CCE*, MAN/77/167 (*Casebook* **11.203–11.205** respectively).

Apart from the general discretion of the Customs & Excise not to collect tax by concession or to waive its collection referred to in the previous paragraph, there are certain situations where the Customs & Excise generally do not collect tax by concession. Such instances of concessionary treatment have no foundation in law and a taxpayer has no right of appeal against the refusal of the Customs & Excise to operate the concession in a given case (see, for example, *Cando 70* (*Canon Street Baptist Church Accrington*) v *CCE*, MAN/78/1 (*Casebook* **11.202**). The *Cando 70* case involved an appeal against the decision of the Customs & Excise refusing to allow a claim for input tax under the concessionary scheme for charities and other voluntary bodies engaged in projects of self-help. The scheme is, however, an example of a published extra-statutory scheme and is designed to enable charities and other voluntary bodies to reclaim input tax in respect of new buildings erected for a qualifying purpose other than in the course of a business. The details of the scheme are published in VAT Leaflet SHP10 (Charities and other bodies engaged in new building projects on a self-build or self-help basis). The scheme is discussed in detail under *Charities* at **15.100.**

The Customs & Excise do not publish a list of extra-statutory concessions as does the Inland Revenue, but examples of other concessions, details of which are available in writing, include:

(*a*) Senior Citizens Railcards which are extra-statutorily zero-rated (see Customs & Excise Press Release dated 16 May 1975). This concession is no longer really necessary, however, following *British Railways Board* v *CCE* (*No 2*), [1977] STC 221 (*Casebook* **3.610**) (see **3.600**, *Characteristics of a two-part tariff*).

(*b*) The waiver of the requirement for tax invoices in the case of petrol costs reimbursed by employers to employees for business mileage (see **5.100**) and Notice No 700, Appendix B.

(*c*) Garages let separately from a house but with the same landlord (see **9.100** PARKING).

(*d*) The provision of meals to staff/visitors in, *inter alia*, school canteens (see **9.600**).

However, as mentioned above the concessions have no statutory authority and if the Customs & Excise chose not to operate a concession the taxpayer has no right of redress. It is, therefore, advisable for taxpayers not to rely on the application of a concession in running his business, but rather to treat any tax not collected as a result of a concession as a bonus.

11.300 Estoppel

A taxpayer who has sought and relied upon representations by an Officer of Customs & Excise as to the correct VAT treatment of a transaction and which are subsequently proved incorrect, may wish to raise a defence of estoppel against any assessment rectifying the Officer's error.

Halsbury's Laws of England (4th Ed, Vol 16) defines *estoppel* at para 1501 as:

"A disability whereby a party is precluded from alleging or proving in legal proceedings that a fact is otherwise than it has been made to appear by the matter giving rise to that disability".

There are said to be four kinds of *estoppel*—in pais, promissory, by deed, or by record (also known as *estoppel per rem judicatem*)—although there is currently debate as to whether the *estoppels* should be combined in a single doctrine of *estoppel* based upon general principles of equity and justice. This Chapter merely considers *estoppel in pais*, that is *estoppel* by representation.

The traditional requirements for an estoppel in pais are:

(*a*) a representation by statement, conduct or silence by the person to be *estopped*;

(*b*) the representation to be relied upon must be clear and unambiguous, that is, reasonably understood by the person to whom it is made in the context in which it is made (*Low* v *Bouverie*, [1891] 3 Ch 82 per Bowen LJ., p 106);

(*c*) the representation must relate to a question of present fact; not intention, belief or future fact nor law (*Jordan* v *Money*, [1854] 5 HL Cas 185). This requirement is complicated however, as a representation may be a representation of fact although it also includes a matter of law (*Lyle-Miller* v *A Lewis and Co* (*Westminster*) *Ltd*, [1956] 1 All ER 247, p 253 per Hodson LJ.);

(*d*) the person raising the *estoppel* must have acted on the representation altering his position to his prejudice (*Freeman* v *Cooke*, [1848] 2 Exch 654, p 663);

(*e*) the representation must not be *ultra vires* the person making the representation;

(*f*) it must be intended by the representor that the representation should be acted upon in the manner in which it was acted upon (*Carr* v *London and North Western Railway Co*, [1875] LR 10 CP 307 per Brett J.). This intention may be inferred from the facts.

In addition to showing that the above is satisfied, a party seeking to rely on an *estoppel* against a statement by a Crown Official was, at one time, faced with the proposition that the Crown could not be bound by statements made by its officers (see *The Trustees of the Will of H K Brodie (Deceased)* v *IRC*, 17 TC 432 per Finlay J. and *The Gresham Life Assurance Society Ltd* v *Attorney General*, 7 TC 36 per Astbury J.) in respect of agreements for future years.

It does appear, however, that this absolute bar is now accepted as no longer applying (per Denning J. in *Robertson* v *Minister of Pensions*, [1949] 1 KB 227).

Notwithstanding the apparent removal of absolute Crown privilege against *estoppel*, there remains the question of whether there can be an *estoppel* against the statutory duty placed on the Customs & Excise to administer and collect VAT in the interest of the public. In *GUS Merchandise Corporation Ltd* v *CCE*, MAN/77/152 (*Casebook* **11.307**) and *POH Medlam* v *CCE*, LON/77/304 (*Casebook* **11.308**), the Tribunals held that no *estoppel* could arise for this reason, finding a "statutory obligation of unconditional character" imposed on the Customs & Excise under ss 1 and 2 and basing their decision on the judgment of Viscount Radcliffe in *Kok Hoong* v *Leong Cheong Kweng Mines Ltd*, [1964] AC 993. It is clear from Viscount Radcliffe's judgment, however, that he did not wish to imply that an *estoppel* would always be prevented from applying against the terms of a statute but only in those cases where social policy dictates, in the interests of the general public, that the statute should prevail. Whether such policy exists to protect the individual appellant or the Crown and taxpayers generally in relation to VAT is open to doubt but until the Courts consider the matter further, *GUS Merchandise* and *Medlam* represent daunting obstacles to pleas of *estoppel* in VAT cases. In this connection it should be noted that the defence of *estoppel* was not pleaded when the *GUS Merchandise* case went on appeal to the High Court (see [1980] STC 480).

In practice, however, it may be that a taxpayer who receives advice from a Customs & Excise Officer, which advice subsequently proves to be incorrect, may rely on the following statement of the Chairman of the Board of Customs & Excise (1 October 1978):

"We have publicly stated .... that where an officer, with the full facts before him, has given a clear and unequivocal ruling in writing, or it is established that an officer knowing the full facts has misled a trader to his detriment, we would apply the correct ruling only from the date the error was brought to the attention of the trader concerned".

Nevertheless, in *Coolisle Ltd* v *CCE*, LON/78/242 (*Casebook* **11.304**) the Tribunal recognised that this statement had no binding legal effect and that it was entirely for the Customs & Excise to decide whether it was or was not bound by that statement according to the particular facts of the case.

Chapter 12

Assessments

12.000 Sources

Section 31—Power of the Customs & Excise to raise assessments.
FA 1976. Section 21(2) and (3)—Persons in a representative capacity.

12.100 General principles

Generally

Basically, VAT is collectable by means of self-assessment (see **17.100**), although s 31(1) gives the Customs & Excise power to raise assessments in their best judgment, where they believe tax to be due as a result of a person's failure:

(*a*) to make returns;
(*b*) to keep sufficient documentation to substantiate the returns: or, where it appears to the Customs & Excise that any returns are incomplete or incorrect.

Obligation to make returns and record keeping

This topic is considered in more detail at **17.300**, but it should be appreciated that it is vital to make returns as otherwise the Customs & Excise can make an assessment based on their estimate of the amount of VAT due and the burden of proof is on the taxpayer to discharge the assessment (see **13.400**, *et seq*). Furthermore, where a person wishes to operate a special scheme he will only be able to do so if he keeps the requisite records (see **16.100**): failure to comply with the requirements can lead to the withdrawal of the scheme treatment (see *Charles Oliver Enterprises Ltd* v *CCE*, MAN/76/67 and *T M Deane* v *CCE*, CAR/77/10—noted at *Casebook* **12.314**).

Best judgment

Although the Customs & Excise has the general power to raise assessments, subject to being within the time limits and to the various points below, the Customs & Excise must raise the assessment to the "best of their judgment" (s 31(1)). The meaning of this phrase has been considered on various occasions by the Tribunals. In *P Friel* v *CCE*, [1977] VATTR 147 (*Casebook* **12.106**), for example, the Tribunal upheld the appeal of the taxpayer as the Customs & Excise had failed to enquire sufficiently into the manner in which the appellant ran his business and in *Mr and Mrs A J Williams* (*trading as Bridge Street Snack Bar*) v *CCE*, CAR/77/191 (*Casebook* **12.107**) the Tribunal again held in favour of the appellant on the basis that it was unreasonable of the Customs & Excise to have based their mark-up after watching the appellant's premises for only two hours at an unrepresentative time of the day. The Tribunal reached a similar conclusion in *Double Luck Restaurant Ltd* v *CCE*, MAN/77/282 (*Casebook* **12.108**) where the Customs & Excise had raised assessments after watching the restaurant from cars outside and based the assessments on the number of persons seen entering.

In *E J Riley Ltd* v *CCE*, MAN/78/266 (*Casebook* **12.110**) the Customs & Excise again lost an appeal because mark-ups had been used based on businesses different from those carried on by the appellant and, therefore, inappropriate for comparison.

However, a Tribunal has stated that the Customs & Excise do not have to spend unlimited time in order to arrive at a perfect assessment and referring to the "best endeavours" cases, has commented that:

> "'arguments by analogy of this kind are never satisfactory, but they do appear to indicate that 'best' does not mean 'perfect' or even 'of an exceptionally high standard' but would if considered by an appellate court to be likely to be interpreted as meaning of 'such standard as a group of reasonable or prudent men carrying out the duties imposed upon the Customs & Excise under Finance Act 1972 would be likely to adopt'."

(*C and A A Ford* v *CCE*, MAN/79/12 (*Casebook* **12.109**)).

Thus, it will be seen that it is open for an appellant to examine the basis upon which the Customs & Excise has made an estimated assessment to see whether it has used its best judgment.

Consideration should also be given to the basis upon which the Customs & Excise use mark-ups (see **12.300**, *et seq*) as if the basis is not representative the assessment may be open to challenge.

Assessment covering more than one period

The question as to whether an assessment can include more than one prescribed accounting period has caused much difficulty in the past as the law on the point was unclear and open to differing interpretation.

However, the position is now clarified in the light of the decision of the Court of Appeal in *S J Grange Ltd* v *CCE*, [1979] STC 183 (*Casebook* **12.101**), where the Court of Appeal, comprising Lord Denning MR, Templeman LJ. and Bridge LJ., held unanimously that an assessment covering 21 months was valid, thereby reversing the decision of Neill J. in the High Court. The Company argued, unsuccessfully before the Tribunal, but with success in the High Court that, to be valid an assessment could only be made under s 31(1) in respect of one quarterly accounting period, the tax assessable in respect of that period being clearly stated in the assessment. In support of its argument the company relied on s 31(2) which refers to an assessment "of an amount of tax due for any prescribed accounting period". Section 31(2) deals with time limits and Neill J. was persuaded that despite any specific reference in s 31(1) (which deals with the power of the Customs & Excise to make assessments) to quarterly periods it was a necessary implication from s 31(2) that tax should be assessed separately for a quarterly period.

In analysing the position in the Court of Appeal Lord Denning accepted that the company's argument "was literally correct", but went on to say:

"But it [the argument] leads to such impractical results that it is necessary to do a little adjustment so as to make the section workable."

The "adjustment" that was made was to read in words so that the assessment was issued under s 31(2) for any prescribed accounting period "which is included in the notice of assessment". So read the section meant, per Lord Denning (Bridge LJ. and Templeman LJ. concurred):

"that, in all cases where it is impossible for the Commissioners to split the assessment up into three-monthly periods, they can assess the amount of tax for any period of time which they specify ... and such assessment will be good."

Thus, the Court of Appeal accepted that an assessment could cover more than one period and reached that conclusion on the basis that the Customs & Excise would otherwise have considerable difficulty in assessing each period separately as they would have to make a guess as to what sales took place in any specific quarterly period.

The principle laid down in *S J Grange Ltd* v *CCE* has been extended by the Tribunals in *Heyfordian Travel Ltd* v *CCE*, LON/77/407 (*Casebook* **12.103**) and *J D Beaman* v *CCE*, BIR/78/80 (*Casebook* **12.104**). In particular, in *S J Grange Ltd*, the Court of Appeal reached its decision on the basis that if it were not possible to have an assessment for more than one period an intolerable burden would be placed on the Customs & Excise in attempting to assess earlier periods separately where the taxpayer's accounts and records were totally inadequate. However, in

Heyfordian Travel Ltd v *CCE* and *J D Beaman* v *CCE* the Tribunals held that assessments covering more than one period could be made notwithstanding that on the facts it would be possible for the Customs & Excise to assess each period contained in the assessment separately. In other words it does not have to be impossible for the Customs and Excise to split a period covering several accounting periods before a composite assessment can be validly issued. Nevertheless, the assessment must specify the period to which it relates, even if the period was more than one prescribed period: it is not possible to attach a schedule to the assessment setting out the periods assessed (see *R E Bell* v *CCE*, LON/78/289 (*Casebook* **12.102**)).

Two assessments for the same period: merger

It is not possible to have more than one assessment for the same accounting period unless the second assessment is raised once further evidence has come to the knowledge of the Customs & Excise after the making of the first assessment (s 31(2)). Thus, in *W R H Jeudwine* v *CCE*, [1977] VATTR 115 (*Casebook* **12.112**) the Tribunal commented that (s 31(1) and (2)):

> "initially authorise the Commissioners if they come to the conclusion that they have got an incomplete or incorrect return, to raise only a single assessment. They can raise that assessment ... but having done that ... they are bound by that assessment unless and until further evidence comes to their knowledge, when they have power to raise an additional assessment."

Following the decision in *W R H Jeudwine* v *CCE*, the Tribunal in *R Scott* v *CCE*, MAN/76/181 (*Casebook* **12.115**) applied the doctrine of merger to two assessments for a single period, holding that neither the first nor second assessment was valid. The facts of the *Scott* case were that, having raised an assessment and refused on the appellant's request for further information, to let the appellant know how the assessment had been arrived at, the Customs & Excise subsequently discovered arithmetical errors in the assessment and issued a second assessment for a higher amount. Applying *Jeudwine*, the second assessment was invalid as the Customs & Excise had no further evidence on which to base it. Furthermore, the first assessment was held to have merged with the second as, "two interests in the same subject matter became vested in the same person without the presence of any intervening interest" and was consequently itself invalid.

A similar decision to that in the Scott case was reached by the Tribunal in *R and M E Blackmore* v *CCE*, LON/78/260 (*Casebook* **12.113**).

The doctrine of merger has also been considered where an application for an extension of time within which to file an appeal was made, after judgment for the VAT due had been obtained in the High Court (see

T S Digwa v *CCE*, [1978] VATTR 119 and *G L and I Hall* v *CCE*, MAN/78/55 (*Casebook* **12.114** and **13.403** respectively).

Accounting for goods

Section 31 (3) enables the Customs & Excise to require a taxable person who has acquired or imported goods in the course or furtherance of his business to show what has happened to those goods. The taxable person must be able to show that the goods have been supplied, will be supplied or have been lost or destroyed. If the taxable person is unable to account for the goods the Customs & Excise may to the best of its judgment assess the tax that would otherwise have been payable.

Consequence of an assessment

Where a person has been assessed under s 31 (1) or (3) the tax, subject to appeal, shall be due and accordingly collectible in the normal way (see **17.400**), unless the assessment is withdrawn or reduced (s 31 (6)).

Representative capacity

FA 1976, s 21 (2) enables the Customs & Excise to assess persons acting in a representative capacity, for example, trustees in bankruptcy, liquidators, receivers and personal representatives, where such representatives fail to make, or make incorrect or incomplete, returns. Section 21 (3) allows a notice of assessment in such circumstances to be treated as properly served on the person for whom the representative is acting.

12.200 Time limits

Subject to the 6 year limit discussed *post*, to be valid, an assessment must be raised within the later of:

(*a*) 2 years from the end of the accounting period (s 31 (2) (*a*)); or
(*b*) 1 year from sufficient evidence (in the opinion of the Customs & Excise) coming to the knowledge of the Customs & Excise to enable an assessment to be raised (s 31 (2) (*b*)).

However, an additional assessment can be made where further evidence comes to the knowledge of the Customs & Excise, providing the assessment is made within 12 months of the additional information coming to the knowledge of the Customs & Excise (s 31 (2)).

Where an assessment covering more than one period is made difficulties can arise in ascertaining whether the assessment has been issued in time (see *S J Grange* v *CCE*, [1979] STC 183), particularly if some of the periods included in the assessment are more than 2 years before the date of the assessment. For example, if on 30 June 1980 the Customs & Excise raised one global assessment for the period 31 August 1976 to 31 December 1979, would the period from 31 August 1976 to 30 June 1978 be validly included in the assessment? In *S J Grange* v *CCE*, where the particular point was not in issue, Lord Denning and Templeman LJ. considered that the two year period began from the first accounting period contained in the assessment whereas Bridge LJ. thought the last period only had to be within the 2 year period. In the above example, therefore, if Bridge LJ. is correct the whole period is validly assessed, whereas if the view of Lord Denning and Templeman LJ. is preferred the assessment would be out of time. This raises a further problem, however, namely whether on Lord Denning and Templeman LJ.'s view the whole assessment is invalid or only that part from August 1976 to 30 June 1978.

As stated the point was not at issue in *S J Grange* v *CCE* and the issue is, therefore, uncertain. However, the Authors believe the view taken by Lord Denning and Templeman LJ. is the more attractive and that, further, as part of the assessment in the example above would, on that view, be out of time, the whole assessment would be invalid.

Assuming that the 2 year limit in (*a*) *ante* has passed the Customs & Excise can still issue an assessment if further evidence comes to their knowledge sufficient to justify the raising of an assessment (see (*b*), *ante*). Thus, if, for example, the Customs & Excise become aware of suppressed takings more than 2 years after the end of the accounting period concerned they still have a further year in which to raise the assessment (subject to the 6 year period (see *post*)). It will be noted at (*b*) that whether there are sufficient facts or not to issue an assessment shall be for the Customs & Excise to decide; however, this power is subject to review by the Tribunal. Thus, in *Macklin Services (Vending) West Ltd* v *CCE*, [1979] VATTR 31 (*Casebook* **12.201**) it was held that as the Customs & Excise had all the facts in their possession throughout the period assessed namely August 1973 to September 1976, the assessment could not be issued under s 31 (2) (*b*). Similar conclusions were reached by the Tribunals in *A Christofi* v *CCE*, LON/77/253 (*Casebook* **12.203**) and *V Lord* v *CCE*, MAN/76/113 (*Casebook* **12.204**). However, by way of contrast in *W J R Wood* (*trading as A1 Cabs*) v *CCE*, CAR/78/183 (*Casebook* **12.206**) the Tribunal held that an assessment was validly raised within the time limit of s 31(2)(*b*) where, although the Customs & Excise had made control visits to the appellant's premises in 1974 and 1975, it was not until a detailed study of the appellant's accounts was made in 1977 that further evidence came to light.

The position, therefore, appears to be that if the Customs & Excise has all the information and have reviewed it, it cannot on subsequently discovering either a mistake in the treatment of a supply or an under-declaration of profits, plead that further evidence has come to light to enable them to raise an assessment within a further year under s 31(2)(*b*); in such circumstances if the 2 year limit has passed no assessment will be able to be made. However, if the Customs & Excise has not studied a person's affairs the mere fact that it has the person's returns ought not to preclude them from raising an assessment (*Wood* v *CCE* (Casebook **12.206**)).

Six year time limit

The Customs & Excise is not generally able to raise assessments under s 31(1) or (3) more than 6 years after an accounting period or more than 6 years after importation. If the person has died, the period is reduced to 3 years from the date of death. However, if the Customs & Excise satisfy a Tribunal that there are reasonable grounds for believing that tax has been lost through the fraud or wilful default or neglect of any person an assessment may be made at any time (or within 6 years of death if the taxable person has died) providing the Tribunal gives leave to raise the assessment (s 31(4)). The members of a Tribunal which hears an application for leave to issue an assessment out of time under s 31(4) may not take part in the hearing of any appeal against the assessment (s 31(5)).

12.300 Estimated assessments

It is somewhat artificial to attempt to discuss estimated assessments in isolation as the general principles, time limits and the comments made under **12.100** and **12.200** equally apply to such assessments. For example, the Customs & Excise must use its best judgment in making assessments. However, certain principles have emerged from the cases, for example, in relation to the basis for calculating a mark-up, or what reduction, if any, must be allowed for pilferage or wastage and these are considered below.

Mark-ups

If the Customs & Excise believe that there has been an under-declaration of profits, it may seek to use a mark-up to calculate the correct amount of tax due. A useful indication of the mark-ups thought to be used by the Customs & Excise is set out in *Accountant's Weekly* and is repro-duced below. In arriving at the mark-up to be used the Customs & Excise may consider mark-ups of related businesses and apply those to a particular person. For example, if the appellant carries on a business as a restaurateur, the Customs & Excise may look at the mark-ups of similar restaurants in the same area and apply those to the person whose affairs are under review. If such a method is used the businesses must be of a similar nature (see *E J Riley* v *CCE*, MAN/78/266 (*Casebook* **12.110**)). Furthermore, the appellant is able to cross-examine the Customs & Excise on figures of related businesses if adduced by the Customs & Excise. The Customs & Excise is not able to plead privilege in respect of confidential information obtained from other traders if it cites figures based on comparative trades (*Alfred Compton* v *CCE*, [1973] 2 All ER 1169, cited with approval in *K W G Goodhew and others* v *CCE*, [1975] VATTR 111 (*Casebook* **12.304**) and followed in *Panayiotis Nicolas Trakka* v *CCE*, LON/75/36 (*Casebook* **12.305**)).

Customs & Excise VAT Mark-ups

Average retail mark-ups alleged by Accountant's Weekly to be used by Customs & Excise in judging the reliability of traders' records. The source is alleged to be a secret list used by Customs & Excise.

AVERAGE RETAIL MARK-UPS

Product	Scotland %	N England %	Midlands %	S & SW %	London & SE %
Batteries (dry)	40	40	—	—	45
Cakes & biscuits	30	20	10	25	20
Carpets	40	40	60	25	65
Cigs & tobacco	9	7–10	8–10	8	7–12
Clothing					
shirts	65	85	65	60	50–100
suits	90	85	75	60	50–100
childrens	50	45	40	45	50–100
womens	70	70	75	70	50–100
	Dept stores	Dept stores	Dept stores		
	80	80	80		
Confectionery	25	20–25	25	20–25	25
Cosmetics	70	50	55	50	55
Cycles	35	30	30	—	—
Electrical goods (excl radio & TV)	50	25	45	50	40
Footwear	40	45	45	45	40
Furniture	50	55	45	75	80
Greetings cards	70	50–60	50	75	40
Hardware	50	40	40	40	40
Household cleaners	40	20	25	—	20
Ice cream	35	50	50	25	30
Jewellery	75	50–100	80	100	75
Newspapers and magazines	35	25–30	30	25	30
Radios & TVs	50 (TV's) 30	30–50	45	50	50
Records	30	35	30	30	40

Soap & soap powder	30	20	20	—	25
Sports equipment	45	40	30	—	45
Stationery	40	35	30	40	35
Tinned goods					
baby foods	25	20	—	—	33
fruit	20	20	30	—	—
meat	25	20	25	—	—
pet foods	40	30	25	35	20
vegetables	20	20	20	—	—
Toys	50	40	60	30	60
Watches	65	70	75	70	—

BEER, WINES AND SPIRITS
AVERAGE RETAIL MARK-UPS

Type	Scotland %	N England %	Midlands %	S & SW %	London & SE %
Beer draught	55	50+	40–60	45	70 Keg 100
Beer bottled					
Grocers	20	45	—	20	20
off licences	20	45	—	20	25
pubs	65	60	60–80	60	80
hotels	65	60–80	—	60	—
Wines					
grocers	36	30	30	20	20
off licences	30	20–25	—	—	20
pubs	70–90	100+	90–100+	90	100+
hotels	95	100	80–100	—	—
Spirits					
grocers	6	10	16	19	12
off licences	18	10	—	—	20
pubs	55–95	100+	90–100+	100	100+
hotels	95	100–120+	80–100+	100	—
Minerals					
grocers	—	25	30	25	20
confectioner	—	25	—	25	—
off licences	30	25	25	25	20
pubs	—	100	75–100+	80–100	100+
hotels	—	100–120	60	80–100	—
Cider					
grocers	—	—	50	—	—
pubs	—	100	65	60	75

Retail mark-ups

Existing information indicates that for some goods, mark-ups vary considerably from area to area and over a wide range of percentages. Even within a comparatively small trading area considerable variations exist. Some of the factors affecting the mark-up applied to a particular description of goods are: location of premises, size of trader, competition in the neighbourhood, type of supplier, quality of merchandise, size of pack, losses and wastage, and health, age and financial situation of the trader. In addition variation can arise due to seasonal change in some traders.

It is not, therefore, possible to publish any authoritative or accurate details of mark-ups applied but it is considered that an approximate summary might serve a useful purpose. The Appendix to this section gives details of approximate average percentage mark-ups for a variety of types of goods in five broad regions of the country. They are averages over the whole range of turnover bands and types of traders unless otherwise stated.

> The averages must only be used as a broad guide to the credibility of the traders' accounts. On no account is a trader or indeed a VAT tribunal to be given any indication that officers have a guide of this kind. Before any conclusion is drawn as to the accuracy of a trader's recorded outputs the mark-ups actually applied by him are to be ascertained and, if practicable, tested. No assessment is to be raised using the average mark-ups listed unless, by chance, the figure coincides with the trader's actual mark-up.

Where two Officers of the Customs & Excise arrive at the same mark-up by using different methods of calculation the Tribunal held that there must be something wrong with the methods used rather than that the methods corroborate the mark-up (*Mrs K Taylor* v *CCE*, [1975] VATTR 86 (*Casebook* **12.301**)).

In *R M Arora and Others* v *CCE*, [1976] VATTR 53 (*Casebook* **12.302**) the Tribunal held that it did not make any difference whether a mark-up was applied to the tax inclusive or exclusive price providing the same approach was used when calculating the tax payable.

If the appellant admits to certain under-declarations in his returns, a contemporaneous statement in writing is required from him if the Customs & Excise are to rely on such admissions (*C M Cunliffe* v *CCE*, MAN/78/227 (*Casebook* **12.303**)).

In another series of cases the Tribunals have considered the position where the Customs & Excise has based mark-ups on visits to the person's premises. In such cases the examination of the person's business must be sufficiently detailed as to enable the mark-up to be accurately calculated. Thus, in *S H Leung* v *CCE*, EDN/77/20 (*Casebook* **12.306**) the Tribunal held that it was unreasonable to calculate a mark-up based on watching the appellant's premises for two Wednesdays only. Similarly, in *Mr and Mrs A J Williams* v *CCE*, CAR/77/191 (*Casebook* **12.107**) it was held to be unreasonable to base assessments on one visit for slightly more than 2 hours by an Officer of the Customs & Excise.

Wastages
The Tribunal is normally prepared to accept arguments by appellants that assessments should be reduced due to wastages; this is particularly so in the case of licensed publicans. An interesting case in which the question of wastage is considered is *R Roocroft* v *CCE*, MAN/76/110 (*Casebook* **12.311**). The standard of care with regard to wastage is not so high where the appellant is an amateur (see *Gloucester Old Boys Rugby Football Social Club* v *CCE*, CAR/77/133 (*Casebook* **12.312**) where the Tribunal remarked that VAT was a tax on supplies and not on inefficiency. These comments were endorsed by the Tribunal in *T G and P Bevan* v *CCE*, CAR/78/308 (*Casebook* **12.313**).

Chapter 13

Appeals

13.000 Sources

Section 39 —Evidence by certificate.
Section 40 —Grounds of appeal; making of returns and payment of tax prior to appeal; interest on tax.
Section 44 —Service of notices.
Schedule 6—Constitution and procedure of VAT Tribunals.
VAT Tribunals Rules 1972 (SI 1972 No 1344)—Rules of procedure before VAT Tribunals.
A right of further appeal is given by virtue of:
Tribunals and Inquiries Act 1972 s 13 and Sched 1—Appeals from certain Tribunals.
The Tribunals and Inquiries (VAT Tribunals Order 1972 (SI 1972 No 1210)
—This Order applies the Tribunals and Inquiries Act to VAT Tribunals.

The following leaflet issued by the President of the VAT Tribunals may also be of use:
VAT Appeals to Value Added Tax Tribunals Explanatory Leaflet.

The President of the VAT Tribunals has also issued Practice Notes to explain certain aspects of procedure before VAT Tribunals under the VAT Tribunals Rules 1972 (SI 1972 No 1344). These notes are reported at [1973] VATTR 215 and [1978] VATTR 266, 278.

13.100 General principles

Conditions precedent to an appeal

For an issue to be capable of being subject to appeal certain basic pre-conditions must be satisfied. These are:

(*a*) there must be a determination of the Customs & Excise on the point at issue (see p 229 *post*);

(*b*) the potential appellant must have sufficient interest in the matter in dispute to be able to bring the matter to appeal, that is, he must have sufficient *locus standi* (see **13.200**);

(*c*) the appellate body itself must have jurisdiction to hear the appeal (see **13.200**);

(*d*) the matter at issue must fall within one of the grounds of appeal (see **13.300**);

(*e*) the time for appeal should not have expired (subject to an extension of such time) (see **13.400**).

Having satisfied these preconditions, the correct procedure must be followed by the appellant (see **13.400**).

Appellate bodies

The primary appellate body established for VAT purposes is the VAT Tribunal. This Chapter will concentrate on appeals before such Tribunals as, due to the relative informality of its hearings, it is common for a taxpayer to appear before VAT Tribunals in person or be represented by a non-legal adviser, for example his accountant.

Appeals from VAT Tribunals, on matters of law only, are made to the Queen's Bench Division of the High Court, usually by way of direct appeal. A further right of appeal is available to the Court of Appeal or by way of a "leapfrog" motion on issues of fundamental importance to the House of Lords. Leave of the court must be obtained before an appeal may be made to the House of Lords. It is to be noted that appeals are to the Queen's Bench Division of the High Court and not the Chancery Division as is the case with income and corporation tax appeals. It has been suggested that this in part explains the court's reluctance to make use of revenue precedents when construing VAT legislation. Appeals from the Court of Appeal are to the House of Lords.

A further reference by UK courts of VAT matters involving EEC law is possible in theory to the European Court of Justice. Such a reference may be made at all stages of the appellate process. No such references have yet been made by a UK court in relation to VAT. References to the European Court are discussed at **13.800**.

Composition of the appellate bodies

VAT TRIBUNALS

The Tribunal staff comprises a President, a panel of Chairmen, in both cases appointed in England and Wales by the Lord Chancellor, in Scotland by the Lord President and in Northern Ireland by the Lord Chief Justice of Northern Ireland and a panel of other members, appointed by the Treasury. The President is required to be a barrister, advocate or solicitor of at least 10 years standing. There is no legal qualification requirement for the Chairmen or other members of VAT Tribunals.

The President determines the number and place of sitting of VAT Tribunals, the number being agreed with the Treasury. At present, there are Tribunal centres in:

(a) London;   (c) Edinburgh;
(b) Manchester;   (d) Belfast.

The centre at which an appeal will be heard is usually determined by the area of the country in which the taxpayer is located. There is, however, power for an appeal to be transferred between centres (see **13.400**).

Appeals may be heard by a Chairman sitting alone or by a Chairman plus one or two other members. The Chairman must be either the President or one of the panel of Chairmen. Decisions are taken by majority with the Chairman having a casting vote on an equality of votes.

HIGH COURT, QUEEN'S BENCH DIVISION

The judges of the High Court, Queen's Bench Division (QBD) comprise the Lord Chief Justice, who is also the President of the QBD, and a number of puisne judges. All judges are appointed by the Crown on the advice of the Lord Chancellor. The qualification for a puisne judge is service as a barrister for at least 10 years.

The court sits at the Royal Courts of Justice in the Strand, London. There are four sittings of the court each year, namely:

(*a*) the Michaelmas Sitting, 1 October–21 December;
(*b*) the Hilary Sitting, 11 January to the Wednesday before Easter Sunday;
(*c*) the Easter Sitting, the second Tuesday after Easter Sunday to the Friday before the Spring holiday; and
(*d*) the Trinity Sitting, the second Tuesday after the spring holiday to 31 July.

There is a procedure for hearing an appeal during the vacations but applications for such hearings are only allowed in cases of urgent need.

Appeals in the High Court are in practice heard by a single judge in VAT appeals (Rules of the Supreme Court Order 55, r 2).

COURT OF APPEAL

The Court of Appeal comprises the Lord Chancellor, who is also the President of the Court, ex-Lord Chancellors, the Lord Chief Justice, the Master of the Rolls, the President of the Family Division, certain Lords of Appeal in Ordinary and, a number of Lord Justices of Appeal. Lord Justices of Appeal are appointed by the Crown on advice from the Lord Chancellor and have a minimum qualification of service as a barrister for at least 10 years or as a judge of the High Court.

The court has the same sittings as the High Court (see HIGH COURT, QBD, *ante*).

Interlocutary matters may be heard by two judges in the Court of Appeal, but final matters require three judges to be present, decisions being taken by majority. The parties may consent to an appeal being heard by two judges alone but in the event of conflicting judgments, the case must be reargued before three judges prior to being permitted to proceed to the House of Lords.

HOUSE OF LORDS

The judicial function of the House of Lords is exercised by the Lord High Chancellor of Great Britain, the Lords of Appeal in Ordinary and any peer of Parliament who is either a member of the Judicial Committee of the Privy Council or a judge of the Supreme Court. Lords of Appeal in Ordinary are appointed by the Crown on advice from the Lord Chancellor and must either have held a high judicial office for at least 2 years or practise as a barrister for at least 15 years.

A minimum of three of the above judges must be present for the hearing of an appeal, the decision being that of the majority.

THE EUROPEAN COURT OF JUSTICE ("ECJ")

The court comprises nine judges chosen, from "persons whose independence is beyond doubt and who possess the qualifications required for appointments to the highest judicial offices" in their respective countries, by the Member States themselves. In practice, there is one judge from each Member State and, although the quorum is seven, all usually consider a reference to the ECJ. A party may not make application for a change in the composition of the court on the ground that a national of its or its opponent's country is or is not sitting.

A feature of the court which differs from the UK appellate process is that the court is assisted by an Advocate General selected out of a panel of four for the particular reference in hand. The Advocate General is also independent of each party and gives a reasoned opinion at the end of the oral proceedings in summary of the facts, review of the legal arguments involved and containing a suggestion as to how the case should be determined. The Advocate General is not restricted in giving his opinion to the issues pleaded by the parties.

The judges of the court are not bound by the opinion of the Advocate General and deliver their combined judgment in open court after deliberating in private. The Advocate General does not attend such deliberations. This procedure is curious to English eyes and may be explained in part by the fact that the European Court of Justice is not an appellate court as such but acts as a court of first and last instance in the interpretation of the Treaty of Rome and Community law generally. There is no appeal from the judgments of the ECJ. The opinion of the Advocate General may be likened, therefore, to a decision at first instance which is subject to review by the judges of the ECJ themselves.

13.200 Locus standi and jurisdiction

All references to "rules" are to the VAT Tribunals Rules 1972 (SI 1972 No 1344) unless otherwise stated.

The appellant

Before a person may bring an appeal before the Tribunal he must have a sufficient interest in the outcome of the point at issue. In the majority of instances, this will not present any problem as the appeal will be against, for example, the refusal by the Customs & Excise to allow a trader's claim for registration, input tax credit, or bad debt relief under FA 1978, 12 or against an assessment to tax. However, shortly after the introduction of VAT doubt was expressed as to the ability of a recipient of a supply to make an appeal. This was notwithstanding the fact that the question as to the amount of tax chargeable on any supply of goods or services is clearly a ground of appeal (s 40(1)(*c*)). This doubt was increased as a result of:

(*a*) the additional requirement that the tax in issue had to be paid (or this requirement waived in cases of hardship) to establish the jurisdiction of the Tribunal itself to hear the appeal (s. 40(3)); and

(*b*) the need for there to be a formal determination of the Customs & Excise in respect of which notice of appeal could be given within the prescribed time limit (VAT Tribunals Rules 1972 (SI 1972 No 1344), rr 3 and 4).

These doubts as to *locus standi* were eventually resolved in favour of the recipient of a supply. It now seems to be settled that a supplier or a recipient of a supply have sufficient financial interest in the outcome of an appeal to be able to initiate an appeal or be heard by a Tribunal.

It is no longer necessary, therefore, for a recipient to join the supplier in his appeal. It also seems possible that a recipient of a supply may rely upon a determination addressed to the supplier by the Customs & Excise in making his appeal (see *Processed Vegetable Growers Association Ltd* v *CCE*, [1973] VATTR 87 (*Casebook* **13.201**), but see also *Davis Advertising Services Ltd* v *CCE*, [1973] VATTR 16).

It is, however, still necessary for the tax to have been paid. In practice, this is unlikely to be a problem as a recipient of a supply is unlikely to wish to appeal to the Tribunal where he has not been charged VAT by the supplier. In such cases, therefore, it only becomes necessary to show that the supplier has accounted to the Customs & Excise for that tax. The supplier then becomes a trustee for the recipient of the supply in relation to that tax and any interest thereon should the recipient be successful in his appeal (see *W J M Mahoney* v *CCE*, [1976] VATTR 241 (*Casebook* **13.203**).

Finally, it is to be noted that the requirement in s 40 (2) that all returns must be made before an appeal may be heard (see *post*) will not prevent an appeal by the recipient of a supply. This is because s 40(2) only requires the appellant to make all returns required of him under s 30(2); the recipient of a supply has no obligation to make any such returns.

Jurisdiction of the tribunal

The following paragraphs will consider certain aspects regarding the extent of the Tribunal's jurisdiction to hear an appeal and the two factors which may prevent such jurisdiction arising.

EXTENT OF JURISDICTION: GROUNDS OF APPEAL

A Tribunal can only hear an appeal made on one of the grounds listed in s 40(1). As to these grounds, see generally **13.300**. This principle is well illustrated by the cases involving the question as to whether the Tribunal may review the exercise by the Customs & Excise of their numerous discretions in the administration and collection of VAT. For example, a fine distinction was drawn in *Barton Townley (Barrow) Ltd* v *CCE*, MAN/75/101, in relation to the exercise by the Customs & Excise of its discretion under the FA 1973, s 4 to allow a late claim for input tax credit in respect of purchase tax suffered on stock held at the commencement of VAT. The taxpayer sought to appeal, under s 40(1)(*d*), against a refusal of such a claim by the Customs & Excise. It was held, however, that no input tax could be treated as arising and, therefore, its amount could not be in dispute as required by s 40, prior to a favourable exercise of the Customs & Excise discretion to allow a late claim under s 4. No appeal lay against the Customs & Excise refusal, therefore.

For a more detailed discussion as to the Tribunal's ability to review the exercise by the Customs & Excise of its discretions given to them, see Chapter 11.

MAKING OF ALL RETURNS (S 40(2))

A bar to the Tribunal hearing an appeal operates where the appellant has failed to make all the returns required of him under s 30(2) and has not paid the amounts shown on those returns as payable by him. The returns required in this respect are those in VAT (General) Regulations 1977 (SI 1977 No 1759), regs 51 and 52 (see Chapter 17).

The date for the compliance with this condition is midnight on the day preceding the day of the hearing (*C W Lacey* v *CCE*, [1975] VATTR

179 (*Casebook* **13.213**)). Tribunals have been willing to accept in the past an appellant's statement that returns have been posted to the Customs & Excise, albeit not received by them, prior to the day of the hearing and have allowed an appeal to proceed on this basis. However, an appellant is well advised not to indulge in this form of brinkmanship if for no other reason than the fact that he may actually be required to prove that this is the case.

Filing improper or conditional returns will not satisfy s 40(2). A conditional return has been held to have been made not only where the declaration on the return was expressed to be made subject to the settlement of the tax in dispute (*D K Wright and Associates Ltd* v *CCE*, [1975] VATTR 168 (*Casebook* **13.211**)) but also where two returns were made for a single prescribed accounting period (*Greenbank Warehouses Ltd* v *CCE*, MAN/76/170 (*Casebook* **13.212**)). The lesson to be learnt here is that, as an incorrect return will satisfy s 40(2), where a taxpayer is in doubt as to the treatment of an item for VAT purposes, he should file a return stating, in accordance with his views, the tax that is due. The Customs & Excise will then assess the taxpayer for any balance of tax they feel is payable and an appeal may then be made in relation to that assessment.

The Customs & Excise has power to waive the requirement under s 40(2) that returns have to be made (*E G Gittins* v *CCE*, [1974] VATTR 109 (*Casebook* **13.216**)).

Finally, it should be noted that it is now a requirement that, before an appeal may be made against an assessment, all returns for the period covered by that assessment must have been made (s 40(1)(*b*) as amended by FA 1980).

PAYMENT OF TAX (S 40(3))

A further bar arises in relation to appeals under s 40(1)(*b*) or (*c*), that is, against determinations of the Customs & Excise as to an assessment or the amount of an assessment under s 31 or as to the tax chargeable on a supply of goods or services or on their importation into the United Kingdom. In such circumstances, no hearing of an appeal may take place before the appellant has paid or deposited with the Customs & Excise the amount of tax in dispute.

The Customs & Excise again has the general power to waive this requirement where it is satisfied that the appellant would suffer undue hardship if he were required to pay the tax prior to the appeal. Should the Customs & Excise refuse to exercise its discretion in this respect, an application may be made by the appellant to the Tribunal under the VAT Tribunals Rules 1972 (SI 1972 No 1344), for a direction that the appeal be heard without the payment of tax. This procedure is discussed further at **13,400,** *post*.

An appellant should carefully consider whether or not to make such payment of tax. This is because it is within the power of the Tribunal to rule that interest should be paid on any unpaid tax should the appellant lose his case. Equally, should the Customs & Excise lose its case, interest may be awarded in the appellant's favour on any tax already paid by him which is ordered to be repaid. When interest is awarded, it is awarded at such rate as the Tribunal may determine. In *Visionhire Ltd v CCE*, [1974] VATTR 62 (*Casebook* **13.601**), the Tribunal indicated that interest should be awarded at the Bank of England minimum lending rate. Such interest may be allowable and is equally not chargeable for income and corporation tax purposes.

EXTENT OF JURISDICTION: MERGER

Where an assessment has become final and binding (because an appeal has not been made within the 30 day time limit) and a judgment debt has been obtained by the Customs & Excise against the taxpayer in the County Court (where the amount due is £1,000 or less) or the High Court, no appeal, or application for an appeal out of time, can be made. In such circumstances, the cause of action (the tax due under the assessment) will have merged with the judgment and the rights of the taxpayer and the Customs & Excise become governed solely by the judgment. The Tribunal has no power to revive the assessment in order to hear an appeal against it. The correct action to be taken by the taxpayer in such cases, therefore, is to apply to the court concerned to have the judgment set aside.

The mere service of a writ in proceedings by way of default action will not exclude the Tribunal from jurisdiction by way of merger. Although a grey area of the law, it is thought that merger will actually take place on the delivery of the judgment in favour of the Customs & Excise rather than the date of the formal drawing up and entering of the judgment (see *T S Digwa* v *CCE*, [1978] VATTR 119 (*Casebook* **13.208**)).

EXTENT OF JURISDICTION: EXCLUSION OF CERTAIN REMEDIES

While VAT Tribunals should apply the rules of natural justice, it is clear that they do not have jurisdiction to hear arguments based on the laws of negligence or equity. Such latter jurisdiction is vested solely in the Supreme Court and the County Courts. This issue has arisen principally in relation to cases where an appellant has attempted to avoid an assessment by seeking to prevent the Customs & Excise going back on a former ruling given by them. The most common line of argument in such cases has been that the Customs & Excise should be estopped from revising their earlier ruling. While Tribunals consistently rejected such arguments (except in the case of *P L Bailey* v *CCE*, MAN/77/163

(*Casebook* **11.306**)) which must be considered as wrongly decided), the more correct approach would possibly have been to refuse to hear such arguments (see in this respect *Coolisle Ltd* v *CCE*, LON/78/242 (*Casebook* **13.206**)). For a general review of *estoppel* see **11.300**.

EXTENT OF JURISDICTION: FUTURE SUPPLIES

A Tribunal does not have the ability to rule as to the treatment of a transaction before that transaction has been effected (see *Parochial Church Council of Emmanuel Church* v *CCE*, [1973] VATTR 76 (*Casebook* **13.205**)). This is in effect a part of the basic rule that an appeal must be against one of the issues listed in s 40(1) all of which presuppose that the event against which the appeal is raised has taken place.

13.300 Grounds of appeal

The issues against which an appeal may be made are set out in 40(1). They are:

(*a*) *Registration*: "the registration or cancellation of registration of any person under this Part of this Act".

For registration, see **2.000.**

(*b*) *Assessments:* "an assessment (i) under subsection (1) of section 32 of this Act in respect of a period for which the appellant has made a return under this Part of this Act; or (ii) under subsection (3) of that section, or the amount of such an assessment".

For assessments and time limits for assessments see Chapter 12.

(*c*) *Supplies or importations:* "the tax chargeable on the supply of any goods or services or, subject to subsection (3) of this section, on the importation of any goods".

Subsection (3) relates to the condition that tax must be paid or deposited prior to the hearing of an appeal. For supply, see **3.000** and importation **6.000**.

One exception to the right of appeal to a Tribunal in relation to imported goods arises where the matter in dispute could be, or has been, referred to arbitration under the Customs and Excise Management Act 1979, 127 (s 40(5)). Section 127 applies to disputes concerning the valuation of goods for duty purposes and provides that an importer may pay the duty demanded by the Customs & Excise and, within 3 months, require the dispute to be referred to arbitration or a referee appointed by the Lord Chancellor.

(*d*) *Input tax:* "the amount of any input tax which may be credited to a person".

For input tax see Chapter 5. Note the distinction drawn in *Barton*

Townley (Barrow) Ltd v *CCE*, MAN/75/101 (*Casebook* **13.257**), referred to on p 224, *ante*.

(*e*) *Taxable supplies:* "the proportion of any supplies that is to be taken as consisting of taxable supplies".

See Chapter 9 as to exemption and **5.300** as to partial exemption.

(*f*) *Special schemes:* "any refusal to permit the value of supplies to be determined by a method described in a notice published under section 30(3) of [FA 1972]".

This relates to special schemes for retailers discussed at **16.200**.

(*g*) *Group election:* "any refusal of an application under section 21 of this Act".

This relates to applications for group VAT registration (see **2.400**) and is an instance where the Tribunal is given specific power to review a Customs & Excise discretion.

(*h*) *Discretionary registration:* "any refusal to act or continue to act on a request under paragraph 11(1)(*b*) to [FA 1972]".

This concerns appeals against actions of the Customs & Excise in relation to the voluntary registration of a person whose taxable supplies do not exceed the statutory registration limits. See **2.300**.

(*i*) *Anti-avoidance direction:* "any direction under paragraph 1, 2 or 3 of Schedule 3 to this Act".

See **3.500**.

(*j*) *Security for tax:* "the requirement of any security under section 32(2) of [FA 1972]".

See **14.200D**. This is another instance of the Tribunal being able to review the discretion of the Customs & Excise.

(*k*) *DIY builders:* "the amount of any refunds under section 15A of [FA 1972]".

See **5.500**.

(*l*) *Goods imported for private purposes*—"a claim by a taxable person under section 16 of the Finance Act 1977".

See p 66, *ante*.

(*m*) *Bad debt relief:* "a claim for a refund under section 12 of the Finance Act 1978".

See **18.000**.

It is to be noted from the above that there is no appeal to the Tribunal against the refusal of any taxable person to issue a tax invoice to another taxable person. As an invoice is now required before a claim to input tax can be made (unless the Customs & Excise otherwise agree) this is a serious omission.

13.400 Procedure

All references to "rules" are to the VAT Tribunals Rules 1972 (SI 1972 No 1344) unless otherwise stated.

VAT Tribunals

The Customs & Excise are given, by Sched 6, para 10, the power to make rules for the procedure to be adopted on appeals to VAT Tribunals. These rules are contained in the VAT Tribunals Rules 1972 as amended. In addition, the Tribunal has issued Practice Notes, reported at [1973] VATTR 215 and [1978] VATTR 266, 278 by way of clarification and comment on certain aspects of these rules. The explanatory leaflet issued by the President of the VAT Tribunals may also be of assistance to a potential appellant.

Time limits

As in all litigation, it is important to observe the time limits set for the lodging of the notice of appeal and the fulfilment of all procedural requirements.

The notice of appeal must be served at the appropriate Tribunal Centre before the expiration of 30 days after the date of the letter of assessment from the Customs & Excise containing the disputed decision. It is important to note here, as indeed with appeals under income tax matters, that it is the date of the document appealed against that is material, not the date of its receipt. It is, however, the date of receipt of the notice of appeal by the Tribunal Centre that will determine whether the appeal is made on time.

It is also important to note that there must be a "decision" of the Customs & Excise before an appeal can be made. It was pointed out by the Tribunal in *Allied Windows (S Wales) Ltd* v *CCE*, [1973] VATTR 3 (*Casebook* **13.104**), that a decision does not include mere guidance given by the Customs & Excise. There must be a specific matter affecting the taxpayer in respect of the VAT consequences of which the Customs & Excise has given a ruling before the time limit for appeal will begin to run. It follows that a letter from the Customs & Excise in relation to a "no names" or general enquiry cannot support an appeal.

Once given, a decision of the Customs & Excise cannot be withdrawn (*Effective Education Association* v *CCE*, LON/76/95 (*Casebook* **13.401**)).

The requirement for service of a notice of appeal within 30 days is subject to two qualifications:

(*a*) the Customs & Excise has the power to extend the time for lodging an appeal to a date 21 days after a date specified by them in writing to the taxpayer (r 4). This is primarily designed to give the parties further time to negotiate a settlement of the matter at issue. If when discussing the VAT treatment of a specific transaction with the Customs & Excise, therefore, a taxpayer considers that the Customs & Excise has gone beyond the stage of giving mere guidance and that he has received a "decision" from the Customs & Excise, he should request the Customs & Excise as a matter of course to extend the time limit for appeal;

(*b*) the tribunal has a general power to direct an extension of any time limit in relation to an appeal (r 18).

The Tribunal may so direct an extension of time either on the application of a party to the appeal or on its own initiative without reference to either party. An extension may be granted before the expiry of the time limit in question and any extension will be on such terms as the Tribunal thinks fit. Such terms may be the payment of costs by the part requesting the extension or the fulfilment of some condition before a specified date, for example, the completion of all returns.

The Tribunal has in fact shown a willingness to grant taxpayers leave to appeal out of time where there has been a complete lack of understanding of VAT matters on the part of the particular appellant or where the taxpayer has been the innocent victim of another's default. In *A J Blackall* v *CCE*, MAN/77/273 (*Casebook* **13.409**), the default was that of the taxpayer's manager and in *W R Hallam* v *CCE*, MAN/78/187 (*Casebook* **13.407**), that of the taxpayer's advisers. In both cases, an extension was granted. Ignorance of the fact that there was a time limit for lodging an appeal was sufficient for the Tribunal to grant an extension in *W J Price* v *CCE*, [1978] VATTR 115 (*Casebook* **13.410**).

However, there must be some reasonable explanation for the failure to make an appeal in time in order for an extension to be granted and, as pointed out by the Tribunal in *R Kyffin* v *CCE*, MAN/78/89 (*Casebook* **13.404**), some material end must be served by allowing the appeal. Extensions will not be granted where there is a judgment debt for the tax in issue outstanding against the taxpayer or where the taxpayer has paid the tax in dispute under a mistake of law.

The "appropriate Tribunal Centre" at which to lodge an appeal is the centre for the area in which the address, to which the disputed decision of the Customs & Excise was sent, is located. If the taxpayer serves his notice of appeal at the wrong Tribunal Centre, it may be returned to him thereby possibly prejudicing the service by him of the appeal at the correct Tribunal Centre within the time limit. However, the President of the VAT Tribunals has commented that if the notice is correct in all other respects it will be posted to the correct Centre by the Tribunal staff. Even here, there will be a time delay before it is received by the correct Centre. Care should be taken, therefore, in addressing the notice to the appropriate Centre. The Centres and their respective catchment areas are set out in VAT Tribunals Explanatory Leaflet and the

Appointment notice of the President of the VAT Tribunals dated 21 March 1980.

The service of a notice will be acknowledged by the "proper officer" of the VAT Tribunal Centre who will also forward a copy of the notice to the Customs & Excise.

A notice of appeal may be withdrawn at any time by notice to the Tribunal Centre.

Content of a notice of appeal

Although the President of the VAT Tribunals has published a recommended form of notice (Trib 1), which is available from any Customs & Excise VAT office), no particular form of appeal is necessary provided that it contains the information required by r 3(2). Rule 3(2) provides:

"3(2) A notice of appeal shall be signed by or on behalf of the appellant and shall—

(a) state the name and address of the appellant and the address to which the disputed decision was sent by the Commissioners,

(b) state the address of the office of the Commissioners from which the disputed decision was sent,

(c) state the date of the letter from the Commissioners containing the disputed decision,

(d) set out, or have attached thereto a document containing, the grounds of the appeal, and ...

(e) have attached thereto a copy of any letter from the Commissioners continuing his time to appeal against the disputed decision and of any letter from the Commissioners notifying to the appellant a date, later than the date of the letter containing the disputed decision, from which his time to appeal against the disputed decision shall run".

In addition to (a)–(c) the Tribunal has requested that a copy of the disputed decision should be sent with the notice in order that the Tribunal may discover, at the earliest possible date, the nature of the disputed decision.

As to (d), the appellant should take some care in setting out his grounds of appeal. In the words of the Practice Notes:

"Although it is not expected or desired that the appellant will set out any elaborate argument in a Notice of Appeal, he should set out the propositions of fact or law on which he relies to reverse the Commissioners' decision with sufficient particularity to enable the Commissioners to see the basis of the case against them".

If the Tribunal considers that the grounds of appeal are insufficiently clear, it may direct that the appellant gives further particulars of his case.

Further, where an appellant wishes at a later stage to rely on additional grounds not set out in his original notice, he will have to make an application to the Tribunal under r 19 for a direction that the notice may be amended accordingly (see also rr 12 and 17). Although the Customs & Excise are unlikely to object to such an application (but may make a cross application for an adjournment of the hearing), the appellant should attempt to be comprehensive in his original notice as to his grounds for appeal).

(As to the requirement in (*e*), see *Time limits, ante.*)

Disclosure of documents

The appellant must serve at the appropriate Tribunal Centre within 30 days of the date of service of his notice of appeal a list of the documents in his possession, custody and power which he intends to produce at the hearing. A copy of this list will be sent to the other party by the proper officer of the Tribunal Centre.

The list must state a reasonable time, commencing not earlier than 7 and ending not later than 14 days after the date of such list, during which and at a reasonable place at which the other party may inspect and take copies of such documents (r 7). Such documents must also be produced at the hearing if called for by the other party. The appellant should, therefore, have at least five sets of copies of such documents available at the hearing (that is, one for each of the Tribunal panel, one for the Commissioners and one for himself).

It will be noted that the appellant is required to produce the list of documents at the same time as the expiry of the time limit given to the Customs & Excise to make their Statement of Case available to the Tribunal (see *Statement of case and disclosure of documents by CCE, post*). It is unlikely, therefore, that the appellant will have seen details of the case against him (other than those of which he is aware from earlier discussions with the Customs & Excise) before he is obliged to compile the list of documents. It is perhaps worth delaying, therefore, until the end of the 30-day period before serving the list on the Tribunal in the hope that the Customs & Excise Case may become available. If the appellant wishes to amend his list at a later stage, he will again be obliged to apply to the Tribunal for a direction that he may do so.

The President of the VAT Tribunals has issued form Trib 2 which may be used to list the documents to be relied upon by the appellant.

The appellant should also, at least 24 hours before the day of the hearing, give notice to the Tribunal Centre of any text books or authorities he will refer to at the hearing.

Statement of case and disclosure of documents

Within 30 days of the date of service of a notice of appeal (or 14 days in the case of an application by the taxpayer for leave to appeal out of time or to appeal without payment of tax), the Customs & Excise must serve at the appropriate Tribunal Centre:

(*a*) a copy of the disputed decision; and

(*b*) a document stating the grounds for that decision and any further grounds they wish to advance in support of that decision (or in the case of an application for extension of time or appeal without payment of tax, the grounds on which they wish to oppose such application).

This Case is not intended to be an answer to the grounds of appeal listed in the appellant's notice of appeal and, therefore, the Tribunal will not normally (unless the appellant agrees) extend the time for lodging such Case even where the Tribunal is requesting further particulars from the appellant in relation to his notice. If, once the further information is available, the Customs & Excise wish to lodge a further or amended Case, it must, if the appellant does not agree, apply to the Tribunal for leave to do so.

Copies of the Customs & Excise Case will be sent to the appellant by the proper officer of the Tribunal Centre.

If the Customs & Excise contend that the Tribunal does not have jurisdiction to hear the appeal, it should inform the Tribunal as soon as practicable after service of the appellant's notice of appeal (r 6(2)). Such notice by the Customs & Excise should set out the basis for such contention and may either:

(*a*) be contained in the Statement of Case;
(*b*) be served with an application that the appeal be struck out under r 16; or
(*c*) be served separately.

Unless method (*b*) is adopted by the Customs & Excise, it is usual for this issue to be dealt with as a preliminary matter at the hearing of the substantive appeal and not separately.

The Customs & Excise is also obliged to lodge its list of documents with the Tribunal within 30 days of the appellant's notice of appeal. The same rules apply here as discussed in *Disclosure of documents, ante*.

Witness statements and summonses

WITNESS STATEMENTS

Witness statements (which may be made on Form Trib 3) are designed to enable written evidence to be given on behalf of either party without the attendance of the witness at the hearing. Such statements must be served at the appropriate Tribunal Centre within 30 days of the notice of appeal and will only be allowed to be read at the subsequent hearing if the other party does not serve a notice of objection to it (Form Trib 4) within 14 days of its service at the tribunal centre (a copy of the statement is sent to the other party by the proper officer of the Tribunal Centre).

Clearly, therefore, witness statements are only of use when the evidence to be given is not controversial. In general terms, it may also be said that witness statements should be avoided unless there are compelling reasons for making use of them. This is because, however uncontroversial evidence may be, it will usually leave a better impression if given orally and it is often useful to have a witness present at a hearing in case further clarification of any points is necessary.

WITNESS SUMMONSES

Witness summonses are only issued by the Tribunal on the application (Form Trib 5) of a party to an appeal or application. If issued to a party a witness summons must be served by him, or he must arrange for the summons to be served, on the person concerned at least 4 days before attendance is required at a hearing.

Witness summonses may be used to obtain for the purposes of a hearing a person's oral evidence or the production of any document in a person's possession, custody or power. Even though the tribunal has the power to require evidence to be given under oath (r 28(2)), witness summonses are unlikely to be of great use in relation to oral evidence. Witnesses who are obliged to attend a hearing must be paid a sufficient sum to cover their reasonable expenses of travelling to and from and their attendance at the hearing.

A person on whom a summons is served may also appeal to the tribunal under r 19 for that witness summons to be set aside.

Notice of the hearing

The parties will receive the following period of notice of a hearing prior to the date of the hearing:

(*a*) at least 14 days in the case of an appeal or application under r 20 for the hearing of an application for an appeal to be entertained without the payment of tax; and

(*b*) at least 7 days in relation to an application by the Customs & Excise to make an assessment (r 21), by either party for a witness summons (r 19) or any other application.

Procedure at a hearing

REPRESENTATION (RULE 25)

The appellant may appear in person or be represented by any person he may appoint for the purpose. Such person need not have legal experience and may be for example, his accountant, an officer of an appellant company or a friend of the appellant.

The Customs & Excise may similarly be represented by any person whom it may appoint.

PUBLIC OR PRIVATE HEARING (RULE 24)

The hearing of an appeal will be in public unless either party makes an application (Form Trib 5 may be used) for it to be heard in private and the Tribunal so directs.

The hearing of an application for a direction will, unless the point at issue is of particular general importance, be in private.

FAILURE TO ATTEND (RULE 26)

If neither party to the appeal or application attends, the Tribunal is obliged to dismiss the appeal or application concerned.

If one party attends, the Tribunal has a choice as to whether it:

(*a*) dismisses the appeal; or
(*b*) proceeds in the absence of the other party.

Where the appeal is dismissed either for failure to attend or on its merits in the absence of one party, the party concerned may apply, within 14 days after the date of the document containing the Tribunal's decision, to have the appeal reinstated or the decision set aside as the case may be. Such application may be allowed on such terms as the Tribunal thinks fit. Such terms usually embody an award, or a further award, of costs against the party who failed to attend (see *J D G Wilkinson* v *CCE*, MAN/77/303 (*Casebook* **13.418**).

ORDER OF APPEARANCE (RULE 27)

It is usual for the appellant to present his case first at the hearing by addressing the Tribunal, presenting documentary evidence to support his case and calling any witnesses to give evidence (or alternatively, by reading out any witness statements to which notices of objection have not been given). The Customs & Excise will then present their case in a similar manner. Both parties have, in the order in which they were first heard, a right to a second address and both may cross-examine the other's witnesses.

The appellant may not be required personally to give evidence but may be cross-examined if he does. The Tribunal may also put any questions to any witnesses called.

EVIDENCE (RULE 28)

The Tribunal has great flexibility as to the evidence it hears and the manner in which it is given. Evidence is not rejected, therefore, merely because it would not be admissible in a court of law (this allows, at least in theory, a party to refer to Hansard in arguing his case). However, although not bound by the usual rules as to the admissibility of evidence, the Tribunal has shown a reluctance to accept hearsay evidence or matters which involve the disclosure of communications between the appellant and his professional advisers (see *Cyril Rawlcliffe* v *CCE*, MAN/78/258 (*Casebook* **13.428**).

Evidence may be given orally or by way of witness statement (see p 233, *Witness statements and summonses, ante*). If given orally, evidence may, at the discretion of the Tribunal, be made under oath or affirmation. An appellant should consider asking to give evidence under oath or affirmation as to directly challenge such evidence, the Customs & Excise would have to imply that the appellant had lied under oath which it may be reluctant to do.

Any document contained in the list of documents served at the Tribunal Centre under r 7 (see **13.400**, p 232, *ante*) is deemed to be an original document or a copy if it appears to be an original or a copy respectively. There is, therefore, no need for formal proof of those facts or as to the due execution of the documents. If any party wishes to challenge any such documents therefore he must apply for a direction of the Tribunal that such documents be formally proved.

Further, until the contrary is proved (s 39):

(1) A certificate of the Commissioners—

(*a*) that a person was or was not, at any date, registered under [FA 1972]; or
(*b*) that any return required by or under [FA 1922] has not been made or had not been made at any date; or
(*c*) that any tax shown as due in any return or assessment made in pursuance of [FA 1972] has not been paid;

shall be sufficient evidence of that fact until the contrary is proved.

(2) A photograph of any document furnished to the Commissioners for the purposes of [FA 1972] and certified by them to be such a photograph shall be admissible in any proceedings, whether civil or criminal, to the same extent as the document itself.

BURDEN OF PROOF

While there is an initial onus of proof on the Customs & Excise to show that they have raised the assessment or exercised their discretion to the best of their judgment, the principal burden of proof lies with the appellant to prove his case against the Customs & Excise. The standard of proof required to displace this burden is that of a balance of probabilities.

The phrase "to the best of their judgment" (see s 31(1)) was considered by the Tribunal in *Ford* v *CCE*, MAN/79/12 (*Casebook* **12.109**), where it was held that perfection was not required of the Customs & Excise but merely a reasonable standard of prudence (see generally **12.100**).

The one clear principle that emerges from the cases on the discharge by an appellant of his burden of proof is that unsupported assertions by the appellant, however reasonable, will not be sufficient unless substantiated by records or other evidence.

Applications to the tribunal

FOR AN APPEAL TO BE ENTERTAINED WITHOUT THE PAYMENT OR DEPOSIT OF TAX (RULE 20)

Such an application must be served within the same time limits as those for the notice of appeal itself and should set out the same information as required in the notice of appeal. Form Trib 6 may be used for this purpose. See, therefore, the section on content of a notice of appeal at **13.400**, p 231, *ante*.

The procedure for the Customs & Excise to submit a Statement of Case and at the hearing of the application is the same as for the substantive appeal except that

(*a*) the hearing will usually be in private; and
(*b*) witness statements may not be used.

FOR THE POSTPONEMENT OR ADJOURNMENT OF A HEARING (RULE 31(1) AND (2))

No form is specified for an application for postponement or adjournment. The Tribunal has accordingly accepted as sufficient a letter written by the appellant or his representative and also a telephone conversation with the appellant.

The Tribunal will not allow an adjournment where the application is merely a delaying tactic by one of the parties concerned or where there is no good reason for the delay. Similarly, where the appellant's representative, in the absence of the appellant, has access to all necessary records to present the appellant's case, or is available to attend at the hearing in his place, an adjournment is unlikely to be granted. Should the appellant's evidence be indispensible, however, the Tribunal has been prepared to allow an adjournment to permit him to attend (see *Mrs P V Malindine* v *CCE*, LON/76/224 (*Casebook* **13.421**).

The Tribunal will also normally permit a postponement at the joint application of the appellant and the Customs & Excise.

OTHER APPLICATIONS

The Tribunal may also, on the application of any interested person or on its own motion, give directions for the following issues:

(*a*) the issue of a witness summons;
(*b*) to set aside a witness summons;
(*c*) to grant any extension of time;

(*d*) the right to take copies of or inspect any document in the list of Customs & Excise documents;

(*e*) the transfer of an appeal or application to another Tribunal Centre;

(*f*) the reinstatement of an appeal which has been dismissed on the failure of an appellant to attend or comply with a direction of the Tribunal;

(*g*) the substitution of another person as the appellant where the original appellant has died or become bankrupt.

The Tribunal decision

CONSENT DECISIONS AND DIRECTIONS (RULE 15)

Where the parties to an appeal or application agree on the terms (which should include terms as to the payment of any interest and costs) of any decision or direction sought of the Tribunal, they may serve particulars of those terms duly signed by them at the appropriate Tribunal Centre. Although the Tribunal is not obliged to follow such terms and may insist on a formal withdrawal of the appeal or proceed to a hearing of the matter, it will usually give a decision or direction in accordance with those terms.

WRITTEN DECISIONS (RULE 29)

Where the parties do not agree an appeal and it proceeds to a hearing, the Chairman may announce the Tribunal's decision at the end of the hearing of an appeal but it is usual for a reserved decision to be made in all but the simplest of cases. In any event, a written decision will be prepared by the Tribunal which decision will contain the Tribunal's findings of fact and the reasons for its decision. Copies of this decision will be sent to the parties.

13.500 Costs

All references to "rules" are to the VAT Tribunals Rules 1972 (SI 1972 No 1344) unless otherwise stated.

General

By r 30, the Tribunal is given the ability on its own motion or at the application of a party to an appeal or application to award costs in favour of either party in respect of his costs "incidental to and consequent upon the appeal or application" in question. If awarded, costs will usually "follow the event" unless the successful party has through his misconduct or for some other reason (for example in *Difevale Ltd* v *CCE*, LON/78/367 (*Casebook* **13.504**)) an appeal would not have been necessary had the appellant produced documents to the Customs & Excise at an earlier stage) made an award inappropriate (see also *Rawlins Davy and Wells* v *CCE*, LON/77/251 (*Casebook* **13.501**)).

An indication of the Customs & Excise policy in relation to costs was given by Mr Sheldon in the following parliamentary answers (Hansard, Vol 954, col 426; see also [1978] VATTR 278):

"In general, Customs & Excise do not seek costs when a taxpayer has been unsuccessful before a VAT Tribunal. However, they have in the past felt justified in applying for costs in a few exceptional cases which have either involved hearings of a substantial nature or have involved misuse of the tribunal procedure resulting in public money being expended to little useful purpose. This policy is currently under review in the light of five years' experience, although it is not evisaged that there will be any major changes ... As regards subsequent appeals to the High Court, Customs & Excise would normally seek costs when they are successful in accordance with the normal rule that costs follow the event. They are, of course, always prepared to consider representations of exceptional hardship or other special circumstances on their merits".

At a later date, the following statement was made in the House (Hansard Vol 958, cols 91–92):

"... the Customs & Excise have concluded that, as a general rule, they should continue their policy of not seeking costs against unsuccessful appellants; however, they will ask for costs in certain cases so as to provide protection for public funds and the general body of taxpayers. For instance, they will seek costs at those exceptional Tribunal hearings of substantial and complex cases where large sums are involved and which are comparable with High Court cases, unless the appeal involves an important point of law requiring clarification. The Customs & Excise will also consider seeking costs where the appellant has misused the tribunal procedure—for example, in frivolous or vexatious cases, or where the appellant has failed to appear or to be represented at a mutually arranged hearing without sufficient explanation, or where the appellant has first produced at a hearing relevant evidence which ought properly to have been disclosed at an earlier stage and which could have saved public funds had it been produced timeously."

Quantum

The Tribunal may award costs either of "such amount as it may determine" or order a taxation of costs by the Taxing Master or District Registrar of the Supreme Court of Judicature.

COSTS SETTLED BY THE TRIBUNAL

The power to send costs to be formally taxed was only added by the VAT Tribunal (Amendment) Rules 1974 (SI 1974 No 1934) with effect from 1 January 1975 and consequently the cases prior to that date give an indication of the basis on which the Tribunal will itself award costs. The following have been allowed by the Tribunal:

(*a*) solicitor's, barrister's or accountant's fees in preparing the case for, and attending, the hearing;

(*b*) the cost (ie salary) and expenses of an employee attending a hearing;

(*c*) where a professional adviser was not engaged there was also allowed in *Jocelyn Fielding Fine Arts Ltd* v *CCE* (*No 2*), LON/78/81 (*Casebook* **13.513**), an additional amount in excess of (*b*). Such an addition was not allowed in *Meshberry Ltd* v *CCE*, LON/78/384 (*Casebook* **13.514**), which decision would seem, in the Authors' opinion, to be preferred as an award of costs should only compensate an appellant for a loss actually suffered.

In all cases, costs can only cover the period after the service of a notice of appeal. As a result, costs incurred in negotiating with the Customs & Excise prior to serving a notice, whether or not an extension of time is granted, are not capable of being covered by an award.

Loss of earnings has also been held to constitute too vague an area for an award of costs to be made.

Where a compromise is reached between the parties and a consent decision or direction made, no order as to costs will be made (The *Cadogan Club Ltd* v *CCE*, LON/77/194 (*Casebook* **13.507**)). This is to be contrasted with an instance where a party withdraws its case. A compromise should, therefore, include an agreement between the parties as to costs.

TAXED COSTS

There are two bases for the taxation of costs, party and party costs and the common fund basis.

Party and party costs include "all such costs as were necessary or proper for the attainment of justice or for enforcing or defending the right of the party whose costs are being taxed". This involves an evaluation of whether the costs were reasonable in principle and amount.

The common fund basis generally gives rise to a higher award.

Costs are usually awarded on a party and party basis unless circumstances are so exceptional as to warrant a common fund basis (see *Mrs D Lawton* v *CCE*, MAN/77/237 (*Casebook* **13.502**)).

Civil debt

Costs once awarded are recoverable as a civil debt (r 30(5)).

13.600 Interest on tax

The Tribunal has power to order the payment of interest by the Customs & Excise on tax which is repaid to a successful appellant or by an unsuccessful appellant where the appeal was heard without the payment or deposit of tax (s 40(4)). Such interest will be at such rate as the Tribunal may determine. The indications are that a commercial rate of interest will be awarded. In *Visionhire Ltd and Others* v *CCE*, [1974] VATTR 62 (*Casebook* **13.601**), the Bank of England minimum lending rate was suggested as the correct rate (see also *Bridge Street Snack Bar* v *CCE*, CAR/77/191 (*Casebook* **13.503**)), and in *Hollingworth* v *CCE*, MAN/77/278, the certificate of the appellant's bankers was accepted as giving the correct rate.

An award of interest will not be stayed, save in exceptional circumstances, merely because one party wishes to appeal against the Tribunal's decision (*Visionhire Ltd and Others* v *CCE*, [1974] VATTR 62 (*Casebook* **13.601**)).

13.700 Further appeals

Appeal under RSC Order 55

An appeal from the VAT Tribunal lies, by virtue of the Tribunals and Inquiries Act 1971, to the Queen's Bench Division of the High Court on points of law. The manner of appeal is usually by way of direct appeal under RSC Order 55 rather than by way of case stated under RSC Order 56.

A notice of appeal must be served on the Chairman of the Tribunal and every other party to the proceedings within 28 days of the date on which the Tribunal decision was given to the appellant (RSC Order 55, r 4). The notice must state the grounds of the appeal and whether the appeal is against the whole or only a part of the decision in question (RSC Order 55, r 3). The appellant may, however, amend the notice without leave by a supplemental notice served not less than 7 days before the day appointed for the hearing of the appeal. Apart from this ability to serve a supplemental notice, the appellant may not rely at the hearing on any grounds other than those stated in the notice of appeal without the leave of the Court. The Court may amend the grounds on "such terms as it thinks fit, to ensure the determination on the merits of the real question in controversy between the parties" (RSC Order 55, r 6).

An appeal before the High Court is by way of a rehearing of the case. Although this does not imply a complete rehearing of the evidence presented before the Tribunal, the Court does have the power to receive further evidence on questions of fact in such manner as it may direct (RSC Order 55, r 7(2)) and may draw any inferences of fact which might have been drawn by the Tribunal. The Court may make any order which could have been made by the Tribunal and may remit the case to the Tribunal for further consideration. This latter is usually exercised where either:

(*a*) the proceedings before the Tribunal were subject to a major, for example, procedural, defect; or

(*b*) where the actual decision of the Tribunal is unclear; or

(*c*) where the Tribunal's findings of fact are incomplete.

Finally, it is the duty of the appellant to furnish the Court with a signed copy of the decision of the Tribunal against which the appeal is made.

Appeal under RSC Order 59

A further appeal lies under RSC Order 59 to the Court of Appeal without leave of the High Court. This appeal is commenced by a notice of appeal served within 6 weeks of the date on which the order of the High Court was perfected, that is, signed and sealed with the seal of the Central Office. The appellant must then produce the judgment or order of the High Court to (and leave one copy of the same duly stamped and endorsed with) the Chief Master within 7 days after service of the notice of appeal.

Appeals allowed in other circumstances

Exceptionally, if:

(*a*) a point of law of general public importance is involved in the decision which point relates to the construction of an enactment, Statutory Instrument or in respect of which the High Court was bound by a previous decision of the Court of Appeal or House of Lords;

(*b*) a sufficient case has been made out to justify an application for leave to make such appeal; and

(*c*) all parties to the proceedings consent to the grant of a certificate,

the High Court judge may, on the application of any party to the proceedings, grant a certificate permitting an appeal to be made direct from the High Court to the House of Lords, "leapfrogging" the Court of Appeal. This certificate should be requested immediately after the judgment although applications may be entertained within 14 days thereafter. Following the issue of a certificate, the parties may then apply within one month by way of petition to the House of Lords for a direct appeal to that House. If granted, no appeal lies to the Court of Appeal.

Leave to appeal from the Court of Appeal

Leave to appeal from the Court of Appeal must first be applied for to the Court of Appeal or, if refused, by petition to the House of Lords. An appeal must be lodged within 3 months of the date of the order appealed against.

13.800 The European Court of Justice

The following paragraphs of this sub-chapter include a highly specialised aspect of the law outside the main scope of this Guide. These paragraphs give only a brief outline of the more relevant points of this topic, therefore, and where further information is required the Authors suggest that reference is made to one of the standard works on the European Court of Justice ("ECJ") and Community law, for example, *Judicial Protection in the European Communities* by H. G Schermers, published by Kluwer.

The relevance of Community law and the European Court of Justice

GENERAL

The European Communities Act 1972, s 2(1) provides that:

"(1) All such rights, powers, liabilities, obligations and restrictions from time to time created or arising by or under the Treaties, and all such remedies and procedures from time to time provided for or by or under the Treaties, as in accordance with the Treaties are without further enactment to be given legal effect or used in the United Kingdom shall be recognised and available in law, and be enforced, allowed and followed accordingly; and the expression "enforceable Community right" and similar expressions shall be read as referring to one to which this subsection applies."

By the introduction of this section the United Kingdom accepted in principle that certain provisions of Community law may be enforced in the United Kingdom. The provisions that may be so enforced are those which *under Community law* are to be given legal effect or used in the United Kingdom *without further enactment*. In the words of Lord Denning MR in *H P Bulmer Ltd* v *J Bollinger SA*, [1974] 4 Ch 401 at 411, the Treaty of Rome is in this respect "like an incoming tide. It flows into the estuaries and up the rivers. It cannot be held back. Parliament has decreed that the Treaty is henceforward to be part of our law. It is equal in force to any Statute."

In the context of VAT, therefore, it is necessary to ask two questions. First, whether there is any Community law which is relevant to VAT and, secondly, if there is, whether such law has direct effect in the United Kingdom.

COMMUNITY LAW RELATING TO VAT

The answer to the first of the questions put in the last paragraph is straightforward. The Council of Ministers has introduced ten Directives to date relating to the adoption of a common system of VAT throughout the EEC (see **18.200**). Of these the most important is clearly the Sixth Directive of 17 May 1977 which laid down a detailed framework of rules which Member States were obliged to follow in the modification of their existing VAT legislation. As far as the United Kingdom was concerned, the final date for compliance with the Sixth Directive was 1 January 1978. As has already been mentioned in this *Guide*, the FA 1977 was designed to introduce the necessary amendments to UK VAT legislation to accord with the provisions of the Sixth Directive. Both the Sixth Directive and all other VAT directives potentially affect VAT legislation in the United Kingdom. If these Directives have direct effect, they must be applied in the United Kingdom and take priority over UK VAT legislation.

DIRECT EFFECT

The question as to whether the above Directives have direct effect in the United Kingdom is more difficult to answer. In this context a distinction has to be drawn between:

(*a*) those provisions of Community law which have direct effect on Member States, that is which oblige States to pass particular legislation, but which do not have direct effect for individuals within those States; and

(*b*) those provisions which have both direct effect on States and grant rights to individuals.

In practice, it is the latter category of provision which will be of use to the individual. If a provision is of the former type, an individual may not seek to rely on it in proceedings before his national courts (although national courts may possibly take notice of the provision, thereby giving it indirect effect). A further obstacle may present itself to an individual in practice in that he may only bring a provision of Community law to the notice of a national court if a national remedy is already provided to him on the point at issue. If there is no national right of appeal against an allegedly invalid national provision, the national courts cannot set aside that provision on the basis that it conflicts with Community law.

The question of whether a provision of Community law has direct effect is a question of the interpretation of Community law and is, therefore, a question to be ultimately determined by the European Court of Justice itself. For an individual to be able to invoke a provision of Community law it would appear that five conditions must be fulfilled. These are:

(*a*) the provision must contain a clear obligation on the Member State;

(*b*) the content of the provision must be such that it has direct effect in relation to the Member State;

(*c*) no further acts by Community institutions or Member States must be needed for the obligation on the Member State to achieve its aim;

(*d*) The provision must be unconditional or any conditions that are present must have been fulfilled; and

(*e*) the Member State should have no discretion in its fulfilment of its obligations under the provision.

In relation to condition (*b*) whether the provision has direct effect on the Member State would itself appear to depend upon the provision in question being clear, unconditional and complete.

Applying the above rules, it would appear possible where a VAT Directive imposes an obligation on the United Kingdom to make certain provision regarding VAT by a certain date and that date has passed, that such provision may have direct effect and may, therefore, be relied upon in the circumstances stated above by taxpayers in the United Kingdom.

An example of an instance where it would appear that a provision of the Sixth Directive has direct effect in the United Kingdom is art 2 of that Directive. Article 2 clearly sets the scope of VAT:

"The following shall be subject to Value Added Tax:
1. the supply of goods or services effected for consideration within the territory of the country by a taxable person acting as such;
2. the importation of goods."

The above article leaves no measure of discretion in Member States' hands. This is in contrast with arts 13 and 14 of the Directive, for example, which do give a degree of flexibility in permitting Member States to exempt certain services "under conditions which they shall lay down". Even with arts 13 and 14, however, it is arguable that if a Member State were to tax the supplies mentioned in those articles, an individual would have the ability to challenge such taxation on the basis that the Member State in question had strayed outside the limits of the discretion given to it in the article.

It should be noted that the Tribunal in *Processed Vegetable Growers Association Ltd* v *CCE*, [1973] VATTR 87 at pp 99 and 100 (*Casebook* **18.202**), rejected the argument put forward by the Customs & Excise that the Second Directive had direct effect in the United Kingdom. The Customs & Excise were attempting in that case to impose a charge to VAT on a taxpayer based on the wording of the Directive. This is clearly a more burdensome task than attempting to cut down the ambit of UK legislation by reference to a Council Directive. It is the Authors' opinion that the decision in *Processed Vegetable Growers* may be incorrect and may not be followed should a similar case come before the courts or a VAT Tribunal in the future.

THE EUROPEAN COURT OF JUSTICE

As indicated above, the role of the ECJ is to interpret the provisions of Community law. This role is fulfilled on references of points of Community law being made to it by national courts. This interpretative function involves not only determining whether a provision has direct effect in national law but also the precise meaning to be placed on that provision. However, once the ECJ has interpreted a provision of Community law it is left to the national court which made the reference of that point to apply the provision to the case in dispute in accordance with such interpretation. The ECJ is not, therefore, an appellate body to which an unsuccessful UK litigant may appeal with a view to the reversal of that UK court's decision but a body solely to which questions involving Community law may be referred for guidance.

References to the European Court of Justice

WHO MAY MAKE A REFERENCE TO THE EUROPEAN COURT OF JUSTICE?

References to the ECJ are made under the Treaty of Rome, art 177 which provides that:

"(1) The Court of Justice shall have jurisdiction to give preliminary rulings concerning:

(*a*) the interpretation of this Treaty;
(*b*) the validity and interpretation of acts of the institutions of the Community;
(*c*) the interpretation of the statutes of bodies established by an act of the Council where those statutes so provide.

(2) Where such a question is raised before any court or tribunal of a Member State, that court or tribunal may, if it considers that a decision on the question is necessary to enable it to give judgment, request the Court of Justice to give a ruling thereon.

(3) Where any such question is raised in a case pending before a court or tribunal of a Member State, against whose decisions there is no judicial remedy under national law, that court or tribunal shall bring the matter before the Court of Justice."

Article 177 (2) and (3) make it clear, therefore, that it is the court or Tribunal in which a question of Community law arises that has the power, or the duty as the case may be, to make a reference to the ECJ. A reference is not made by the parties to the proceedings. Thus, although a party may request the UK court or tribunal concerned to make a reference in a particular case, that party has no rights before the ECJ and cannot submit a case to it before a reference has been ordered by the court or Tribunal (see *Milchwerke Heinz Wöhrmann und Sohn* v *EEC Commission*, [1963] CMLR 152 at p 158).

There has been considerable debate as to whether a domestic Tribunal constitutes a "court or Tribunal" for art 177 purposes. The phrase "court or Tribunal" is to be interpreted in accordance with Community law and the leading decision, *Vaassen-Göbbels* v *Beambtenfonds Voor het Mijnbedriff*, [1966] CMLR 508, suggests that a Tribunal would fall within this phrase where:

(*a*) the power to nominate members of the Tribunal and lay down rules of procedure is in the hands of a government Minister;

(*b*) the Tribunal is a permanent body which settles disputes in a manner similar to that adopted by ordinary courts of law; and

(*c*) the Tribunal is bound to follow the rules of law.

Adopting these criteria, it would appear that a VAT Tribunal would be within art 177 and may, therefore, make a reference to the ECJ. However, as yet no procedural rules have been laid down for such references by VAT Tribunals and it may be that, while such power of reference exists in theory, in practice a reference would not be made until after the decision of the Tribunal has established the primary facts of the case (see MANNER IN WHICH A REFERENCE IS MADE ETC., *post*).

It is clear that the High Court and the Court of Appeal may make a reference to the ECJ under art 177 (2) although they are not bound to do so. The House of Lords, as the court of final instance in the United Kingdom, is required to make a reference to the ECJ where a point of Community law is involved which it is necessary to resolve to enable the House to give judgment (art 177 (3)). In practice, however, no reference is made by the House of Lords where the point at issue is sufficiently clear for the House of Lords to resolve itself (that is, where the *acte clair* principle applies (see MANNER IN WHICH A REFERENCE IS MADE ETC, para (*b*), *post*)).

THE MANNER IN WHICH A REFERENCE IS MADE: THE DISCRETION OF THE COURT

The Rules of the Supreme Court Order r 114 lays down the procedure for references from the High Court and the Court of Appeal to the ECJ. Such references may be made by the court on its own motion or on the application of the parties.

The High Court and the Court of Appeal in determining whether a reference is necessary adopt the following basic guidelines established in *H P Bulmer Ltd* v *J. Bollinger SA*, [1974] 4 Ch 401:

(*a*) The point at issue must be conclusive of the case, that is, its resolution must be necessary to determine whether judgment is to be given in favour of the appellant or the defendant. Thus, once the ECJ has given its ruling, all that would remain for the UK court to do would be to give judgment in accordance with that ruling.

It follows from this that where there is no agreement between the parties as to the questions to be referred, it is unlikely that the court will make a reference—see *DDSA Pharmaceuticals Ltd* v *Farbwerke Hoechst AG* 16 CMLR 50.

(*b*) *Acte clair* principle—where the point at issue is clear and free from doubt, the UK court should not overload the ECJ with a reference to it if the UK court itself can resolve the point raised.

(*c*) Previous ECJ ruling—where a substantially similar point has been the subject of a previous ECJ ruling, it may not be necessary to make a further reference. However, as Lord Denning MR. pointed out in the *Bulmer* case, the ECJ is not bound by its own decisions and there- fore if new factors have been brought to light a further reference may be required.

(*d*) Fact and law—a reference should not normally be made before the essential facts of the case have been determined. Further, where a party would fail under UK law on another point at issue in the case, no reference should be made to the ECJ.

The House of Lords is under a duty to obtain a ruling on points of Community law (art 177 (3)) and is, therefore, only concerned to follow guidelines (*a*) and (*b*), *ante*.

Should the High Court or the Court of Appeal refuse to make a reference to the ECJ under RSC Order 114, an appeal may be made against that refusal, with leave, to the Court of Appeal or the House of Lords as the case may be. An appeal may also be made, without leave, where an order for a reference is made by a court. Such appeals must be lodged within 14 days of the decision being entered.

Community law which does not have direct effect on UK law

There will be areas of Community law, and in particular of the Sixth Directive, which do not have direct effect in relation to UK law. The question arises, therefore, as to the extent to which such Community law may be taken into account in interpreting the parallel provisions of UK law designed to cover that area of Community law. The answer to this question lies in the following two basic principles of UK law.

First, UK statute law over-rides all other forms of law. Such other forms of law will include international conventions and Community law which does not have direct effect. Secondly, where a particular provision of UK law is unclear or ambiguous, it is to be interpreted if possible in such a manner as will not involve a breach of the United Kingdom's international treaty obligations in relation to that area of law. From these basic principles, three conclusions may be drawn:

(*a*) if a provision of UK law is unambiguous it is to be given effect even if contrary to Community law which does not have direct effect in the United Kingdom;

(*b*) if a provision of the law is ambiguous, however, the court should consider the alternative interpretations of that provision that are available. If an interpretation is consistent with the apparent obligation or meaning of the equivalent provision of Community law, that interpretation should be preferred by the UK court; and

(*c*) if the Community law is itself also unclear, it is possible that a reference may lie to the ECJ under art 177 to resolve that uncertainty.

Finally, in determining whether a provision of UK law is ambiguous, it is the generally accepted view that it is not possible to have regard to the relevant Community law provisions. However, this does not prevent the appellant from looking to that provision and mentioning as part of his argument any ambiguity that he discovers, provided that he does not acknowledge its origin before the Tribunal or court.

Chapter 14

Conduct of Enquiries

14.000 Sources

Section 32—Power of the Customs & Excise to require security for VAT.
Section 33—Recovery of VAT including power to levy distress.
Section 35—Power given to the Customs & Excise requiring the furnishing of information.
Section 36—Powers to take samples.
Section 37—Powers of entry and search.
Section 38—Penalty provisions.
Section 41 (as amended by FA 1976, s 22)—Priority in Bankruptcy.
Section 127—Power to exchange information with Inland Revenue.
VAT (General Regulations) 1977 (SI 1977 No 1759)—Regulations made pursuant to s 33: further provisions relating to distress.

14.100 General principles

The central management, administration and collection of VAT is vested in the Board of Commissioners. The Board comprises a Chairman, two Deputy Chairmen and Commissioners. Each Commissioner is the head of a Directorate, there being two Directorates concerned with the administration and collection of VAT respectively. The administrative directorate is based in London and is responsible for matters of policy and the control directorate is based in Southend and is responsible for the collection of the tax. Further details of the general structure of the Board are available as set out in a Guidance Note issued in May 1979 by the CCAB, the contents having been agreed with the Customs & Excise (see BTR No 6 1979 p 525, *et seq*).

A taxable person is most likely to be involved with local VAT offices (LVO) which are run by an Assistant Collector, and comprise about one hundred staff. A chart is produced below which sets out the approximate equivalent ranks of Customs & Excise in comparison with the Inland Revenue and the Civil Service generally.

(1) *Customs & Excise*	(2) *Inland Revenue*	(3) *General Service*
Collector	Senior Inspector	Assistant Secretary
Deputy Collector	Principal Inspector	Senior Principal
Assistant Collector in charge of an LVO (a Principal)	Inspector (Higher Grade)	
Surveyor	Inspector(S)	Senior Executive Officer
Senior Officer	Inspector	Higher Executive Officer
Officer	Tax Officer Higher Grade	Executive Officer
Assistant Officer	Tax Officer	Clerical Officer

(*Note:* The Customs & Excise ranks in column (1), other than Collector and Deputy Collector, relate to staff in LVOs and sub-offices. In Headquarters Offices the General Service titles in column (3) are used. Similarly, the Inland Revenue ranks in column (2) relate in the main to staff at local tax offices.)

Each LVO consists of eight to ten Surveyors each of whom is in charge of a District. The surveyors in charge of Districts are responsible for organising control visits and generally supervising the collection of VAT at a local level.

Commencement of enquiries: control visits

Taxable persons will be familiar with the control visits made by Customs & Excise Officers. These control visits are normally made every 2 or 3 years and are to enable the Customs & Excise to keep a check on traders to ensure that they are collecting and accounting for VAT correctly. The visits will normally be made by prior appointment, but for further consideration of this see **14.200**.

Experience of the Customs & Excise has shown that on average about one-third of persons visited under-declare the VAT due by an average of over £400, and that approximately 5 per cent over-pay VAT by an average of £250. It is, therefore, likely that any enquiry which arises will be as a result of a control visit.

If the Customs & Excise raises queries the taxpayer may wish to conduct negotiations and correspondence with the Customs & Excise himself or he may appoint a professional adviser to do so. Where a person is represented by a professional adviser the Customs & Excise will correspond directly with that adviser where he contacts the Customs & Excise on behalf of his client. However, where any document or letter relates to the subject of proceedings the original letter or document will be sent to the taxpayer. In addition, certain documentation is issued by computer and these documents are always sent direct to the taxpayer, for example certificates of registration and quarterly returns.

It may be that any enquiries of the Customs & Excise, resulting, for example from a control visit, can be answered and settled by mutual agreement. If the queries on a person's VAT Returns relate to profit margins and mark-ups the person's professional adviser may be able to negotiate an acceptable settlement with the Customs & Excise. However, care must be taken to ensure, so far as possible that, if it is accepted that the taxpayer's turnover is greater than that returned to the Customs & Excise, the agreed increased turnover only applies from the date of the settlement. This is because if the settlement relates to an earlier period additional difficulties can arise. For example, assuming that there is no question of fraud, a settlement relating to an earlier period can lead to the Inland Revenue raising additional income tax or corporation tax assessments, for that earlier period. In this respect, it should be borne in mind that the information may be exchanged between the Inland Revenue and Customs & Excise: this disclosure is authorised by s 127 (see Exchange of Information at **14.200**, *post*). Thus, although it may be cheaper to settle a claim in terms of professional fees and the compliance costs of a settlement, rather than take the matter to appeal before a Tribunal, considerable thought must be given to the other tax consequences of such a settlement.

If a dispute with Customs & Excise cannot be resolved amicably, a taxpayer should be aware of the extent of the statutory powers of the Customs & Excise to obtain information. This is particularly important in cases where the Customs & Excise is alleging fraud.

14.200 Powers of Customs & Excise

Furnishing information

The Customs & Excise is given power in s 35(1) to make regulations requiring taxable persons to notify it of changes in their circumstances so as to enable the Customs & Excise to keep an up to date register of traders. Regulations have been made under the VAT (General) Regulations 1977 (SI 1977 No 1759) regs 4–7, by which persons must give notice to the Customs & Excise of, *inter alia*, changes affecting registration.

Further, the Customs & Excise have power to require any person who is concerned, in whatever capacity, in the supply of goods in the course or furtherance of any business, including a person to whom a supply is made to furnish them with such information relating to the goods, or to the supply as they may specify (s 35(2)(*a*)). It will be noted that this gives a very broad power to the Customs & Excise as it may require any information relating to the supply of the goods as it may specify.

It will be seen that s 35(2)(*a*) referred to above relates to the supply of goods, but similar although narrower powers are given to the Customs

& Excise in s 35(3)(*a*) in relation to supplies of services. In particular the Customs & Excise may require information regarding the consideration for the supply of the services or the name and address of the person to whom the supply is made.

Right of the Customs & Excise to call for documents

GOODS

In relation to a supply of goods a person authorised by the Customs & Excise has power to call for documents to be produced by every person who is concerned (in whatever capacity) with the supply.

The documents must relate to the goods or the supply. The documents must be available to the authorised person for inspection and he is empowered to take copies, to make extracts from them or to remove them at a reasonable time and for a reasonable period (s 35(2)(*b*)). In practice the documents and books will normally be examined at the person's place of business by prior appointment. If the Customs & Excise does enforce its statutory rights and remove books or documents, the books are normally returned quickly and are not usually held for more than 1 month. If books are retained by the Customs & Excise, copies will be supplied, if required. Further, where the Customs & Excise has removed documents, it normally allows the trader access to them to enable him to check any assessment raised (see *Abedin* v *CCE*, [1979] STC 425 (*Casebook* **13.414**)).

The definition of an authorised person for the above purposes is contained in s 46(1) and means "any person acting under the authority of the Commissioners". Documents for the purpose of s 35 include, in addition to a document in writing, any maps, plans, drawings, photographs, disc, tape, soundtrack or other device in which sounds or other data are embodied so as to be capable of being reproduced, films, negatives and other devices for recording visual images.

If any documents are removed by the Customs & Excise and are lost or damaged, the Customs & Excise must compensate the owner for any reasonable expense of replacing or repairing them (s 35(5)).

In addition to the above power to enter and remove documents, the Customs & Excise may, in certain circumstances, enter premises at any time, by force if necessary, acting under a warrant issued by a Justice of the Peace (see *Power of entry and search, post*).

SERVICES

Similar provisions to those outlined above in relation to goods apply to a supply of services, except that the documents which may be called for can only be documents relating to the consideration for the supply (s 35(3)(*b*)).

Right of the Customs & Excise to take samples

Section 36(1) enables a person authorised by the Customs & Excise to take samples from a supplier so that a check can be made to see if VAT is being correctly accounted for in respect of the goods. The power is exercisable if it appears to the authorised person that the Customs & Excise may not be receiving the full amount of VAT due to it because a mistake is being made or a fraud perpetrated. The Customs & Excise is liable to pay compensation if the goods taken by way of sample are not returned within a reasonable time and in good condition. Reasonable time for this purpose will depend upon the type of goods concerned and there is no fixed time limit that the Customs & Excise in practice applies.

Power to require security

The Customs & Excise is given power in s 32 to require security for VAT in two instances. First, where a person's input tax exceeds his output tax, so that a repayment of VAT is due from the Customs & Excise to him, the Customs & Excise may require security for the amount of the repayment. The security to be given would normally be in the form of a bank guarantee or bond guaranteed by a bank. Secondly, the Customs & Excise may require security as a prerequisite to a person making taxable supplies where it appears necessary for the protection of the revenue. That is to say, if the Customs & Excise has reason to believe that a taxable person will not account for VAT or may be in a position so that he is unable to pay the VAT due (eg, because he may spend it) they may require security for any potential liability to VAT. However, the terms of a surety must not be so onerous as to effectively put a person out of business (see *S Evans* v *CCE* CAR/79/124 (*Casebook* **14.201**)).

Exchange of information

Section 127 enables the Customs & Excise and the Inland Revenue to exchange information. The information may be disclosed to the respective Commissioners or an authorised officer of the respective Commissioners. The information can only be disclosed to the Commissioners themselves, to the authorised officer on whose behalf the information was obtained, or for the purpose of any proceedings.

In practice it was intended that disclosures should occur infrequently and it was not envisaged that wholesale exchanges of information would take place (see the remarks of the Financial Secretary to the Treasury during the committee stage of the Finance Bill 1972—Standing Committee E, 27 June 1972). However, the practice has been extended as explained by Robert Sheldon in a Parliamentary reply, when he said:

"Section 127 of the Finance Act 1972 already provides full statutory authority for the Inland Revenue and the Customs & Excise Department to supply each other with information to assist in the performance of their duties, but because of undertakings given during the passage of the legislation, exchanges of information have been made only under head office arrangements and not directly between local offices. It seems likely that exchanges between local offices directly, could be of real help in checking tax evasion and I propose to authorise such an exchange of selected information as an experiment in one selected area for a year, with a view to extending the arrangement generally if the result is worth while. In selecting an area it is desirable to choose a conurbation where the area covered by a VAT office corresponds fairly closely to an area covered by a group of tax districts and with this in mind, Leeds has been selected for this purpose."

The results of the experiment are still being analysed and it is not yet known whether the practice will be extended to other areas (see the reply of Mr Peter Rees to a Parliamentary question, Hansard 6 December 1979, Vol 975, col 286).

Power of entry and search

ENTRY

The Customs & Excise has a general power to enter premises used in connection with a business at any reasonable time in order to enable them to exercise the powers given to them in the FA 1972 (s 37(1)). It is under this authority that control visits are made. Further, the Customs & Excise may enter premises to inspect the premises or any goods on the premises at a reasonable time, where an authorised person has reasonable cause to believe the premises are used in connection with a supply of goods (s 37(2)). Either of the above powers of entry is exercisable by an authorised person, ie, a person acting under the authority of the Customs & Excise. The entry under s 37(1) or (2) must be at a reasonable time and normally the Customs & Excise will only enter premises in such circumstances by prior appointment. However, there is no need to make an appointment. For the purpose of s 37(2) an authorised person must have reasonable cause for the belief that the premises are used in connection with the supply of goods: it is not sufficient that he honestly believed he had reasonable cause (see the remarks of Lord Scarman in *R v IRC ex parte Rossminster Ltd*, [1980] 2 WLR at p 62, when he was considering similar wording to that in s 37(2) contained in TMA 1970, s 20C).

ENTRY AND SEARCH OF PREMISES UNDER WARRANT

Where a Justice of the Peace is satisfied that the conditions set out below are met, he may issue a warrant in writing authorising any authorised person to enter the premises at any time within 14 days of the issue of the warrant. The conditions on which the Justice of the Peace must be satisfied are:

(*a*) there is reasonable ground for believing an offence relating to VAT has been, is being or is about to be committed on the premises; or

(*b*) there is reasonable ground for believing evidence of an offence will be found on the premises.

The Justice of the Peace must satisfy himself on the above points on evidence given before him on oath. It is interesting to note, however, that there is no indication as to who should give the information on oath before the Justice. It is, presumably, therefore, possible for anyone to give the information, whether he is an authorised person or not. The warrant must, however, name the premises which are to be searched, although it would appear that it is not necessary for the warrant to name the authorised person who is to execute it. This is because s 37(3) refers to the warrant "authorising any authorised person" to execute it—the wording should be contrasted with that contained in TMA 1970, s 20C which refers to authorising "an officer of the Board" which words have been held to mean that the officer must be named in the warrant (*R v IRC ex parte Rossminster*). It is to be noted that some interesting comments on the issuing of warrants generally are to be found in the judgments of the House of Lords in *R v IRC ex parte Rossminster*. Although this case considered points arising on the issue of warrants under TMA 1970, s 20C, it nevertheless considers the meanings of some similar phrases to those that appear in s 37.

The authorised person in possession of the warrant may enter the premises at any time, if necessary, by force. He may then, under the authority of the warrant:

(*a*) take other persons with him, if necessary; and

(*b*) seize and remove documents or anything else on the premises which he has reasonable grounds for believing may be needed as evidence of the committal of the offence; and

(*c*) search or cause to be searched any person on the premises who the authorised person has reasonable grounds to believe has or is about to commit an offence, or may be in the possession of documents or other things. However, only a woman may search another woman or girl. On the other hand, there would appear to be no grounds to prevent a woman searching a man! (s 37(3)).

If the Customs & Excise acts in excess of its authority under the warrant, it is open to the aggrieved person to bring an action in trespass against the Customs & Excise, and, if successful, may be entitled to punitive damages (see the obiter dicta of Lord Wilberforce and Lord Diplock in *R* v *IRC ex parte Rossminster*, at [1980] 2WLR pp 39 and 50 respectively).

14.300 Recovery of tax

Once it has been established that VAT is due to the Customs & Excise it remains for the Customs & Excise to obtain payment. The tax due is recoverable as a debt due to the Crown (s 33(1)). It should be noted that s 33 also provides in sub-ss (2) and (2A) for the recovery of tax where no supply actually takes place and where an invoice has been issued even though there has been no supply, for example, where a trader fraudulently issues an invoice in order to obtain input tax relief.

Distress

The Customs & Excise are given power by s 33(3) to make Regulations authorising the distraint of goods and chattels of any person refusing or neglecting to pay any tax due from him. Regulations have been made and are contained in the VAT (General) Regulations 1977 (SI 1977 No 1759), regs 58 and 59. In particular, reg 58 enables a Collector of Customs & Excise to authorise the distraint of goods where payment has not been made after being demanded by the Collector or a Senior Executive Officer. The Collector must issue a warrant authorising the distraint, but distraint cannot be made until 30 days after the tax is due. Thus, before distress can be levied there must first be a demand for payment by the appropriate person (see *ante*) and the taxpayer must refuse or neglect to pay; even then the distress cannot be levied until 30 days have elapsed from the date the tax is due, as determined under s 31(6). A taxable person may still be able to appeal against an assessment notwithstanding that distress has been levied; as long as the distress is lawfully carried out at a time when it is lawfully authorised, the fact that an appeal takes place subsequently does not make the distress unlawful (*P J Davies* v *CCE*, MAN/79/9 (*Casebook* **14.301**)).

In practice the Customs & Excise rarely exercise their powers under s 33 and when they do it is only after careful consideration by senior officials (see the statement issued by the CCAB on 30 June 1978).

Once a warrant authorising distraint has been issued the authorised person may break open a house or premises and seize goods or chattels of the person in default. However, if the authorised person is to break into the premises to levy distress he must be present when the warrant is issued (reg 58(3)). Having seized the goods they must be kept by the Customs & Excise, acting through the authorised person, for 5 days at the cost of the taxpayer. If the taxpayer has not paid the tax due plus the costs of keeping the goods and the Customs & Excise's charges by the time the 5 days have elapsed the goods will be sold at public auction. The sale proceeds will be used to account for the tax due, plus the costs of keeping the goods including the Customs & Excise's charges and any expenses, for example, auctioneer's fees. Any surplus will be returned to the taxpayer.

Similar provisions apply to diligence in Scotland (reg 59).

Priority in bankruptcy

Where a company or person is declared bankrupt or a person dies insolvent, any VAT due during the period of 12 months before the "relevant date" as defined in s 41(2) has priority in the bankruptcy as a preferred creditor (see **15.600E**).

14.400 Penalties

The penalty provisions relating to VAT are contained in s 38 and are considered in detail below. It should be noted that the general provisions relating to proceedings for penalties or mitigation of penalties of the Customs and Excise Management Act 1979 ("CEMA"), ss 145 to 155 are applied to VAT by s 38(8). The following are the more important aspects of those sections:

(*a*) no proceedings may be instituted without the consent of the Customs & Excise, except that proceedings in a Magistrates' Court may be instituted in the name of a Customs & Excise Officer (CEMA 1979, s 145);

(*b*) any service must be served:

(i) personally; or

(ii) left at the person's last known address, place of business, or (in the case of a company) at its registered or principal office (CEMA 1979, s 146);

(*c*) proceedings should, unless otherwise provided, be commenced within 3 years of the commission of the offence (CEMA 1979, s 147);

(*d*) where liability to tax has been incurred jointly by two or more persons, each shall be liable for the full amount of any penalty and may be proceeded against jointly or severally as the Customs & Excise think fit (CEMA 1979, s 150);

(*e*) the Customs & Excise may mitigate penalties by staying proceedings, restoring forfeited goods (subject to such conditions as they may impose) or by mitigating or repaying any penalty even after judgment has been obtained. Further, they may order the release of any person before the term of his imprisonment has expired (CEMA 1979, s 152);

(*f*) special rules may apply to the proving of documents and certain other matters (CEMA 1979, ss 153 and 154).

It must be remembered that the above procedural rules only apply (in the context of VAT) for the purposes of penalties imposed under s 38.

The offences

The table below gives a brief description of offences in relation to VAT and their respective penalties and detailed discussion of the respective offences follows the table.

Table of offences and penalties in relation to VAT

Offence	*Penalty*
1. Fraudulent Evasion (s 38(1)).	£1,000 or three times the tax, whichever is greater, or two years' imprisonment (maximum), or both.
2. Deceit (s 38(2)(*a*)).	£1,000 or two years' imprisonment (maximum), or both.
3. Recklessly giving false information (s 38(2) (*b*)).	£1,000 or two years' imprisonment (maximum), or both.
4. Deemed offence under 1–3 above (s 38(3)).	£1,000 or three times the tax, whichever is greater, or two years' imprisonment (maximum), or both.
5. Receiving goods or services where the supplier evades the tax (s 38(4)).	£1,000 or three times the tax, whichever is greater.
6. Failure to comply with the registration requirements (s 38(5)).	£1,000 or three times the tax, whichever is greater.
7. Breach of the Security Provisions (s 38(5)).	£1,000 or three times the tax, whichever is greater.
8. Wrongful issue of an invoice.	£1,000 or three times the tax, whichever is greater.

Offence	*Penalty*
9. Failure to comply with record keeping requirements or to furnish information	£100 plus £10 per day that the offence continues.
10. Late payment of tax or submission of a quarterly return.	£100 plus £10 or ½% per day of the tax due for the quarter, if greater.

1. FRAUDULENT EVASION OF TAX

An offence is committed where a person knowingly evades payment of tax, or is knowingly involved in the evasion of tax by another person (s 38(1)). The penalty is set out in the table at 1. above. It will be seen that a person must have the *mens rea* (an intention to commit the offence) before he can be liable. However, where a person argues that he did not know he was committing an offence he can have the knowledge imparted to him and be guilty of an offence under s 38(3) (see Item 4, *post*).

2. DECEIT

An offence is committed where a person, with intent to deceive, produces, furnishes or sends, or otherwise makes use of a document which is false in any material particular (s 38(2)(*a*)). Two elements are essential before this offence can be committed, therefore. First the person must have an intention to deceive and secondly the document must be false in a material particular. There is no definition of "to deceive" for this purpose but the generally accepted meaning is set out in the obiter dicta of Buckley J. (as he then was) in *Re London and Globe Finance Corporation Ltd*, (1903) 1 Ch 728, at p 732, when he said "To deceive is, I apprehend, to induce a man to believe that a thing is true which is false, and which the person practising the deceit knows or believes to be false.", and was cited with approval by Lord Radcliffe in *Welham* v *DPP*, (1960) 1 All ER 805. For further discussion on the matter see generally *Halsbury's Laws of England*, Fourth Edition, para 1328. Secondly, the document must be false in a material particular. A particular may be material if it tends to make something else more credible. Thus, statements made of a circumstantial nature only may be material if they support other statements (see *R* v *Tyson*, (1867) LRI CCR 107). The penalty for the offence is set out at Item 2 in the table, *ante*.

3. RECKLESSLY GIVING FALSE INFORMATION

An offence is committed where a person, furnishing any information for the purposes of the VAT legislation, makes any statement which he knows to be false in a material particular or recklessly makes a statement which is false in a material particular. For the meaning of "material particular", see 2., *ante*.

For a case where the authorities on recklessness were reviewed, see *R v Grunwald and Others*, [1960] 3 All ER 380, in particular the remarks of Paull J. at p 384 where he said:

> "A man may honestly and strongly hold an opinion with which others disagree. Provided that he bases that opinion on facts which he has reason honestly to believe exist and makes the statement or gives that promise because of the existence of those facts, then, in my judgment, that statement or promise is not reckless. He has reckoned, although he may have reckoned wrongly or may even have been somewhat careless in the conclusion to which he has come. Carelessness, in my judgment, may not in itself be sufficient to constitute recklessness, although, of course, it is one of the factors which have to be taken into account. Clearly, a statement or promise cannot be both careful and reckless. On the other hand, I do not think that it is necessary to find dishonesty. A statement or promise may be reckless although the person making it, in some somewhat vague way, thinks that the statement is true and the promise is warranted."

Paull J. concluded that three tests were required to be satisfied, namely

> "(i) that the statement or promise was in fact made; (ii) that it was a rash statement to make or a rash promise to give; and (iii) that the person who made the statement or gave the promise had no real basis of facts on which he could support the statement or the promise."

4. DEEMED OFFENCE

It is provided in s 38(3) that where a person's conduct must have involved the commission of one or more of the offences described at 1–3, *ante*, then whether or not the person knew of the provision of the offence or offences he shall be guilty of an offence in any event. The section, therefore, deems an offence to have been committed if a Court is satisfied that the person by his conduct has evidenced the commission of an offence. The inclusion of this offence met with resistance from the opposition during the passage of the Finance Bill 1972 through Parliament, but it was justified by the government of the day as being necessary, "to cover the case where it can be proved that an offence has been committed but it is not clear to what extent it was committed in a particular accounting period within the total time concerned." (Hansard, Standing Committee E, 14 June 1972 col 850).

The offence is curious in that whereas *mens rea* (an intention to commit the offence) is required for the actual commission of the principal offences described at 1.–3., *ante*, the court can impute *mens rea* under s 38(3). The offence carries the penalty shown on the table at p 259, *ante*.

5. RECEIVING GOODS OR SERVICES WHERE THE SUPPLIER EVADES TAX

It is an offence for a person to acquire possession of or deal with goods, or accept the supply of services, where he has reason to believe that

tax on the supply of the goods or services has been or will be evaded
(s 38(4)). This offence would, therefore, be committed by a person
who, for example, employs a contractor to carry out work for him and
who pays the contractor "cash" on the basis that no VAT is added to
the price and where he believes VAT is being evaded. The penalty for
the offence is £1,000 or three times the tax due, whichever is the greater.

6. FAILURE TO COMPLY WITH THE REGISTRATION REQUIREMENTS

A person commits an offence if he fails to comply with the registration
requirements of Sched 1 (see **2.100**, s 38(5)). The penalty for the
offence is £1,000 or three times the tax evaded by the failure.

7. BREACH OF THE SECURITY PROVISIONS

A person commits an offence (s 38(5)) if he supplies goods in breach
of the security provisions of s 32(2), ie where the Customs & Excise
require security before supplies may be made (see **14.200**). The penalty
for committing the offence is £1,000 or three times the tax evaded by
the contravention.

8. WRONGFUL ISSUE OF A VAT INVOICE

If a person who is not authorised to issue a VAT invoice does so, he
commits an offence and will be liable to a penalty of £1,000 or three
times the tax shown on the invoice, whichever is the greater (s 38(6)).
The only persons who may issue an invoice showing VAT on the supply
are:

(a) a registered person; or
(b) a body corporate treated for the purposes of s 21 as a member
of a group; or
(c) persons within s 23(3)—basically persons acting temporarily in
a representative capacity, for example personal representatives of a
deceased person; or
(d) persons executing a power of sale over the goods within Sched
2, para 6; or
(e) a person acting on behalf of the Crown.

Any person, other than those listed above will, therefore, commit an
offence under s 38(6) if he issues an invoice showing VAT due on it.

9. FAILURE TO COMPLY WITH RECORD-KEEPING REQUIREMENTS OR FURNISH INFORMATION

Subject as in 10., *post* a person commits an offence when he fails to
comply with the record-keeping requirements of s 34, as to which see
Chapter 17. Further, an offence is committed if a person fails to furnish
information or produce documents under s 35, as to which see **14.200**

(s 38(7)). Either of the above offences will make the person liable to a penalty of £100 plus a penalty of £10 per day for which the failure continues. Any penalty under this provision will run until the date of the hearing before the Magistrates (see *M J Grice* v *P J Needs and A G D Hale* [1979] STC 641 (*Casebook* **14.401**)).

10. LATE PAYMENT OF TAX OR SUBMISSION OF QUARTERLY RETURN

F A 1980, s 14 has increased the penalty in respect of an offence under s 38(7) where the offence is the:

(*a*) late payment of tax; or
(*b*) the late submission of a quarterly return.

With effect from 1 August 1980 the penalty in respect of these offences will be £100 plus the greater of £10 or one-half per cent per day of the tax due for the period. The change will not affect any taxable persons whose quarterly VAT amounts to £2,000 or less. The provision has been introduced to expedite the payment of VAT where larger sums are involved.

Chapter 15

Special Categories of Supplier

15.000 Agents

15.000A Sources

Section 24(1) —Enables the Customs & Excise to recover VAT from a UK agent of a non-resident trader and further makes the UK agent responsible for carrying out the non-resident's obligations for VAT.

Section 24(2) —Enables the Customs & Excise to treat a taxable person who imports and supplies goods on behalf of a non-taxable person as a principal.

Section 24(2A)—Enables a person who would be a taxable person (because his supplies exceed the registration limit) to be treated as a non-taxable person where he only supplies goods through a UK agent.

Section 24(3) —Enables the Customs & Excise to treat an agent as principal where the supplies are made in the agent's name.

In addition the following Customs & Excise Notices and associated Leaflets may be helpful:

710 —Supplies by or through agents.
700/4/79—Overseas Traders and UK VAT.

15.000B General principles

Section 24(3) enables the Customs & Excise to treat a supply made through an agent in his own name as being a supply to and a supply by, the agent, thereby effectively treating the agent as a principal. The Customs & Excise have a discretion in this matter, however, and cannot be forced to afford an agent such treatment. In practice, the Customs & Excise will usually treat the agent as a principal in such circumstances.

15.000C Whether an agency exists

It is a question of fact as to whether or not an agency exists, but the Tribunals have suggested certain principles that might assist in the determination of this point. In particular, in *Aberdeen Office Services v CCE*, EDN/77/12 (*Casebook* **15.004**) the Tribunal said that the term agent meant no more than "one who acts on behalf of another". Further, in *New Way School of Motoring v CCE*, LON/78/317 (*Casebook* **15.002**), the Tribunal approved the four-fold test laid down by Lord Wright in

Montreal and A G for Canada, (1947), 1 DLR 161, for determining whether a person was an independent contractor as opposed to an agent, ie:

(*a*) the degree of control exercised over the "agent";
(*b*) whether the "agent" owned his own tools;
(*c*) the chance of profit for the "agent";
(*d*) the risk of loss to the "agent".

In Notice No 710 the Customs & Excise indicates its own view as to agency, namely that:

"An agent/principal relationship exists if both parties agree that it does and if the arrangement between them is that the agent shall act on behalf of his principal in relation, for example, to the passing on of a supply of goods or services, or the making or receiving of a payment passing between the principal and a third party."

Normally, the parties wishing to establish an agency relationship would be advised to do so in writing and in clear terms for the protection of both parties.

15.000D Registered buying agent

Where an agent acts as a buying agent and is himself a taxable person, if the invoice is made out in the agent's name, the agent may himself issue an invoice to his principal. The agent will not suffer any VAT himself if he is a fully taxable person as the invoice to and from him will "match" and the VAT due on the invoice to him is deductible from that shown on the invoice issued by him.

If the agent is acting for a principal who is not a taxable person he need not, necessarily, issue an invoice to the principal. The principal will be unable to recover the VAT on the supply in any event and he may simply reimburse the agent for the cost of the goods plus VAT: the agent must not claim a deduction for the VAT in such circumstances.

Where the agent merely acts as an intermediary and brings the parties, who are known to each other together, the supplier may issue an invoice direct to the buyer in the normal way.

It should be noted that a non-taxable person cannot issue a VAT invoice, and indeed it is an offence to do so (see **14.400** and s 38(6)). Accordingly, special rules apply to agents who are not taxable persons (see **15.00F**).

15.000E Registered selling agent

Where the agent acts as a selling agent for a principal similar provisions to those outlined above for buying agents apply. If the agent and the principal are both taxable persons and an invoice is issued to the agent in his name the agent may himself issue a corresponding invoice to the principal.

If the agent is acting for a seller who is not a taxable person, he need not charge VAT, but he must be satisfied that the principal is not a taxable person. In such circumstances the agent must have evidence that he is making the supply as agent, for example, an agreement with the principal, or a declaration from the principal stating that he is not a taxable person (see Notice No 710, para 5(*b*)). The agent must keep separate records of any such supplies and must be able to distinguish them from other supplies made by him.

Where the agent merely acts as an intermediary and brings the parties, who are known to each other, together, the supplier may issue an invoice direct to the purchaser in the normal way.

An agent who is not a taxable person must not issue invoices and special rules apply—see below.

15.000F Unregistered agents

An agent who is not a taxable person cannot issue tax invoices; indeed it would be an offence to do so, see Chapter 14 at p 262. Accordingly where an agent who is not a taxable person acts as an undisclosed agent the principal will be at a disadvantage because the agent will receive the invoice from the seller (if a buying agent) and will not be able to issue an invoice to his principal with the result that the principal will be unable to obtain credit for the VAT on such a purchase. In this situation the agent may wish to apply for voluntary registration (see **2.100**).

15.000G Overseas traders with UK agents

The position of overseas traders and their obligations to register for VAT is considered at **2.700**. Further, the importation of goods into the United Kingdom by non-residents is dealt with at **6.600**. However, it may be of assistance to deal briefly with some of the points made earlier again in the context of UK agents. Esssentially, three possible situations exist:

(1) Overseas trader who appoints a UK agent to import and sell goods on his behalf

Where an overseas trader is not required to be registered because his taxable supplies in the United Kingdom are below the limit, he may appoint a UK agent to import goods and sell them on his behalf. If the agent is a taxable person he will be treated as a principal for VAT purposes (s 24(2)) which will enable him to be able to issue a VAT invoice to UK purchasers. The agent will operate the postponed accounting system in the usual way (see **6.600**). Where the supplies exceed the limit for registration the non-resident would normally become liable to be registered but s 24(2A) enables him to avoid registering himself if he makes no other supplies in the United Kingdom other than through the import agent.

A difficulty that arises with this method of operating is that the non-resident will be liable to VAT on the agent's fees. The agent's fees cannot be zero-rated unless title to the goods has passed outside the United Kingdom in which case they can be zero-rated under Group 9, item 11(c) (the fees will not qualify for zero-rating under Group 9, items 5 or 6 as the agent's services do not fall within Sched 2A). It should be noted that Notice No 710, para 12 is no longer correct on this point as the notice describes the position prior to 1 January 1978. Since the non-resident is not registered he cannot recover the VAT on such agent's fees. The problem can be resolved, however, by the non-resident applying to be registered, see VAT Leaflet 700/4/79, para 2(b).

(2) Overseas trader with no place of business in United Kingdom but making supplies in the United Kingdom

Where an overseas trader makes taxable supplies in the United Kingdom but has no fixed place of business in the United Kingdom he may, nevertheless, appoint a UK agent to act on his behalf in VAT affairs. In such circumstances he will be registered at the UK agent's address (see **2.700**).

(3) Overseas trader with place of business in the United Kingdom

Such a person must register at his UK place of business if his supplies exceed the statutory limit and agency will not be relevant.

15.000H Disbursements

VAT is generally payable on the total value of the supply of goods or services. However, sometimes a supplier incurs expenditure as agent for his customer. These payments are disbursements and do not fall to be included in the value of the supply made to the customer. These "agency disbursements" must be distinguished from "general disbursements" incurred by a supplier, for example telephone, postage, photocopying and travel expenses, which are included in the total value of the supply to the customer and which form a part of the cost of supplying the goods or services, the leading case on the point being *Rowe and Maw* v *CCE*, [1975] STC 340 (*Casebook* **15.006**). In Notice No 710 at p 7, the Customs & Excise list three types of "agency disbursements" namely:

(*a*) payments which are clearly the liability of the client (eg estate duty payable by him, vehicle excise duty payable by him for his car, stamp duty payable by him on a contract to be made by him);

(*b*) bills paid on behalf of the client for goods or services ordered directly by the client from the party supplying them, eg delivery charges by a carrier employed by the client to send goods to an auctioneer, when the charges are to be deducted by the auctioneer from the proceeds of sale;

(*c*) payments for goods or services which the client has, explicitly or by clear implication in the contract between himself and the agent, instructed the agent to order on his behalf from another party, provided that those goods or services are additional to what is normally and necessarily covered by the service that is being rendered to the client, and that the client knows they are being supplied by a third party.

If a supply falls within any of the items described at (*a*)–(*c*) above, the supply is really between the client and the third party. Accordingly, the rules outlined earlier will apply ie if the invoice is issued in the name of the agent, the agent should (if a taxable person) himself issue an invoice to his principal. Certain suppliers incur "agency disbursements" on a regular basis, for example, solicitors and it may be that special concessionary rules have been negotiated with the Customs & Excise, for example special treatment is afforded to solicitors in respect of Counsel's fees.

15.100 Charities

15.100A Sources

Schedule 4, Group 16—Zero-rates certain supplies made by charities.
In addition the following Customs & Excise Notice and associated Leaflets may be of some assistance:
700   —Scope and coverage, p 58 *et seq.*
701/1/79—Charities.
SHP 10   —Charities and other bodies engaged in new building projects on a self-build or self-help basis

15.100B General principles

In general charities have no special treatment for VAT. If a charity engages in business activities and its supplies exceed the statutory limit it must register and account for VAT in the usual way. The meaning of business for VAT purposes is considered at Chapter 4, but an example of a business activity carried on by charities is the sale of Christmas cards. Non-business activities include certain religious activities (for example donations to clergy and offertories) and the provision of voluntary services without charge (see VAT Leaflet 701/1/79). Furthermore, the Customs & Excise has indicated that where a charity supplies goods or services to distressed persons consistently below cost for the relief of their distress, such supplies are not treated as made in the course or furtherance of a business. The Customs & Excise regard supplies as being consistently below cost for this purpose where the supplies are always made for a consideration which is less than the cost of the goods or services to the charity. The cost of the goods to the charity is the actual cost exclusive of capital expenditure on capital assets (see VAT Leaflet 701/1/79, p 7). Emblems given to the public, for example "poppies" or "flags" in respect of voluntary donations, are also regarded as not being a business activity; however, the donations must be entirely voluntary and there must be no obligation to make a specified payment for the emblem.

However, certain limited supplies made by charities are specifically zero-rated in Sched 4, Group 16 and some supplies may be exempt.

15.100C Zero-rated supplies

Supply of goods donated for sale

The supply by a charity, established primarily for the relief of distress, of any goods which have been donated for sale, subject to certain conditions, is zero-rated (Sched 4, Group 16, item 1). In particular, where a charity receives donated goods for sale by it the proceeds are zero-rated provided that the goods have not been donated from the stock of a taxable person, in which case the goods are only zero-rated if the cost to the donor is less than £10. Furthermore, the sale must be by the first donee of the goods, so that if one charity gives goods it has recieved by way of gift to another charity and the second charity sells the goods, VAT is chargeable on the sale at the standard rate.

Moreover, to be zero-rated the charity must have been established primarily for the relief of distress, which is defined as meaning the relief of poverty or the making of provision for the care or mitigation or prevention of, or the care of persons suffering from or subject to, any disease or infirmity of disability affecting human beings including in the care of women before, during and after childbirth (Sched 4, Group 16, Note (3), see **8.1600**). Thus, to qualify for zero-rating under this item, the charity must broadly speaking be for the relief of poverty or to help the sick and many charities will not, therefore, be entitled to claim this relief, for example, educational charities.

The item includes sales by qualifying charities of goods at bring and buy sales, jumble sales and similar activities, so that such sales are zero-rated.

Export of goods

The export of any goods by a charity is zero-rated (Sched 4, Group 16, item 2). Since exports of goods are zero-rated under s 12(6) and (7) (see Chapter 7) if the Customs & Excise is satisfied that the goods have been exported and that certain conditions have been complied with it is arguable that because these requirements have not been included in Group 16, item 2, a charity may zero-rate exports without meeting the conditions of the Customs & Excise imposed under s 12.

Medical or scientific equipment and voluntary contributions

The supply to a charity of medical or scientific equipment out of funds provided by a charity or voluntary contributions made to it is zero-rated. The medical or scientific equipment must be solely for use in medical research, diagnosis or treatment and must be donated by the charity to a designated Regional or Area Health Authority or similar body or a hospital or research institution. The relief is *not* given if:

(*a*) the supply of the equipment is to a person other than the donor (ie the charity);
(*b*) the activities of the hospital or research centre are carried on for profit;
(*c*) the donee of the equipment has contributed wholly or partly to the funds used for the purchase.

Further, the importation of such medical or scientific equipment by the charity for donation to one of the bodies of persons specified above may be zero-rated, if the correct procedure on importation is followed (see Notice No 701 (Scope and Coverage), p 60 and VAT Leaflet No 701/6/79 (Donated Medical and Scientific Equipment)).

15.100D Exempt supplies

Charities are governed by the normal principles of exemption and may make exempt supplies within Sched 5 (see Chapter 9). Attention is particularly drawn to Sched 5, Group 7 (Health) in relation to supplies by charities from hospital trolleys or shops which supplies are exempt (see VAT Leaflet 701/1/79, p 6).

15.100E Projects of self-help

A special concessionary scheme is operated for charities and other voluntary bodies who are engaged in the construction of a new building on a self-help basis (see Leaflet SHP 10 (Charities and other bodies engaged in new building projects on a self-build or self-help basis)). The purpose of the scheme is to enable charities or voluntary bodies to obtain credit for input tax suffered on the construction by the body of a new building. The bodies would not be able to obtain relief without the benefit of the scheme as they are not carrying on a business where they construct the building themselves. The arrangement covers buildings to be used mainly for activities which benefit the aged, the sick, the disabled, the needy or the young, or which are for the social, cultural or artistic benefit of the community. The Customs & Excise list as examples the construction of a church hall, village hall or scout hut. The arrangements only apply to the construction of a building, and not the conversion, extension, alteration or reconstruction of an existing building.

The goods which are eligible for relief are builder's materials or hardware, sanitary ware or other articles of a kind ordinarily installed by builders as fixtures. For consideration of this expression see **8.800**.

To qualify for the benefit of the scheme a separate entity, the project organisation, must be set up, comprising in the case of an unincorporated association at least three individuals. The project organisation must undertake the project and make construction services to the charity or voluntary body for which it receives payment to meet expenses. Alternatively, the project organisation must sell or grant a lease of at least 21 years of the building to the body. In these circumstances the Customs & Excise will register the project organisation, which must be responsible for its own affairs and finances, maintain its own bank account and keep its own records.

As stated, the scheme is concessionary and the Customs & Excise cannot be made to operate it in favour of any particular body and will not do so where all the conditions are not satisfied (see *Widnes Spastic Fellowship* v *CCE*, MAN/77/132 (*Casebook* **15.101**) and other cases noted thereat). Leaflet SHP 10 should accordingly be consulted before setting up a project organisation to ensure that all the conditions of the Customs & Excise are satisfied.

15.200 Clubs and associations

15.200A Sources

Section 23(2)   —Power given to the Customs & Excise to make Regulations to determine who
shall be responsible for carrying out statutory obligations in relation to VAT
where the business is carried on by, *inter alia*, clubs and associations.

Section 23(2A)—Enables registration to be in the name of the Club. No account to be taken
of change in members.

Section 45(2)   —Deems the provision by clubs, associations or organisations for a subscription
or other consideration of facilities or advantages to be the carrying on of
a business.

Section 45(3)   —Political, religious and similar bodies.

Schedule 5, Group 6, item 6—Exempts the provision of the facilities of a youth club to its
members.

VAT (General) Regulations 1977 (SI 1977 No 1759), reg 6—Regulations made pursuant to
s 23(2) above.

In addition the following Customs & Excise Leaflet may be helpful:

701/5/79—Clubs and associations: liability to VAT.

15.200B Facilities or advantages of membership

Section 45(2) deems the provision of the facilities or advantages of
membership of a club, association or organisation for a subscription,
or other consideration, to be the carrying on of a business for VAT purposes.

The Tribunals have considered many cases concerning the question of
whether or not a club is providing facilities or advantages to its members
(see *Casebook* **15.200**, *et seq*) and in *Club Cricket Conference* v *CCE*,
[1973] VATTR 53 (*Casebook* **15.204**) the Tribunal said that "facilities"
should be given its normal meaning of "opportunities to do something
more easily". Before the changes in s 45, introduced as a result of the
EEC Sixth Directive in F A 1977, it used to be material whether a club
or association provided "facilities" or "advantages", but such a distinction is no longer of importance. However, for a case in which the
difference between the two was analysed see *The Royal Highland and
Agricultural Society of Scotland* v *CCE*, [1976] VATTR 38 (*Casebook*
15.206).

15.200C Admission fees

Section 45(2)(*b*) deems the admission to premises in return for a fee
to be a business activity for VAT purposes. Accordingly, many activities
run by clubs and associations are brought within the charge to VAT, for
example entrance fees to play bingo or to listen to lectures (eg where
a prominent or famous member of a club gives a lecture to raise funds
for the club, the entrance fees going to club funds).

15.200D Apportionment of subscriptions

The result of a club being deemed to be carrying on a business is that if its supplies exceed the statutory limits (see **2.100**, *et seq*) it must register for VAT. Normally, the supplies made by the club are the provision of the facilities of membership in return for the payment of a subscription, with the result that the club's subscriptions become liable to VAT. The extent of the liability will depend on the type of facilities provided as explained below.

In *CCE* v *Automobile Association*, [1974] STC 192 (*Casebook* **15.211**) (which decision was followed in *Barton* (*Alpine Garden Society*) v *CCE*, [1974] STC 200 (*Casebook* **15.212**)) the Tribunal held that the supply of the magazine *Drive* and *Handbook* to members was a zero-rated supply under Sched 4, Group 3 and that, therefore, only a part of members' subscriptions was chargeable at the standard rate. Following this decision the Customs & Excise issued a statement to the effect that it is possible for subscriptions to be apportioned between zero-rated or exempt supplies on the one hand and standard-rated supplies on the other, see 1974 BTR, p 464). Further, VAT Leaflet 701/5/79, para 3 provides that:

> "Organisations which consider that any of the supplies which they make in return for membership subscriptions are zero-rated or exempt under Schedules 4 or 5 of the Finance Act 1972 may apportion their subscriptions so that part which is properly attributable to positive-rated supplies is charged with tax. The supplies which they make means identifiable goods or services which clubs, associations etc supply to their members. The most common form of apportionment is in respect of zero-rated literature supplied to members.
>
> Relief from the tax cannot be granted for subscriptions on account of an association receiving zero-rated or exempt supplies from third parties. For example, a sports club cannot zero-rate part of its members' subscriptions because this income is used to pay for a structural alteration to its premises. The builder has supplied zero-rated construction services to the clubs, but the club is not supplying such services to its members.
>
> Apportionment of the membership subscriptions to cover the value of the supplies should normally be carried out by the organisation. While there are no specific rules one method, which is generally acceptable to Customs & Excise, is to apportion the total subscription income to reflect the relative cost to the organisation of providing various supplies to members. There is no objection to calculations for the current financial year being based on the accounts for the previous financial year, providing the method is applied consistently. The calculations should be retained and may be inspected by a visiting Customs & Excise Officer. Any organisation which wishes to use another method of apportionment should put proposals supported by accounts and other relevant documents, in writing, to the local VAT office.
>
> The Customs & Excise does not consider apportionment to be justified if the value of the zero-rated or exempt supplies is trivial compared with the value of the membership benefits as a whole represented by the annual subscription."

However, although a club makes zero-rated supplies it must be remembered that zero-rated supplies are taxable supplies and if the value of a club's supplies, including zero-rated supplies exceeds the statutory limits in Sched 1 it must register for VAT although the Customs & Excise may grant exemption from registration under Sched 1, para 11(1)(*a*) (see **2.100**, *et seq*).

15.200E Loans from members

In some clubs members, or prospective members, are required to make loans to the club or association on joining, or annual loans once admitted to membership. The Customs & Excise have argued that such loans are really part of the subscription and accordingly subject to VAT but in *Dyrham Park Country Club* v *CCE*, [1978] VATTR 244 (*Casebook* **9.503** and **15.218**) the Tribunal held that the total value of the subscription and the loans should be apportioned according to the proportion the facilities supplied bore to the total consideration given by members. However, in *CCE* v *Exeter Golf and Country Club*, [1980] STC 162 (*Casebook***15.219**) the High Court held that interest foregone on interest free loans required to be made by members of the club constituted a part of a notional subscription from the members, so that the market value of the interest foregone formed a part of the subscription and fell to be valued under s 10(5). The position with regard to loans made by club members would, therefore, appear to be that if a member is required to make loans to the club, the value of the loan will form part of the subscription and be liable to VAT to the extent that the loan is attributable to the provisions of facilities (*Dyrham Park Country Club* v *CCE*). If the loan is interest free, the interest free element must also be taken into account. However, if a member makes an interest free loan in addition to his subscription and there is no obligation on him to make the loan it is doubtful that either the loan or the interest free element of it, can be regarded as a payment for the provision of facilities or advantages of membership; accordingly such a loan, in the Authors' view, should not be liable to VAT.

15.200F Receipts

A club or organisation may provide many different kinds of facilities to members for which additional charges may be made. Alternatively, it might take part in a variety of fund raising activities. Some of the main types of receipt are considered in outline below (it being assumed that the club is a registered taxable person):

Subscriptions or joining fees

These are liable at the standard rate unless suitable for apportionment following *CCE* v *Automobile Association* (see **15.200D**).

Bar proceeds

These are liable at the standard rate. However, attention is drawn to the case of *Gloucester Old Boys Rugby Football Social Club* v *CCE*, CAR/77/133 (*Casebook* **15.220**) where the Tribunal was satisfied that it would be unfair to accept the Customs & Excise proposed commercial rate mark-up of bar-profits as there was no evidence of dishonesty on the club's part, although it was accepted that the bar had been run less efficiently than a proper commercial enterprise. The Tribunal commented, that VAT "was a tax on supplies made by a taxable person and not a tax on inefficiency".

It would seem, therefore, that where a club runs a bar with a volunteer labour force, the standards expected of it should not be as high as where paid professional staff are used.

Donations

These are not taxable if the payments are entirely voluntary and the donor receives no direct benefit (see VAT Leaflet 701/5/79).

Match, court, green and competition fees

These are liable at the standard rate on the gross receipts. Where the court fees include payment for the use of lights the full amount is still chargeable as there is no separate supply of electricity (see *St Annes-on-Sea Lawn Tennis Club Ltd* v *CCE*, [1977] VATTR 229 (*Casebook* **3.612**). It should be noted that *High Wycombe Squash Club Ltd* v *CCE*, [1976] VATTR 156 (*Casebook* **8.702**) is of doubtful authority in the light of the *St Annes-on-Sea Lawn Tennis Club* case and *British Railways Board* v *CCE* (No 2), [1977] STC 221 (see *Casebook* **3.612**, *Editorial Note*).

Lotteries

These are exempt under Sched 5, Group 4 if the conditions contained therein are satisfied (see **9.400**). Broadly speaking, to be exempt, the lottery must be an arrangement for the distribution of prizes by chance and no element of skill must be present. The value of the exempt supply is the total proceeds of sales less the amount of cash prizes. In this connection it should be noted that "Spot the Ball" competitions are now regarded by the Customs & Excise as being games of skill and therefore, not exempt (see Customs & Excise Statement, *Taxation*, 17 November 1979).

Discos, dances and socials

Standard rate is payable on the gross receipts. No deduction is allowable for overheads, for example the cost of the disco or band.

Jumble sales/admission charges

Normal rules apply to the sales of the various items sold, for example sales of books will be zero-rated. The charging for admission to premises is itself a deemed business (s 45(2)(*b*)) and admission proceeds are, therefore, standard rated.

Bank interest

This is exempt under Sched 5, Group 5, item 2 (see **9.500**) and need not be brought into account in calculating partially exempt supplies (see VAT (General) Regulations 1977 (SI 1977 No 1759), reg 68 and Customs & Excise Notice No 706, para 3(*a*)).

15.200G Political, religious and similar bodies

It will be seen from p 272, *ante* that the provision of facilities or advantages to members is deemed to be the carrying on of a business under s 45(2)(*a*). However, special rules are contained in s 45(3) relating to bodies whose subjects are of a political, religious, philanthropic, philosophical or patriotic nature. In particular s 45(3) provides that such bodies shall not be treated as carrying on a business simply because members subscribe to them, providing that the payment of the subscription does not afford facilities or advantages other than the right to take part in the management of the bodies or receive reports of their activities. The scope of this section was considered by a Tribunal in *South Church Workman's Club and Institute Ltd* v *CCE*, MAN/78/40 (*Casebook* **15.203**), where it was held that the subscriptions of members in fact entitled members to the general facilities and advantages of membership in addition to the right to participate in the club's management.

The section was introduced as a result of the adoption by the United Kingdom of the EEC Sixth Directive. In particular, the subsection has its origin in art 13(A)(*l*) of the directive which enabled (art 13(A)(1)(*l*)) Member States to exempt, *inter alia*, the:

"supply of services and goods closely limited thereto for the benefit of their members in return for a subscription fixed in accordance with their rules by non-profit making organisations with aims of a political, trade union, religious, patriotic, philosophical, philanthropic or civic nature, provided that this exemption is not likely to cause distortion of competition."

Section 45(3) has not adopted the exact wording of art 13(A)(1)(*l*) but the limitation in s 45(3), to the benefit of the exemption to those bodies which do not afford general facilities or advantages to members in return for a subscription (but only allow members to participate in management or receive reports) is Parliament's attempt to satisfy the requirement of art 13(A)(1)(*l*) that the exemption shall not cause distortion or competition. On the basis that once a body provides more than the mere right to participate in management or receive reports (as in *South Church Workman's Club and Institute Ltd*) with the result that its subscriptions are treated as being received in the course or furtherance of a business under s 45(2)(*a*), the legislation meets the requirements of the EEC Sixth Directive (the restriction of the exemption effectively preventing distortion and competition because, once more than the limited rights of membership referred to in s 45(3) are granted, the body is within the general rule of s 45(2)(*a*)).

15.300 Local authorities

15.300A Sources

Section 15—Enables local authorities and other bodies to recover VAT in respect of non-business activities.

Section 19—Enables the Treasury to direct that the supply of goods or services by a government department to be treated as made in the course or furtherance of a business.

Section 20— Provides that the £13,500 registration limit does not apply so that local authorities must register if any business is carried on regardless of turnover.

Notice 749 "Local Authorities and similar bodies covered by Finance Act 1972 Section 15"—may be helpful.

15.300B Local authorities

A local authority is basically in no different position from any other business for VAT purposes, so that it must charge VAT on supplies it makes in the course or furtherance of its business in the usual way (for example see *Rawlins Davy and Wells* v *CCE*, LON/77/251 (*Casebook* **15.301**)). Similarly, a local authority will be able to recover or obtain credit for input tax suffered on goods supplied to it for the purpose of its business. One difference between local authorities and other businesses, however, is that the registration limits contained in Sched 1 (see **2.100**) do not apply, so that if a local authority makes any business supplies in the course or furtherance of a business it must charge VAT on them (s 20). The reason for this is that special rules apply (see *post*) to enable, *inter alia*, a local authority to recover input tax in respect of goods or services received by it in a non-business capacity (Hansard, Standing Committee E, 8 June 1972, col 648).

As stated above, a local authority is able to obtain a refund in respect of VAT charged to it on goods or services supplied to it other than for the purpose of a business carried on by it (s 15). Thus, local authorities obtain input tax relief for non-business activities. Section 15 applies to other bodies, in addition to local authorities, a list of which is given below. For the purpose of s 15 a local authority means (s 15(6)):

> "The council of a county, borough, county district, district, parish or group of parishes, community or group of communities, the Greater London Council, the Common Council of the City of London, the Council of the Isles of Scilly and any joint committee or joint board established by two or more of the foregoing, and in relation to Scotland, the Council of a county, county of a city, large burgh, small burgh, district and any combination and any joint committee or joint board established by two or more of the foregoing."

Other bodies to which s 15 applies are:

(*a*) a local authority;
(*b*) a river authority, a river purification board, the Conservators of the River Thames and the Lee Conservancy Catchment Board;
(*c*) a drainage board within the meaning of the Land Drainage Act 1930;
(*d*) any statutory water undertakers within the meaning of the Water Act 1945, and a regional water board and water development board within the meaning of the Water (Scotland) Act 1967;
(*e*) the London Transport Executive and a passenger transport authority or executive established under Part II of the Transport Act 1968;
(*f*) a port health authority constituted under Part I of the Public Health Act 1936, and a port local authority constituted under Part X of the Public Health (Scotland) Act 1897;
(*g*) a police authority and the Receiver for the Metropolitan Police District;
(*h*) a development corporation within the meaning of the New Towns Act 1965 or the New Towns (Scotland) Act 1968, a new town commission within the meaning of the New Town Act (Northern Ireland) 1965 and the Commission for the New Towns;
(*i*) a general lighthouse authority within the meaning of the Merchant Shipping Act 1894, Pt. XI to the extent that its activities relate to the provision, maintenance or management of the lights or other navigational aids;
(*j*) the British Broadcasting Corporation;
(*k*) Independent Television News Limited; and
(*l*) any body specified for the purposes of the section by an order made by the Treasury. Orders have been made specifying the following bodies:

(i) the Scottish Special Housing Association (VAT (Refund of Tax) Order 1973 (SI 1973 No 552)).

(ii) Welsh National Water Development Authority
North West Water Authority
Yorkshire Water Authority
Anglian Water Authority
Thames Water Authority
Southern Water Authority
Wessex Water Authority
South West Water Authority
Severn-Trent Water Authority
(VAT (Refund of Tax) (No 2) Order 1973 (SI 1973 No 2121))
(iii) the Commission for Local Administration in England
the Commission for Local Administration in Wales
the Commission for Local Administration in Scotland
the Commission for Local Authority Accounts in Scotland
(VAT (Refund of Tax) Order 1976 (SI 1976 No 2028))

Business or non-business activities

As a local authority must charge VAT on supplies made by it in the course or furtherance of any business, it is necessary to be able to distinguish between activities of a local authority which are regarded as business activities and those which are not. A list of the Customs & Excise views on the matter is contained in notice 749, at Appendix B.

A local authority's ability to claim input tax in respect of supplies for the purpose of its business will be governed by the normal rules for partial exemption (see **5.300**). Exempt supplies must be taken into account accordingly, although many of the local authority supplies will not be exempt because they will not be made in the course or furtherance of a business, for example health, housing and education.

15.300C The Crown

Section 19 enables the Treasury to make a direction to a Government department to the effect that supplies of goods or services made by it shall be treated as made in the course or furtherance of a business carried on by it. Thus, Government departments can be made to charge VAT on supplies of goods or services in such circumstances notwithstanding that no business is in fact carried on. The reason for the provision is to prevent Government departments which are in competition with registered taxable persons obtaining an unfair advantage. A list of the directives that have been made is contained in the *London Gazette* 21 November 1975 which list is fairly extensive.

15.400 Partnerships

15.400A Sources

Section 22—Provisions relating to registration, changes in partners and liability of the partners.
VAT (General) Regulation 1977 (SI 1977 No 1759)
    reg 4(4)—Notification of, *inter alia*, any change of partners to be given.
      reg 5—Provision dealing with who should give notice on behalf of partnership.
VAT Tribunal Rules 1972 (SI 1972 No 1344)
    r 10—Appeal can be in partnership name.

15.400B General principles

Generally a partnership is in exactly the same position as any other category of supplier and must charge VAT on supplies made by it in the course or furtherance of its business. Most VAT cases on partnership have arisen as a result of a dispute as to whether or not, in given circumstances, a partnership existed or not. In determining whether or not there is a partnership, the Tribunals have accepted the definition in the Partnership Act 1890, s 1, namely that a partnership is the relationship which subsists between persons carrying on business in common with a view of profit (see *Pollingford Farms* v *CCE*, LON/76/103 (*Casebook* **15.403**).

It will of course be a question of fact as to whether or not persons are regarded as carrying on business in partnership, but it is relevant to consider the intention of the parties (see *Daniels and Blackmore* v *CCE*, CAR/78/251 (*Casebook* **15.404**), where the Tribunal referred to the decision in *Cox* v *Hickman*, 8 HLC 268 with approval). In *Daniels and Blackmore* v *CCE*, the Tribunal, however, having cited *Cox* v *Hickman* with approval, appears to have ignored the intentions of the parties in reaching its decision. For cases generally on whether a partnership exists or not, see *Casebook* **15.403**, *et seq*.

In some instances one or more of the partners engaged in the partnership might carry on a separate business independently on their own account. Whether the separate activity can be properly regarded as outside the partnership is a question of fact, but the relevance of the problem is likely to arise where the separate business is below the statutory limit for registration, so that VAT is not being charged on those supplies. In such circumstances the Customs & Excise may be anxious to show that all the activities are in reality carried on by the partnership so that VAT is payable on the "separate independent activities" too. Such a point arose in *P T and V Marner* v *CCE*, MAN/77/140 (*Casebook* **15.410**) where a wife maintained that she ran the catering side of a public house separately from the partnership comprising herself and her husband which was responsible for running the public house. On the facts it was held that the catering was a separate business carried on by Mrs Marner alone. A similar point was considered in *D H Miller v CCE*, [1977] VATTR 241 (*Casebook* **15.411**); *F V E Good* v *CCE*, [1974] VATTR 256 (*Casebook* **15.413**) and *P Kenealy* v *CCE*, LON/ 77/208 (*Casebook* **15.414**). In both *Good* v *CCE* and *Kenealy* v CCE, however, the Tribunal declined, on the evidence available, to accept the taxpayers' contention that a separate business was carried on.

In considering whether a separate business is carried on by a partner independently of the partnership the Tribunal has considered the relevance of financial accounts which cover both the partnership activity and the alleged separate business. In *Marner* v *CCE*, for example, the Tribunal noted that financial accounts encompassing all activities were prepared, but placed more importance on the fact that separate operating accounts were maintained.

Although general principles of VAT apply to partnerships the very nature of a partnership requires that certain special rules for VAT should apply, more particularly in relation to registration, changes in the partnership, liability of individual partners, and on whom the responsibility for submission of partnership details should fall, and these are considered in turn below.

15.400C Registration

Section 22(1) provides, *inter alia*, that the registration of persons carrying on business in partnership may be in the firm's name. This raises a point of difficulty immediately because where two persons are, for example, carrying on business together in two separate partnerships each with a different trade, is it possible to register both partnerships separately in their respective partnerships names? Section 22(1) would appear to indicate that this might be possible, but the High Court decided otherwise in *CCE* v *Glassborrow and Another* (*trading as Bertram and Co*), [1974] STC 142 (*Casebook* **15.401**). In that case the appellant and his wife were engaged in business in partnership as estate agents under the name "Bertram and Co" and they also began a new partnership together in land development and applied for that partnership to be registered separately as "Glassborrow and Glassborrow". The Customs & Excise maintained that both partnerships were covered by the one registration in the name of "Bertram and Co" and refused the second application. The Tribunal found in favour of the taxpayers but on appeal the High Court held that the scheme of the tax was to register persons and the same persons were, therefore, only entitled to one registration. Section 22(1) is only able to permit the one registration to be in the name of the firm rather than the names of individual partners. Thus, the taxpayers in the *Glassborrow* case were only entitled to the one registration as "Bertram and Co".

The decision in the *Glassborrow* case leads to the effect that if, for example, A, B, C, and D are engaged in business together in partnership as estate agents, and C and D carry on business in partnership as antique dealers, and both partnerships are registered in their respective partnership names, on the deaths say of A and B, C and D are left as the only two partners in each partnership with the result that one of the registrations will have to be cancelled, as they can have only one registration to cover all businesses. If the antique business in the above example had previously been below the statutory limit for registration, the effect of A and B's deaths would be that the aggregate supplies of both businesses would be liable to VAT: see *J O W and E M Harris* (*trading as Structural Maintenance and Repair Co*) v *CCE*, CAR/76/ 220 (*Casebook* **15.402**). This principle only applies, however, where the partners in each partnership are identical; thus if the partners in a partnership were XYZ and in another partnership WXYZ, both partnerships should register separately.

However, the principle established in *Glassborrow* has been held not to apply to a limited partnership (see *M Saunders* v *CCE*, LON/79/226 and *T G Sorrell* v *CCE*, LON/79/298 (*Casebook* **2.202**)).

15.400D Change of partners or business

Apart from the particular result of a change in partners described under **15.400C** generally a change in partners is ignored for VAT (s 22(1)). Notification of a change must, however, be given (see **15.400F**).

15.400E Liability of partners

Partners are generally jointly and severally liable for all partnership debts, including tax. This principle applies equally to VAT due from the partnership, except that where an individual partner is only a partner for a part of the prescribed accounting period, his liability is restricted to such proportion of the total VAT due "as may be just" (s 22(2)).

15.400F Responsible person

Section 35(1) gives the Customs & Excise power to make Regulations to provide who shall be responsible for giving notices required under FA 1972 to enable the Customs & Excise to keep their records up to date. Regulations have accordingly been made; the VAT (General) Regulations 1977 (SI 1977 No 1759) and, reg 5 thereof relates to partnerships. In particular, reg 5 provides that it shall be the joint and several liability of all the partners to give any notice required under FA 1972 provided that if a notice is given by one partner the other partners need not also give notice. It is no longer the senior partner alone who is responsible for giving notice. The application to be registered must be given on Form 1 of Schedule 1 to the Regulations (Form VAT 1) and Form 2 of Schedule 1 (Form VAT 2) must also be completed, giving the full name, address, and signature of each partner (reg 4(1) and (2)).

Notice is also required to be given of any change in partners or the business carried on by the partners or any other event which may necessitate the variation of the register kept by the Customs & Excise, within 21 days of the change or other event (reg 4(4)).

The submission of partnership returns is also, on general principles, the joint and several liability of all partners, although compliance by one partner will be sufficient.

Any appeal against an assessment may be made in the partnership name (VAT Tribunals Rules 1972 (SI 1972 No 1344), r 10).

Where a partner also holds an office the partnership may be liable to account for VAT on fees paid to the individual partner, as comprising a part of the partnership's business. For detailed consideration of this see **4.200**, *ante*.

15.500 Pension funds

Where a company sets up a pension fund for the benefit of its employees it will normally wish to make a claim for input tax relief in relation to its costs of setting up and administering the fund. However, often the company which sets up the pension fund is not a trustee of the fund.

Nevertheless, the company may, even though it is not a trustee, be responsible for meeting the costs of setting up the fund and for putting the trustees in funds to enable the trustees to pay their costs of administering the trust fund. The difficulty the company is faced with, in such circumstances, is that the costs of administering the pension fund are borne by the trustees, albeit perhaps with monies received from the company, so that tax invoices are in the names of the trustees and not the company—in such a situation the company is merely indemnifying the trustees in respect of their expenditure, and, subject as below, cannot obtain relief for the trustees' input tax. However, following the decision of the Court of Appeal in *CCE* v *British Railways Board*, [1976] STC 359 (*Casebook* **5.105** and **15.501**) the Customs & Excise now accepts that where a company, which is registered in respect of the business carried on by it, is sole trustee of a pension fund set up for the benefit of its employees it can claim a deduction for input tax relief in respect of the expenditure in setting up the fund and the annual costs of administering the funds.

Where, however, the company is not a sole trustee of a pension fund for its own employees, it is the view of Customs & Excise that only the VAT incurred in setting up the fund will be deductible (being expenditure incurred by the company) and not the VAT incurred in respect of annual costs as such costs are borne by the trustees, even where the company is obliged to reimburse the trustees' expenditure under the terms of the Trust Deed. No input tax relief is available to the company, in respect of the trustees' annual expenditure because the company does not incur the expenses of running a pension fund for the purpose of its business, where it is not the sole trustee of the fund (see *Linotype and Machinery Ltd* v *CCE* [1978] VATTR 123 (*Casebook* **5.106** and **15.502**)).

Where a company is not the sole trustee of a pension fund it may nevertheless be possible to obtain relief for input tax on annual expenditure incurred by the trustees and reimbursed by the company by appointing another company within the group as the trustee of the pension fund and making a group registration to include the trustee company. However, if this is done, the Authors understand that it is the view of the Customs & Excise that a claim for any unpaid VAT can be made against the assets of the pension fund. This view is based upon the wording of s 21(1) which says that all members shall be jointly and severally liable for any VAT due from the representative member. However, the trustee company will only be acting as trustee and would not have any right to the trust property, which it holds for the benefit of the beneficiaries. Accordingly, the Authors incline to the view that the Customs & Excise cannot recover VAT due from the representative member out of the assets of the fund because the trustee company does not own such funds.

15.600 Receiverships, liquidations and trustees in bankruptcy

15.600A Sources

Section 23(3)—Enabling provisions relating to those who carry on the business of certain persons.
Section 24(3)—Supplies through agents.
Sections 37 and 38—Entry and search and penalties.
Section 41—Priority of VAT.
Schedule 2, paras 6 and 7—Sales under exercise of a power of sale; supplies on cessation of business.

Bankruptcy Act 1914, s 33—Preferential debts.
The Law of Property Act 1925, s 109—Status of receivers.
Companies Act 1948,
   ss 94 and 319—Preferential debts.
   s 369—Receivers and managers appointed out of court.
FA 1976, s 22—Priority of VAT.
CEMA 1979, ss 145–155—Entry and search and penalties.
VAT (General) Regulations 1977 (SI 1977 No 1759), regs 4(4), 7, 52 and 56—Notification of Customs & Excise on carrying on business; liability to account for and pay tax.

In addition the following Customs & Excise Notice may be helpful:
700, para 70.

15.600B Companies

Generally

A company continues to be the taxable person in respect of supplies made by it following the appointment of a receiver or liquidator to it. Further, neither a receiver nor a liquidator will usually act in his own name but in that of the company to which he is appointed. This means that the Customs & Excise cannot treat supplies made to the company as made to and supplied by the receiver or liquidator, as the case may be (s 24(3)).

The VAT (General) Regulations 1977 (SI 1977 No 1759), reg 56, does not apply to a receiver or liquidator of a company, notwithstanding the reference to receivers and liquidators in that Regulation. Regulation 56 provides that:

"56. Where any person subject to any requirements under this Part of these Regulations dies or becomes incapacitated and control of his assets passes to another person, being a personal representative, trustee in bankruptcy, receiver, liquidator, or person otherwise acting in a representative capacity, that other person shall, if the Commissioners so require and so long as he has such control, comply with those requirements: provided that any requirement to pay tax shall only apply to that other person to the extent of the assets of the deceased or incapacitated person over which he has control, and save to the extent aforesaid this Part of these Regulations shall apply to such person, so acting, as if he were the deceased or incapacitated person."

Although reg 56 refers to a "person" (which would usually include both an individual and a company) the context of reg 56, which relates to persons who die or become incapacitated, would suggest that "person" in that Regulation should be restricted to individuals. A receiver or liquidator cannot, therefore, be obliged to comply with the accounting and payment requirements of the VAT (General) Regulations 1977 (SI 1977 No 1759). However, as is discussed, *post*, this does not absolve a receiver from all obligations in relation to the payment of VAT.

For the above reason also, the VAT (General) Regulations 1977 (SI 1977 No 1759), reg 7 cannot apply to receivers appointed to companies.

Regulation 7 requires the notification of the Customs & Excise when a taxable person dies, becomes bankrupt or incapacitated and allows the Customs & Excise to treat any person carrying on such taxable person's business as a taxable person for the purposes of the Act. The Customs & Excise does consider, however that an obligation falls upon a receiver or liquidator to inform it of his appointment (see Notice No 700, para 70). Although this obligation cannot arise under reg 7, it may possibly result from reg 4(4) which provides that:

> "(4) Every registered person except one to whom paragraph 8, 9, or 10 of Schedule 1 to the Act applies shall, within 21 days after any change has been made in the name, constitution or ownership of his business, or after any other event has occurred which may necessitate the variation of the register or cancellation of his registration, notify the Commissioners in writing of such change or event and furnish them with full particulars thereof."

Receiverships

THE STATUS OF A RECEIVER

Prior to the liquidation of a company the status of a receiver depends upon the Law of Property Act 1925, s 109(2) and the terms of his appointment. Section 109(2) provides that:

> "A receiver appointed under the powers conferred by this Act, or any enactment replaced by this Act, shall be deemed to be the agent of the mortgagor; and the mortgagor shall be solely responsible for the receiver's acts or defaults unless the mortgage deed otherwise provides."

In practice, it is not usual for the mortgage deed to alter the basic provision under s 109(2). A receiver will usually be, therefore, the agent of the mortgagor.

Following the placing of the company in liquidation, the status of its receiver is in doubt. However, it would appear that from the date of the passing of the resolution, or the presentation of the petition for the winding up of the company, as the case may be, the receiver ceases to be the agent of the company (see *Gosling* v *Gaskell*, [1897] AC 575 and *Thomas* v *Todd* [1926] All ER 564, the case of *Re Northern Garages Ltd*, [1946] ChD 188 being considered to be anomalous). Given that a receiver ceases on the effective date of the liquidation of a company to be its agent, three possibilities exist as to his status from that date. These are:

(*a*) agent for the mortgagee—It seems from the authorities (*Cox* v *Hickman*, 8 HLC 268 and *Gosling* v *Gaskell*) that a receiver does not automatically become, by operation of law, on the liquidation of the company, the agent of the mortgagee in respect of money collected by him in the course of his receivership. Lord Halsbury LC referred to such monies in *Gosling* v *Gaskell* as follows:

"The company is still the person solely interested in the profits, save only that it has mortgaged them to its creditors. It receives the benefit of the profits as they accrue, though it has precluded itself from applying them to any other purpose than the discharge of its debts. The trade is not carried on by, or on account of, the creditors, though their consent is necessary in such case, but the trade remains the trade of the company. The company is the person by, or on whose behalf, the business is carried on."

If contrary to the above, a receiver is to be treated as agent for the mortgagee following the liquidation of the company, it would seem to follow the *Gosling* case that such agency, or trustee relationship cannot arise in respect of monies as they are received by the receiver. Those monies are collected on behalf of the company. Such relationship will only arise immediately after, and not affect the nature of, such receipt;

(*b*) as principal—The above passage from Lord Halsbury's judgment would also appear to remove any possibility of the receiver being treated as collecting monies on his own behalf. The beneficial ownership of the monies remains with the company;

(*c*) as a mere "conduit"—The remaining possibility is that the receiver is no longer an agent following liquidation but a mere conduit through which the monies due to the company are collected and paid to the mortgagee in satisfaction of the company's debt. This is the interpretation that is most widely believed to be correct.

The result of the above analysis is that the position of a receiver is likely to be similar whether or not the company to which he has been appointed has been placed in liquidation.

WHERE THE RECEIVER IS AGENT FOR THE MORTGAGEE (PRE-LIQUIDATION) OR A MERE CONDUIT (POST LIQUIDATION)

All supplies in such circumstances will be made on behalf of the company and no personal liability will attach to the receiver for VAT in respect of those supplies. The provisions of Sched 2, para 6 and the VAT (General) Regulations 1977 (SI 1977 No 1759), reg 52 will not apply as the supply is made by the company and not the reciever.

This lack of personal liability was accepted by the Customs & Excise in *Re John Willment (Ashford) Ltd* v *CCE*, [1979] STC 286 (*Casebook* **15.602**), where it was also common ground that:

(*a*) no personal liability attaches to a receiver in respect of VAT under the Companies Act 1948, s 369(2) (which provides that the receiver of the property of a company appointed out of court shall be personally liable on contracts to the same extent as if appointed by the court);

(*b*) money collected as VAT is not impressed with any trust in favour of the Customs & Excise (the case of the *Attorney General* v *Antoine* [1949] 2 All ER 1000 regarding PAYE was referred to);

(*c*) the Customs & Excise have no right to demand VAT by virtue of the Law of Property Act 1925, s 109(8). This is because s 109 does not give a taxing authority a right to sue a receiver for tax but protects a receiver against suit from the mortgagee if he applies monies in discharge of taxes (*Liverpool Corporation* v *Hope*, [1938] I KB 751).

Although not personally liable for VAT on supplies made by the company during his tenure, *Re John Willment* decided that a receiver is under an obligation to pay such VAT to the Customs & Excise when collected by him. In other words, the receiver cannot collect VAT and pay it over to the mortgagee in settlement of the mortgage debt because to do so would be to involve the company in a criminal liability, namely, the failure to pay VAT (see ss 37 and 38(8) which applies Customs and Excise Management Act 1979, ss 145—155 to VAT and Chapter 14).

Finally, where the receiver is appointed under a debenture imposing a fixed charge on specified assets of the company, he is not obliged under s 41(1)(*d*) to pay VAT which has become due within the 12 months before the date of his appointment. This is because monies received in such circumstances are not postponed to the payment of preferential debts under the Companies Act 1948, s 94 or 319, as the case may be.

WHERE THE RECEIVER IS AGENT FOR A PERSON OTHER THAN THE COMPANY

In such an event, it would appear that the provisions of Sched 2, para 6 and the VAT (General) Regulations 1977 (SI 1977 No 1759), reg 52 would apply. As a result, the receiver would be personally liable for VAT in respect of sales by him.

Schedule 2, paragraph 6 states that:

"Where in the case of a business carried on by a taxable person, goods forming part of the assets of the business are, under any power exercisable by another person, sold by the other in or towards satisfaction of a debt owed by the taxable person, they shall be deemed to be supplied by the taxable person in the course or furtherance of his business."

Regulation 52 states that:

"Where goods are deemed to be supplied by a taxable person by virtue of paragraph 6 of Schedule 2 to the Act, the person selling the goods, whether or not he is registered under the Act, shall within 21 days of the sale—

(*a*) furnish to the Controller a statement showing—

(i) his name and address and, if registered, his registration number,

(ii) the name, address and registration number of the person whose goods were sold,

(iii) the date of the sale,

(iv) the description and quantity of goods sold at each rate of tax, and

(v) the amount for which they were sold and the amount of tax charged at each rate;

(*b*) pay the amount of tax due; and

(*c*) send to the person whose goods were sold a copy of the statement referred to in (*a*) above,

and the person selling the goods and the person whose goods were sold shall exclude from any return which either or both may be required to furnish under these Regulations the tax chargeable on that supply of those goods."

A typical example of the operation of the above provisions would be the sale by a receiver of property on behalf of a bank "as mortgagee". In such a case, although the supply remains that of the company to which the receiver was appointed, a liability attaches on the receiver to account for VAT on that supply out of the sales proceeds.

Liquidations

The position of a liquidator of a company may be briefly stated. Supplies during a liquidation continue to be made by the company itself although it is controlled at that stage by its liquidator. As a result, the company remains liable for the tax and not the liquidator. This is the case, notwithstanding the VAT (General) Regulations 1977 (SI 1977 No 1759), reg 56 (see under *Generally, ante*).

15.600C Individuals: Trustees in bankruptcy

The position of a trustee in bankruptcy is to be distinguished from that of a receiver appointed in respect of a company. Section 23(3) empowers the Customs & Excise to make Regulations:

"... for persons who carry on a business of a taxable person who has died or become bankrupt or incapacitated to be treated for a limited time as taxable persons, and for securing continuity in the application of this Part of this Act in cases where persons are so treated."

Such Regulations are contained in the VAT (General) Regulations 1977 (SI 1977 No 1759), reg 7 which provides that:

(*a*) until some other person is registered in respect of taxable supplies made or intended to be made by the bankrupt, the Customs & Excise may treat the trustee in bankruptcy as a taxable person if he carries on the business of the bankrupt. In such case, the Act and all the Regulations and Orders made under it apply equally to the trustee; and

(*b*) the trustee shall within 21 days of commencing to carry on the business of the bankrupt, inform the Customs & Excise of that fact and such date of commencement.

The trustee is only treated as a taxable person if he elects to carry on the business of the bankrupt.

If he does not so elect, the business is treated as ceasing and all its assets are deemed to be supplied in the course or furtherance of the bankrupt's business before the cessation (Schedule 2, para 7).

Regulation 56 applies to a trustee in bankruptcy, however, and thus limits the trustee's liability for VAT to the extent of the assets over which he had control.

15.600D Priority of tax

Section 41 and the FA 1976, s 22 include as a preferential debt under the Bankruptcy Act 1914, s 33 on the bankruptcy of an individual, or the Companies Act 1948, s 94 or 319, on the appointment of a receiver or the winding up of a company, VAT which has become due within 12 months before "the relevant date".

"The relevant date" means:

(*a*) in relation to the Bankruptcy Act, s 33, the date of the receiving order or the individual's death as the case may be;

(*b*) in relation to the Companies Act, s 319, the date of the winding up order or of the appointment of a provisional liquidator where the company is compulsorily wound up and, in any other case, the date of the passing of the resolution for the winding up of the company (s 319(8)(*d*)); and

(*c*) in relation to the Companies Act, s 94, the date of the appointment of the receiver or when possession is taken by him of any property on behalf of the debenture holders.

The tax which has become due at the relevant date means tax which is unpaid at that time whether or not the time for its payment is before or after that date (FA 1976, s 22(*a*)). Similarly, tax need not have been assessed prior to the relevant date to be within s 41.

Where the relevant date does not fall on the first day of a prescribed accounting period, the 12 month period covered by s 41 will begin and end during a prescribed accounting period of the trader in question. Tax in respect of the first and last prescribed accounting periods covered by the 12 months must be apportioned, therefore, to determine the amount of tax that is to be included as a preferential debt under the section. The apportionment requires the percentage of the tax for each "split" period which is equal to the percentage that the part of that period that falls within the 12-month period bears to the total length of the split accounting period to be included as a preferential debt.

Two final points must be noted in relation to the priority of tax.

First, the Crown may set off a debt due from one of its departments to a taxpayer against a debt due from that taxpayer to another such department. Thus, a liquidator may find, as was the case in *Re Cushla Ltd* v *CCE*, [1979] STC 615 (*Casebook* **15.601**), that input tax repayable to the company from the Customs & Excise is not repaid but is set against another liability of the company to the Crown (in *Cushla*, a debt due to the Inland Revenue).

Secondly, s **41** does not apply to receivers appointed under fixed charges. Monies coming into such a receiver's hands from the sale or possession of property covered by the fixed charge are not subject to the payment of preferential debts. However, the principle established in *Re John Willment* (*Ashford*) *Ltd* v *CCE*, [1979] STC 286 (*Casebook* **15.602**), will apply to the VAT in respect of supplies affecting that property (see **15.600B**, WHERE THE RECEIVER IS AN AGENT FOR THE MORTGAGOR, *ante*).

Chapter 16

Special Types of Transaction

16.000 Second-hand or margin schemes

16.000A Sources

Section 14—Enabling provision relating to relief for certain second-hand goods.
VAT (Special Provisions) Order 1977 (SI 1977 No 1796)
  arts 4 and 5—Details of relief for certain second-hand goods.
VAT (Cars) Order 1980 (SI 1980 No 442)—Details of relief for second-hand cars.

The following Customs & Excise Notices and associated Leaflet contain the conditions relating to the operation of the second-hand schemes:

711—Second-hand cars.
712—Second-hand works of art, antiques and scientific collections.
713—Second-hand caravans and motor-cycles.
720—Second-hand boats and out-board motors.
721—Second-hand aircraft.
722—Second-hand electronic organs.
712/1/78—Goods sold at auction: premium payable by buyer.

16.000B General principles

The VAT (Special Provisions) Order 1977 (SI 1977 No 1796), art 5 provides that VAT shall be charged only on the excess of the sale proceeds over the acquisition price of certain items specified in art 4 of that Order. Thus, where art 5 applies, VAT is only payable on the supplier's margin and not on the full sale price of the item in question. This has led to the provisions of arts 4 and 5 being known as introducing a "margin scheme" for certain categories of goods. The goods specified in art 4 are:

(*a*) works of art, antiques and collector's pieces;
(*b*) used motor cycles;
(*c*) used caravans;
(*d*) used boats and outboard motors;
(*e*) used electric organs; and
(*f*) used aircraft.

Similar treatment is extended to used motor cars by the VAT (Cars) Order 1980 (SI 1980 No 442), art 6.

To qualify for such treatment, certain conditions must be fulfilled. These are:

(*a*) the acquisition of the item in question by the supplier seeking to qualify under the VAT (Special Provisions) Order 1977 (SI 1977 No 1796), art 5 must have been one of the following:

(i) a supply on which no tax was chargeable;

(ii) a supply on which tax was chargeable in accordance with arts 5 or 6;

(iii) a transaction which was treated under any Order as neither a supply of goods nor of services; or

(iv) in relation to works of art, antiques and collector's pieces only, an importation on which no tax was chargeable.

These conditions, (*a*)(i) to (iv), do not apply, however, to the sale of a second-hand motor car;

(*b*) the sale must not be a letting on hire;

(*c*) no tax invoice or similar document showing the VAT charged must be issued in respect of the sale; and

(*d*) the supplier must keep "such records and accounts as the Customs & Excise may specify in a notice published by them for the purposes of this Order or may recognise as sufficient for those purposes" VAT (Special Provisions) Order 1977 (SI 1977 No 1796), art 4(3)(*c*) and VAT (Cars) Order 1980 (SI 1980 No 442), art 6(2)(*d*)). In the case of cars, however, this requirement only applies to car dealers seeking to rely on article 6. A "car dealer" is defined as a person who carries on a business which consists of or includes the sale of motor cars.

16.000C Record requirements

All the Notices, detailed in **16.000A**, contain a similar requirement in relation to record keeping. This is in addition to the usual records required to be kept for VAT purposes (see **17.300**). The general requirement is that a stock book be kept containing the following information:

Part A

1. Stock number in numerical sequence.
2. Date of purchase.
3. Purchase invoice number.
4. Seller's name and address and VAT registration number, if any.

5. Registration number of vehicle.
6. Type and make.
7. Chassis number.
8. Engine number, if any.
9. Month and year of vehicle's first registration in the United Kingdom.
10. Name and address of last owner recorded in the vehicle registration document (if different from 4).
11. Last licensing authority,

Part B

12. Date of sale.
13. Sales invoice number.
14. Buyer's name and address.
15. Details of any change to particulars 7 and 8 in Part A.

Part C

16. Purchase price (inclusive of any tax but excluding the value of a surrendered vehicle excise licence).
17. Gross selling price (inclusive of tax), or method of disposal if not sold.
18. Margin on sale—item 17 less item 16.
19. Tax rate at the tax point for the sale.
20. Tax on the margin due to the Customs and Excise.

Note (*a*) 5 to 11 are peculiar to second-hand cars, caravans and motor-cycles. In all other cases, details of the unique number of the item, its type, class and make are required.
(*b*) 6 and 15 are not required for second-hand works of art etc.

It is for the taxpayer in all cases to show that he qualifies for the operation of one of the above margin schemes (*D A Pody* v *CCE*, LON/75/124 (*Casebook* **16.001**)), and the majority of cases under this heading have centred on the question as to whether the taxpayer's records meet the requirements of the Customs & Excise as set out in 1–20, *ante*. In a number of cases the issue has arisen as to whether a taxpayer who has failed to keep adequate records at the time of the transactions in question can reconstruct such records at a later date in order to comply with the requirements of the scheme. This issue has been considered by three Tribunal Centres, London in *J J Woodward* v *CCE*, LON/77/247 (*Casebook* **16.002**), Manchester in *M Callaghan* v *CCE*, MAN/77/187 (*Casebook* **16.003**), and Cardiff in *W E Mead* v *CCE*, CAR/77/344 (*Casebook* **16.110**). The leading case is possibly that of *W E Mead* v *CCE* where the Tribunal noted that the Customs & Excise was given a discretion to accept records such as it recognises to be sufficient for the purposes of the scheme. It was held, therefore, that provided that the information available could establish the margin between the cost and proceeds of sale of the items in question, it was adequate for the purposes of applying the scheme. Of the two other cases mentioned above, the Tribunal in *M Callaghan* v *CCE* also found reconstructed records sufficient.

In *J J Woodward* v *CCE* such records were held incapable of replacing contemporaneous records which were required by the rules of the scheme. The authority of these cases is now of some doubt, however, following the case of *J H Corbitt* (*Numismatists*) *Ltd* v *CCE*, [1980] STC 231 (*Casebook* **11.101**). In the *Corbitt* case, the question of whether the taxpayer's records satisfied the conditions specified by the Customs & Excise was not in dispute as they clearly did not. This is also likely to be the position where a taxpayer attempts to reconstruct accounts after the event as the implication from the relevant Customs & Excise Notices is that accounts should be kept at the same time as sales are made. The House of Lords decided in the *Corbitt* case that the Tribunal does not have the power to review the exercise by the Customs & Excise of its discretion as to whether records not satisfying the specified conditions are nevertheless sufficient for the purposes of the schemes. Thus, if the Customs & Excise take a reasonable view that reconstructed records are not sufficient, it would seem that a taxpayer cannot challenge such a decision.

16.000D Gross purchase cost and sales price

Two cases illustrate that when operating a margin scheme, the taxpayer should simply take the cost charged to him for the item without any addition for subsequent improvements (*Wyvern Shipping Co Ltd* v *CCE*, [1979] STC 91 (*Casebook* **16.009**)) and the gross sales price received for that item without any deduction for expenses (*C G Todd* v *CCE*, LEE/74/31 (*Casebook* **16.005**)). This accords with the general principle that VAT is chargeable by reference to turnover and not profit figures.

This point requires further clarification in relation to auction sales, however. At auction sales, the auctioneer often charges a premium to both the seller and the buyer of the item sold. Such premiums are deducted by the auctioneer out of the sale proceeds after, in the case of the buyer's premium, having added that premium to the price. In *Jocelyn Fielding Fine Arts Ltd* v *CCE*, LON/78/81 (*Casebook* **3.509**), a case which led the Customs & Excise to alter its former practice in this area (see VAT Leaflet 712/1/78 (Goods sold at auction: premium payable by buyer)), it was held that the buyer's premium was not a real addition to the sale proceeds as the seller was not entitled to retain that additional amount. Consequently, for the purposes of the margin scheme, the seller should account for VAT only on the difference between the cost of the article and its sales price less the premium paid to the auctioneer by the buyer.

16.100 Special schemes for retailers

16.100A Sources

Section 30(3)—Enabling provision for the special schemes for retailers of goods and services.
VAT (Supplies by Retailers) Regulations 1972 (SI 1972 No 1148)—Basic provisions regarding
the special schemes for retailers and caterers.

The following Customs & Excise Notices and associated Leaflets contain the conditions
relating to the operation of the special schemes for retailers and caterers:

727—Special schemes for retailers.
727 A–J—Retailers: special scheme A–J.
5/75/VMC—New arrangements for retail pharmacists from 1 April 1975.
727/1/80—Accounting for VAT on Teleflorist transactions.
727/2/80—Accounting for VAT on Interflora transactions.
727/3/80—Retail schemes C and D: tolerance in turnover limits.

16.100B Generally

If no special provision were made, retailers would be obliged to keep
a record for VAT purposes of each item sold by them. This would present
considerable difficulties given the number of small sales made by retailers
and the fact that a retailer is not required to issue tax invoices to non-
taxable persons or even taxable persons except, in the latter case, where
one is specifically requested. To overcome these difficulties, the Customs & Excise is given power by s 30(3) to make special provision
through Regulations for:

"... taxable supplies by retailers of any goods or of any description of goods or of services
or any description of services as may be determined by or under the regulations and,
in particular,—

(*a*) for permitting the value which is to be taken as the value of the supplies in any
prescribed accounting period or part thereof to be determined, subject to any limitations or restrictions, by such method or one of such methods as may have been described in any notice published by the Commissioners in pursuance of the regulations
and not withdrawn by a further notice or as may be agreed with the Commissioners;
and
(*b*) for determining the proportion of the value of the supplies which is to be attributed
to any description of supplies; and
(*c*) for adjusting that value and proportion for periods comprising two or more prescribed accounting periods or parts thereof."

Regulations have been introduced for retailers generally and for
caterers supplying food both on and off premises (for a discussion of
the Regulations as they affect caterers see **16.100E**). These Regulations
are the VAT (Supplies by Retailers) Regulations 1972 (SI 1972 No
1148) as amended.

The word "retailers" is not defined in the Act or the Regulations
but is interpreted by the Customs & Excise to mean "anyone (not necessarily a shop-keeper) whose business consists mainly of supplying

goods or services direct to the public, without tax invoices" (Notice No 727, para 3). Thus a retailer is a person whose customers are mainly non-taxable persons.

The above Regulations for retailers only affect the calculation of the majority of a retailer's outputs. His inputs and certain more unusual supplies by him have to be accounted for in the usual way. Furthermore, special schemes for retailers provide only a means of estimating outputs. Such schemes cannot be entirely accurate and a retailer may find that he pays more tax through operating a scheme than he would if he accounted for VAT in full in the normal manner. A retailer in this position must weigh the advantage of the reduced cost of not maintaining a full record of all his transactions against such higher tax cost.

16.100C Methods available

The Regulations permit a retailer to calculate the value of his non zero-rated supplies in any prescribed accounting period either:

(*a*) by using a method described in any Notice published by the Customs & Excise; or
(*b*) by using any other method agreed with the Customs & Excise.

In relation to (*a*), the Customs & Excise have published Notice No 727 (Special Schemes for Retailers) (which was revised in October 1977) setting out the general rules for nine schemes (Schemes A–J) that may be used. Supplements 727A–727J to Notice No 727 describe the detailed rules in relation to each of these schemes. These schemes are almost universally used; method (*b*) above is extremely rare.

Refusal

Regulation 3 allows the Customs & Excise to refuse to permit a retailer to make use of a special scheme, apparently for any reason. Regulation 3 mentions specifically, however, the case where the retailer could reasonably be expected to account for tax in the normal way as one where such a refusal would be appropriate.

Notification and change of scheme

A retailer using a scheme must notify the Customs & Excise of the scheme used on each VAT return (reg 5). A special box is provided on Form VAT 100 for this purpose.

Regulation 4 provides that, save as the Customs & Excise may allow, only one scheme may be operated at a time. The Customs & Excise do allow more than one scheme to be used where a business is divided into separate, identifiable, parts. For example, certain schemes may be run in parallel to cover different departments or different shops. A special scheme and the normal method of accounting for VAT may similarly be run in parallel in these circumstances. If more than one scheme is used, separate accounts and stock records must usually be kept for each part of the business. Notice No 727, para 25 gives further details as to the combination of schemes that are possible and the modified rules which apply where more than one scheme is used.

Changes from one scheme to another are not allowed within 1 year of the adoption of a scheme and can only be made at an anniversary of the adoption of the original scheme without the consent of the Customs & Excise (reg 6; see *P and M Summerfield* v *CCE*, BIR/74/24 (*Casebook* **16.109**), where a change after 6 months was permitted).

A number of cases have come before the Tribunal where retailers have attempted to adopt a retrospective change of scheme having discovered that they were paying more tax than would have otherwise been payable under another scheme. Although a retrospective change is not impossible *per se* (*E W A Charles* v *CCE*, LON/77/388 (*Casebook* **16.107**)), special circumstances are required before such change can be made. In the *Charles* case, the retailer's mistake as to the most beneficial scheme to use was found not to constitute a special circumstance.

If a retailer intends to cease to make use of any special scheme, he must inform the Customs & Excise accordingly. In such case, the retailer may be required to pay tax on such proportion of his supplies in the final period of use of the scheme as the Customs & Excise consider fair and reasonable (reg 7).

Change in tax rate

The Customs & Excise may also prescribe rules adjusting the treatment of transactions under the special schemes where there is a change in the tax rate (reg 9). Such rules are contained in the supplements to Notice No 727.

16.100D The nine special schemes

These schemes are set out in Notice No 727 and its supplementary Notices. All such Notices have binding effect.

The operation of all nine schemes falls into two parts. First, it is necessary to calculate the gross takings of the retailer. This may be done using either a standard or an optional method. Secondly, the resultant gross takings figure must be applied through one of the nine schemes to give a total amount of VAT payable on such takings.

Gross takings

The standard method of calculating gross takings operates on a pure cash basis. It may not be suitable, therefore, where the retailer makes sales on credit or has account customers. The standard method does have the advantage, however, of giving automatic credit for bad debts as supplies for which no consideration is received will not be shown in the amount of total cash takings.

The optional method adds to the total cash receipts, the value of supplies on credit to achieve the final figure for gross takings. A retailer is required to notify the Customs & Excise if he wishes to use the optional method.

The calculations required under the standard and optional methods are more fully detailed in Notice No 727, paras 15 and 16.

In operating either method certain additional kinds of transaction must be excluded. These are discussed in Notice No 727, Pt VII, paras 32–59. Further, a daily record of gross takings covering all types of transaction must be kept. These aspects of the special schemes are summarised in Customs & Excise Notice No 727, Pt VII, paras 32–59 to which reference must be made in each case.

Choice between the schemes

Having made the basic decision to operate a scheme, the retailer must then choose which scheme most closely meets the requirements of his particular business. In certain respects, this choice of schemes may be narrowed as certain schemes suit only particular types of business operation. For example, scheme A cannot be used where the retailer makes supplies to which more than one rate of tax applies and scheme C is not available where annual turnover is more than £50,000. Further, only schemes A, F and in certain circumstances B, can be used where supplies include services. Schemes C, D and G cannot be used in relation to goods manufactured or grown by the retailer in question.

The following guidance as to the scheme to adopt has been given by the Customs & Excise (Notice No 727, para 22):

Are all the goods or services that you supply subject to the same rate of tax? If so (and if you cannot calculate tax in the normal VAT way). Scheme A is the scheme you should use. None of the other schemes will work for you.

Are you selling goods at two rates of tax, and services (if any) at the higher of the two rates, with the lower of your two rates applying to not more than 50% of your total takings for both rates? Scheme B is probably the best scheme for you. But only you know your own business, so look also at the other schemes, especially Scheme C and Scheme D. If you are able to use one of those, it may suit you better.

Do you sell goods, or goods and services at more than one rate of tax which you can distinguish at the point of sale?

Scheme F is specially designed for you, and it covers services as well as goods.

Whether or not you find that you can use Scheme B or Scheme F, if you sell goods at more than one rate of tax you should have a look at the other schemes and consider these questions too:—

Is your taxable turnover £50,000* a year or less?

* (See VAT Leaflet 727/3/80)

Scheme C is a simple scheme for small businesses of this kind. You never have to do any stocktaking for VAT purposes, and there is very little extra calculation to do when your goods are affected by changes in the rates or scope of VAT.

Is your taxable turnover £125,000* a year or less?

* (See VAT Leaflet 727/3/80)

If your business is too big for Scheme C, then Scheme D might suit you very well. Initial stocks do not have to be included in the calculations and there is no stocktaking to do at times of tax changes. If you can deal easily with stocktaking then you should also consider Schemes E, H and J.

Is your taxable turnover greater than £125,000 a year?

Schemes E, H and J are available for businesses of all sizes, but they are likely to be more suitable for the larger businesses which have the accounting resources to deal with them.

Scheme G may suit you as your business is too big for Scheme D.

Are you selling goods or services at more than one rate of tax in a business with separate departments having separate accounts and stock records?

If so you should consider whether it would be advantageous to use one of the permitted mixtures of schemes.

Are you selling goods at more than one rate of tax and able to separate your gross takings, e.g., by calculating notional figures for goods at different tax rates?

If so, you can use Scheme F; or Scheme A for your supplies at one rate, plus any other scheme you are eligible to use for your other supplies.

Retail florists should also refer to VAT Leaflets 727/1/80 (Accounting for VAT on Teleflorist transactions) and 727/2/80 (Accounting for VAT on Interflora transactions).

The schemes in detail

Once again, it is useful to refer to Notice No 727 for a summary of the basic details of the nine schemes. Full details are contained in the individual scheme supplements to Notice No 727. As explained in **16.100C**, certain of the schemes may, in certain circumstances be run in parallel. Notice No 727, para 24 provides:

"Scheme A. This is a scheme for calculating output tax on supplies of goods or services (or both) which are all subject to the same rate of tax. For this scheme you will only need to keep a record of your daily gross takings for those supplies, as well as the record of inputs and the VAT account which are explained in Notice No. 700.

Scheme B. This is a scheme for calculating output tax on supplies of goods at two, and not more than two, different rates of tax (zero counting as a rate of tax) and of services (if any) at the higher of those two rates. It is a condition of the scheme that your takings for the goods you sell *at the lower of your two rates* (e.g., zero, if one of your rates is the zero rate) must not amount to more than half (50%) of your total takings for goods at both rates and services (if any) at the higher of the two rates. You must be able to record the total VAT-inclusive amounts you expect to realise from selling those goods *subject to the lower of your two rates* which you receive into your business for retailing in each tax period. You then subtract those amounts from your gross takings for all the goods and services you supply under the scheme, and the remainder will be assumed to be the value of your supplies of goods and services (if any) at the other rate.

Scheme C. This scheme is intended for the small retailer of goods, whose total taxable turnover in a year does not exceed £50,000,* and who sells goods at more than one rate of tax (zero counting as a rate of tax). It is limited to businesses whose trade classification, shown on their certificate of registration (Form VAT 4), is from 8201 to 8239. If you use this scheme, you must keep a record of the VAT-inclusive prices which you have to pay to your suppliers for the goods you buy for re-sale. A separate column is needed for each of the tax rates you deal in. At the end of the tax period, you have to total the columns and add a fixed mark-up to the total of each positive rate column. Output tax is then calculated by applying the correct VAT fraction to each result. The fixed mark-up you will have to use will depend upon your kind of business, e.g., whether you are a grocer, a florist, etc. The details are in Supplement 727C (Revised October 1977). You must also keep a record of your gross takings to complete your VAT return.

Scheme D. This is a scheme for calculating output tax on supplies of goods at more than one rate of tax (zero counting as a rate of tax). It is for retailers whose total taxable turnover does not exceed £125,000* in a year. This scheme splits your gross takings for the tax period in proportion to the total amounts payable by you to your suppliers for goods received in your shop for retailing at each tax rate during the period. You apply the correct VAT fractions to the results to arrive at your scheme output tax. Stocks are not included in the calculation, and each tax period is dealt with separately. But to correct for differences in buying and selling patterns over the year, you must carry out, every year, an annual adjustment of your calculations.

A retailer using this scheme whose business mark-ups are, on average, higher for the zero-rated goods he sells than those he uses for positive-rated goods may find that he will pay more output tax than if he were using one of the schemes that use retail selling prices to calculate output tax. So, if you are in that position and you are considering Scheme D you will have to decide whether the the saving in paperwork is worth that possible disadvantage. You may find that the arrangement described in paragraph 26 will enable you to choose Scheme F, or Scheme A plus one of the schemes that you are eligible to use.

Scheme E. This scheme is for calculating output on supplies of goods at more than one rate of tax (zero counting as a rate of tax). You must record the total VAT-inclusive retail selling prices of all the goods you receive in the tax period for retailing, to arrive at a separate total for each positive tax rate. Initial stocks must be included as goods received for retailing in the first period in which you use the scheme. You must apply the correct VAT fractions to your totals to give the scheme output tax at each positive rate. You must also keep a record of your gross takings in order to complete your VAT return.

---

* See VAT Leaflet 727/3/80: Retail schemes C and D—tolerance in turnover limits.

Scheme F. This is for retailers who supply goods or services (or both) at more than one rate of tax (zero counting as a rate of tax) and who can distinguish between the rates at the point of sale. You must add up, each tax period, your gross takings for supplies at each different tax rate in the tax period, and apply the correct VAT fractions to the results to give your scheme output tax at each positive rate (see also paragraph 26 about calculating notional gross takings for supplies at different rates of tax).

Scheme G. This scheme is for calculating output on supplies of goods at more than one rate of tax (zero counting as a rate of tax). It is for retailers whose taxable turnover exceeds £125,000 in a year. For each of the first three tax periods you use the scheme you split your gross takings in proportion to the total VAT-inclusive amounts, payable by you to your suppliers for the goods at each rate of tax which you had in stock when you began to use the scheme and which you have received since for retailing. (If you are changing to Scheme G you can use in place of stock the goods you received for retailing in the three months immediately before the change.) This gives your assumed takings, including VAT, for goods supplied at each tax rate. You must then apply the correct VAT fractions to those takings to arrive at your provisional output tax.

Next, to allow for the effect of ignoring your different profit margins on different lines of goods, you must increase the provisional output tax by:

one-eighth, unless you qualify for the one-twelfth addition;
or
one-twelfth, if you are concerned *only* with *two positive* rates of tax, or two positive rates of tax and the zero rate where your supplies of zero-rated goods are insignificant, i.e. the cost to you of the zero-rated goods is not more than 2% of the cost of all the goods covered by Scheme G.

The increased amount is the output tax actually due under the scheme.

For every tax period after the first three, you must split your gross takings for the period in proportion to the total VAT-inclusive amounts payable by you to your suppliers for goods at each rate received in the twelve months up to the end of that tax period. Initial stock is no longer taken into account. Output tax is again calculated by applying the VAT fraction for each positive rate and adding one-eighth, or one-twelfth, as the case may be.

The addition of one-eighth or one-twelfth to the provisional output tax may sometimes mean that a retailer using this scheme will pay more output tax than if he were using one of the other schemes. This can happen, for example, if the mark-ups used in the business for standard-rated goods are lower than, or do not differ from, those used for zero-rated goods. So if you are considering Scheme G you will have to decide whether the saving in paperwork is worth that possible disadvantage to you. You may find that the arrangements described in paragraph 26 will enable you to choose Scheme F, or Scheme A plus one of the other schemes which you are eligible to use.

Scheme H. This scheme is for calculating output tax on supplies of goods at more than one rate of tax (zero counting as a rate of tax). For each of the first three tax periods you use the scheme you split your gross takings in proportion to the total VAT-inclusive amounts payable by your customers for the goods at each rate of tax which you had in stock when you began to use the scheme and which you have received since for retailing. (If you are changing to Scheme H you can use in place of stock the goods you received for retailing in the three months immediately before the change.) These calculations must take account of the different selling prices of the goods you supply. They give your assumed takings, including VAT, for goods at each rate. You must then apply the correct VAT fractions to arrive at your scheme output tax. For every tax period after the first three, you must split your gross takings for the period in proportion to the total VAT-inclusive amounts payable by your customers for goods at each rate which you received in the twelve months up to the end of that tax period. Initial stock is no longer taken into account. Output tax is again calculated by applying the VAT fraction for each positive rate.

Scheme J. This scheme is also for calculating output tax on supplies of goods at more than one rate of tax (zero counting as a rate of tax). You split your gross takings for each tax period in proportion to the total VAT-inclusive amounts payable by your customers for the goods at each rate of tax which you had in stock at the beginning of your VAT year and which you have received since for retailing. These calculation must take account of the different selling prices of the goods you supply. They will give your assumed takings, including VAT, for goods at each rate. You must then apply the correct VAT fractions to reach your provisional scheme output tax. At the end of your VAT year, you must record the total amounts payable by your customers for all goods remaining in stock, and calculate your output tax for the year by reference to initial and closing stock, receipts of goods and gross takings for the whole year. If the result of that calculation is more that you have already paid in the year you must pay the difference to Customs and Excise; if it is less, you can reclaim the difference from Customs and Excise.

16.100E Caterers

A retailer who supplies food for consumption both on and off premises will make a proportion of zero rated supplies. The VAT (Supplies by Retailers) Regulations 1972 (SI 1972 No 1148), reg 10 requires such retailer to either:

(a) keep such records as will enable all zero-rated supplies to be identified to the satisfaction of the Customs & Excise; or
(b) if he can show to the Customs & Excise that it is impracticable to keep such records, estimate the proportion of his taxable supplies that is attributable to zero-rated supplies.

If (b) is adopted, and the business changes significantly or the caterer otherwise has evidence that the estimate is no longer accurate, he must inform the Customs & Excise. Tax will then be accounted for in accordance with the caterer's revised estimate from a date notified to him by the Customs & Excise. The Customs & Excise may impose their own estimate where they disagree with a further estimate made by a caterer on a change of circumstances.

In operating either of the above arrangements, the caterer must include the following in his gross takings:

(a) all cash, including VAT, received in the provision of food to customers and staff;
(b) the tax inclusive cost of food applied for personal use;
(c) amounts charged on supplies against the use of credit cards, vouchers, coupons and trading checks.

The cost of free meals to staff should not be included.

16.200 Leasing

16.200A Sources

Schedule 2, para 1—The letting of goods is treated as a supply of services.
Schedule 4, Groups 9 and 10—Possible zero rating of supplies of goods on hire.
VAT (General) Regulations 1977 (SI 1977 No 1759),
    reg 18—Time of supply of the continuous supplies of services.
    reg 38—Temporary importation of goods on hire.

In addition the following Customs & Excise Notice may be helpful:

702, para 23(*b*)—Temporary importation of goods on hire.

16.200B Generally

The letting of goods on hire is a supply of services (Sched 2, para 1
(1)(*b*)). This has two practical consequences. First, the place of the
supply will be determined not by reference to where the goods are situated, but the country in which the supplier, that is the lessor, belongs.
Secondly, VAT will be payable only when rental payments are received
or a tax invoice for such payments issued (VAT (General) Regulations
1977 (SI 1977 No 1759), reg 18).

The majority of lease transactions will be straightforward and few VAT
problems will arise. The more complex financial leasing transactions do,
however, require further comment.

16.200C Financial leasing

It is common, where a trader wishes to use an item of expensive
equipment such as a computer, or plant, for example a ship or lorry,
for that equipment to be purchased by another party ("the financier")
and then let on hire to the trader. The financier does this in part to benefit
from first year allowances in respect of such equipment which allowances he may set against his profits for the purposes of corporation tax.
If the equipment is particularly expensive, more than one financier may
be involved. This type of arrangement is referred to in this subchapter
as a "financial lease".

In a financial lease, the lessee may be given the right to renew the
lease or be appointed the lessor's agent to sell the equipment at the
end of the initial rental term. Further, where there is a sale of the
equipment, it is not unusual for a substantial part of the proceeds to
go to the lessee by way of sales commission or rebate of rentals. The
VAT treatment of this and financial leases generally is discussed in the
following paragraphs.

Initial purchase of the equipment

Where the intended lessee has already entered into a contract to purchase the equipment, such contract will require novation in order for the equipment to be purchased by the financier. As discussed in **3.100**, a novation is thought to have the effect for VAT purposes of cancelling out the initial supply to the trader and replacing it with a supply to the financier. This will not affect the supplier in substance but will shift the potential ability to reclaim VAT on that supply as input tax from the trader to the financier. The supplier will accordingly be required to issue a new invoice to the financier and a credit note to the trader cancelling out the original invoice issued to him.

Where the leasing arrangement provides for the continuing purchase of equipment to become subject to the lease, it is common for the lessee to be appointed the agent of the financier for the purchase of that equipment. The normal agency rules as to invoicing will apply in such circumstances (see **15.000**).

Multiple financiers

Where there is more than one financier involved in the letting of equipment to the trader, it has to be considered whether those financiers are to be treated for VAT purposes as:

(*a*) a partnership;
(*b*) a joint venture (although there is doubt as to whether a joint venture can be regarded in law as some form of relationship which falls short of a partnership, the Customs & Excise appears to recognise that a joint venture between financiers may exist); or
(*c*) individually.

Where a joint venture does exist, the Customs & Excise permits the "lead" joint venturer to account for VAT as though it were the sole owner/financier of the equipment in question. Settlements between the lead and the other joint venturers will then be disregarded. The Customs & Excise also ignores sales of interests in a joint venture by joint venturers other than by the lead joint venturer. If the lead joint venturer drops out, however, the equipment is regarded as supplied by him to the new lead joint venturer on his departure from the joint venture.

If a partnership is involved, it should register separately and will be treated as would a normal partnership for VAT purposes (see **15.400**).

Foreign element

UNITED KINGDOM LESSOR

Following the changes in the income and corporation tax rules as to capital allowances in respect of leased plant and machinery introduced by FA 1980, Part III, Chapter II, it is now less likely for a UK financier to lease equipment (other than ships or aircraft on time charter) to a non-UK resident lessee. However, a letting of goods on hire for use outside the United Kingdom throughout the term of the lease will be zero-rated under Sched 4, Group 9, item 2 if the goods are either:

(*a*) exported by the lessor from the United Kingdom; or
(*b*) not in the United Kingdom at the time of the supply (which will be the earlier of the time a tax invoice is issued or a rental payment is made).

The above position is unlikely to be affected in practice by the proposed EEC Tenth Directive. This Directive (see **18.200**) will shift the place of supply of goods (other than transport) on hire from the place the lessor belongs to the place where the goods are made available to the lessee. If the goods are made available to the lessee in the United Kingdom, they will not be used outside the United Kingdom throughout the term of the lease and would not, therefore, satisfy the present conditions of Group 9, item 1 above. On the other hand, if the goods are made available outside the United Kingdom, they are likely to satisfy those conditions with the effect that under the law as it exists at present the supply would be zero-rated. This position will remain under the EEC Tenth Directive, which proposes that such a supply would not be subject to VAT in the United Kingdom.

NON-UK LESSOR

Although a lease generally falls to be treated as a supply of services (which supply will not be subject to VAT where the lessor belongs outside the United Kingdom as the supply, under present rules, will be outside the United Kingdom (but see the proposed EEC Tenth Directive; UNITED KINGDOM LESSOR, *ante* and **18.200**)), where goods are leased to a UK lessee a charge to VAT will nevertheless, be imposed on the importation of those goods into the United Kingdom (s 1(1) and see generally Chapter 6).

The VAT (General) Regulations 1977 (SI 1977 No 1759), reg 38 restricts the value of the importation and thereby the VAT chargeable on such importation, however, in certain circumstances. Regulation 38 provides:

"**38**. Where goods are imported, and
(*a*) the Commissioners are satisfied that the goods are on hire or loan to the importer from an overseas supplier; and
(*b*) the proper officer is satisfied that the goods are to be re-exported; and
(*c*) such conditions as the Commissioners may impose are complied with,
the Commissioners may remit such amount of tax as represents the difference between the tax ordinarily payable on importation and such tax as would have been payable had the charge made for the hire or loan been the value of the goods, and may further remit any amount of value added tax that is shown to their satisfaction to have been charged in another member state of the Community in respect of the hiring or loan and not to be eligible for refund in that state: provided that if in their opinion such charge is less than would normally be made or if no charge is made, the Commissioners may assess that value having regard to charges made for the hiring of similar goods for a similar period in the United Kingdom."

Where reg 38 applies, VAT will only be charged on the amount of the hire charge, that is, the aggregate of all rental payments under the lease. Credit may also be claimed for any VAT paid in another EEC Member State in respect of the lease in question. Such credits will be rare, however, as VAT should only be charged in the State in which the goods are used (see the EEC Sixth Directive, art 9(2)(*d*)).

The only condition that the Customs & Excise would appear to have published to date in connection with reg 38 is that where the importer is an "exempt person" (a term, it is assumed, to mean a non-taxable person), he must initially pay VAT on the full value of the goods at the time of their importation (Notice No 702 para 23(*b*)). Such VAT as exceeds the VAT charged under reg 38 may then be repaid to the importer when the goods are subsequently exported. A lessee should make a repayment claim in such circumstances.

16.200D Particular types of goods

In all cases where goods are supplied on hire, consideration should be given as to whether the actual item leased is of a type which would qualify for zero rating. The following may be relevant in this respect:

Sched 4, Group 9, item 2

This item applies to equipment supplied for use outside the United Kingdom. This is discussed in **16.200C**, *Foreign element*.

Sched 4, Group 10, items 1, 2 or 3

These items relate to the supply of the following ships and aircraft:

(*a*) any ship which is neither:
   (i) a ship of a gross tonnage of less than 15 tons; nor
   (ii) a ship designed or adapted for use for recreation or pleasure;

(*b*) any aircraft which is neither:

(i) an aircraft of a weight of less than 8000 kilogrammes; nor

(ii) an aircraft designed or adapted for use for recreation or pleasure.

(*c*) any lifeboat when supplied to the Royal National Lifeboat Institution.

For a general discussion on the above items in Group 10, see **8.1000**.

16.200E Rebate of rentals and Sales commission

Rebate of rentals

Although styled as a rebate of rentals, such a payment by the lessor/ financier at the end of the term of a lease is a means of allowing the lessee to share in the sale proceeds of the equipment. The financier offering such a rebate will have calculated his return under the lease on the basis that the equipment will have a negligible value at the end of lease term.

If the lessee sells the equipment on behalf of the financier and retains out of the proceeds an amount "by way of rebate of rentals", two transactions will be involved. First, the sale of the equipment for the gross proceeds and secondly, a supply of sales services by the lessee to the financier for, arguably, the amount of the rebate. Where the lessee is a taxable person, VAT will be chargeable therefore on the amount of the rebate. In the absence of any express provision requiring the financier to pay VAT in addition to allowing a rebate of rentals, the rebate should be treated as a VAT inclusive amount, therefore, and three twenty-thirds (3/23rds) of the rebate accounted for to the Customs & Excise as VAT. The lessee should issue a tax invoice to the financier accordingly.

If the lessee does not sell the equipment on behalf of the financier but merely returns the equipment to the financier and receives a rebate of rentals or the rebate is apportioned and only a part is attributed to the sales activities, it would seem arguable that the rebate, or the part not apportioned to the sales activities, as the case may be, should not be subject to VAT. This is because in such circumstances the rebate is merely a payment to the lessee for which no reciprocal consideration is given by the lessee in the form of a supply.

It is understood that, in practice, many financiers issue credit notes to lessees for VAT on an amount equal to any rebate of rentals made to those lessees. An attempt is, thus, made to rewrite the consideration for the earlier hire of the equipment. Although this is consistent with the argument that the rebate is a true return of earlier rental payments, the Authors doubt whether this is in fact correct. Certainly, the Customs & Excise has recently begun to examine the treatment of the rebate of rentals in more detail and are known to disagree with the issue of such credit notes.

Sales commission

Where the lessee acts as the financier's selling agent for the equipment at the end of the term of the lease, the VAT treatment of any sales commission received by the lessee is more clearly defined. In such circumstances, there is a supply of the equipment by the financier for the full proceeds of sale and a supply of services by the lessee to the financier for an amount equal to the sales commission. Where the lessee is a taxable person, the commission will be a VAT inclusive amount (unless otherwise provided). The lessee should issue a tax invoice accordingly.

16.300 Hire purchase, conditional sale and credit sale agreements

16.300A Sources

Section 7—Time of supply.
Schedule 2, para 1(2)—Supply of goods under a contract where the property in the goods passes at a future time to be a supply of goods.
Schedule 5, Group 5, item 2—Supplies of credit.
VAT (Special Provisions) Order 1977 (SI 1977 No 1796)
arts 10 and 11—Treatment of sales of certain repossessed goods.
VAT (Cars) Order 1980 (SI 1980 No 442)
art 7—Treatment of sales of certain repossessed goods

In addition the following Customs & Excise Leaflet may be helpful:

700/5/79—Sale of repossessed and surrendered goods by finance companies, insurers and mortgagees.

16.300B Definitions and nature of the supply

Hire purchase agreements

Under such agreements, the hirer takes possession of the goods and is given an option to purchase, usually for a nominal sum, the hired goods at the end of the hire period. As such the supply is one of goods

(Sched 2, para 1(2)(*b*)). In addition to the supplier and the hirer (that is the recipient of the supply) a third party finance company may also be involved in the transaction. In such case, the supplier sells the goods to the finance company which then supplies the goods on hire purchase to the hirer.

Conditional sale agreements

Under such agreements, the possession of the goods passes to the purchaser but title to the goods only passes on the occurrence of some future event, usually under the full payment of the price. Again, this is a supply of goods (Sched 2, para 1(2)(*b*)).

Credit sale agreements

Such agreements involve a supply of goods, the title to and possession of the goods passing on execution of the contract but the price being left outstanding for a period. This is also a supply of goods.

16.300C Time of supply

Under all the above agreements, the general rules as to the time of the supply of the goods remains unchanged. Thus, the goods will be treated as supplied and VAT in respect of the full price (see **16.300D**), will be payable on the earliest of:

(*a*) the removal of the goods;
(*b*) the making available of the goods to the recipient;
(*c*) the issue of a tax invoice; or
(*d*) the payment of the price,

(s 7(2) and (4)), but in relation to (*c*) and (*d*) only to the extent invoiced or paid respectively (see generally **3.300**).

   The credit element of the consideration for the supply (see **16.300D**) will be treated as supplied whenever a payment for that credit is received. The Customs & Excise has indicated, however (VAT News No 13), that where a supplier finds such treatment difficult to operate, he may apply to the Customs & Excise for the time of supply of the credit and the goods to be aligned.

   It will be appreciated that under these rules VAT in respect of the entire transaction may become due to the Customs & Excise before the supplier has recovered such VAT from the purchaser of the goods. To overcome this problem, some suppliers require the initial instalment of the price to be increased to cover the amount of the VAT due in respect of the sale.

16.300D Tax value

All of the agreements under discussion involve an element of credit being extended to the recipient of the supply. If a separate charge is made for such credit and is disclosed to the recipient of the supply, that charge will be exempt under Sched 5, Group 5, item 2(*b*). Such disclosure should ideally be made in the agreement itself.

Fees on the exercise of an option to purchase under a Hire Purchase Agreement, documentation fees and administrative charges in connection with actually transferring title to the goods to the purchaser under all agreements considered under this heading are also exempt if of less than £10 in aggregate and are specified in the agreement (Sched 5, Group 5, item 2(*c*)). If over £10 such fees will be standard rated, unless the supply is made to a person who belongs outside the EEC when they will be zero-rated under Sched 4, Group 9, item 6.

The amount on which any VAT will be chargeable (and whether VAT is chargeable depends, of course, upon the nature of the goods and whether or not they are supplied for export) will be, therefore, either the aggregate of all payments to be made under the relevant agreement or, where either Group 5, item 2(*b*) or (*c*) applies, that aggregate amount less the value of such exempt supplies.

16.300E Repossessions

Two issues arise on the repossession of an article. First, the treatment of the original transaction and secondly, the treatment of any sales of the articles by the repossessing party.

The original transaction

In fixing the total price for the goods to be sold or hired the supplier will calculate the principal and interest elements in each instalment paid by the hirer or purchaser. For example, in a hire purchase contract with a one year term the "rule of 78" is often applied. This may be illustrated as follows:

"Where the basic price for the goods is £1,000 and the interest charged is £200, the VAT charge will be £150, giving a total price of £1,350. Following the rule of 78, where there are twelve instalments the first instalment will comprise a repayment of 12/78ths of the amount of the interest charged, the second 11/78ths, the third 10/78ths and so on."

In the case of a repossession of the goods, a part of the original transaction is effectively cancelled. The VAT already accounted for by the owner to the Customs & Excise on that part is consequently repaid to it and a credit note for that VAT is issued by the owner to the hirer. To continue the above example:

"If default takes place following the payment of the third instalment, 33/78ths of the interest charged will have been repaid, in the present example £84.61 of the £200 interest charged. Therefore, of the £337.50 paid in the first three instalments, £84.61 comprised interest and the balance of £252.89 capital. This balance represents 21.99 per cent of the payments (excluding interest) due and therefore 78.01 per cent of the VAT charged should be refunded. A repayment of £117.01 VAT will be made by the Commissioners."

The same principles as illustrated above apply, of course, where the hire term is longer than 1 year and in practice, the Customs & Excise is prepared to follow whatever method the owner uses in computing the interest elements of each repayment to determine the amount of VAT available for credit.

Subsequent sales

By virtue of VAT (Special Provisions) Order 1977 (SI 1977 No 1796), arts 10 and 11 and the VAT (Cars) Order 1980 (SI 1980 No 442), art 7, the sale of certain repossessed articles will be treated as neither a supply of goods nor services. The articles in question and the conditions for the relief are detailed at **3.100,** pp 28–29.

16.400 Commodities

16.400A Sources

Section 26—Enabling provision in relation to Orders concerning terminal markets.
Schedule 4, Groups 1 and 9, items 5, 6 and 11—Possible zero-rating of certain supplies connected with commodities.
VAT (Terminal Markets) Order 1973 (SI 1973 No 173)—Transactions affecting commodities entitled to be zero-rated.

In addition the following Customs & Excise Leaflet may be helpful:

701/9/80—Terminal markets: dealing with commodities.

16.400B Generally

Without specific provision to the contrary, dealings in commodities would be subject to the usual VAT rules concerning the supply of goods. This applies to both actuals and futures trading. The phrase "actuals trading" is used in this sub-chapter to cover transactions where the purchaser of a commodity intends to take delivery of that commodity at some fixed date. "Futures trading" on the other hand is used in relation to a transaction where a quantity of a commodity is bought or sold by a person in the hope that that commodity (or the contract of purchase or sale itself) may subsequently be sold or bought at a future date at a profit. For the purposes of the discussion in this sub-chapter, it is assumed that a futures contract will not lead to the delivery of the commodity in question. The nature of the commodity in a futures contract is not, therefore, of primary importance. Instead, the market is used as a means of earning profits for the investor or trader on that market.

In the same way that the stock exchange provides a market for shares, certain "terminal markets" have been created to facilitate the dealing in commodities. These markets are limited to one principal commodity. Dealings on these terminal markets are usually effected through brokers who may or may not be members of the markets in question.

In part due to the volume and complexity of dealings on terminal markets, provision was made by s 26 to enable the Treasury to modify the general rules of VAT in relation to dealings on terminal markets by persons "ordinarily engaged in such dealings". In particular, the Treasury is given power to:

(*a*) zero-rate or exempt a supply of goods or services on a market;
(*b*) register bodies representing persons ordinarily engaged in dealings on a market;
(*c*) disregard dealings of persons so represented in determining their liability to be registered for VAT and to disregard for all purposes dealings between such persons; and
(*d*) refund to such persons as are specified in any order, input tax attributable to specified dealings on the markets.

16.400C The VAT (Terminal Markets) Order 1973 (SI 1973 No 173)

Section 26 powers

The Treasury has exercised certain of its powers under Section 26 above by the introduction of the VAT (Terminal Markets) Order 1973 (SI 1973 No 173). This order zero-rates certain transactions effected on the markets listed in that Order. These markets are set out in column 1 of the table below. Dealings on any other terminal market cannot benefit from zero-rating under the Order and will, therefore, be governed by the general rules relating to VAT. It is understood that the Treasury is reluctant to add further markets to the Order.

Persons benefiting from the Order

The Order specifies those persons who may benefit from the Order, when engaging in one of the transactions listed under *Transactions zero-rated under the Order, post* as,

(*a*) members of the market in question; and
(*b*) persons who ordinarily engage in dealings on such markets.

Categories (*a*) and (*b*) are defined in the Order as "market members". In practice, however, the Customs & Excise restrict the ambit of the second category of persons to members and associate members of the relevant market associations. Details of those associations are given in the second column of the table below. It is arguable that the Customs & Excise practice in this respect is not in accordance with the Order.

TABLE

(1) Terminal market	*(2) Persons entitled to benefit under the Order*
London Metal Exchange	Ring dealing members and other members of the Exchange.
London Rubber Market	For actuals transactions—class P (producer members), class A (selling agent and importer members), class B (broker members) and class C (dealer members) of the Rubber Trade Association of London. For futures transactions—floor and associate members of the London Rubber Terminal Market Association.
London Cocoa Terminal Market London Coffee Terminal Market London Sugar Terminal Market London Vegetable Oil Terminal Market London Wool Terminal Market London Gold Market London Silver Market	Full and associate members of these markets' Associations.
London Grain Futures Market	Any member of the Grain and Feed Trade Association.
London Soya Bean Meal Futures Market	Full and associated members of the GAFTA Soya Bean Meal Terminal Market Association.
Liverpool Barley Futures Market	Any member of the Liverpool Corn Trade Association.

Transactions zero-rated under the Order

The following transactions are zero-rated under art 3 of the Order:

ACTUALS TRADING

A sale between market members of a commodity ordinarily dealt in any one of the listed markets is zero-rated provided that:

(*a*) if the market is the London Metal Exchange, the sale is between members entitled to deal in the ring;

(*b*) if the market is the London Cocoa Terminal Market, the London Coffee Market, the London Soya Bean Meal Futures Market, the London Sugar Terminal Market, the London Vegetable Oil Terminal Market or the London Wool Terminal Market, the sale is registered with the International Commodities Clearing House Limited;

(*c*) if the market is the London Grain Futures Market, the sale is registered in the Clearing House of the Grain and Feed Trade Association Limited; and

(*d*) if the market is the Liverpool Barley Futures Market, the sale is registered at the Clearing House of the Liverpool Corn Trade Association Limited.

FUTURES TRADING

Futures transactions, which include dealings in options, are zero-rated if they involve, as either seller or buyer, a market member and do not lead to the delivery of the commodity in question. "Delivery" is not defined in the Order but is interpreted by the Customs & Excise as taking place when instructions are given for the goods to be physically removed from the warehouse in which they are located.

BROKERS' AND AGENTS' SERVICES

The services of a market member when acting as a broker or agent are zero-rated on the specified terminal markets where the basic transaction to which they relate is itself zero-rated under ACTUALS TRADINGS AND FUTURES TRADING, *ante*.

Where a broker shares his commission in return for the introduction of business, that part of the commission paid over to the person making the introduction is standard rated. Only that part retained by the broker is entitled to be zero-rated under the Order.

A broker's services not within these rules may be zero-rated by virtue of Sched 4 (see **16.400D**, *Brokers and agents, post*).

Rewriting the transaction

If for any reason it is discovered at a later stage that a transaction was incorrectly zero-rated under the Order, for example, because delivery is subsequently called for in a transaction involving a non market member, VAT must be accounted for on that transaction in the normal way.

Accounting

The Customs & Excise permits a trader not to record transactions on a terminal market listed in the Order which are zero-rated. This is, however, on an "all or nothing" basis. If the trader wishes to record certain zero-rated transactions, he must record them all.

VAT Leaflet 701/9/80

The Customs & Excise has published VAT Leaflet 701/9/80 (Terminal Markets dealing with Commodities) which may be of assistance in the interpretation of the Order.

16.400D Other provisions affecting commodities

Where a transaction affecting commodities is not zero-rated under the VAT (Terminal Markets) Order 1973 (SI 1973 No 173), the following should, nevertheless, be borne in mind.

Brokers and agents

The "international" services of brokers may be zero-rated under Sched 4, Group 9, item 11 (c) where the commodity in question is to be supplied outside the United Kingdom.

The Customs & Excise also appears to accept that brokers' services are financial services within Sched 2A, para 5. This is the case whether the transaction is an actuals or futures transaction. As a result, if the broker's client belongs outside the United Kingdom, the broker's fee may be zero-rated under either Sched 4, Group 9, item 5 or 6.

Food

If the commodity falls within one of the items of Sched 4, Group 1 (Food), its supply will be zero-rated. Brokers' fees in connection with such transactions will remain taxable at the standard rate, however, unless they are entitled to be zero-rated under one of the provisions mentioned under *Brokers and agents, ante*. Categories of food zero-rated under Group 1 which may be relevant in this respect include cocoa, coffee, soya bean meal, grain and sugar.

16.500   Eurobond issues

16.500A Sources

Section 8B—Determination of the country in which a person belongs.
Schedule 2A, para 5—Financial services.
Schedule 4, Group 9, items 5 and 6—Possible zero-rating of certain financial supplies.
Schedule 5, Group 5, item 4—Exemption of dealings in secondary securities.
VAT (General) Regulations 1977 (SI 1977 No 1759), reg 68(4)—Determination of partial
    exemption calculations without regard to certain financial supplies.

16.500B Generally

There are two basic types of eurobond issue. These are the European
style issue, principally used by English and European managers, and the
American style issue, used by US orientated managers.

In a European style issue, a group of managers headed by a lead
manager, manages the issue of bonds by the borrower of euro-currency
(the issuer) and arranges for the issue to be underwritten by a group
of underwriters. The managers also offer to sell the bonds to a selling
group usually comprised of banks, financial institutions and dealers. The
managers act throughout their above functions as agents for the issuer.
The underwriters agree to take up any bonds not purchased by the selling
group. The selling group will either retain the bonds or sell them to investors in the market.

The American style issue follows the broad pattern of the European
style issue but with the distinction that the underwriters will subscribe
for the bonds as principals, for sale by them to the selling group.

The VAT position of the parties mentioned above is discussed
under **16.500C—16.500F**.

16.500C The issuer

In this section it is assumed that the issuer belongs in the United
Kingdom. Where the issuer belongs outside the United Kingdom, issues
by him will not be subject to VAT.

A eurobond is a secondary security within the meaning given to that
term in the Exchange Control Act 1947, s 42 that is:

"any letter of allotment which may be renounced, any letter of rights, any warrant conferring an option to acquire a security, any deposit certificate in respect of securities (but

not including a receipt by an authorised depository for any certificate of title deposited in pursuance of this Part of this Act), and such other documents conferring, or containing evidence of, rights as may be prescribed".

Thus, the issue of a eurobond will be an exempt supply within Sched 5, Group 5, item 4 where the purchaser of the bonds, that is the members of the selling group in a European style issue and the underwriters in an American style issue, "belongs" in a country which is a member state of the EEC. Where the purchaser belongs outside the EEC, however, the issue will be zero-rated under Schedule 4, Group 9, item 6 (see Note (6) to that Group). No distortion in the issuer's ability to recover input tax should arise where the issue is exempt, however, as the value of such a supply may usually be disregarded in any partial exemption calculation (VAT (General) Regulations 1977 (SI 1977 No 1759), reg 68(4)(a)).

In the perhaps unlikely situation where a United Kingdom issuer appoints a lead manager who belongs outside the United Kingdom, the provisions of s 8B (reverse charge on supplies received from abroad) must be considered. If the issuer is a taxable person, s 8B will require the issuer in such circumstances to account for VAT on the managers' services as if it had itself supplied those services in the United Kingdom. For a further discussion of s 8B, see **10.200**.

16.500D The manager

It is understood that it is the Customs & Excise practice to assess the VAT treatment of the managers' services by reference to the position of the lead manager. It is assumed below, therefore, that the lead manager belongs in the United Kingdom with the result that the managers' supplies are within the scope of VAT.

Where the managers receive a fee from the issuer for their services in managing the issue, that fee will be regarded as paid in respect of the provision of a financial service within Sched 2A, para 5. The fee will be zero-rated, therefore, under Sched 4, Group 9, items 5 or 6 where the issuer belongs in a country outside the United Kingdom (Note (4) will not prevent such supplies from falling under item 5 as the making of arrangements for the issue of a secondary security is not an exempt supply under Sched 5, Group 5).

In some issues, managers may not be paid a fee as such but will be permitted to subscribe for bonds at a discount ("the selling group discount"). The managers then sell such bonds for their face value in the market. It is understood that, if this is done, the Customs & Excise regards the selling group discount as being outside the scope of and, therefore, not subject to, VAT. The Customs & Excise's view is based upon the argument that the arrangement between the manager and the issuer is merely an agreement to subscribe for bonds at a specified price. While this view is unlikely to be challenged by managers, it is perhaps too simplistic an approach to the transactions in question. Services are supplied by the manager, both in arranging the issue and negotiating its terms on behalf of the investors. The consideration given for such services is the foregoing by the issuer of the full price of the bonds. It is suggested that such consideration should be valued under s 10(3) at its market value. That market value is presumably equal to the selling group discount. If the selling group discount is subject to VAT, it will of course be a VAT inclusive amount. Where the fee is standard and not zero-rated (this will depend on the country in which the issuer belongs (see above)) the VAT element of the discount will be three twenty-thirds of the total discount.

Finally, where a manager subscribes for bonds as a principal, a subsequent sale by him of those bonds will be either an exempt supply (Schedule 5, Group 5, item 4), if the purchaser belongs in the EEC, or zero-rated under Sched 4, Group 9, item 6 if the purchaser belongs outside the EEC.

16.500E The Underwriters

The VAT treatment of the underwriters' services will be similar to that discussed in relation to the managers above. In summary this is as follows:

(*a*) where the underwriter belongs in the United Kingdom and the issuer belongs in the United Kingdom—the underwriters' fee is standard rated;

(*b*) where the underwriter belongs in the United Kingdom and the issuer belongs outside the United Kingdom—the fee is zero-rated under Sched 4, Group 9, items 5 or 6;

(*c*) where the underwriter belongs outside the United Kingdom and the issuer belongs in the United Kingdom and is a taxable person, s 8B will apply to the issuer;

(*d*) where the underwriter subscribes for bonds at a discount instead of receiving a fee, the discount is arguably to be treated as a VAT inclusive fee. Whether any VAT is accountable for on such fee in such circumstances then depends upon the rules in (*a*) and (*b*), *ante*.

(*e*) the subscription for bonds by an underwriter where an issue is unsuccessful will not involve any further supply by the underwriter even if such subscription is at a discount;

(*f*) a subsequent sale of bonds by an underwriter will be either exempt or zero-rated depending upon whether the purchaser belongs in the EEC or outside the EEC respectively.

16.500F Selling group

The selling group will purchase bonds and either hold them to maturity or sell them on the market. The first of these alternatives will not involve a supply by the selling group. The second will be either an exempt (Sched 5, Group 5, item 4) or zero-rated (Sched 4, Group 9, item 6) supply depending upon whether the transferee belongs in or outside the EEC respectively.

16.600 Off-shore activities

16.600A Sources

Section 12—Exportation of certain goods; zero-rating of certain supplies.
supplies.
Schedule 4
Group 9, items 3, 5 and 6 ⎫
Group 10, items 1 and 5 ⎬ —Zero-rating of scientific etc. activities, the supply of ships,
Group 15, item 2   ⎭   freight and personnel, and self-supplies.
VAT (General) Regulations 1977 (SI 1977 No 1759), reg 37—Temporary importation of goods.
In addition the following Customs & Excise Leaflet may be helpful:
3/75/VLB—Off-shore oil and gas installations.

16.600B Generally

The United Kingdom includes only the UK mainland and its territorial waters. UK territorial waters extend 3 miles seaward (the "three mile limit") of the low water mark on the mainland or any island, rock or sand bar which is above high water level and over which the United Kingdom has sovereignty. The base lines for calculating the 3 mile limit are set out in the Territorial Waters Order in Council 1964. As a result, operations outside the 3 mile limit of the territorial waters, for example in a designated area of the UK continental shelf, will be treated as would operations in any country other than the United Kingdom. It follows that operations in the territorial waters should be treated in the same way as operations on the UK mainland.

In this subchapter, the adjective "off-shore" is used to imply that the activity or installation in question is performed or located outside the 3 mile limit.

The limitation of the United Kingdom to the mainland and its territorial waters has the consequence that the supply of goods or services by a UK supplier to an operator's off-shore installation will represent an import or export, as the case may be, with the attendant VAT consequences (see Chapters 6 and 7). The transfer of goods by the operator himself from the United Kingdom, however, will amount to a self-supply and will usually not be subject to VAT.

In relation to the exportation of goods to an off-shore location care must be taken to ascertain the actual exporter of the goods as only that person will be entitled to zero-rate the supply of those goods under either s 12(2) or (6). Thus, if an operator takes delivery in the United Kingdom of equipment to be shipped by him for use offshore, the supply will not be zero-rated even though the goods are in fact subsequently exported. This is only likely to be of concern (except in cash flow terms) to partially exempt operators. An operator in this position would appear to have two options. Either to take delivery outside the United Kingdom, the supplier actually exporting the equipment, or alternatively, to take delivery in the United Kingdom through a separate company which is not subject to a group election and which makes no taxable supplies. In the latter case, the recipient company may rely on Sched 4, Group 15, item 2 to establish registration, zero-rate the shipment to its off-shore installation and reclaim all input tax paid on the supply of the equipment to it (see further, in relation to Group 15, **8.1500**).

Where an operator imports items into the United Kingdom for use off-shore and exports them to the off-shore installation within 6 months of their importation (or such longer period as the Customs & Excise may allow), those items may qualify for exemption from tax on importation under the rules relating to temporary importations (see VAT (General) Regulations 1977 (SI 1977 No 1759), reg 37 and Chapter 6).

Special entry arrangements apply to the continuous importation of natural gas and crude oil by pipeline.

16.600C Off-shore installations

The supply, repair or maintenance of a ship which is neither of gross tonnage of less than 15 tons, nor designed or adapted for use for recreation or pleasure, is zero-rated under Sched 4, Group 10, item 1. A ship will include an off-shore oil and gas platform if it is mobile. "Mobile" is interpreted by the Customs & Excise as "designed to be moved from place to place, whether under its own motive power or otherwise" (see VAT Leaflet VLB/3/75 (Off-shore oil and gas installations)). This is perhaps a generous interpretation as, in the light of *T M Hagenbach v CCE*, LON/74/49 (*Casebook* **8.1001**), it is open to doubt whether an installation which does not have its own motive power is capable of being called a "ship" within Group 10. A supply of an installation not within Group 10 will be standard rated unless exported by the supplier (see paragraph **16.600B**).

16.600D Support activities

Such activities will commonly take one of three forms. First, the transport of freight or passengers between the United Kingdom and the off-shore installation. This will be zero-rated under Sched 4, Group 10, item 5 (Transport). Secondly, the supply of personnel. This will be zero-rated under Sched 4, Group 9, items 5 or 6 where the person receiving the supply belongs outside the United Kingdom. Thirdly, the performance of services on the off-shore installation. Such services will usually be regarded by the Customs & Excise in practice as "scientific services" within the ambit of Sched 4, Group 9, item 3. They may also, therefore, be zero-rated.

16.700 Compensation and ex gratia payments

16.700A Sources

> Section 6(2)—Definition of a supply.
> Section 8B—Reverse charge to VAT on the receipt of certain services from abroad.
> Schedule 2
>   para 5(2)—Deemed supply on the transfer of assets.
> Schedule 2A—Those supplies treated as supplied where received.
> Schedule 3
>   para 7(*b*)—The value of Sched 2, para 5(2) supplies.
> Schedule 4, Group 9, items 5 and 6—Certain zero-rated supplies.
> VAT (Cars) Order 1980 (SI 1980 No 442), arts 6 and 7—Free gift of cars; special scheme for second-hand cars.

In this section, four types of compensation payments are considered. First, payments to compensate a person for refraining from carrying on a part of his business. Secondly, payments to terminate a contract before its specified expiry date. Thirdly, ex gratia payments following a termination of a contract by mutual agreement. Fourthly, payments to employees.

16.700B Compensation payments for restraint of business activities

Such payments are made in respect of the surrender by the payee of the right to continue to trade freely and are, therefore, in respect of a supply of services by the payee (s 6(2)(*b*)).

Such a supply is also arguably within Sched 2A, para 4. Paragraph 4 includes the:

> "acceptance of any obligation to refrain from pursuing or excercising, in whole or part, any business activity or any such rights as are referred to in paragraph 1 above".

Schedule 2A, para 1 includes:

"transfers and assignments of copyright, patents, licences trademarks and similar rights".

As was mentioned in **10.200**, para 4 is different from its counterpart in the EEC Sixth Directive. While the equivalent provision to para 4 in the EEC Sixth Directive is not limited to "such rights as are referred to in paragraph 1" but extends to Schedule 2A, paras 1–7, "business activity" in the EEC Sixth Directive would appear to be a more limited phrase, again extending to only those supplies mentioned in paras 1– 7. If para 4 is to be read subject to the EEC Sixth Directive (as to this see, generally, **13.800**), it would seem that compensation payments to refrain from exercising an activity within any of the paragraphs of Sched 2A fall within para 4 of that Schedule.

The above has the following consequences:

(*a*) if the payer and payee both belong in the United Kingdom, the supply will be taxable at the standard rate;
(*b*) if the payer but not the payee belongs outside the United Kingdom, the supply will be zero-rated under Sched 4, Group 9, items 5 or 6; and
(*c*) if the payee but not the payer belongs outside the United Kingdom, the payer must account for tax on the payment under s 8B if he is a taxable person (see **10.200** for a general discussion of s 8B).

16.700C Compensation for the termination of a contract

Such payments are also within s 6(2)(*b*) and are subject to tax. There would appear to be no scope for zero-rating such payments. This applies where the compensation is in the form of liquidated damages under the contract itself, where the payment is agreed in settlement by the parties or is ordered by a court.

16.700D Ex gratia payments following the termination of a contract

The question for consideration in connection with such payments is whether they may truly be said to be ex gratia or whether in substance they are payments of compensation and ought to be treated as falling within **16.700C**. This is a question of fact that will depend upon the circumstances surrounding the payment in any given case. If the payment is ex gratia, there will have been no supply by the payee which may attract tax and, therefore, the payment will not be subject to VAT.

16.700E Payments to employees

Where an employer makes a cash payment to an employee, no VAT consequences will result. This is because although the employee may be seen to have provided a "supply" (for example the performance of past or future services or the giving up of a claim against the employer), such supply will not be made in the course or furtherance of a business carried on by the employee.

The transfer of property to an employee does have potential VAT implications for the employer. Schedule 2, para 5(2) provides that a supply of goods is to be treated as made "if goods forming part of the assets of the business are transferred or disposed of so as no longer to form part of those assets". A transfer of assets to an employee by way of compensation for loss of office, as an ex gratia payment or in lieu of emoluments will fall within para 5(2). The treatment of such a transfer will vary, however, depending upon whether the employee gives consideration for the transfer and the nature of the asset transferred.

The value of a supply under para 5(2) for which no consideration is given is fixed in Sched 3, para 7(*b*) as the cost of the goods to the person making the supply, that is the employer. Cost may, of course, differ from the market value of the item at the time of its transfer to the employee. Where a consideration is given for the transfer, for example, where an employee is given the opportunity to purchase the asset at its written down value, the valuation rules in s 10(2) or (3) will prevail. If the employee purchases the item for money (whether or not at an undervalue) and gives no other consideration, s 10(2) will require that price to be taken. The Customs & Excise may not substitute a higher value. If the employee provides another form of consideration, for example, the promise not to bring a claim against the employer, s 10(3) will fix the value of the employer's supply at its market value at the date of the supply.

These valuation rules may work to the disadvantage of the employer. The optimum is, perhaps, a situation where the employee pays a nominal consideration (£1?) for the transfer of an item to him which would otherwise have been transferred to him purely on an ex gratia basis. This reduces the value of the supply from original cost (Sched 3, para 7(b)) to £1 (s 10(2)).

The final factor to be taken into account in this connection is the nature of the asset transferred. If the asset falls within Scheds 4 or 5, it will be zero-rated or exempt accordingly. If the asset transferred is a car and it is transferred for no consideration, such a transfer is treated as neither a supply of goods nor services (VAT (Cars) Order 1980 (SI 1980 No 442), art 7(*c*)). As a result, no VAT will be chargeable on such transfer. It is also possible that an asset will fall within one of the categories of goods which qualify for the operation of a margin scheme. The most likely instance of such an item would be a company car which is transferred to an employee for a consideration. Where a margin scheme applies the value of the supply will be reduced to the excess of the consideration (see *ante*) for which the item is transferred to the employee over the consideration for which it was acquired by the employer.

16.800 Management services

16.800A Sources

The following Customs & Excise Leaflet contains the conditions relating to management services:
700/6/80—Management services.

16.800B Generally

Where one party has agreed to provide a package of services for another it is necessary to determine the precise nature of such agreement and the relationship it creates between the parties. If the agreement creates an agency between the parties, whether disclosed or otherwise, the overall VAT treatment of the underlying provision of goods or services will not be affected. Additional VAT will only be payable on the agent's fee. An example of such an arrangement would be where one group company is appointed purchasing agent for the group as a whole in order to take advantage of bulk purchases at reduced cost. For a general discussion of the treatment of agents for VAT purposes, see **15.000.**

Where an agency is not established and one party ("the manager") agrees to provide a package of services for another ("the recipient"), VAT will usually be chargeable on the whole management fee charged to the recipient whether or not such management fee includes any element of profit. This follows from the general principle of VAT that VAT is charged on the consideration paid for a supply without any deduction for disbursements or costs incurred by the supplier. Thus, there will be a number of supplies by third parties to the manager on which VAT may or may not be payable (if it is, the manager may potentially recover it as input tax) and a single supply by the manager to the recipient on which VAT is chargeable. It would not appear to be possible to break down the manager's supply into its constituent parts in order to charge VAT according to the nature of those parts.

16.800C Treatment and interpretation

The Customs & Excise has issued a VAT Leaflet 700/6/80 (Management Services) which sets out at some length their interpretation of the treatment of management charges generally. This leaflet notes that a further distinction has to be drawn where the manager and the recipient are joint owners or joint employers of any property or the personnel involved in the supply of management services. In such a case, where the manager has agreed to act as the payer, for example of rents or rates on the property owned or the salary of the person employed by them, any settlement between the manager and recipient will be ignored for VAT purposes. This would seem to be correct following the, otherwise apparently conflicting, cases of *Commonwealth Telecommunications Bureau* v *CCE*, LON/75/25 (*Casebook* **3.111**), and *The Heart of Variety* v *CCE*, [1975] VATTR 103 (*Casebook* **4.205**).

16.800D Provision of management services

In practice, management charges will most commonly arise where a service company is established by a partnership or by a group of companies to carry out administrative functions and possibly employ the staff on behalf of the partnership or group. In such instances, VAT will be chargeable on any fee payable.

Two cases illustrate such provision of management services. First, in *Smith and Williamson* v *CCE*, [1976] VATTR 215 (*Casebook* **3.109**), a company established by a partnership provided financial services to clients of the partnership and also employed the partnership staff. In return, the partnership allowed the company to share its offices. Office expenses were notionally apportioned between the partnership and the company. At the end of each year the company invoiced the partnership for a net amount being its fee after having set off the amount notionally apportioned to it in respect of its occupation of the office accommodation. On appeal it was held that the company had contracted to supply services to the partnership for the gross amount of its fee and that no set off was permissible in ascertaining the amount on which VAT was payable.

The second case, *CCE* v *Tilling Management Services Ltd*, [1979] STC 365 (*Casebook* **16.801**), involved the provision by a group management company of general services to other group members. As no charge was made for such services to other group members, losses arose in the management company which were surrendered to other group companies for corporation tax purposes. At the request of the company's auditors, a payment for such group relief was made to the management company. On appeal before the High Court, it was held that such payment represented a consideration for the provision of the management services.

The *Tilling* case led to the issue, by the Consultative Committee of

Accountancy Bodies, of the following statement in respect of payments for group relief and management services within a group of companies:

"Group relief and management services

Memorandum issued in June 1979 on behalf of the Councils of the constituent members of the Consultative Committee of Accountancy Bodies in connection with VAT on management services for group relief following the case of *CCE* v *Tilling Management Services Ltd.*

1. The accountancy bodies have raised with the Customs and Excise Authorities their disquiet as to the VAT position arising in respect of group relief under section 258 of the Income and Corporation Taxes Act 1970 following the case of *CCE* v *Tilling Management Services Ltd* (Q.B.D., July 7, 1978).

2. Tilling Management Services Limited ("TMS") entered into an agreement with its parent company to supply management services to the group in consideration for the procuring of payments to TMS for the group relief which it surrendered.

3. TMS was assessed to VAT on the basis that it had supplied services for its parent and other group companies. Customs and Excise contended that the management services were rendered in consideration for the procuring of payments to TMS for the surrender of group relief, the quantum of which was the amount of those payments.

4. TMS appealed to a VAT Tribunal which found in favour of TMS. On appeal by Customs and Excise to the High Court the Tribunal decision was reversed, it being held that there was consideration for the management services.

5. The Customs Authorities have now confirmed that it remains their view that group relief payments do not give rise to taxable supplies of goods or services for VAT purposes. Where an agreement between two companies links, as is intended by section 258, the surrender of a tax loss to a group relief payment is not considered that this occurrence of itself results in a VAT charge. Similarly, if a tax loss is surrendered but no group relief payment is made, the Customs Authorities would again see no supply for VAT purposes if this is all that happens.

6. However, when considering whether or not an activity constitutes a supply of services for VAT purposes the Customs Authorities have to determine whether there is any consideration, either monetary or non-monetary, for the activity, and then place a value on the consideration. Thus, if Company A agrees to provide, for example, management services to Company B it is necessary to consider whether there is any consideration for those services.

7. In some cases, however, an agreement to render management services might be related to some other occurrence. For example, Company A might agree to provide management services to Company B if Company B agrees to procure a payment of group relief for Company A. In such a case Company A has agreed to perform certain services in return for a non-monetary consideration—the consideration being Company B's promise to procure a group relief payment—and it is therefore necessary to value the consideration in order to determine the amount of VAT due. This was the position in the *Tilling* case, and it was agreed that the value of the management services being provided was the amount of the group relief payments which were made. The group relief payments as such were not taxable but they represented the consideration for a supply of management services.

8. Dealing with four specific examples put to the Customs Authorities:

(*a*) If Company A incurs a tax loss and surrenders it to Company B under section 258 without any payment the Customs Authorities do not see any taxable supply of goods or services for VAT purposes.

(*b*) If Company A incurs a tax loss and surrenders it to Company B under section 258 with a payment or credit to current account for the surrender of the tax loss, again the Customs Authorities do not see any taxable supply of goods or services.

(*c*) It is possible, in cases (*a*) and (*b*) above, that Company A might render management services to Company B without a separate charge being made for those services. The position here depends on whether there is any arrangement linking the provision of management services to, say, the procurement or making of group relief payments. If there is, then the Customs Authorities would see a non-monetary consideration for the management services which would have to be valued to determine the amount of VAT due. If there is no such arrangement, then if the management services are provided free of charge there is no taxable supply.

(*d*) Again, Company A may render management services to Company B and make a charge for those services, at the same time surrendering group relief, with or without payment. In such a case there is clearly a taxable supply of management services, but what has to be determined is whether the money charge is the full consideration for the supply. If there is an arrangement linking the supply of management services to the procurement or making of group relief payments then once again there would be a non-monetary consideration which would have to be valued. In such circumstances VAT would be due on the full consideration, *i.e.* on the sum of the monetary and non-monetary considerations. However, if there is no link between the management services and the group relief payments, then VAT will be due only on the charge actually made for the management services.

9. The Customs Authorities have also confirmed that where services are rendered between companies within the same VAT group registration then no liability to VAT arises.

10. Whilst, therefore, there are circumstances when VAT might arise the Customs Authorities stress that the mere surrender of group relief, whether in return for a payment or without charge, under the provisions of section 258 does not, in their view, give rise to a supply for VAT purposes and is, therefore, outside the scope of the tax. Moreover, it is not the intention of the Customs Authorities to bring transfers of group relief, as such, within the scope of the tax. C.C.A.B., June 19, 1979.

Finally, it should be noted that the Customs & Excise regards the provision of inter-group management services as falling within Sched 2A. This enables a supply of such services to be zero-rated under Sched 4, Group 9, items 5 or 6 when supplied to a person who belongs outside the United Kingdom and will result in a s 8B charge where such services are received in the United Kingdom by a taxable person from a supplier who belongs outside the United Kingdom.

16.900 Gaming machines

16.900A Sources

F(No 2)A 1975, s 21—The VAT treatment of the supply of gaming machines.

In addition the following Customs & Excise Leaflet may be helpful:

9/78/VAH—VAT on gaming machine takings.

16.900B Generally

A gaming machine is defined in F (No 2) A 1975, s 21 (4) as a machine which satisfies the conditions that:

(*a*) it is constructed or adapted for playing a game of chance by means of it;

(*b*) a player pays to play the machine (except where he has an opportunity to play payment-free as the result of having previously played successfully), either by inserting a coin or token into the machine or in some other way; and

(*c*) the element of chance in the game is provided by means of the machine.

VAT is charged in respect of the playing of such machines where the owner of the machine is a taxable person and the supply of the machine forms a part of his business. The value on which the tax is based (necessarily a VAT inclusive amount) may be simply stated as the value put into the machine by the player less any winnings paid out by the machine. Complications arise, however, through the use of tokens and the possibility that any tokens won may be exchanged for goods. Tokens are, therefore, to be taken as having a value:

(i) if they can be used to play the machine, equal to the value purchased on the machine by the token; and

(ii) if not within (i) but which can be exchanged for money, equal to the amount of such money.

Tokens which are within neither (i) nor (ii) are ignored; they can clearly not be regarded as winnings.

Where goods are exchanged for tokens, such an exchange represents a separate supply from the provision and playing of the machine. VAT is chargeable on that exchange accordingly. The exception to this appears to be where a token not within (i) or (ii) is exchanged for goods. In such case, the value of the goods is regarded as winnings for the purposes of VAT on the supply of the machine and the supply of the goods is disregarded.

VAT Leaflet 9/78/VAH (Gaming machine takings) may be of use in this area.

Chapter 17

Accounting for VAT

17.000 Sources

Section 30   —Accounting for and payment of VAT
Section 30(2)—Invoices.
Section 32(1)—Provision of evidence.
Section 34   —Records
Section 35   —Production of documents.
FA 1980, s 16—Use of computers.
VAT (General) Regulations 1977 (SI 1977 No 1759)
   regs 2, 8–11—Invoices.
   regs 7, 51–57—Accounting for and payment of VAT.

In addition the following Customs & Excise Notice has legislative effect in relation to record keeping:

700, Part VI, paras 49–63.

17.100 General principles

Although the Customs & Excise is given power to assess tax due (s 31), VAT is collected primarily through a system of self-assessment by taxable persons. To ensure that such self-assessments may be easily verified by the Customs & Excise, formalised records and documentation are required to be kept by taxable persons. These records may be divided into three categories. First, the tax invoice which evidences a supply. Secondly, books and accounts recording a taxable person's transactions. Thirdly, the VAT return prepared from those books and accounts with reference to prescribed accounting periods. These three categories will be discussed at **17.200, 17.300** and **17.400** respectively.

Further more specialised accounting systems apply to retailers who would otherwise have difficulty in complying with the above formal requirements for each supply made by them. These "special schemes for retailers" are discussed at **16.200**.

17.200 Tax invoices

Generally

VAT (General) Regulations 1977 (SI 1977 No 1759), reg 8 (made under the authority of s 30(2)) introduced the concept of a "registered taxable person". This is defined in reg 2(1) as a taxable person who is in fact registered for VAT (the definition of a taxable person, of course, also includes a person who is required to be registered). Such registered taxable person is obliged when making a supply to a taxable person to issue, unless the Customs & Excise otherwise allow, an invoice or other document giving certain information (reg 8(1)). This invoice or document is defined as a "tax invoice".

Under sections 16(1) and (2) of the Finance Act 1980, a taxable person is permitted to provide another with a tax invoice by recording the necessary information in a computer and transmitting that information by electronic means, that is, without delivering any document to that other person. However, before taking advantage of this provision, the taxable person (and in certain cases the person receiving the transmission) must give at least one month's notice to the Customs & Excise and comply with any requirements that the Customs & Excise might impose.

Information required on a tax invoice

The information a tax invoice must contain is set out in reg 9 and is:

(*a*) an identifying number;
(*b*) the date of the supply;
(*c*) the name, address and registration number of the supplier;
(*d*) the name and address of the person to whom the goods or services are supplied;
(*e*) the type of supply by reference to the following categories:

- (i)   a supply by sale,
- (ii)   a supply on hire purchase or any similar transaction,
- (iii) a supply by loan,
- (iv) a supply by way of exchange,
- (v)   a supply on hire, lease or rental,
- (vi) a supply of goods made from customer's materials,
- (vii) a supply by sale on commission,
- (viii) a supply on sale or return or similar terms, or
- (ix) any other type of supply which the Customs & Excise may at any time by notice specify.

(*f*) a description sufficient to identify the goods or services supplied;
(*g*) for each description, the quantity of the goods or the extent of the services, the rate of tax and the amount payable, excluding tax;
(*h*) the gross amount payable excluding tax;
(*i*)   the rate of any cash discount offered;
(*j*)   the amount of tax chargeable at each rate, with the rate to which it relates; and
(*k*) the total amount of tax chargeable.

The Customs & Excise does have the power, however, to accept a tax invoice which does not contain all the above information (regs 9(1) and 10. In relation to reg 10, see *When an invoice is not required, para (e), post*).

When an invoice is not required

There is no requirement to provide a tax invoice in any of the following instances:

(*a*) any zero-rated supply (reg 11(*a*));

(*b*) any supply on which tax is charged although it is not made for a consideration. This would, for example, include the personal use of a business asset (reg 11(*c*));

(*c*) any supply to which an order made under s 3(9) applies. This refers to orders restricting the ability to claim input tax relief on certain goods or services specified in the order. It would apply, for example, to certain motor cars or business entertainment (reg 11(*b*));

(*d*) any supply to which an order made under s 14 applies. This relates to second-hand goods the subject of a margin scheme, for example antiques (reg 11(*d*));

(*e*) if the registered taxable person in question is a retailer, he may if he wishes not issue an invoice unless the customer requests that an invoice be issued to him. If an invoice is requested and the supply does not exceed £25, a simplified invoice may be issued. Such simplified invoice will contain only the information listed under *Information required on a tax invoice* paras (*b*), (*c*) and (*f*) the rate of tax in force at the time of the supply and the total amount payable including tax. A simplified invoice should cover only supplies taxed at one rate of tax and cannot include zero-rated or exempt supplies (reg 10);

(*f*) where a registered taxable person operates a system of self-invoicing with the approval of the Customs & Excise, the document issued by that registered taxable person is treated as a tax invoice (reg 8(3)). There is, therefore, no further obligation on the supplier of the goods or services to issue a tax invoice. The operation of a self-invoicing system does not absolve the supplier from liability to account to the Customs & Excise for the tax should the customer default however (*T A Landels and Sons Ltd* v *CCE*, MAN/78/52 (*Casebook* **5.201**);

(*g*) an authenticated receipt issued by a supplier to which reg 21 applies is treated as a tax invoice if it contains the information required by reg 9(1) and no other tax invoice is issued. Regulation 21 applies to a supplier of goods or services together with goods in the course of the construction, alteration, demolition, repair or maintenance of a building or any civil engineering work under a contract which provides for such supplies to be made periodically (reg 8(4)).

Documents not to be treated as a tax invoice

A consignment, delivery or similar document (or any copy thereof) issued by a supplier in respect of a supply of goods on sale or return or approval shall not be treated as a tax invoice if issued before the normal time of supply in such cases. That is, before it becomes certain that the goods have been appropriated to the contract. The document must, however, be endorsed to the effect that it is not a tax invoice (reg 9(2)). Pro forma invoices used to offer goods or services to potential customers would also fall within this category (see VAT Notes 1980–81 issued by the Customs & Excise).

Also, a consignment, delivery note or similar document issued prior to the 14 day period given by s 7(5) for the issue of an invoice is not to be regarded as a tax invoice.

Exempt or zero-rated items

Where an invoice in respect of a standard rated supply also covers exempt or zero-rated items, it must total such supplies separately (reg 9(3)).

Time limits

A tax invoice or similar document treated as a tax invoice under the heading *When an invoice is not required, paras (c)* or *(g), ante,* is required to be issued within 30 days of the time of the supply (reg 8(5)). As to the time of supply, see generally **3.300**.

17.300 Records

Section 34(1) provides that every taxable person shall keep such records as the Customs & Excise may require. Details of such records are set out in Notice No 700, Pt VI. The information kept in such records will be disclosed to the Customs & Excise through the completion of VAT Form 100 (Return of Value Added Tax) after the end of each prescribed accounting period. Such information may also be required to be disclosed through the obligation to produce documents to the Customs & Excise under ss 32(1) or 35(2), (3) and (4). These sections and the Customs & Excise powers to call for information and documents generally are discussed in **14.200**.

Such records are required to be kept for a period of 3 years. All auxiliary documentation such as orders, invoices, delivery notes, correspondence and other documents relating to the business are required to be retained for a similar period.

If the Customs & Excise agree, the above information may be kept in microfilm form or on a computer. To obtain the Customs & Excise's approval the information must be capable of being readily converted into a legible form for inspection by the Customs & Excise on request. Records contained on a "computer" will only be admissible in evidence, however, if the conditions in the Civil Evidence Act 1968, s 5(2) are satisfied (s 34(5)). These conditions are:

(*a*) that the document containing the statement was produced by the computer during a period over which the computer was used regularly to store or process information for the purposes of any activities regularly carried on over that period, whether for profit or not, by any body, whether corporate or not, or by any individual:

(*b*) that over that period there was regularly supplied to the computer in the ordinary course of those activities information of the kind contained in the statement or of the kind from which the information so contained is derived;

(*c*) that throughout the material part of that period the computer was operating properly or, if not, that any respect in which it was not operating properly or was out of operation during that part of that period was not such as to effect the production of the document or the accuracy of its contents; and

(*d*) that the information contained in the statement reproduces or is derived from information supplied to the computer in the ordinary course of those activities.

"Computer" for these purposes means (Civil Evidence Act 1968, ss 5(6) and 10(1)):

"... any device for storing and processing information, and any reference to information being derived from other information is a reference to its being derived therefrom by calculation, comparison or any other process."

If a mechanical or electronic form of record keeping is employed, the local VAT office should be informed at the design stage of the system to ensure that no problems will be involved in relation to Customs & Excise approval of the system.

Notice No 700 para 50 contains the following advice to taxable persons in respect of record keeping requirements:

"**Records**

50. (a) *General*. You must keep records and accounts of all taxable (including zero-rated) goods and services that you receive or supply in the course of your business,

including any taxable self-supplies and goods applied to non-business or personal use. You must also keep a record of all the exempt supplies you make. All these records must be kept up to date and must be in sufficient detail to allow you to calculate correctly the amount of VAT that you have to pay to, or can reclaim from, Customs and Excise and to complete the necessary tax returns. Your records do not have to be kept in any special manner but they must be in a form which will enable Customs and Excise officers to check the completeness and accuracy of your returns. If they do not satisfy the requirements set out in this Notice, Customs and Excise have power to direct you to make the necessary changes.

You must also keep, at your principal place of business, a list of your branches.

(b) *Information to be recorded*. Briefly, you must keep records of all operations connected with your business which affect the amount of VAT you have to pay or may reclaim. For example you must record every input of goods or services on which you are charged VAT by your suppliers, every importation or removal from bonded warehouse and all the taxable outputs of your business, including zero-rated outputs, gifts and loans of goods, taxable self-supplies and any goods which you acquire or produce in the course of your business but apply to personal or non-business use. You must also record such things as errors in your accounts, amended tax invoices or credits given or received."

This general statement is amplified in the Notice No 700, paras 51–63. These paragraphs deal exclusively with Customs & Excise practice. Due to their importance, they are set out in full below. References to other paragraphs of the Notice have been replaced in the following quotation, however, with references to chapters of this *Guide*.

Tax on imported goods or goods removed from bonded warehouse

51. If you use the postponed accounting system (Chapter 6) to account for tax on imported goods or on goods removed from bonded warehouse you must observe the requirements of Notices No. 702 and No. 186 as to the keeping of records.

Tax on services received from abroad

52. If you receive certain services from abroad for the purpose of your business you must account for VAT due on them (**10.200**). You should do this by recording the amount of VAT on the "TAX DUE" side of your VAT account. This tax may, however, be deducted as input tax, subject to the limitations of the partial exemption rules (**5.300**). It should be included with other input tax on the "TAX DEDUCTIBLE" side of the VAT account (paragraph 63). To support the amount shown in your VAT account you should hold an invoice issued by the person supplying the services.

Retention of copies of tax invoices

53. Unless you are a retailer issuing less detailed tax invoices (**17.200**), a copy must be kept of all tax invoices which you have issued. Cash and carry wholesalers must retain a copy of all till-rolls and product code lists.

Recording of outputs and output tax

54. (a) *General.* (*This sub-paragraph does not apply to your outputs if your are a retailer using one of the special schemes described in Notice No. 727. (But it does apply to retailers' outputs which are excluded from those special schemes.)*) You must keep a record of all your taxable (including zero-rated) and exempt outputs. So far as applicable it must contain information corresponding to that required on tax invoices (**17.200**

above). If you issue invoices which give all the necessary details and file copies in such a way that they can be readily produced if required, the record need be no more than a summary to enable you to produce separate totals of different classes of outputs. You must also keep a record of any goods which you send out on sale or return, approval or similar terms and of the dates when the tax becomes chargeable.

(b) *Goods given away or applied to non-business or personal use.* Where you give away, or apply to non-business or personal use, goods which you have acquired or produced in the course of your business, you need record only the following:

date when the goods were given away, or taken, or set aside for non-business or personal use;
description and quantity;
tax-exclusive cost of goods;
rate and amount of tax chargeable.

(c) *Self-supplies.* If you are a motor manufacturer, vehicle converter or dealer, and use motor cars you have produced or acquired in the course of your business, you must record for each car:

the date when it was applied to business use (the tax point);
the value on which tax is chargeable;
the rate and amount of tax chargeable.

If you are a partly exempt trader who self-supplies certain printed matter (or a trader who would be exempt but for the self-supply), your records must be kept as required by Notice No. 706.

Analysis of output tax and of outputs

55. Your records must show separately, for each tax period:

(a) the amount of tax chargeable;
(b) the total value of all taxable (including zero-rated) outputs; and
(c) the value of exempt outputs.

Under (a) you should show the *net* amount of tax after deducting any tax on credits allowed to your customers in the tax period. This amount should be carried to your VAT account.

The values to be shown in (b) and (c) are the *gross* amounts, excluding any VAT, charged to your customers, ie without allowance of any deduction for cash discounts but less any credits allowed in the tax period.

Information about completing Box 11 of your tax return is contained in Appendix H (Notice No 700). If you have chosen to use the alternative basis B your records will need to show the total value of all your outputs.

Evidence of input tax

56. (a) *General. In your own interest you should obtain and preserve tax invoices.* All invoices for taxable inputs (including zero-rated inputs) whether they are tax invoices or not, must be filed in such a way that, given the invoice date and the supplier's name and address, they can be readily produced to Customs and Excise. Nobody except a registered taxable person may issue a tax invoice; if you receive an invoice from an unregistered person and knowingly use it with a view to obtaining deduction of input tax, you are committing an offence. You should have no difficulty in finding out from suppliers whether they are registered or not but if you are in doubt you should consult your local VAT office.

(b) *Retailers buying from cash and carry wholesalers.* If you are a retailer buying from a cash and carry wholesaler you will need tax invoices to support your claims for input tax deductions. If the cash and carry wholesaler provides tax invoices in the form of till-rolls on which the goods are represented by product code numbers you should get an up-to-date copy of the wholesaler's product code list and keep it with the till-roll invoices, so that both are readily available for inspection when required.

(c) *Evidence of tax on imported goods or goods removed from bonded warehouse.* You or your agent should ensure that official evidence is obtained, where required, of VAT chargeable on imported goods (Notice No 702) and goods removed from bonded warehouse (Notice No 186). This evidence serves the same purpose as a tax invoice from a taxable supplier in the United Kingdom and without it you may be unable to prove a claim for deduction of input tax. The evidence should be annexed or cross-referenced to the relevant invoice from your supplier and both should be preserved.

(d) *Evidence of tax on services received from abroad.* If you receive a supply of services from abroad (**10.200**) you should hold the relative invoice from the person supplying the services. This evidence serves the same purpose as a tax invoice from a taxable supplier in the United Kingdom and without it you may be unable to prove a claim for deduction of input tax.

Recording of inputs and input tax

57. (a) *General.* You must record all taxable (including zero-rated) inputs in such a way that the details of each transaction and the amount of VAT are entered in full or can readily be found by referring to:

the supplier's invoice;
evidence of services received from abroad;
official evidence of VAT on goods imported or removed from bonded warehouse.

If invoices etc have been received which give all the necessary details, and are filed in such way that they can be readily produced if required, your record need be no more than a summary to enable you to produce a separate total of taxable (including zero-rated) inputs. For example an add-list would be acceptable if it shows tax and values separately itemised in the order in which the tax invoices are batched or filed. Alternatively, depending upon your circumstances, you may prefer to adopt the arrangements described in sub-paragraph (c).

(b) *Non-deductible inputs.* As explained (at **5.400**) the tax on certain inputs is not deductible as input tax. You must keep a record of these inputs if they concern your business, but non-deductible input tax must not be included in the total carried to your VAT account. The value should not be included in Box 12 of your return unless you have chosen to use the alternative basis B for completing Boxes 11 and 12 as explained in Appendix H (Notice No 700).

(c) *Cashbook accounting for inputs.* If it is your normal accounting practice to claim input tax according to the time when you pay your suppliers you may find it convenient to adapt your cashbook payments record to serve also as a record of inputs. An example showing how this may be done by incorporating an additional "tax" column is given at Appendix F (not reproduced in this *Guide*). If you are using the special schemes explained in Notice No 727 (**16.200**), your cashbook would only provide figures for inputs and input tax; it would not provide the figures required for calculation of output tax under Schemes B, C, D, E, G, H or J.

If you change to this method of accounting you must exclude items of tax which you have already claimed on a previous return.

Analysis of input tax and inputs

58. (a) *Input tax.* For each tax period you records must show separately:

(i) the amount of tax due on goods imported or removed from bonded warehouse and on services received from abroad. This amount with certain exceptions listed in Notice No 702 should also be carried to the VAT account (paragraph 63) as "TAX DUE". (Notice No 702 also explains how you can determine the amount of tax due on imported goods if official evidence is not provided and Notice No 186 on goods from bonded warehouse); and

(ii) the amount of input tax on other goods and services (including any tax actually paid at import or on removal from bonded warehouse). This amount is to be shown net after deduction of any tax credits allowed by your suppliers in the tax period.

The total amount of deductible input tax, ie (i) plus (ii), should be carried to your VAT account. If you are not entitled to be treated as a fully taxable person (**5.300**) you should carry only the deductible part of your input tax to the account.

(b) *Inputs.* Your records must show for each tax period the total value (excluding tax) of all taxable (including zero-rated) inputs. Goods imported or removed from bonded warehouse and services received from abroad should be included in the total. The value to be shown is the gross amount charged by your suppliers (ie without any deduction for cash discount) less any United Kingdom VAT charged and less any credits allowed by your suppliers in the tax period.

Information about completing Box 12 of your tax return is contained in Appendix H (Notice No 700). If you have chosen to use the alternative basis B your records will need to show the value of all your inputs.

Record of credits allowed to customers

59. *If you are a retailer accounting for output tax on your supplies by one of the special schemes described in Notice No 727 this paragraph does not apply except where the credit involves a tax invoice.* You must keep a record of all credits allowed to your customers in respect of taxable (including zero-rated) supplies and exempt supplies. When a credit relates to a tax invoice, the record must either show the details in (**17.200** above) or else show clearly (eg by cross-reference to filed copies of credit notes) where those details can be found.

For credits relating to zero-rated or exempt supplies, the record must show the date and amount of the credit and whether it was in respect of an export, a zero-rated supply in the United Kingdom or an exempt supply. If filed copies of credit notes provide a complete and conveniently accessible record no separate record need by kept for VAT purposes.

Where a tax adjustment has to be made, you must adjust your records of outputs and output tax for credits allowed in whatever way you find most convenient, provided that the nature of the adjustment and the reason for it are clear from the accounts or supporting documents.

Record of credits received from suppliers

60. You must keep a record of all credits received from your suppliers in respect of taxable (including zero-rated) inputs. Where a credit relates to a tax invoice, the record must either show details (see **18.000C**) or else show clearly (eg by cross-reference to filed credit notes) where those details can be found.

For credits relating to zero-rated supplies the record need only show the date and amount of the credit. If filed credit notes provide a complete and conveniently accessible record no separate record need be kept for VAT purposes.

Adjustment of input tax

61. If you receive a credit relating to deductible input tax your record of input tax must be adjusted. The reason for the adjustment must be clear from the accounts or supporting documents. Whatever the method, the result must be that at the end of each tax period the deductible input tax entered in your VAT account and the tax return is the net amount, after deducting any tax credits received in the period.

If it is your practice to issue debit notes to suppliers from whom credit is due and to adjust your commercial records at that stage, you may adjust your tax record as well. The debit notes must bear details similar to those required for credit notes. If you later receive credit notes from your suppliers they should be compared with the debit notes and any errors corrected. When this procedure is adopted care must be taken to ensure that adjustments are made once only and that the debit and credit notes are not both used as accounting documents. When a debit note is issued by you, as a fully taxable person, you are not obliged to adjust the original VAT charged to you provided that the supplier agrees that you need not do so. However, if either the supplier or yourself wishes to adjust the original VAT charge both of you must do so.

Adjustment of errors

62. (a) *Errors in tax invoices*. If the amount of tax on a tax invoice which you have issued is higher than the amount properly due you must nevertheless account for that amount in your records unless you correct the error with your customer by issuing a credit note. If the amount of tax is too low, you must account for the correct amount of tax due, whether or not you correct the error with your customer (eg by issuing a supplementary invoice for the amount undercharged).

If the amount of tax shown on a tax invoice is too low and you are unwilling or unable to recover the whole of the balance due from your customer it will be necessary to make a tax adjustment. The amount of the tax adjustment may be calculated from the total tax-inclusive amount actually charged.

If an error in the amount of tax chargeable is corrected with the customer (eg by issuing a credit note or supplementary invoice to the customer) the correction should be allowed to "work through" your accounting system. It should then be reflected in an adjusted total of output tax due from you at the end of the tax period in which the error was corrected. Adjustments of this kind, if they relate to tax due in previous tax periods, need not be carried separately to the VAT account or declared separately on the tax return.

If you issue a credit note or supplementary invoice to correct an error in a tax invoice it must, where practicable, bear a reference to the number and date of that tax invoice and show clearly both the correct and incorrect amounts of tax.

(b) *Others errors*. All other errors affecting tax due from you or repayable to you, which are discovered after you have sent in your return for the tax period in which they occurred, should be recorded separately as underdeclarations or overdeclarations of tax in previous periods. The totals should be carried to your VAT account for adjustment in your next return.

The VAT account

63. (a) *Summary of tax records*. For each tax period you must summarise your records under the following heads:

> output tax (including tax on any goods applied to non-business or personal use);
> tax due but not paid on:
>> imported or warehoused goods:
>> services received from abroad;
> deductible input tax;
> tax adjustments affecting:
>> amounts due;
>> amounts repayable.

These summaries must be entered in a special book or ledger opening to be known as the VAT account, showing the TAX DUE, the TAX DEDUCTIBLE and the NET AMOUNT for payment or repayment.

A simple VAT account is illustrated at Appendix F (not reproduced in this *Guide*). Other forms of account containing the same information will be acceptable to Customs and Excise.

17.400 The VAT return

Generally

VAT is accounted for by reference to "prescribed accounting periods". Such periods are usually of 3 months duration but a taxable person who expects to receive regular net repayments of tax may operate prescribed accounting periods of only 1 month (reg 51(1)(*a*)). Such treatment is, however, at the discretion of the Customs & Excise and is not permitted where VAT registration has been voluntary.

Taxable persons will be allocated to one of three groups of prescribed accounting periods (usually referred to as "stagger groups") depending upon their trade classification. These trade classifications are listed in Customs & Excise Notice No 41 and the correct classification is required to be specified by the taxable person in his application for registration (Form VAT 1). The particular stagger group and the dates to which the prescribed accounting periods will run will be notified to the taxable person in his certificate of registration issued by the Customs & Excise. The stagger groups are:

Stagger Group 1—Three month periods ending on 31 March, 30 June, 30 September and 31 December;

Stagger Group 2—Three month periods ending on 30 April, 31 July, 31 October and 31 January;

Stagger Group 3—Three month periods ending on 31 May, 31 August, 30 November and 28 February.

The first and last prescribed accounting period of a taxable person may be for a period of less than 3 months depending upon the date of registration and cancellation respectively. A taxable person may also make application in writing to his local VAT office for his prescribed accounting periods to accord with his financial year. Similarly, where a taxable person's accounting system is not based on a calendar year, he may apply for any accounting method other than the usual 3 months prescribed accounting period system to be considered for adoption.

Who must file the return

The basic obligation to file a return falls on all persons who are registered or should be registered for VAT purposes (reg 51). This obligation is extended by regs 52 and 56 to cover persons treated as making taxable supplies under Sched 2, para 6 (goods sold under a power of sale) and reg 7 (persons acting on death, bankruptcy or incapacity of taxable persons). As noted under **15.600**, however, it is suggested that no personal liability to account for VAT attaches to a receiver or liquidator appointed in respect of and acting as agent for a company. Regulation **56** must be read subject to this qualification, therefore.

Time for filing the return

Unless the Customs & Excise otherwise permit, a return must be made not later than the last day of the month following the end of the pre-scribed accounting period to which it relates. This applies whether the prescribed accounting period is one or 3 months long. A final return must also be made by a person within one month of the effective date of the cancellation of his registration (reg 51(4)).

Contents of a VAT return

The aim of the return is to arrive at a net figure for each prescribed accounting period for the amount of tax due by or to the taxable person in question. In reaching such figure, the taxable person must declare the tax due on his outputs for the period (Boxes 1 and 2 of the return form VAT 100) and determine the amount of input tax reclaimable for that period (Box 6). Clearly, both of these items may involve the taxable person in making a decision as to whether tax is chargeable or reclaim-able in respect of specific items. In such cases, the taxable person must take a firm and reasonable view. A return which is qualified or provisional is, as discussed below, an incorrect return (see *Unqualified returns, post*).

Box 1, outputs, of the return should simply be the total VAT shown on all invoices issued in the period. If an error is found in those invoices before the end of the period in question, it should be corrected within the figure in Box 1. This correction will be automatic where a credit note is issued. If the error is not found until after the end of the period, it must be recorded in Box 3, underdeclarations, or Box 7, overdeclara-tions, in the return for the next period. The Customs & Excise may allow a person to estimate a part of his output tax for a period if they are satisfied that he cannot account for the exact amount in that period (reg 54). In such cases, the amount should similarly be adjusted to the exact amount through Box 3 or 7 in the next period or such later period as the Customs & Excise may allow.

Box 6 must show only input tax recoverable by the taxable person. This will involve the taxable person in omitting VAT charged to him on items specifically excluded from credit (see **5.400,** for example, motor cars and business entertainment) and operating any percentage adjustment required where he also makes exempt outputs (see **5.300**).

Assistance in the completion of Boxes 11 and 12 is given by the Cus-toms & Excise Notice No 700, Appendix H.

As with output tax, the Customs & Excise may allow a person to estimate a part of his deductible input tax for any period. Adjustments through Box 8 or 4 must be made in the following prescribed accounting period or such later period as the Customs & Excise may allow (reg 55(2)). Bad debt relief claims (see **18.000**) should also be included in Box 8.

To be eligible to make a claim to input tax relief in a return, the taxable person should (unless the Customs & Excise otherwise allow) hold the documentation specified in reg 55(1). That is:

> "... if the claim is in respect of—
>
>   (*a*) a supply from another registered person, the document which is required to be provided under Regulation 8;
>   (*b*) a supply under section 8B (1) of the Act, the relative invoice from the supplier;
>   (*c*) an importation of goods, a document showing the claimant as importer, consignee or owner and showing the amount of tax due on the goods and authenticated or issued by a proper officer; or
>   (*d*) goods produced in the United Kingdom or the Isle of Man which have been removed from warehouse, a copy, authenticated by the proper officer, of the document on which an undertaking to account for tax has been given, or, if tax was paid on such removal, the document which evidenced that payment."

Unqualified returns

A VAT return is not properly made if it is qualified in any way. A return would be qualified if, for example, it is expressed to be subject to a particular item being allowable as an input or is provisional pending receipt of further information (see *D K Wright and Associates Ltd* v *CCE*, [1975] VATTR 168 (*Casebook* **13.211**)). Two differing returns submitted for a single period would also amount to a qualified return (*Greenbank Warehouses Ltd* v *CCE*, MAN/76/170 (*Casebook* **13.212**)).

Consequences of filing an improper return or failing to make a return

Such consequences are threefold. First, the person in question becomes liable to a penalty of £100 plus £10 per day of default or one-half per cent of the tax due for the period, whichever is the greater (s 38(7A)). For a discussion of penalties and their enforcement, see **14.400**. Secondly, the Customs & Excise are entitled to assess the person concerned for the amount of tax which, to the best of their judgment, they consider is due from him (s 31) (see further Chapter 12). Thirdly, a VAT Tribunal has no jurisdiction to entertain an appeal from a person who has not made all the returns he is required to make and paid the amount of tax shown due on those returns (s 40(2)). The Customs & Excise has the power, however, to waive this requirement in order to permit an appeal to proceed (*E G Gittins* v *CCE*, [1974] VATTR 109 (*Casebook* **13.216**)).

Payment of tax

If required to make a return, the person concerned is also required to pay to the Customs & Excise the net tax, if any, shown on that return to be due from him. Unless the Customs & Excise otherwise allow, payment must be made by the last day of the month following the end of the prescribed accounting period to which the return relates (regs 51 and 53(*b*).

If such person fails to pay such tax by the due date, the consequences would appear to be, first, that he commits an offence under s 38(7). The penalty for such offence is £100 plus £10 per day of default or one-half per cent of the tax due, whichever is the greater. Secondly, the Tribunal has no jurisdiction to hear any appeal from such person in relation to any issue concerning VAT (s 40(2)). This lack of jurisdiction is not capable of waiver by the Customs & Excise. There is no provision to allow interest to be charged on that outstanding tax, however, in addition to the penalties mentioned above.

Chapter 18

Miscellaneous

18.000 Bad debts and credit notes

18.000A Sources

FA 1978 s 12—Bad debt relief.
VAT (Bad Debt Relief) Regulations
  1978 (SI 1978 No 1129)—Detailed provisions relating to the giving of relief.

In addition the following Customs & Excise Notice and Leaflet may be helpful:

700, paras 46–48
8/78/VAC—Relief from VAT on bad debts.

18.000B Bad debts

FA 1978, s 12 introduced a new relief for suppliers who have accounted for VAT on a supply but have not received payment for such supply from the recipient of the supply. The relief is, however, limited as before relief may be claimed, the following conditions must be satisfied:

(*a*) goods or services must have been supplied for a consideration in money and the claimant must have accounted for and paid to the Customs & Excise the VAT in respect of that supply;

(*b*) the debtor, that is the recipient of the supply, must have become insolvent. Thus, if the debtor is an individual, he must have been adjudged bankrupt or the court must have made an order for the administration of his estate in bankruptcy. If the debtor is a company, the debtor must be subject of a creditors' voluntary winding up or the court must have made an order for its winding up and the circumstances are such that the company is unable to pay its debts;

(*c*) the claimant must have proved in the insolvency for the amount of the consideration payable in respect of the supply, less the amount of the VAT thereon;

(*d*) the consideration given for the supply must not have exceeded the open market value of the supply;

(*e*) in the case of a supply of goods, the property in the goods must have passed to the recipient. Bad debt relief is not available under FA 1978 where title has been reserved by the supplier pending full payment for the goods. Such reservation of title to goods until payment is received in full is now common, however. The Consultative Committee of Accountancy Bodies referred this issue to the Customs & Excise, therefore, whose reply is contained in the following CCAB Guidance Note (TR 388) of 1 May 1980:

"1. The legislation regarding bad debt relief is contained in Section 12 Finance Act 1978. Sub-Section 2(c) provides that a refund of VAT is not available unless 'the property in the goods has passed to the person to whom they were supplied.' The legislation is explained in leaflet number 8/78 VAC which gives a reservation of title contract as an example of a case where ownership of the goods has not passed to the customer.

2. Under Section 2 Finance Act 1972 tax is payable by the person making the supply and becomes due at the time of supply, which for goods sold under reservation of title would, in accordance with Section 7 of that Act, normally be the time the goods are removed or made available to the purchaser or the time they are invoiced if within 14 days thereafter.

3. The difficulty in which some traders find themselves is that when goods are sold under reservation of title VAT has been charged and is therefore payable to Customs but, if the customer becomes insolvent, bad debt relief is not available.

4. However, it often happens that if the reservation of title extends to the proceeds of sale of the goods (as was the case in Aluminium Industrie Vaasen BV v. Romalpa Aluminium Ltd. [1976] 1 WLR 676) the rights of the vendor are not, in fact, of any value because the proceeds of sale are no longer available. Hence the vendor is precluded from obtaining relief for VAT on the debt, whilst at the same time he has no means of recovering the amount owing to him.

5. The accountancy bodies have referred the above difficulty to HM Customs and Excise, who have replied as follows:

'We take the view that, subject to the other qualifying conditions being fulfilled, there is entitlement to bad debt relief in such cases if title has passed to the insolvent debtor *by the time the relief is claimed*.

Moreover we would regard title as having passed in such cases if it has been formally transferred to the liquidator as agent for the debtor company. We have already instructed our officers to this effect' ."

(*f*) The insolvency must have occured after 1 October 1978.

It is also to be noted that only the original supplier may make a claim under s 12. No relief is given to persons to whom a debt has been factored.

Under subs 12(3) the Customs & Excise is given the power to make Regulations in relation to:

(*a*) the manner and form of any claim under s 12;

(*b*) the evidence and records required for such claim;

(*c*) the calculation of the consideration where a set-off lies between the claimant and debtor or part payment has been received; and

(*d*) the repayment of any relief where the Regulations are not complied with.

Such Regulations are contained in the VAT (Bad Debt Relief) Regulations 1978 (SI 1978 No 1129), which Regulations are discussed under the following headings.

The claim form

No special form is used for a claim for bad debt relief. Instead, the amount is shown in box 8 (other over declarations made on previous returns) in the normal VAT return, Form VAT 100. The special box on the form is also ticked to indicate that box 8 includes a figure for bad debt relief. This entry is made in the prescribed accounting period in which the supplier receives an acknowledgement from the debtor of his claim in the insolvency (in the case of claims to the Official Receiver, Form VAT 996 may be used for this purpose).

Evidence required

In addition to the acknowledgement of the debtor mentioned under *The claim form, ante*, the following evidence is required to be produced:

(*a*) a copy of the tax invoice in question; or

(*b*) where no tax invoice was required to be issued, a document showing the time and nature of and consideration for the supply; and

(*c*) records or other documents showing that the tax has been accounted for and paid.

Such documents must be retained for a period of three years from the date of making the claim and shall be produced to any authorised person for inspection or temporary removal for inspection during that period.

Set-off

If a debt is due from the claimant to the debtor, the claimant may claim VAT on only the net amount of the debt outstanding. This is the case whether a formal right of set-off exists or the debtor merely has a lawful claim to the amount due.

Part payment

A part payment by the debtor only causes a problem where different rates of tax apply to the supplies in question (this, of course, includes zero-rated and standard rated supplies) or a supply was exempt. Regulation 7 provides, therefore, that the payment by the debtor is to be allocated to the supply that was first made to him unless such payment has already been specifically allocated to a particular supply. In this latter case, provided that the payment covers the whole of the consideration for the supply to which it was allocated, it is disregarded for the purposes of the relief.

Repayment of relief

A repayment of VAT previously refunded by way of bad debt relief is only required in two circumstances. First, if the claimant fails to keep the required documentation (see *Evidence required, ante*) for the requisite 3 year period. Secondly, if the claimant makes a further claim in the insolvency which claim, together with the amount previously claimed, exceeds the amount of the outstanding debt due to the claimant from the debtor less the tax thereon, the whole relief is repayable. It is to be noted in the second case that it is the whole of the relief that is repayable, not the excess relief claimed.

18.000C Credit notes

Credit notes should only be issued to correct a genuine error or to cancel a supply where the goods in question have been returned to the supplier, for example, because they were faulty. Credit notes cannot be issued to rewrite the VAT treatment of a transaction merely because the recipient of the supply has failed to pay the amount shown on the original invoice (see *Peter Crispwell and Associates* v *CCE*, CAR/78/131 (*Casebook* **18.003**)). If a credit note is not issued for a *bona fide* reason, it is void as being against public policy (*Temple Gothard and Co* v *CCE*, LON/78/238 (*Casebook* **18.002**)).

If a credit note is issued to adjust the previous treatment of VAT (and the supplier and recipient may agree not to alter that position), it should contain the following information:

(*a*) an identifying number and date of issue;
(*b*) the supplier's name;
(*c*) the recipient's name and address;
(*d*) the reason for the credit;
(*e*) a description sufficient to identify the goods or services for which a credit is being allowed;
(*f*) the quantity and amount credited for each description;
(*g*) the total amount credited excluding VAT;
(*h*) the rate and amount of VAT credited, totalled separately where more than one rate of tax applies; and
(*i*) the number and date of the original tax invoice if possible.

If the original goods are merely replaced by identical goods, the supplier has a choice as to whether to either issue a credit note in respect of the original supply and adjust his return accordingly and treat the replacement goods as a new supply or let the original account stand and ignore the subsequent supply. The former is perhaps the more correct procedure.

18.100 Changes in the rate of tax

18.100A Sources

Section 9(3)—Enabling provision relating to changes in the rate of tax.
Section 42—Adjustment of contracts on changes in the rate of tax.
F(No 2)A 1979 s 1(4)—Apportionment of supplies spanning 18 June 1979.

18.100B General principles

The Treasury may by Order increase or decrease the rate of VAT at any time by a factor of 25 per cent (s 9(3)). Any such change is, however, subject to confirmation by a further Treasury Order within a period of 1 year or it will lapse at the end of that year.

Where there is a change in the rate of VAT, it is necessary to ascertain the tax point in respect of each supply potentially affected by such change. This is because the rate of tax applying at the tax point will determine the amount of tax chargeable on that supply.

Thus, in the case of a supply of goods, if the goods have been either removed, made available to the recipient, invoiced or paid for before the change in the rate of tax, the old rate of VAT will be payable in respect of the supply (s 7(2)). Similarly, where services have been performed in full or payment is received or a tax invoice is issued before a change, the old rate will apply (s 7(2)). Where a continuous supply of services is involved with the consideration for those services payable periodically, VAT (General) Regulations 1977 (SI 1977 No 1759), reg 18(1) treats such services as being successively supplied whenever a payment is received or (subject to the exception in reg 18(2) in respect of invoices for a period not exceeding 1 year) a tax invoice is issued. As a result, the rate of tax in respect of each payment will depend upon whether it is received (or invoiced) before or after the change. It is to be noted that reg 18(3) provides that an invoice covering a period of up to one year issued under the protection of reg 18(2) and necessarily showing the rate of tax on all payments in that period will cease to be valid. A new invoice would, therefore, have to be issued.

Regulation 17 should also be noted in connection with supplies of goods and services. Reg 17 provides that where any contract specifies that any part of the consideration is to be retained pending satisfactory performance of the contract by the supplier, a supply is treated as made whenever a payment is received or a tax invoice is issued by the supplier, whichever is the earlier.

Further reference should be made to **3.300** for a general discussion of the time of a supply. And note should be made of the power of the Customs & Excise, given by s 7(6A), to agree an earlier tax point in relation to a supply.

The above rules would operate to the detriment of a supplier or recipient (depending upon whether there is a rise or fall in the rate of tax) where a contract for a fixed price is entered into before the date on which a change has effect but where the tax point in relation to the supply will fall after that date. Section 42 provides, therefore, that unless the contract otherwise provides, the price specified in that contract shall be amended to take into account the alteration in the tax rate.

It is to be noted that on the recent change in rates with effect from 18 June 1979, specific provision was made in F(No 2)A 1979, s 1(4) for the apportionment of a supply made wholly or partly before that date in order that different rates of tax might be charged on the relevant parts of the supply falling either side of the date of change. This section was principally designed to provide relief where the consideration for a supply was payable in arrear, either not periodically or not in respect of a supply of services.

18.200 EEC Directives

It was mentioned in **13.800** that where an EEC Directive contains a provision which has direct effect in the United Kingdom, UK law must arguably be interpreted subject to that provision. If UK law conflicts with that provision, therefore, the Directive should prevail and must be applied accordingly. A Directive can only have direct effect, however, from the date by which the United Kingdom is required to comply with such Directive. It is important, therefore, to be aware of the terms of all current Directives and whether the time for their implementation has passed.

Ten Directives relating to VAT have been introduced to date. These are:

EEC First and Second Directives (11 April 1967)

These directives established the principle of the harmonisation of VAT legislation in Member States and the basic structure for a common system of VAT throughout the Community. These directives were repealed by the Sixth Directive and are now, therefore, of only academic interest.

EEC Third, Fourth and Fifth Directives

These Directives extended the date for implementation of the First and Second Directives to 1 January 1973.

EEC Sixth Directive (17 May 1977)

Following the adoption by member states of a system of VAT in accordance with the First and Second Directives, the Sixth Directive was aimed at the harmonisation of those individual systems to produce a uniform system throughout the EEC. Member States are permitted, however, to retain their own VAT systems in relation to small undertakings and, subject to limitations, to derogate from the directive in order to simplify the levying of tax or to avoid fraud or tax avoidance.

The Sixth Directive was originally to be implemented by Member States by 1 January 1978. The changes to FA 1972 necessary to implement this Directive in the United Kingdom were introduced by FA 1977.

A derivation table showing the inter-relationship of the Sixth Directive and FA 1972 is set out in the Appendix to this Guide.

EEC Seventh Directive (draft 11 January 1978)

This Directive was made pursuant to the Sixth Directive, art 32. The draft proposes a uniform system to be adopted by member states for "used goods". The system in fact permits a taxable person reselling used goods (other than cars, trailers, pleasure boats, motor cycles and private aircraft) to choose one of two schemes. These are either to charge tax on 30 per cent of the selling price or on the difference between the purchase and selling price of the goods in question. "Used goods" are defined as goods which have completed a "commercial cycle" by reaching a final consumer and which then are sold by such consumer and re-enter a further commercial cycle.

This Directive was adopted by the Council on 6 December 1979.

EEC Eighth Directive (6 December 1979)

This Directive establishes a system whereby a taxable person "established" in one Member State may recover VAT suffered in another Member State in which he is not "established" and in which he has not supplied goods or services in the same period (certain transport and ancillary services and deemed supplies are excluded in determining whether supplies have been made in the country in question). A person is "established" in a country if he has in that country the seat of his economic activities, a fixed establishment from which business trans-actions are effected or, if neither exists, in which he is domiciled or has his normal place of residence. A taxable person will only be able to recover tax which is generally recoverable as input tax in the country in which it is incurred.

Member States are to comply with this Directive by 1 January 1981. Germany has, however, been operating the recovery scheme since 1 January 1980. Forms for reclaiming tax suffered in Germany and details of the German scheme may be obtained from *Bundesamt für Finanzen, Friedhofstrasse 1 D – 5300, Bonn 3*. The form must be completed in German and forwarded to the German authorities with the original tax invoices or import documents. The UK claimant must also obtain from his local VAT office and submit with the claim a certificate of his UK status. In general, applications can be made covering periods of 3 months to 1 year and must be made not later than 6 months after the end of the calendar year in which the VAT was incurred. Claims by a representative member of a group of companies must contain the names of all group members included in the claim.

EEC Ninth Directive (26 June 1978)

This Directive extended the date for compliance with the Sixth Direc-tive for those Member States which had not already adopted it, to 1 January 1979.

EEC Tenth Directive (draft 14 December 1979)

This Directive (draft) concerns the hiring of tangible moveable property. The Directive proposes that goods, other than forms of transport, shall be treated as supplied in the country in which the goods are actually made available to the hirer. This alters the current treatment which is to treat the supply as made in the country in which the supplier belongs.

18.300 Inter-relationship of VAT and other taxes

The Inland Revenue issued a Press Release on 7 May 1973 (Income tax, corporation tax and capital gains tax : treatment of VAT). The follow-ing paragraphs in this subchapter are based on that Press Release.

There are three basic categories into which a person may fall. First, the non-taxable person. Secondly, the fully taxable person. Thirdly, the taxable person who makes some exempt supplies.

18.300A The non-taxable person

Such persons will suffer VAT in relation to items of income and capital expenditure and will be unable to recover such VAT from the Customs & Excise. As a result, the following will apply to give that person a measure of relief:

(*a*) income or corporation tax—if the item purchased is allowable as a deduction for income or corporation tax purposes. The amount of the deduction will be the VAT inclusive amount of the purchase price of the item. Where a deduction is not allowed, for example because it relates to non-allowable entertainment expenditure, the VAT element of that expenditure will similarly not be allowable;

(*b*) capital allowances—if the expenditure qualifies for capital allowances, the amount that may be claimed as such will be inclusive of VAT;

(*c*) capital gains tax—the base cost of an item for the purposes of capital gains tax will include any VAT element of the purchase price.

18.300B The fully taxable person

Such a person will initially pay VAT on supplies to him and will only be unable to recover that tax if it is paid in relation to an item in respect of which input tax is specifically not recoverable. For example, input tax on motor cars and business entertainment may be precluded from recovery under the VAT (Cars) Order 1980 (SI 1980 No 442), art 4 and VAT (Special Provisions) Order 1977 (SI 1977 No 1796), art 9 respectively. Where no recovery is possible, the taxable person will be in the same position as the non-taxable person in **18.300A**. The converse will be the case, however, where recovery of input tax is possible. This is to avoid a double relief for the same expenditure. Thus:

(*a*) income tax or corporation tax—allowable expenditure will be VAT exclusive;

(*b*) capital allowances—allowable expenditure will be VAT exclusive;

(*c*) capital gains tax—the base cost for the asset will be VAT exclusive. Similarly, any VAT charged on the subsequent disposal of the asset will not be included in the disposal proceeds. This is because that VAT does not accrue to the person disposing of the asset but must be accounted for to the Customs & Excise.

The position in relation to bad debts, which include an element of VAT, requires clarification. If the VAT in respect of a bad debt is not recoverable from the Customs & Excise under the bad debt relief provisions (FA 1978, s 12, see **18.000B**), the amount of that VAT may be included in the amount of the debt claimed as a trading expense in the period in which it is known that the debt has become irrecoverable. Conversely, if the VAT is recoverable from the Customs & Excise, it cannot be claimed as a trading expense.

Finally, if a trader does not make a claim to input tax, possibly because his records are not sufficient to enable such claim to be made, he may treat that input tax as a cost in accordance with **18.300A**.

18.300C The taxable person who makes exempt outputs

Such a person may be unable to recover a part of the input tax on supplies to him in addition to any specific disallowance of input tax relief on specific types of supply. As discussed in **5.300**, the calculation of the recoverable input tax of a partially exempt person may:

(*a*) be on a straightforward proportional basis;
(*b*) be linked in relation to certain identifiable input expenditure to an identifiable exempt output; or
(*c*) follow another method agreed with the Customs & Excise.

If (*a*) applies, the reclaimable proportion of each input will follow the rules in **18.300B** and the non-reclaimable proportion, the rules in **18.300A**.

If (*b*) applies, the position in **18.300A** will apply in relation to that particular item of expenditure.

In relation to (*c*), the Inspector of Taxes will consider any reasonable arrangement for allocating the VAT cost in accordance with the general principles in **18.300A** and **18.300B**.

Appendix

Derivation tables: interrelationship of the FA 1972 and the Sixth Directive

A direct cross reference between the Act and the Sixth Directive is often not possible. The following tables merely give an indication, therefore, of where the similar provision is covered in the Directive or the Act, as the case may be.

FA 1972: Sixth Directive

Act	Directive	Act	Directive
1	2	11(2)	11B(1)(a), (2)
2(1)	2	(3)	11B(1)(b)
(2)	4(1), (2), 24(2)	(4)	11B(2)
(3)	10(1), 12(1),	12(2)	12(4)
	21(1), 22(5)	(3)	14
(4)	10(3), 21(2), 23	(6)	15
3(1)	24(5)	13	13, 14, 15, 16
(2)	17(1), 18(2)	14	32
(4)	17(5)	15	4(5)
(5)	18(4)	16(1)	15(10)
(6)	18(3)	17	16, 23
4(1)	17(1), (2), (5)	18	23
(3)	19(1), (3), 20	19	4(5)
5	17(3), (4)	20	4(5)
6(2)	2, 5(1), (4),	21	4(4)
	6(1)	22	4(4)
(3)	5(8)	24(1)	22(7)
(4)	6(2)	(3)	6(4)
(6)	5(7), 6(3)	25	24
7	10(2), 12(1)	26	28(2)
8	8	28	20(2)
8A	9	29	11
8B	9(2)(e), 22(7)	30	22(2)–(6), (8),
9	12(1), (3), (5)		(9)
10	11A(1)(a)	32	22(8)
(2)	11A(3)(b),	34	22(2)
	24(2)	45(1)	4(2)
(3)	11A(1)(d)	(3)	13A(1) (f)

Act	Directive	Act	Directive
Sched 1	22(1), 24(2)	Sched 4	
	24(6)	Group 9, item 5	9(2)(e)
		6	9(2)(e)
Sched 2, para 1	5(1), (4)(b)	7	17(3)(c),
2	5(5)		13B(a)
3	5(2)	8	17(3)(c)
4	5(3)(a)	9	17(3)(c),
5	5(6), (7), 6(2)		13B(d)
7	5(7)	10	15(3)
		11	15(13), (14)
Sched 2A	9(2)(e)	Group 10	15(5)–(9)
			9(2)(c)
Sched 3, para 4	11A(3)(a)	12	15(11)
5	11B(4)	Sched 5, Group	
7	11A(1)(b)	1	13B(b), (g), (h)
8	11A(1)(c)	2	13B(a)
10	11C(2)	3	13A(1)(a),
11	11A(1)(a)		13B(e)
		4	13B(f)
Sched 4	28(2)	5	13B(d)
Group 9, item 1	9(2)(a)	6	13A(1)(i), (j)
2	9(2)(d), 9(3)	7	13A(1)(b), (c),
3	9(2)(c)		(e)
4	9(2)(c)		

Sixth Directive: FA 1972

Directive	Act	Directive	Act
1	—	6(3)	6(6)
2	1, 2(1), 6(2)	(4)	24(3)
3	—	(5)	—
4(1), (2)	2(2)	7	—
(3)	—	8	8
(4)	21	9(1)	8A
(5)	19, 20, 15	(2)(a)	Sched 4, Group 9, item 1
5(1)	6(2)	(b)	—
(2)	Sched 2, para 3	(c)	Sched 4, Group 9, item 3, 4
(3)(a)	Sched 2, para 4		Group 10, item 11
(b), (c)	—	(d)	Sched 4, Group 9, item 2
(4)(a)	6(2)	(e)	Sched 4, Group 9 items 5 & 6, Sched 2A, s 8B
(b)	Sched 2, para 1(2)(b)	(3)	Sched 4, Group 9, item 2
(c)	6(2)	10(1)	2(3)
(5)	Sched 2, para 2		
(6)	Sched 2, para 5(2)		
(7)(a)	6(6)		
(b)	Sched 2, para 5		
(c)	Sched 2, para 7		
(8)	6(3)		
6(1)	6(2)(b)		
(2)	Sched 2 para 5(3)		

Directive	Act	Directive	Act
10(2)	7	13B, (h)	Sched 5, Group 1
(3)	2(4)	C	—
11A(1)(a)	10	14	12(3)
(b)	Sched 3, para 7	15(1)	12(6)
(c)	Sched 3, para 8	(2)	VAT (General) Regulations 1977 regs 44–50
(d)	10(3)		
(2)	—		
(3)(a)	Sched 3, para 4	(3)	Sched 4, Group 9, item 10
(b)	10(2)		
(c)	—		
B(1)(a)	11(2)	(4)	12(6)
(b)	11(3)	(5)–(9)	Sched 4, Group 10
(2)	11(4)		
(3)	11(2)	(10)	16(1)
(4)	Sched 3, para 5	(11)	Sched 4, Group 12
(5)	VAT (General) Regulations 1977 reg 41	(12)	12(6)
		(13)	Sched 4, Group 9, item 11(a)
C(1)	FA 1978 s 12		
(2)	Sched 3, para 10	(14)	Sched 4, Group 9, item 11(c)
(3)	—		
12(1)	2(3), 7, 9	16	17
(2)	F (No 2) A 1979, s 1	17(1)	3(2), 4(1)(a)
		(2)	4
(3)	9	(3)	5
(4)	12(2), Sched 4	(4)	5, see Eighth Directive
(5)	9		
13A(1)(a)	Sched 5, Group 3	(5)	4
(b)	Group 7	(6)	—
(c)	Group 7	17(7)	—
(d)	—	18(1)	VAT (General) Regulations, reg 55
(e)	Sched 5, Group 7		
(f)	—		
(g)	—	(2)	3(2)
(h)	—	(3)	—
(i)	Sched 5, Group 6	(4)	3(5)
(j)	Group 6	19(1)	4(3)
(k)	—	(2)	—
(l)	see 45(3)	(3)	4(3)
(m)	—	20	4(3)
(n)	—	21(1)	2(3)
(o)	—	(2)	2(4)
(p)	—	22(1)	Sched 1
(q)	—	(2)	30, 34
(2)	—	(3)	30(2)
B(a)	Sched 5, Group 2	(4)	30(2)
(b)	Group 1	(5)	2(3), 30
(c)	—	(6)	30(2)
(d)	Sched 5, Group 5	(7)	24(1), 88(2)
(e)	Group 3	(8)	30, 32
(f)	Group 4	(9)	30
(g)	Group 1	23	2(4), 17, 18

Directive	Act	Directive	Act
24(1)	—	24(7)	—
(2)	see Sched 1, para 1	(8)	—
		(9)	—
(3)	—	25–31	—
(4)	2(2), 10(2)	32	14, see Seventh Directive
(5)	3		
(6)	Sched 1, para 11	33–38	—

Index

Note Most entries in this Index give references in both light and bold print. Those in light print refer to pages in the *Guide*, while the figures in bold print refer to the relevant cases in the *Casebook*.

POWER, HEAT, REFRIGERATION AND VENTILATION—
supply of, 32, 275, **3.612**, **8.702**
time of supply, 35
POWER OF ATTORNEY—
non-resident trader, given by, 22
PREMISES—
hot dog stall as, 124, 125, **8.103**
meaning of, 124, 125, **8.103**
ownership of, 124, **8.102**, **8.104**
PRESCRIBED ACCOUNTING PERIODS, 340
PRINTED MATTER—
definition of, 49
self-supplies, 27, 49
PRIVATE OR NON-BUSINESS USE OF BUSINESS ASSETS—
value of supply, 41
PRIVATE VESSELS—
relief on importation of, 93
PROCEDURE BEFORE VAT TRIBUNAL—
discovery,
appellant by, 232
Customs and Excise, by, 232, 233
documents, disclosure of, by lists, 232, 233
hearing,
adjournment or postponement of, 237, **13.421**
burden of proof, 236
documents, use of, at, 236
evidence, 235–236, **13.428**
failure to attend, 235, **13.418**
notice of, 234
order of appearance at, 235
public or private, 235
representation at, 234
notice of appeal, *see* NOTICE OF APPEAL
Statement of Case, by Customs and Excise, 232–233
witnesses,
statements, 233–234, 236
summonses, 234, 237
PROFESSIONAL ASSOCIATIONS, *see* TRADE UNIONS AND PROFESSIONAL BODIES (EXEMPTION)
PROFESSIONAL EFFECTS—
relief on importation of, 93
PROJECTS OF SELF-HELP—
discretion of Customs and Excise with regard to,
nature of, 271
relief for,
conditions for, 271, **15.101**
extent of, 271
PUBLIC OFFICES—
salary in respect of, as supply in course or furtherance of a business, 55–56, **2.216**
PURCHASE TAX, 100

QUEEN'S BENCH DIVISION, *see* HIGH COURT

RAILCARDS—
Senior Citizens, 206, **3.610**
students, 45–46, 3.610
RECEIVERS—
agent, as
mortgagee, for, 286–288
person other than company, for, 288–289
assessment of, 213
fixed charges, appointed under, 288, 291
generally, 285–286
more conduit, as, 287–288
personal liability of, 287, **15.602**
status of,
after liquidation, 286–289
prior to liquidation, 286
trustees in bankruptcy and, 280
RECORDS—
generally, 333, 334–335
importance of, 209, **12.314**
practice of Customs and Excise, 335–339
retention of, *see* RETENTION OF RECORDS
RECOVERY OF INPUT TAX, *see also* "FOR THE PURPOSE OF ANY BUSINESS CARRIED ON OR TO BE CARRIED ON"
agent, supplies to or by, 64–65
do-it-yourself builders, by, 64
employees, supplies contracted for by, 65–66
generally, 63
imported goods for private use, 66
indemnity payments, 64
non-registered taxable persons, by, 63–64
recipient of supply carrying on more than one type of activity, 66
REFRIGERATION, *see* POWER, HEAT, REFRIGERATION AND VENTILATION
REGISTRATION FOR VAT—
application for, 13
cancellation of, *see* DEREGISTRATION
clubs and associations, by, 273
companies organised in divisions, 18–19

RETURNS—*continued*
  final, 21
  improper, 342–343
  making, as pre-condition of appeal,
    date for compliance, 224–225, **13.213**
    improper or conditional returns, 225,
      13.211, 13.212
    waiver of, 225, **13.216**
  obligation to make, 209
  time for filing, 341
  unqualified, 342
  who must file, 340–341
RIVER AUTHORITIES, 68
ROMALPA CONTRACTS, 31, 32
ROYAL NATIONAL INSTITUTE FOR THE BLIND,
  130
ROYAL NATIONAL LIFEBOAT INSTITUTION,
  144
ROYAL PHOTOGRAPHIC SOCIETY OF GREAT
  BRITAIN, 183, 184
ROYALTIES, 36

SALE OR RETURN—
  time of supply, 30, 34
SCHOOLS, 174, **6.601, 6.602**
SCOTLAND, 5
SEA—
  exportation of goods, by, 105
  importation of goods, by, 88
S 15 BODIES, 67–69, 278
SEEDS, *see* FOOD (ZERO-RATING)
SELF-SUPPLIES—
  cars, 27, 49
  consideration, absence of, 47, **3.702**
  generally, 26–27
  off-shore installation, transfer of goods
    to, by operator as, 321
  partnerships and, 48
  printed matter, 27, 49
  supply, as, 47
  time of supply, 35
  value of supply, 40
SERVICES—
  exportation of, *see* EXPORTATION OF SER-
    VICES (ZERO-RATING)
  importation of, *see* IMPORTATION OF SER-
    VICES
  supply of, *see* SUPPLY OF SERVICES
SEWERAGE SERVICES AND WATER (ZERO-
  RATING)—
  provisions of Schedule 4, 126–127
SHIPS, *see also* TRANSPORT
  classifying, 146

SHIPS—*continued*
  crew member, over-the-counter export
    sales to, 108, 110
  handling, 145–146
  leasing of, 307
  meaning of, 143–144, **8.1001**
  off-shore installations as, 321
  storage of, 162, **9.123**
  stores for retail sale on, 103
  surveying, 146
SOLICITORS—
  Client account, interest on, 170,
    9.505
SOURCES—
  general
    Customs and Excise, 2–4
    EEC legislation, 1
    Finance Acts, 1
    Statutory Instruments, 2
  particular,
    accounting for VAT, 330
    agents, 264
    appeals, 219
    assessments, 209
    bad debts, 344
    business, 51
    charities, 268
    clubs and associations, 272
    commodities, 312
    compensation, 322
    conditional sale agreements, 309
    credit sale agreements, 309
    Crown, the, 277
    enquiries, 250
    Eurobond issues, 317
    ex gratia payments, 322
    exemption, 156
    exportation, 103
    gaming machines, 328
    hire purchase agreements, 309
    importation, 84–85
    input tax, 62
    international supply of services, 185
    leasing, 304
    local authorities, 277
    management services, 325
    margin schemes, 292
    off-shore activities, 320
    partnerships, 280
    rate of tax, changes in, 348
    registration, 10
    second-hand cars, 292
    supply, 24
    zero-rating, 120